Acknowledge

Much courtesy has been received over many years from the staff of the Vatican library and archives, especially from Monsignor Charles Burns; from those of the British museum, when the archives and library were still there and more recently from the staff at the new installation; from the Public Record Office, formerly in Chancery Lane and now at Kew; from the staff of the Institute of Historical Research, London; from the staff of Lambeth Palace Library, especially Dr R.J. Palmer and Miss Melanie Barber; from Mr John H. Hopkins, former librarian, and Mr E.B. Nurse, the present librarian, of the Society of Antiquaries of London. Most of my research in the Jesuit archives in London, and much of it in Rome, was done while I was head archivist in both places, but thanks are due to the late Edmund Lamalle, S.J., former archivist at the Archivum Romanum, S.J., and to Thomas McCoog, S.J., present archivist in London. I must acknowledge much kindness and encouragement from Professor V.A. McClelland, present editor of *Recusant History*, Miss Penelope Renold and many others.

Abbreviations

add.	additional
a.l.s.	autograph letter signed
BL	British library
BPA	British province archives
Cal.	Calendar
CRS	Catholic Record Society
Dnb	*Dictionary of national biography*
Dom.	domestic
ed.	edition
Eliz.	Elizabeth
endd.	endorsed
HMC	Historical Manuscripts Commission
HMSO	Her Majesty's Stationery Office
Harl.	Harleian – indicates a fond in the BL.
MF	microfilm
misc.	miscellaneous
ms	manuscript
n.	note
no.	number
n.d.	no date
n.s.	new style
NY	New York
o.s.	old style
PRO	Public Record Office
Sal. Cal.	Salisbury Calendar, i.e. of the mss at Hatfield belonging to the marquess.
SP	State papers
VEC	Venerable English College, Rome

Bibliography

Since all the sources are included in the notes, and sometimes given more than once in full to assist the reader's convenience, the example of Lawrence Stone in *The crisis of the aristocracy, 1558–1641*, is here followed in not giving a separate bibliography. The following works seem to deserve special mention as bibliographical in nature, or containing bibliographies bearing on the present study, or as indicating works to illustrate the larger context.

J.B. Black, *The reign of Elizabeth 1558-1603* (Oxford 1959), pp 497-519.

T. Clancy, S.J., *Papist pamphleteers* (Chicago 1964), pp 235-41.

P. Milward, *Religious controversies of the Elizabethan age: a survey of printed sources* (London 1977).

Penry Williams, *The later Tudors: England 1547-1603* (Oxford 1995), pp 560-80.

Francis Edwards, S.J., *Robert Persons* (St Louis 1995), pp xiv–xviii.

Paul E.J. Hammer, *The polarisation of Elizabethan politics: the political career of Robert Devereux, 2nd earl of Essex, 1585-1597* (Cambridge 1999), pp 405-27.

Thomas McCoog, S.J., *The Society of Jesus in Ireland, Scotland and England, 1541-1588* (Leiden, New York, Köln, 1996), pp 281-98.

The death of Cecyl Lord Burghley. 4. Aug.[1598] aetat. Anno. 77.

... William Cecil, Lord Burghley, Lord High Treasurer of England, being spent with continuall discontentment of minde, the gout and old age, gave himself over to sorrow and anguish of heart; and writing a letter to the Queene, earnestly besought her that he might lay down his Offices of Magistracy. Upon this she visited him now and then, comforting him with most kinde words. But within a few days, when he had lived long enough to nature, long enough to his glory, but not long enough to his Countrey, he rendered his soule to God by so quiet a death, that the greatest adversarie he had, said that he envied him for nothing so much as for such a death in so great glorie, whereas for the most part the Managers of the greatest affaires have more sad ends. Certainly, he was a most excellent man, who (to say nothing of his reverend Presence, and undistempered countenance) was fashioned by nature, and adorned with learning, a singular man for honesty, gravities, temperance, industrie, and justice. hereunto were added a fluent and elegant speech, (and that not affected but plaine and easie) wisedome strengthened by experience, and seasoned with exceeding moderation, and most approved fidelitie, but above all, singular piety towards God. To speak in a word, the Queene was most happy in so great a Councellor, and to his wholesome counsels the State of England for ever shall be beholden.

W. Camden, *Annales* ... (1635 ed.), p. 494

I

Introduction

This book attempts to set out the larger historical context of the gunpowder plot which began about 1570. Certain events between 1570 and 1601 contain much that explains important aspects of the gunpowder plot of 1605. It is safe to say that controversy will never cease since the evidence, much of which has been destroyed by chance, and also by design, one must suppose, will never be complete for earlier plots any more than for the last and greatest. So more than one interpretation is possible. Earlier plots must be considered independently of the gunpowder plot, but as they led up to it as to a grand finale, it is relevant to begin with something about the plot of 1605. The general verdict on that plot is likely to colour any approach to others that preceded it. Alan Haynes' *Invisible power*, of 1992, a study of 'the Elizabethan secret services' between 1570 and 1603, covers the whole period of the present work. Haynes dealt with the subject in a readable and popular way, treating the subject mainly from the point of view of the hunter. His overall view is that the plots were genuine. The present work rounds up the evidence to suggest that they were not. Clearly this goes against accepted traditions at many points. While taking the hunter into its view – it could hardly do otherwise – it views the field mainly from the eye-level of the hunted. The evidence for an unusual view must be carefully weighed. Otherwise it could be dismissed as special pleading.

Is there such a thing as Establishment history? Certainly much history of the Jacobethan period puts forward an interpretation of the times which avoids the darker corners. While not uncritical enough to endorse the Edward German picture of Merry England without demur, it leaves the reader with the overall impression that all was well and everybody happy except for a few obstinate religious dissenters. These either pined for a past which was gone for ever – the papists – or looked to a future which demanded more than they could decently be given – the puritans. Exploring the darker corners gives only one side of the picture. But it is an important side. A picture without shadows and dark areas as well as highlights cannot be a picture at all.

The over-optimistic view of the times does not always look closely enough at archival sources while making use of them. It can skim over difficulties or queries arising from handwriting. Admittedly we are in a mine-field here. Standard history – Establishment history, if the phrase is not unkindly loaded – tells us the story mainly through the eyes of official sources and government. This mainstream view has always been challenged but only with limited success. It shows great resilience especially at the present time. Perhaps it is because it seems necessary to convince the indigenized strangers among us, as well as the natives, that our past has been as glorious and largely impeccable as our present is desirable. There is a great deal of truth in what is far from wholly legend especially regarding more recent centuries. It would be more comfortable to leave the legend alone. Your author takes no pleasure in disturbing the mythology for its own sake. However, the claims of truth must take precedence over political correctness, at least in works which the general public may never see and some kinds of publication never want to notice.

It is timely to call to mind that, even without dramatic new discoveries, the evidence, incomplete as it is, and because it is incomplete, allows alternative solutions. There is no such thing as English history; only English histories. Many living in the time, who had nothing to gain from the official interpretation, thought it likely if not certain that the Jacobethan plots, including the gunpowder plot, were at least largely contrived by government. The only contrivers with sufficient daring, intelligence and influence were William and Robert Cecil, father and son, although they needed their allies in government. The last plot of the series, the gunpowder plot, was exploited to discredit and destroy personal enemies and those of the kind of state they had established with remarkable and even phenomenal success. This book is about the other plots which led up to it: some decidedly important if not as important as the gunpowder plot. It presents the seamy side of Elizabethan history. It does not claim that this is the only side there is.

The gunpowder plot has so far been treated, whether in general histories or as a subject in its own right, as an event having little if anything to do with what went before even during the ascendancy of Sir Robert Cecil. If it has any connection with earlier events, then it must appear as the culmination of a long tradition of popish treason. One may also see it as the consummation of another tradition not yet generally acknowledged by English-speaking historians. This will become clear as the narrative advances. Much has been published on the plot of 1605, most recently Antonia Fraser's notable production of 1996. But many questions still remain unanswered which call for further investigation. The subject is elusive and emotionally explosive, with a powder train laid to it by those who resent any tampering with traditional mythology.

Some largely unnoticed if not always unknown evidence for earlier plots is offered here. Some of it has come to light from under record office tiles, so to speak, as was supposed to have happened in the Ridolfi plot, or behind the panelling in more recent years, like the Clarke-Thornhill manuscripts found at Rushton. Progress towards truth often comes from reconsidering from another point of view what has hitherto been taken for granted, or ignored because it did not fit the standard thesis. At the end of the investigation it may be concluded that this work no more than others is enough to displace entrenched views. It is conceded that as an alternative to standard historical solutions it must be taken to include a questionmark in text and title. A like sign of doubt should come from all new tellers of the old tale too. Undoubtedly, the backing of long supportive historical convention leaves older and more familiar narratives well ensconced; but this is not the same as unassailable.

Taking into account the incomplete, doctored evidence for all the Jacobethan plots as they have come down to us, one understands without accepting, and appreciates without converting, the scholarly effort of Dr Mark Nicholls, *Investigating gunpowder plot* of 1991, which sets out anew the standard tradition. There is no better brief to date in defence of Robert Cecil and his associate ministers. But it seems to omit too many questionmarks and brushes aside too easily points of evidence on the other side. But Dr Nicholls and Antonia Fraser were both fully justified in offering a counterthesis to the theme of my *The real story of the gunpowder plot?* published in 1969. In spite of the questioning title, the text, for the sake of continuous narrative and smoother reading for a popular audience, hurried the reader along in a story suggesting too little doubt or query. It was an exposition intended for nonexpert appreciation; a plain presentation of the most obvious meaning of the evidence as it presented itself to the author. All the same, it was based on extensive research in original sources and took into account practically all previous printed works on the subject. Allowing for continuing obscurities and lacunae in the evidence sufficient to preclude final certainty, its main thesis still stands up to close scrutiny.

This solution looks back, after careful investigation, from the gunpowder plot to a similar explanation for all, or nearly all, the many plots preceding it. *The real story ...* was cast in a form too light to impress Academe, and it contained the errors of a book written too quickly. But as Chesterton observed, anything worth doing is worth doing badly. The book before you attempts to improve on what was a preamble to a more definitive work on the master plot. This will never cease to be of interest and significance in the island story; and not only to the good people of Lewes, the only place left in Britain, it seems, which still remembers the original villains with all the traditional gusto.

Of great assistance in preparing this book was A.J. Loomie's 'Guy Fawkes in Spain; the Spanish treason in Spanish documents' printed in the *Bulletin of the Institute of Historical Research* in 1971 as Special Supplement 7. An article, 'Still investigating gunpowder plot', by F. Edwards, which appeared in volume 21 of *Recusant History* in 1993, set out to confirm and supplement major points of the thesis offered in *The real story ... ?* Important background is provided in Dr Nicholls' doctoral thesis on 'Percies and politics' (Cambridge 1985) and other highly informative studies in the field.

How comes it that historians still differ among themselves on the interpretation of even well-known and long-studied events? The question seems naive but is valid. As E.L. Woodward pointed out in his essay on bias in the teaching of history, 'You reach more quickly in history than in any of the studies which can rightly claim the name of science, the limit of demonstration' (*History*, 19, pp 234–44). The natural scientist can pursue his object of study by direct contact in a continuous and unbroken line; seeing the thing evolve before him and go back to any point in it to revise or confirm his thesis. For the historian, the evidence is broken, discontinuous, always secondhand, and incomplete especially for the most interesting problems. It is not even easy to define evidence in every situation. When is it completely trustworthy? When is it only hearsay or gossip, or an attempt by interested parties to obscure the real truth for purposes of propaganda, usually political or religious? Everyone is tempted to dismiss as unreliable or trivial anything which spoils the thesis.

It is always important to weigh the document itelf. Who wrote it? Is it a copy, transcript, autograph or decipher? Have marginal additions been incorporated in the printed text without note? One must approach all official statements on this kind of subject and in this period with a spirit of incredulity. Successful politicians, arguing necessity, have always been slippery creatures. The investigator has to walk on black ice without losing his balance; analysing the complications, defining the status quaestionis and providing clues to areas for further research to anyone interested in probing further.

Some reminder of what should be our undogmatic non-slumbering approach to the subject was given to us in *The Times* of 29 December 1990 where we read with apprehension that when a new history syllabus came into operation, it would ensure that, 'at seven children should be able to retell the story of the gunpowder plot ... recognise the difference between a fairy tale character and an historical personality', and for good measure be able to distinguish between fact and value judgments. Far from acknowledging a controversial element, there was to be no question, apparently, about the basic facts of the plot; nor was there any difficulty in distinguishing the good from the bad. Papists and more particularly Jesuits are still in some danger of being recast in their time-honoured, dishonoured, role of villains. Antonia Fraser's study, if widely accepted, should at least make this less likely. Not all have approved her revision.

One could hope that nowadays the prejudices and crude emotions which accompanied historical writing in the past are much diminished if not eliminated. The religious spirit does not invariably assist the cause of truth. Writing in 1905, Philip Sidney complained, 'It is this common ignorance that has helped Jesuits, and other interested persons, in their task of trying to obscure the history of the [gunpowder] plot as much as possible ... to call into question the accuracy of the facts, and by hook or by crook trying to clear the name and fame of Father Henry Garnet, and other Jesuit priests.' Sidney wrote *A history of the gunpowder plot* ... for the Religious Tract Society in times that were still so highly polemical that even to question the complicity of the Jesuits seemed like a general attack on true religion. In this day and age Garnet and his fellow Jesuits have received the more impartial hearing their case demands, at least from Antonia Fraser. The unsatisfactory nature of the evidence against them is more clearly recognised even by critics not overfriendly. The determination of Robert Cecil and his coministers to implicate them is a factor which should arouse suspicion of his influence and intervention at other points in the story. *Qui nimis probat nihil probat* – or perhaps proves something to the advantage of the adversary.

The bibliographies of Mark Nicholls and Antonia Fraser for the gunpowder plot contain much that is relevant to the present study. Works more immediately touching on the present theme will be found in footnotes to the text. The late Rev. W.K.L. Webb, S.J., examined most of the material to hand in detail and produced an interesting manuscript study which also sheds light on aspects of the present thesis. He agreed with the present writer that the latest plot contained much that amounted to government contrivance. The fact that he disagreed with much of the thesis set out in *The real story ...* is a useful reminder that there is no such thing as a uniform history of these times accepted even among Jesuits. True, no Jesuit knowing the authentic history of his order from reliable foreign sources, especially those in Rome, could suppose that the Jesuits were involved as organisers or even approvers of assassination plots. But there is no unanimity on other important details. Fr John Gerard thought the celebrated confession of Thomas Wintour, giving a sketch history of the gunpowder plot on 23/25 November 1605, was a forgery. Fr Herbert Thurston took it as genuine. I consider the signature forged, the rest written by Wintour.

Undoubtedly, the gunpowder plot constitutes a watershed in English history. Any time before this non-event, as Hurstfield once described it, even if reconciliation with Rome would not have been a realistic possibility, Catholicism might have come to be tolerated at least in holes and corners; and perhaps more openly, provided it did not make itself conspicuous. After the plot, the papists came increasingly to occupy the position of the Jews in Nazi Germany. Like the burning of the Reichstag, allegedly by Jews, even the fire of London was attributed to the Jesuits and commemorated for ever in the Monument, a prominent structure in the City of London. They were despised and hated but also feared. Without visible influence but credited with the incalculable propensity for destruction to be attributed to a powerful and unscrupulous secret society, they were vowed to evil whatever their hypocritical surface colouring. This reputation of Jesuits and papists generally as advocates of treason, assassination and plot had its consummation after the gunpowder plot; but the ground had been preparing over a long period. This book is the story of that preparation.

Any vindication of the Jesuits in the present study is incidental to the larger issues, although the writer, as a Jesuit himself, cannot regard this lesser aspect as trivial. One is likely to be accused of special pleading or providing ammunition in a continuing apologetic war. This is unavoidable. No apology is offered. The attempt is to portray man the political animal revealed in a certain type of statecraft: which hopefully is not the only kind there is. No one will be naive enough to suppose that such procedures are nowadays obsolete or only exist in the pages, shall we say, of John Le Carré. The temptation to cut ethical corners still influences the lives of public administrators and private citizens alike. Sixteenth-century people were taken up with the peculiar problems of politics and religion, personal and public, in an age which had little regard for individual conscience or conviction; least of all, it may be said, in England and Spain. Our own age differs from the condition of early seventeenth-century England only in more fortunate parts of the world; and even in this country perhaps only for the time being. History can repeat itself. It is difficult for us to enter into an understanding of earlier attitudes. These were determined sometimes by a desire to survive physically without excessive loss of spiritual integrity, and sometimes by cynicism in some who had abandoned the struggle; who accepted the basic demand of the Cecilian state system: conform or be obliterated.

To understand fully the mentality of those living in Jacobethan England one would probably need to have had experience of life under one of the dictatorial regimes still abounding in the world. One might take refuge in the thought that the first earl of Salisbury would never have done such a thing. What he might have done in connection with the gunpowder plot becomes more plausible from considering what he did in previous plots. Who can say what a 'great statesman' will do when he feels driven by necessity to find the answer to a problem which can only be readily solved by a moral bypass? Furthermore, son Robert was only continuing the policy of a father and a regime which began with the accession of Elizabeth I. William and Robert Cecil perfectly understood the words of Edward Forset who saw the use of 'wicked men' by magistrates on occasion as an analogy of God: 'himself infinitely good, extracteth good out of evil'. This only reflects the doctrines set forth in the politician's primer for the modern age, Niccolo Macchiavelli's *The prince*. It was in Italy that Walsingham acquired his early training and distinguished himself as a student.

Reflecting more precisely on the all-important and recurring question of what is evidence, everyone who looks for a solution of these plot mysteries comes up against sources which contradict one another. A thesis emerges after concluding that some sources are relatively trustworthy, others less so, some not at all. Everything may have something to tell us. There is a subjective element in deciding the relative value of evidences: one reason why there is no unanimity among scholars. One could despair of ever finding the truth about almost anything, especially when the subject, like ours, involves the emotions. Counsels of despair must be resisted. The north face of the Eiger will always attract climbers even with the possibility of falling off. New paths and ways ahead are there to be attempted. So in history there will always be room for reappraisal. The wood can look different from another viewpoint above the trees. In spite of the confusion apparent from one angle, a pattern can emerge from another. A test of validity in any proffered solution has to be consistency. Consistency presupposes a gradation of credibility in the evidence offered. True, what one accepts or rejects as spurious depends partly on personal bias; but bias is not the same thing as dishonesty or even prejudice. This simply rejects what is known to be true but spoils the thesis. Writing history should not be an occupation for mere propagandists even if most of us, truth to tell, have an axe to grind; at least a hidden one.

So the gunpowder plot was not a unique and isolated event in our history, sticking up on its own like Ayer's Rock in the middle of Australia. It was only the last of a lengthy series of plots which began in the reign of Elizabeth I and ended with a final spectacular after a long gap following the death of the second Cecil in 1612. This final spectacular in the reign of Charles II, the Oates plot, ended in fact as a damp squib. Is there a thread of continuity which linked them all? What typified all the plots? Three answers are possible. One, and that still favoured by most because it is hallowed by long tradition, is that they were engineered by the enemies of the regime. Most of the time these were papists – not necessarily in the sense that they approved as a community, but that a few headstrong characters claimed to be acting for the rest. An older tradition, officially fostered for centuries, was that the papists approved of them openly or secretly in sufficient numbers to make the whole community reasonably suspect and therefore justifiably subject to the most extreme rigours of draconian laws. The third approach recognises that individual Catholics were present in nearly all of them. But one asks, what sort of Catholics were they? Were the apparent ringleaders also the real organisers? Or only agents provocateurs? The complications begin.

The technique of denigration

At the trials of the lay gunpowder plotters, and later of Henry Garnet, the Jesuit, every effort was made by the attorney general, Edward Coke, to make the Jesuits not only accomplices but principal contrivers of the plot. Papists were not alone in thinking this went too far. Coke admitted during Garnet's trial on 28 March 1606, 'There was a particular apology spread abroad for this man, and another general for all Jesuits and priests, together with this imputation, that king-killing and queen-killing was not indeed a doctrine of theirs, but only a fiction and policy of our State thereby to make the popish religion ... despised and in disgrace.'[1] This other tradition continued as a kind of descant above the popular tune. The Jacobethan plots have not only been looked upon askance by Catholic scholars. Martin Hume declared, 'the accusations that have been repeated by nearly every English historian from Elizabeth's time to our own, of widespread and numerous plots by Catholics to assassinate the Queen at this period, are to a large extent unsupported by serious evidence ... In accordance with the usual practice, it was the policy of the English government at the time to blacken the character and methods of the national enemy as much as possible ... '[2] Again, plots 'like that for which Dr Parry suffered and that of Moody and young Stafford, were more or less bogus plots, in which agents-provocateurs were sacrificed to the exigencies of party politics ... Much of the stuff was obviously untrue, but it was made the most of in England for two reasons. Anything that aroused horror and detestation of Spain, and of those Englishmen who were assumed to have sold their bodies and souls to her, was useful – as we have seen in the report of the parliament of 1593 – in keeping alive the patriotism of the country, inciting its liberality in the matter of supplies for defence against so dastardly a foe, and in attracting to the Protestant side those waverers who declined to continue their identification with a cause which allowed regicide to be used for its ends.'[3] David Jardine likewise wrote critically of English policy-makers in the same period. 'The practice of those days was to hold the people in leading-strings on political subjects, and so much light only was given respecting occurrences of state as the Privy Council thought convenient and useful for the attainment of their objects. Where the whole truth would not produce the intended effect, a part only was pub-

1 *The trial of Guy Fawkes*, edited by Donald Carswell (London 1934), p. 135.   2 Martin Hume, *Treason and plot* (London 1901), p. 113.   3 Ibid., pp 88-9.

lished; and where the part would not exactly suit the purpose, no scruple was made of garbling and altering it.'[4]

So we are heartened by such authorities in upholding a right to be suspicious of what is presented as evidence whether in connection with the gunpowder plot or any other. The unreliability of evidence in such cases, Jardine reminds us, 'was well illustrated in the official account of the Gunpowder Plot published immediately after its occurrence. Before the trials of the conspirators, an anonymous narrative entitled *A discourse of the manner of the discovery of the gunpowder plot* was printed by the king's printer, and published by authority of the government. This publication which was industriously ascribed to the pen of the king, and was called the "King's Book", was not only dispersed profusely in England, but was sent, together with the king's speech on opening the parliament, to the ambassadors at foreign courts, translated into several languages, and circulated with the utmost diligence in every part of Europe. A careful comparison of this relation with Bacon's acknowledged narratives of the treasons of Lopez and of the earl of Essex, in Queen Elizabeth's time, produces a strong impression that all of them were composed by the same hand. The resemblance is not confined to the similarity of the style and language; the whole scheme of the *Discourse* is the same as that of the "Declaration of the earl of Essex's treasons", viz., to surround fictions by undoubted truths with such apparent simplicity and carelessness, but in fact with such consummate art and depth of design, that the reader is beguiled into an unsuspecting belief of the whole narration.'[5]

'Consummate art and depth of design' is something which appears in many of the plots of the period. Nevertheless, even in the most sophisticated contrivances, as one could take them, there are curious inconsistencies; flaws that must leave even the most credulous, or perhaps one should say more justly, even the most friendly, receptive and optimistic reader somewhat dismayed. One feature of all these plots, which convey at least a superficial impression of authenticity, is that they occurred during what one might call the Cecil domination. Between 1558 and 1612, for reasons which have been often explored, England came under the influence of a great dynasty in a way which has never happened in quite the same way before or since. The reign of the Cecils, father and son, and the term 'reign' is scarcely metaphorical, dominated the scene of Queen Elizabeth until 1598, when William Lord Burghley died. Her remaining years and those of James I were overshadowed by his son Robert, first earl of Salisbury, until his death in May 1612. These two methodical, patient and intelligent men, masters of statecraft, though not overendowed with moral conscience as ordinary mortals would understand it, determined to an extraordinary degree not only the course of history but also of historiography.

The easiest way to arrive at a plausible picture of the Jacobethan age is to confine one's reading to the official correspondence, minutes and letters of the Cecils and their faithful colleagues and subordinates. Burghley's extensive and frequent memorials and

---

4 David Jardine, *A narrative of the gunpowder plot* (London 1857), p. vii.   5 Ibid., p. viii.

analyses of the political situation in Europe as well as Britain at any given time are masterly as summaries from his point of view. The consistent picture emerging portrays his honour, devotion to duty, selflessness and loftiness of ideal. Robert wrote much less in this genre but conveyed the same impression of devotion to duty, undoubtedly true, and transparent integrity, often false. It is difficult to challenge their claims if only because the evidence for a contrary or more critical point of view is relatively scanty; not only in official but even in unofficial family sources. This is not surprising. As secretaries of state, father and son kept, or did not keep, and controlled, the main sources of documentary evidence. These included the acts of the privy council and the reports of ambassadors as well as the remaining public records. There were two principal ways whereby the secretaries of state could gain control of private records. Anyone charged with treason – and very few in the period once charged achieved acquittal – had his property, including family records, confiscated to the crown. Both Cecils were also in turn masters of the court of wards. This gave them an additional opportunity for manipulation and control through the heirs. They not only held as wards a significant number of heirs in their minority to vast feudal estates and rich titles, but also had thus the opportunity to weed out embarrassing items in their family archives.

From the mere absence of documents, that is, of evidence, one can suspect much but prove nothing. Private records, or what is left of them, tend to tell much the same story as the public. But gaps amounting to a gaping abyss in the lives of such as Edward de Vere, seventeenth earl of Oxford, Thomas Arundell, first Baron Arundell of Wardour, Thomas Howard, fourth duke of Norfolk, Robert Dudley, earl of Leicester, and Sir Francis Walsingham, to name a few important examples, make it difficult to believe in the aggregate that all these lacunae are simply the result of time's random ravages. An interesting example of the way in which records could be manipulated so that only what was wanted was recorded or allowed to survive was uncovered by Professor Joel Hurstfield, no hostile witness. 'From two different sources we have evidence which appears to demonstrate that Burghley refused to take advantage of the rare opportunity now at hand' – the mastership of the court of wards – so that 'in all the time he was master ... he reserved to his own use but three', and 'of no other wardship grant to Burghley has it been possible to discover a single trace.'[6] But 'if we turn away from the neat and careful entries of the clerk of wards and call in some of the unofficial and informal materials of family papers ... from these sources ... we can build up a significant list of wards to whom he stood guardian ... In all he gained the wardships of eight noblemen, an unique achievement in Tudor England.' This success, as Hurstfield makes clear, was due to Burghley's singular influence over the queen.

Elizabeth's acceptance of Burghley, and later of his son, in almost all they proposed and did, was the all-important factor in the history of the times. Becoming the royal confidant par excellence was a dangerous proceeding as was proved in the lives of Cardinal Wolsey and Thomas Cromwell. But Wolsey failed because he recognised

6 Joel Hurstfield, *The queen's wards* (London, 1958), p. 249.

another loyalty, however perfunctorily, that to Rome, while Cromwell failed because he came to treat too casually a king whom in time he took too much for granted. The Cecils, father and son, were too wily or wise to overstep the mark. Ruling virtually as kings, they were never so foolish as to behave in the royal presence as anything but subjects. Elizabeth and James both realised their dependence on these great subjects even if they also understood the importance of not letting their greatness eclipse their own. They were not allowed to become overmighty and they were too shrewd to attempt it. Their sovereignty was a quiet affair. James owed his English kingship much more to the influence of Robert Cecil than did Elizabeth to William. Nevertheless, Elizabeth had known William as a friend when she had hardly any other in the difficult times from 1550. Robert Cecil had made his preference regarding the succession clear to James long before the queen's death and revealed himself early as the most important single factor in deciding it should be Scottish.[7]

Neither Elizabeth nor James I were wise enough to penetrate every shift and wile of these their mightiest subjects. The present study confirms the fact. So their popular image is largely saved. But they were astute enough to realise that they could not rule, for all their despotism, without the virtual consent of at least the greatest officers of state. The outstanding quality of the Cecils, an aspect of their political savoir faire, was that they knew when to stop. They did not stop before their own nests were very comfortably feathered. But they well knew how to stop all and sundry coveting similar nests; and this a long distance before men on the way up came anywhere close to serious rivalry with themselves. As for those who had already arrived, or were on the way to arriving, and might seriously threaten the Cecil dominance, it is noteworthy, and scarcely coincidental, that many found themselves involved in plots and treason. In this way they were effectively removed from the scene if only by imprisonment. This remarkable phenomenon is surely worth investigating.

Elizabeth and James accepted, James perhaps too completely, the principle of not muzzling the ox that grinds the corn. Both monarchs were well aware of the faults of those around them. But as Elizabeth wrote to James VI on 11 September 1592, 'I am not so unskilful of a kingly rule that I would wink at no fault, yet would be open-eyed at public indignity. Neither should all have the whip though some were scourged.'[8] Much of the history of the times depended on the favour of the sovereigns for the chosen few. It was fairly easy to deceive or convince Elizabeth and James with regard to alleged enemies since they both had behind them practical experience of plotting against the throne. Elizabeth had witnessed the peril of Wyatt's rebellion in the time of Queen Mary, coming near to involvement herself. If Mary had been served by the Cecils, and if they had truly espoused her cause, it is questionable whether Elizabeth would ever have come to the throne.

7 John Bruce, editor, *The correspondence of King James VI with Sir Robert Cecil and others in England*, Camden Society 1861, Old Series, pp 7-8.   8 Elizabeth I to James VI, 26.11.1592, Camden Society, vol. 46 (1849) p. 77.

James had even more direct contact with attempts by factions to snatch him even if they did not amount to attempts to kill him. His was a genial spirit many ways, and well might Elizabeth in a letter of 21 January 1592, warn him of, or rather rebuke him for, his dangerous leniency shown recently to certain rebels. 'I have beheld of late a strange, dishonourable and dangerous pardon, which, if it be true, you have not only neglected yourself but wronged me, that have too much procured your good to be so evil guer-doned with such a wrong as to have a free forgiveness of aught conspired against my person and estate ... Think me, I pray you, not ignorant what it becometh a king to do, and that will I never omit.'[9] Or as she summed it up in a letter of 26 November 1592, 'Weed out the weeds lest the best corn fester!'[10] Not that Elizabeth was always as harsh as her words. She showed great reluctance in bringing William Cecil's earlier rival, the fourth duke of Norfolk, to the block in 1572. And the lord treasurer and his friends had to chafe for another fifteen years before the Scottish queen was safely dispatched. Both sovereigns realised that it was not their business to descend too deeply into the foren-sic details of treason trials any more than it was their business to make a personal inspection of the palace drains. They might bring attention to bear on unpleasant smells. A ruler left the sordid, nauseous and unamusing things of life as far as possible to ministers. This was what they were for. Meanwhile the sovereign got on with the important if not the main task of court amusements. So it was quite possible for min-isters who enjoyed the complete confidence of the crown to bend the truth consider-ably, especially if their untruthfulness was at least ostensibly directed to saving the state from harm. How far did ministers go in their management and exposition of treason-able practices all too frequent in this period? We shall try to see.

It will be evident by now that a third possible explanation of many, perhaps most, if not all of the treasonable plots popping like boiling mud in thermal springs is that they were at least largely contrived by government. It had a very sufficient motive. One important factor in the background of plots leading to the gun-powder plot was the emergence of a conscious effort to destroy the influence of the Catholic reformation – the counter reformation as it is usually denoted. In England as in other places the ref-ormation was not only a religious movement. Primarily concerned with religion, nowhere was it effectively promoted without the support of princes and politicians with an eye to substantial material advantage. The counter reformation likewise was a religious movement which also relied heavily on the support of rulers and politicians working likewise with mixed motives. No religion, church or sect could prevail with-out the support of the secular arm. Or expected to. In England the movement aimed at the Catholic reformation came to include an important secular and non-religious aspect which at government level could be taken to eclipse purely religious considera-tions. Macchiavellian rather than humanist, theistic rather than Christian, pragmatist more than Protestant, it branded Catholicism not as heresy but as treason. The idea was originally invented by Henry VIII and Thomas Cromwell but it was revived to do

9 S. to s., 21.1.1592, ibid., p. 73.   10 Ibid., pp 73, 78.

deadly service against the ancient faith by Sir William Cecil and his allies with the tacit approval at least of Queen Elizabeth and of her successor, to look no further.

It was fundamentally absurd that a religion which the western world had recognised for more than a millennium as embodying two ultimate authorities, namely the pope as the spiritual head of christendom and the emperor or the local monarch as temporal head, and both under Christ, should be branded as treason. Tensions there had been between the two powers, inevitably. Henry II and Thomas à Becket, Gregory VII and Barbarossa, and many less spectacular confrontations. All the same, the system worked well enough. After 1559 it became a legal fiction in England that all English papists were traitors *ipso facto* by reason of their religion; a charge that had nothing in it of justice and was strenuously resisted by the papists themselves. It had to be shown, however, that whatever their outward profession, Christians still loyal to the Roman connection were in fact unworthy of civic trust. This was proved by their alleged constant proneness to acts of treason and rebellion. The 'proof' lay in the plots occurring serially with almost monotonous frequency throughout two reigns until the death of the second Cecil in 1612. After this time there was little of the kind to record, as we recall, until the Oates plot of 1678. This failed, one could believe, not because of any surplus of goodwill or sincerity in the land where papists were concerned but because the technique of exploiting and organising these plots had been lost. The political scene and ambience were no longer closed and closeknit enough to prevent unpalatable truths leaking out so that all but the most prejudiced had to accept the fact that this plot was a fabrication.

The idea that the earlier plots were largely contrived by government still does not go down well. One can admit that there is room for more indulgent reinterpretation. Nevertheless, it becomes fairly clear that our leading statesmen at that time were perfectly adapted to the task of bending evidence to suit the needs of statecraft. It is difficult to believe that either of the Cecils or Leicester had much personal religion even if they mouthed pieties with the best. They well understood the importance of religion for most of the people round them. It was still for most the skeleton to which clung the flesh of daily life. The government well understood the uses to which religion might be put: indeed, needed to be put in matters of state. In this age religion was not the opium of the people but often the whip in the hand of the pharaohs. The ruling caste was opposed to toleration in matters of conscience. This in any case was poorly understood in most parts of Europe especially those under Spanish domination. Sir William took religion seriously as an instrument of state policy, but his personal approach beneath the surface was probably as lighthearted throughout his life as when he revealed what could be taken as his true feelings in a well-known story retailed in G. Peck's *Desiderata curiosa*. This concerned his student days at Gray's Inn and the successful if somewhat cynical exploitation of a fellow-student's superstition to recover property lost in gambling.[11]

11 Conyers Read, *Mr Secretary Cecil and Queen Elizabeth* (London, 1912), pp 30-1, quoting Peck's *Desiderata curiosa*, p. 5, tells the story retailed by Cecil himself revealing a side of his make-up later

Cecil's pragmatic approach to religion in his maturity, largely coinciding with the queen's, appeared clearly enough in 'An antidote against Jesuitism' penned for her enlightenment most probably in 1583. He speaks admiringly of King Philip of Spain as a prince 'whose closet hath brought forth greater victories than all his father's journeys, absolutely by ruling his subjects a people all one-hearted in religion, constantly ambitious, politic and valiant, the king rich and liberal and, which I like worst of all, greatly beloved amongst all the discontented party of your highness subjects'.[12] Robert Cecil, left behind him, it seems, no such plain statement of his views but his dislike of having more than one approved religion in the State is sufficiently evidenced.[13] He, like his father before him, rejected firmly what had been called the Gelasian principle of the two swords, the separation of the spiritual from the temporal in the state. As under Elizabeth, so under James, there would be only one sword with two edges, so that both powers were in one hand and turned sharply against all enemies public or private. The distinction of spiritual and temporal thus became blurred for all practical purposes. Churchmen in the past enjoyed great influence in the state; but from this time the Church became increasingly a subordinate department of secular government. True, the clerics continued to enjoy their original titles of bishops, priests and deacons, but since the sacrament of holy order was abolished by the thirty-nine Articles of 1563 these could not mean what they meant when England was Catholic. Moreover, the lord chancellor, the keeper of the king's conscience, was now always a layman.[14]

metamorphosed but probably not lost. 'The sixth of May, 33 H. 8, being nineteen years old, he ... student in Gray's Inn, where he profitted, as before at Cambridge. But as his years and company required, he would many times be merry among young gentlemen, who were most desirous of his company for his witty mirth and merry temper. Among the rest I heard him tell this ... That a companion of his ... enticed him to play. Whereupon in a short time he lost all his money, bedding and books to his companion; having never used play before. And being afterwards among his other company, he told them how such a one had misled him; saying he would presently have a device to be even with him. And he was as good as his word. For with a long trunk he made a hole in the wall, near his playfellow's bedhead and in a fearful voice spake thus through the trunk: "O mortal man, repent! Repent of thy horrible time consumed in play, cozenage and such lewdness as thou hast committed or else thou are damned and cannot be saved!" Which being spoken at midnight, when he was all alone, so amazed him as drove him into a sweat of fear. Most penitent and heavy, the next day, in presence of the youths he told, with trembling, what a fearful voice spake to him at midnight, vowing never to play again. And calling for Mr Cecil, asked him forgiveness on his knees, and restored all his money, bedding and books ... Many other the like merry jests, I have heard him tell ...' A great pity that they are lost!   12 'An antidote against Jesuitism', Inner Temple, Petyt mss, Series 538, vol. 43, ff. 304-14. It is in Burghley's hand, as given in the title, and dated '158-' and would appear to be a draft. The finished version, 'An excellent treatise against Jesuits and recusants written by the earle of Salisbury or rather the lord treas. Burleigh, and dedicated 'To Queen Elizabeth' is in ibid., vol. 37, ff. 177 et seq.   13 P. M. Handover, *The second Cecil*, (London 1959), chapter 29, 'I love not to yield to any toleration'.   14 Ibid. Evidence for the firm control of the Anglican bishops exist in many places. See V. J. K. Brook, *A life of Archbishop Parker* (Oxford 1962) passim; P. Collinson, *Archbishop Grindal* (London, 1979), 235-6; references in *Salisbury Calendar*, v, to Lincoln pp 37-41, Durham p. 35,

The Cecils with complete ruthlessness and an astonishing degree of success managed to cut off the heads of every opposing growth even if they did not always succeed in pulling out the root. Since the popish enemy was for them the most significant, they endeavoured as far as they could, to give all opposition and opponents a popish air whether this was true or not. So the fourth duke of Norfolk, implicated in the Ridolfi plot of 1571, was made out to be a Catholic although in fact he never wavered from his Anglican faith; or for that matter from his allegiance to Elizabeth.[15] Norfolk's principal crime was to attempt to maintain himself in a position of independence of William Cecil. Admittedly, such independence could have been disastrous for the kind of influence which Cecil considered necessary to carry out his grand design. When rivals similarly threatened Robert Cecil, or he thought they did, he too proved only too well how completely he had learned his lessons in Realpolitik from his gifted father. All this is what this book is about.

Sir William allowed no friend or friendship to stand between him and the goal he had set before him. Indeed, anyone who impeded his onward march soon ceased to be a friend. Not that Sir William gratuitously made enemies or revealed his hand except when confident of emerging victorious. The will to win was revealed early in his long and successful career. On 21 July 1563, he penned a meaningful letter to Sir Nicholas Bacon, lord keeper of the great seal. Bacon had resented what he took to be Cecil's cavalier attitude in writing up the letters which duty allotted to him as principal secretary. Cecil used his discretion in recent wording to the point where he had substantially altered the meaning of what the council intended so that Bacon refused to sign the letters. Cecil took it heavily. 'I know not upon what just ground your lordship should use me thus strangely, as you many times do in open speech and not in private ... Indeed so manifestly was your displeasure showed, as the greatest part of my grief is that there were so many sorts of hearers that perchance mislikes not to see and hear so strange dealing ... I required your Lordship to hear me speak but ye would not ... I confessed the letters were otherwise in some points but not contrary.'[16]

Significantly he reminded Bacon that 'what he had written was so also ordered by the queen's Majesty ... not contrary to the resolution but more to the purpose.' He resented the fact that such criticism made him out to be a 'falsary'. 'Though I lack the wit, the great wealth, the credit that you easilier get than I can, I will never ... lack any portion of truth, plainness or honesty that you have.' Cecil had held himself in from speaking his mind in what might have been a stormy meeting the day before, but Bacon should not suppose that this was due to intimidation. 'For I assure you, my Lord, what weakness soever you find in my understanding, you shall find me in that quarrel no baby, nor one that will learn of you more than I have, but to call on God

Peterborough pp 11-12, Canterbury p. 18, all of 1594. **15** F. Edwards, *The marvellous chance* (London 1968), referred to subsequently in the notes to these chapters as *The m. c.* For Norfolk's Anglicanism, see pp 177, 190-1, 368. **16** W. Cecil to the lord keeper, 21.7.1563; BL, Lansdowne ms 162, ff. 69r-70v.

and his grace to serve him and my sovereign lady the queen for whose service with some earnestness I find these privy nips ... I am no clerk to write your resolutions, nor letters for you or the council. There be clerks for that purpose. Yet have I for service never refused to do that which to such offices doth belong.'[17]

He could not resist a final, typical flourish reminding his addressee of the great sacrifices he was making for the realm. 'For service I have forborne wife, children, kin, friends, house, yea all mine own to serve, which I know not that any other hath done in my time.' Sir William ended by expressing his readiness 'to honour and love' the lord keeper as he should, but he would not put up with further provocation.[18] It was a rare kind of letter for Cecil. The indications are that Sir Nicholas took the point since we hear of no renewed protest. The same kind of determination descended to Sir Robert, son of Mildred Cooke. His father established for the office of principal secretary, after his showdown with Bacon, virtually the powers of a grand vizier. Son Robert performed as effectively when he too came to assume the office. Small wonder that the Cecils left an indelible mark on English history. Their imprint lies on all the plots which led to the gunpowder plot.

17 Ibid.   18 Ibid.

The Ridolfi plot

The Ridolfi plot of 1571 was in many ways the prototype of all the successful plots that followed right up to the gunpowder plot, the crowning masterpiece of the series. This first *tour de force* of Cecilian statecraft has been examined in detail with the evidence, the lack of it, and the contradictions which make it reasonable if not necessary to believe that Ridolfi, a papal agent, was turned round.[1] This happened after a couple of instructive weeks as Sir Francis Walsingham's house prisoner in the late autumn of 1569. Roberto Ridolfi, a Florentine banker, had extensive contacts with English families noble and prestigious including Thomas Howard, the fourth duke of Norfolk of his house. Ridolfi was picked up soon after the northern rising of 1569 in which his activity could have been taken as ambivalent at least. As the queen claimed, no doubt at William Cecil's prompting, she 'could, if she were so disposed to proceed severely' have 'convinced him of much more' than he had confessed. But he was released on two important conditions. 'Bound by writing ... to her Majesty's use in the sum of £1,000', he also undertook 'not to deal directly or indirectly in any matters appertaining to her Majesty, or the state of this realm, otherwise than he shall be licensed by her Majesty, or have her assent by declaration of some of her privy council. Neither shall he impart to any person the matters whereof he hath been examined since his restraint.'[2] Conyers Read omitted the latter parts of this quotation and only reproduced in full the other letters of this correspondence in his life of Walsingham. He admitted, 'it is a little hard to understand why Ridolfi got off so easily'.[3]

Ridolfi's 'escape' is not at all difficult to understand on the thesis that he was the principal executive of a skilfully contrived plot which was designed by William Cecil to eliminate the duke of Norfolk and the queen of Scots. Among other circumstances, it would explain what appears to be a serious oversight when Ridolfi was allowed to leave England, on 25 March 1571, with his bags unexamined. These contained, as was later alleged, names of the principal noblemen of England who were ready to help a

---

1 For the Ridolfi plot, see Neville Williams, *Thomas Howard, 4th duke of Norfolk* (London 1964); Edwards, *The m. c.*, see n. 15 above. For Ridolfi's stay with Walsingham, see Conyers Read, *Mr Secretary Walsingham and the policy of Queen Elizabeth*, Oxford 1925, i, p. 165. F. Edwards, *The dangerous queen* (London 1964), pp 164-6, referred to subsequently in this chapter as *The d. q.* 2 Ibid. 3 C. Read, op. cit., p. 167.

Spanish invasion to overthrow Elizabeth and put the Scottish queen married to Norfolk in her place. How could the true Protestant Norfolk always claimed to be up to the moment of death, and genuine man of honour, have stooped to such a conspiracy? An effort was made to represent him as a Roman Catholic, and therefore a man capable of any villainy. From the evidence the idea is absurd.

Norfolk's consistency in his Anglicanism was evident throughout his life. By the end of May 1572 he knew that he must die. The man he asked for as his comforter at the end was Alexander Nowell, dean of St Paul's, a lifelong friend.[4] In his scaffold speech on 2 June he declared, 'I take God to witness, I am not, nor never was, a papist since I knew what religion meant. I have had friends, yea, familiar friends, and peradventure servants, that have been papists, with whom I have borne. But I call God to witness I am none. I utterly defy the pope and his religion, and I hope to be saved only by my faith in Christ Jesus. I utterly abhor all man's traditions. And if at any time I did give countenance to any papist whereby any good man was offended, or the Church, I ask them mercy. There is no man that alloweth better of this religion than I do.'[5] This was the duke's last word on the subject. A Christian believer would not wish to go before judgment in the next life with a gross lie on his lips. The argument has nothing to do with the truth of Christianity, of course, but only with Norfolk's belief in it. Sir Thomas Smith was sent to France early in 1572 to justify English policy towards Norfolk and Queen Mary. The queen-mother of France, Catherine de Medici, raised the obvious point of Norfolk's religion as an argument against his participation in the plot. Smith claimed that his Protestantism was only a sham. 'His doings declareth what he was; the bringing up of his children all in papistry, the chief officers and most in credit with him all papists.'[6] Norfolk did appoint a Catholic tutor for a short time but he was dismissed as soon as he knew of his religion.[7]

Perhaps the Ridolfi plot is best approached, in this study abbreviated from two books, by following the trial of the duke in Westminster Hall on 16 January 1572. The court which tried him was that of the lord high steward. This only came into existence to try a peer of the realm when parliament was in recess. When parliament was sitting, a nobleman would be tried before his peers in the high court of parliament. The lord high steward, who, like his court, only came into existence for this special purpose, was the sole judge of the court. It was his warrant that summoned the prisoner to the bar, and his indictment that removed the case from any lower court. The peers who assisted him as 'triers' were determined by him both as to person and number.[8] The earl of Shrewsbury was the lord high steward on this occasion, a man whom Burghley could trust to steer the court to the correct verdict. He was to preside later over the court that would try Mary, queen of Scots. The twenty-six triers in 1572 could be relied on to

4 *The m. c.*, p. 367.   5 Ibid., p. 368. L. Cheyne, 'Account of the duke of Norfolk's speeches on the scaffold'; BL, Add. ms 48, 027, ff. 114r-16v.   6 *The m. c.*, p. 355.   7 Cf. *The d. q.*, p. 309. See 'A declaration of the duke's intent'; BL, Cotton ms Calig. C. ii, ff. 551r-64v. This was written after Norfolk's death by a Protestant servant or friend to vindicate him. The writer showed an intimate knowledge of his household.   8 For the court of the lord high steward, see *The m. c.*, p. 211.

give him the utmost assistance: the earls of Sussex, Huntingdon, Hertford – the two latter had some claim to the throne – the Dudleys, the earls of Warwick and Leicester, Lord Burghley himself and a full supporting cast and chorus that would not be likely to sing out of tune. As David Jardine commented, 'There can be no doubt that the nomination of persons so circumstanced to decide on a capital charge was a gross indecency.'[9]

The heads of the legal profession were prominent: Sir Robert Catline, lord chief justice, Sir James Dyer, lord chief justice of the common pleas, and Sir Edward Saunders, lord chief baron of the exchequer. Sir Francis Knollys, Sir Walter Mildmay and others of the privy council were also there. More importantly, taking a more direct part in the proceedings were Nicholas Barham, the queen's sergeant, Gilbert Gerrard, attorney-general and Thomas Wilbraham, attorney of the court of wards. They all of them knew their duty to the state and to their careers. The trial was public so that some who watched may have written up the anonymous accounts on which more than one narrative was based.[10]

The lengthy indictment read by the clerk of the crown may be reduced to four main heads. Firstly, contrary to Elizabeth's order upon his obedience he attempted to marry the Scottish queen, knowing her title to the English throne which could only be to Elizabeth's prejudice. Secondly, he helped with money persons involved in the northern rebellion after they had been attainted with treason and had fled to Flanders. Thirdly, he used Roberto Ridolfi as his agent to incite foreign powers to invade England. Fourthly, he had sent pecuniary relief to Lord Herries and other Scots, the queen's public enemies. The most serious charge claimed that he had intended not merely to depose the queen but to bring about her death, raise sedition and civil war in England, and 'endeavour a change and alteration of the sincere worship of God, well and religiously established'.[11]

Before attempting to plead, the duke asked to be allowed counsel for answering the indictment. Catline pointed out that no counsel was allowed in cases of high treason. The accused had to answer 'to his own fact only'. According to Staunford, writing in 1557, although the answer to the indictment, a plea of guilty or not guilty, had to be made without counsel, 'if his answer be such that it exceedeth his skill in law to plead it, he shall have counsel assigned to him, notwithstanding it be against the King'. But Staunford justified the principle introduced by the Tudors, it seems, that counsel was not allowed easily, and by this time not at all. If the accused had counsel, 'they might be so wary in their speech that it would occupy too long time before the truth would appear'. The defendant's words should be 'plain and simple, and thus the truth may be sooner discovered than by the artificial discourse of learned men'. So while 'the artificial discourse of learned men' could be used to secure a conviction, it could not

9 David Jardine, *Criminal trials*, i (London 1832), p. 231.   10 Sources for the trial of Norfolk in *The m. c.*, p. 210, n. 1. The longest and best(?) account is in Joseph Brown, *The trial of Thomas, duke of Norfolk* (London 1709). It is not overpartial to him.   11 For the indictment, see *The m. c.*, p. 212.

be called upon to defend the accused.[12] Not only was Norfolk denied counsel but, as he told the court, he had only fourteen hours notice before coming to trial. 'I am hardly handled. I have had ... neither book of statutes nor so much as the breviate of statutes. I am brought to fight without a weapon.'[13] The duke was not an intellectual and had only an average memory impaired by recent hardship. 'Here is too much for me to answer without book. My memory is not so good to run through everything as they do that have their books and their notes lying before them.'[14]

By way of comfort and in answer to a further question, Catline assured the duke that as far as the charges went, 'All be treasons if the truth of the case be so in fact'.[15] The statute of Edward III was that under which Norfolk was tried and not the more recent statute of 1571. This maintained as treason the upholding of the right to the throne of anyone claiming succession to Elizabeth. There was a further section in that act aimed at any who supported invasion from abroad. Possibly, since conciliatory gestures were now being made towards France, it was not considered politic to refer to an act which made large claims for Elizabeth's right to the throne of France. For the rest traditional doctrine demanded an overt act to establish treason. Mere thought and intention even in expression was not enough. But as Jardine observed, by Elizabeth's day there had been so many 'refined and forced constructions that' by the time of Norfolk's trial 'it had already become impossible for any man to say what case when it happened ought to be called treason'.[16] A man charged with treason now who reached a court was taken to be a public enemy to be eliminated. As W.S. Holdsworth put it, 'The dangers to the queen's life from the constant Roman catholic plots, and the certainty that possibly the existence of the English state, and certainly its orderly development, were bound up with [Elizabeth's] safety, led the nation to acquiesce in any measures that could be devised to preserve it. Hence the constructive extensions of this clause of the statute came to be not only acquiesced in, but even approved as [a] necessary means of defence in a time of national emergency.'[17] It becomes intelligible that advantages to the regime, providing a ready means of eliminating enemies, might have persuaded it to take the risk of manufacturing plots even when there were none.

After Norfolk's plea of 'not guilty', the first task of Sergeant Barham and the attorney general was to show that the duke's attempt to marry the queen of Scots was treasonable. It rested on the fact that when Mary married the dauphin in 1558 she assumed the arms of England quartered with those of France and Scotland. After strong English protest, a clause renouncing the claim had been included in the treaty of Edinburgh of 1560 which Mary, as it happened, never ratified. It was now assumed for present purposes that, since Mary had never formally renounced the claim, she must be anxious to pursue it even to the extent of turning Elizabeth off her throne. In

---

12 For the procedure on counsel, see William Staunford, *Les plées del coron* (London, 1557), quoted Jardine, p. 145, note, and *The m. c.*, p. 213.   13 *The m. c.*, p. 214; Brown, p. 15.   14 Ibid., p. 215 and Brown, p. 98.   15 *The m. c.*, p. 215.   16 For the definition of treason, see ibid., p. 216 and Jardine, p. 235 quoting Luder.   17 W. S. Holdsworth, *A history of English law*, viii (London 1937), ch. 5, p. 310. *The m. c.*, p. 217.

fact Mary had no such intention. John Leslie, her ambassador in England, made it clear to the privy council at a meeting in May 1569 that this was 'une invention forgée' to incense Elizabeth against her enforced guest. The 'Donation faicte par Marie Stuarte au Roi Henri II' of 4 April 1557 included the all-important condition 'advenant le cas qu'elle décedde sans hoirs procréez de son corps', referring to herself. With the birth of Prince James and the appearance of an heir there could be no question of rights to be given away or transferred to others. In a letter to Elizabeth of 15 May 1569, Mary insisted that she had never made any contract with Henri, Anjou or anyone else with any intention 'de fàre chose à votre préjudice'.[18]

Leicester was proposed at one time as a suitable spouse for Mary but she wanted none of it or him; which explains the earl's animosity which lasted for the rest of his life – and hers. So a marriage between an English peer and the Scottish queen could not in itself be taken as treason, or as containing an implicit intention to use her right to oust the present queen. But for the purposes of the present legal argument, it was. Norfolk undoubtedly erred in one important respect. He did not take Elizabeth into his confidence or explain his intentions to her while pursuing his marriage plans. Not a carpet knight in any sense, and knowing he lacked the smooth courtier's tongue, he had left it to others, including Leicester, to state his case to the queen. But none of them had any interest in seeing Norfolk succeed in a step which would have given him even more influence over them. He was already the only duke in the house of lords. Elizabeth offered him several cues to make a clean breast of it but he missed them all. If she was reluctant to admit that Norfolk had sinister motives, it was difficult to resist the suggestions of those who made the most of what appeared to be the duke's deviousness. Surely his lack of trust in his sovereign could only conceal the most sinister intentions?[19]

The prosecution had a valid point, therefore, when Barham asserted that Norfolk, against Elizabeth's 'express commandment upon his allegiance, against his own faith and promise to the contrary, practised to join ... in marriage with the said queen of Scots'. The further charge was mere construction that he could not have done this without 'an intent of his to advance and maintain that unjust title of the Scottish queen ... and to join himself in marriage with her' so that he meant 'to maintain a present title to the queen's crown'. Norfolk was pressed to admit that 'he knew that she so claimed, but with circumstance'. He recognised that Barham was trying to make Mary the queen's enemy, which would make him a traitor. He resisted the charge, but reminded the court, 'sore troubles, sore cares, closeness in prison evil rest, have much decayed my memory' so that it was for his accusers to do him the justice he could not do himself. He also reminded his hearers that, faced with the dilemma of 1569 after the northern rising, when some of his advisers urged him not to come to the court since

18 For Mary's right to the English throne, see *The dangerous queen*, pp 125-6, and p. 126, n. 3. 19 For Norfolk's failure to take Elizabeth into his confidence regarding the marrriage to Mary, see *The m. c.*, p. 217. But Cecil leads him on by telling Ross that he approves of the marriage project. See Ross to (?), 11.10.1570, BL, Cotton ms Cal. C. iii., f. 102r/v and *The m. c.*, p. 139 and n. 2.

his enemies were out to destroy him, he had given the indication of a clear conscience in presenting himself at Windsor. 'I needed not to have been here at this time ... I have chosen rather to come here to be tried by you than with needless and cowardly running away to have left a gap open for my enemies slanderously to lay to my charge in my absence what they maliciously invent.'[20]

Norfolk's 'lack of good utterance' and poor memory left him having to revise his original plea and plead guilty to neglect of duty towards Elizabeth but 'in cases inferior to treason'. Barham reminded him, quite untruly, of Mary's secret treachery towards Elizabeth. Norfolk, having no means of knowing what the truth was, could only repudiate her alleged activities in this area. He also remembered that after ambassador Sir Nicholas Throckmorton's protest in France, any French claim to England had been 'laid down ... After this there grew amity' between Elizabeth and Mary so that any previous enmity could be taken as ended. If Mary did not ratify the treaty of Edinburgh, this had nothing to do with any present claim to the English throne. Barham ignored all this and merely underlined the duke's admission that Mary had once claimed the crown presumably with a view to present occupation. He also accused Norfolk quite unjustly of moving to London the commission which had been considering Mary's case at York in 1568 so that her alleged infamies insisted on by Moray would not be brought to light. In fact the move had been ordered from London since the case was taken to be of more than ordinary difficulty: which it was.[21]

Barham succeeded in confusing the duke with a letter from the bishop of Ross in 1568 which proved Norfolk had betrayed Elizabeth's secrets to the rival queen as well as sought her hand in marriage. The letter was an obvious fabrication: another example of 'marvellous chance'. For the best of reasons, the duke could not remember any such letter and insisted on his loyalty to his queen. He threw out a challenge which the prosecution could not dare to accept. 'If the bishop of Ross or any other can say otherwise, let them be brought before meface to face. I have often desired it, but I could not obtain it.' Avoiding the challenge, Barham merely repeated the main charge. If the duke knew Mary's faults and did not love her, he could only have desired her out of ambition for the claim coming thereby to the present possession of Elizabeth's crown.[22]

Since there was no danger of a challenge to the authenticity of any document produced as evidence, Barham could feel safe enough in producing yet another document of doubtful worth: an alleged examination of the bishop on 3 November 1571. This claimed that Norfolk was prepared to try his cause by rebellion in 1569, something which contradicted facts and more authentic sources.[23] This document was at variance with everything else that Ross wrote concerning Norfolk's reaction to the northern rising and preceding events of 1568. If it was not forged it could have been written by Ross at Burghley's dictation as the confession of someone else: a technique to be used

---

20 Ibid., pp 217–19 and Brown pp 18, 23.   21 Ibid., p. 120 and n. 1, 2; Brown, p. 27.   22 For another example of 'marvellous chance' or plain fraud, see *The m. c.*, pp 223–5.   23 For a discussion of Ross' examination of 3.11.1571, see ibid., pp 228 and n. 2 and p. 229.

more than once in these years. It is the last paragraph in Burghley's hand which claims it was Ross' confession: hardly an impartial witness. It was Burghley who obliged Robert Hickford to authenticate a compromising letter of 8 February 1571 supposed to be written by the Scottish queen. In fact we only have the alleged copy in Hickford's hand. What Hickford wrote by way of authentication was, 'This copie being conferred word by word with the originall copie is agreing in all points with the sayd originall.' It must be clear to any impartial observer that this is dust thrown in the eyes of hopefully gullible posterity. There was no original. If there had been, we cannot suppose Burghley would not have cherished and preserved it.[24] And it would hardly have occurred to anyone coming after him to be less careful.

Norfolk only admitted in his examinations receiving one visit from Ross and this concurred with what Ross himself confessed. They spoke about some £2,000 of the Scottish queen's still in Norfolk's keeping, and at the end, the duke asked Leslie not to come again in view of his compromising office as Mary's ambassador. Norfolk now pleaded again for the ambassador to be brought to the court to vindicate the truth of what he was saying. The judges desired no such thing. The statutes of Edward VI required two witnesses in a treason trial, but a law of Philip and Mary was taken by the judges to repeal the previous laws, so no witnesses needed to be called. In spite of his inability to do more in his own defence, this was spurned as being only the duke's word.[25] Adding insult to injury, Barham now admitted a certain Cavendish to inform the court that he had been used by the duke as a go-between to Mary on several occasions 'to labour the cause of his marriage with her with all diligence'. More serious, the duke had revealed a strong suspicion, if not foreknowledge, that the rebellion of the northern earls was about to break. Hoping to take advantage of the duke's admittedly poor memory, the prosecution made a mistake in this which, in a court interested in justice, should have put the accused on the road to acquittal.

The duke rounded on Cavendish in a momentary blaze of anger. Cavendish had assured him that in the matter of marriage, Leicester and Sir Nicholas Throckmorton would both speak for him to Elizabeth. In fact Leicester, no doubt to further Norfolk's downfall, first put him in touch with Cavendish, his minion. The duke neither liked nor trusted him, but lent him money vicariously he could not afford, although he was warned by friends to 'take heed' of him. He 'dealt with Dyer and Strange very maliciously'. What the duke was supposed to have said at Kenninghall, he dismissed as lying.[26] One thing was clear by this time. The duke's memory was too good to allow of further witnesses. Burghley with his own foxy cunning, seeing that the duke had caused something of a reaction, made an intervention. 'My Lord, did you ever desire to have any proofs or witnesses produced for your part to prove anything that might make for you ?' Norfolk gave the obvious reply. He had 'divers times prayed' for any

24 For Mary's alleged letter of 8.2.1571 and the roles of Ross and Hickford, see *The d. q.*, ch. 6. A photograph of part of the letter is reproduced at p. 400. It is in Hickford's hand not Cecil's.   25 *The m. c.*, p. 230 and Jardine, i, p. 233 and n. 168.   26 Ibid., pp 231-2 and Brown, p. 73.

means that would help his case. Burghley persisted, 'I ask it because I have not heard it reported to her Majesty that you made any such request to have any special witness examined or proofs heard on your part.' With only fourteen hours' prior notice of the trial Norfolk could only have left such things to the decency of a court truly interested in justice to provide on its own initiative. But he must have known that the law no longer allowed such help.[27]

Norfolk admitted lending money to the queen of Scots and offering advice for the conduct of her affairs in Scotland. But even an intention to marry her could not be construed as treason. 'There is a maxim in law', he declared, 'that penal statutes must be construed strictly and no penal statute ought to be extended further than the very words. Now in all that my accusers have deposed or said against me, there is not one word, how false so-ever they be, that say I went about any hurt to her Majesty's person, or that I levied, or practised to levy, any power against her, or to do any of those things that are contained for treasons within the words of the statute.' Undeniably, 'If I had intended any such rebellion or treason, I would not have ... come hither to put my head in the halter in the Tower.'[28]

The charge that Norfolk assisted the rebels who fled to Flanders after the northern rising could not convincingly be reduced to treason. Although Blackstone laid down the important principle two centuries later, expert opinion took it to be valid in the earlier period: the relief of a 'rebel fled out of the kingdom is not treason; for the statute is taken strictly, and a rebel is not an enemy; an enemy being always the subject of some foreign prince, and one who owns no allegiance to the crown of England'.[29] Even if Norfolk had dealt in some way with the distribution of relief in Flanders from the Vatican, 'there was no proof or even suggestion that the money was sent by the pope to support any treasonable design; and if ... Norfolk under these circumstances approved of, and promoted the relief of these unfortunate persons, one of whom, the countess of Westmorland, was his own sister, his conduct could not in law amount to treason ... '[30] In any case, there was nothing to disprove Norfolk's claim, 'I never dealt with money nor heard of it. I dealt not at that time with Barker' – his steward – 'nor heard anything of the rebels since they went into Flanders.'[31]

Another charge was that Nofolk had conveyed some £600 in bullion across the Scottish border to help the queen's enemies in the summer of 1571. In the first place, Burghley's charge remains quite unproven that the duke was directly concerned with the conveyance of this money although his servants were certainly involved. Robert Hickford, the servant principally involved, was undoubtedly subjected to pressure to make him say the right thing to sustain the charge. The use or threat of torture on witnesses was denied by the prosecution. This was a lie.[32] The vital evidence was provid-

27 Ibid., p. 232.   28 Ibid., and Brown, p. 69.   29 Ibid., p. 233; William Blackstone, *Commentary on the laws of England* (London, 1765-69), iv, p. 83. Quoted Jardine, p. 244.   30 *The m. c.*, ibid.; Jardine, p. 244.   31 Ibid.   32 The transfer of the £600 is described in detail in *The m. c.*, pp 155-67. For the use and threat of torture, see ibid. pp 226-8. See also *Treasures of the Tower of London: torture and punishment*, pamphlet published by HMSO (London, 1975).

ed once again by the 'marvellous chance' which turned up key documents, or alleged their existence, on at least four occasions in the story of the duke's undoing. Everything turned on defining the 'queen's enemies'. Châtelherault, Herries, Hume, Buccleuch and other Scottish lords may well have carried out destructive raids into England, a well-established, seasonal Scottish sport, but Sussex, in the roughest spirit of the game, carried out reprisals, which have been called notorious, in the spring of 1570. It was all over by June. There had been no declaration of war; and those Scots who supported Mary were in no legal sense 'the queen's enemies'.[33]

The whole case for the prosecution, then, as Jardine justly concluded, rested on Norfolk's implication in Ridolfi's plot. Deprived of access to the evidence of voluminous confessions and examinations – his steward, William Barker, was examined more than twenty times – Norfolk made the most of all the commonsense arguments which were available to him. They were considerable; and in a court bent on justice should have been conclusive. Had Norfolk really intended to assist Ridolfi's projected Spanish invasion, he would have made some previous preparation. He had only eight armours in his house and a hundred arquebuses – and no money. Ten thousand men, including horsemen, were supposed to land at Harwich. But Harwich was not a port in the duke's territory. Furthermore, 'I am of not so little skill that I would have three or four thousand horsemen land in Essex, the unfittest place for horsemen to land in all England, a country best inhabited of noblemen, gentlemen, and other ability to resist them. And who would land horsemen in Essex, a country as full of lanes, woods, ditches and marshes? ... Again in respect of religion, I would not have landed them in Essex that came to destroy religion, and so should have found but little assistance.'[34]

Avoiding the defence of commonsense and coming to the 'evidence', the attorney of the court of wards reminded him that there were several witnesses in independent agreement so that there was only one verdict possible – guilty! 'The bishop of Ross at this time was in custody, and these men also that have confessed against you were also in custody; kept asunder in several places, and severally examined, agreed all in one, and your own confessions agree with them. How can this be imagined and false?' The duke, unequal to the task of penetrating effectively the combined wiles of Burghley and Walsingham, knew that he had somehow been tricked but could only object, 'They have not agreed in confession against me, but one of them told another, and so from hand to hand it went among them.' Undoubtedly telling in its effect on the court was the attorney's objection, 'If you had been a good subject, being then a prisoner in your own house, when such dangerous matter came to your understanding, you would have opened it that the queen's Majesty and her council might have provided to withstand them. But you did it not!'[35]

One must conclude, in view of all that we know of his general integrity, his genuine loyalty to Elizabeth, and perhaps above all, his unswerving devotion to his Protestant faith, which he maintained to the end on the scaffold on 2 June 1572, that the duke

33 *The m. c.*, p. 234.   34 Ibid., p. 235; Brown, pp 99-100.   35 *The m. c.*, ibid.; Brown, p. 92

knew too little of the Ridolfi affair to take it seriously; seriously enough to make an issue of it in the council. But at the end of the court hearing it must have seemed even to those friends who remained that, even if he had taken no part in it, he had been remarkably negligent; negligent enough to justify the verdict which the leading councillors clearly wanted, and which it would have been personal ruin to refuse.

The production of dubious and spurious documents by way of evidence began early in the process of trapping the duke. It will be recalled that Ridolfi was allowed to depart for Europe with his baggage unexamined about 25 March 1571; baggage which contained clear proof of his intention to foment an invasion of England, with the names of nobles allegedly prepared to support the same. He was supposed to have approached practically all the nobles of importance in the course of peddling his plot. He did not pretend that all those he approached were favourable. It is surely remarkable that of those who disapproved not one gave any warning to the government. So he was allowed to proceed on his way to offer his plot to Flanders, Spain and the papacy. Another man who preceded him by a little to Europe was Charles Bailly, a Fleming by birth and upbringing, who was employed in the entourage of the bishop of Ross as a cipher clerk and messenger. As a messenger he went to Flanders to arrange with Sir Francis Englefield for the importation of a book printed without licence in Louvain into England, clearly a forbidden enterprise on both sides of the narrow seas. He was travelling without a passport, no doubt hoping to use diplomatic status and pay his way past any stubborn formalist. Alba's government had no desire to provoke Elizabeth, and so withheld consent, at her ministers' request, for reprinting a book which defended the Scottish queen. Bailly imported it apparently in printed sheets together with certain harmless letters from the exiles by way of Dover. But with the rest were three letters far from harmless, if they were genuine, and indeed, if they existed at all. In trying to sort out a significant incident, we are up against Burghley wearing his most impenetrable persona.

Scarcely by chance, after crossing to Brussels, Ridolfi met up with Bailly, whom he knew to be an important member of Ross' household. Ridolfi obliged the young Burgundian to assist in addressing the three compromising letters in the first place to Ross. They were in a cipher supplied by Bailly himself. Two of the letters were directed to peers of the realm, mentioning Ridolfi's safe arrival, and that certain 'instructions' had been communicated to Courteville, Alba's secretary. Bailly, by his own account, was not happy to be made use of in this way, but he evidently felt Ridolfi's pressure to be irresistible. 'And then he showed me a letter for my lord [Ross] written with his own hand, partly in cipher and partly out of cipher, which being closed up, he set upon the one the number of "30", and upon the other, "40". And of these three letters, with my other letter, written likewise with his own hand, as I think, he made a packet, commanding me expressly to deliver it to Monsieur De Gourdan, Captain of Calais, and to desire him at the first commodity to send it into England.'[36] Bailly's

36 *The m. c.*, pp 35, 37.

account is far from clear but it seems there were three letters, one for Ross and the other two marked each with a number for a peer. There was also a fourth letter. What was this ? Ridolfi refused to tell Bailly the destination of the letters marked with '30' and '40'.

Why did Ridolfi tell Bailly to leave the three letters at Calais rather than take them across with him to England which was their destination? Knowing the kind of reception Bailly would get when he got to Dover, did he take pity on his relative youth and innocence and hope to spare him an ordeal? If he did he was badly mistaken. Certainly, when Bailly arrived back in England on 12 April all was in readiness for him. Cecil and Walsingham would have been grimly amused to see the book in question reprinted which had no right to be there. Its arrival was not unexpected. It is likely that the spy William Sutton had been keeping young Bailly in his sights.[37] His surveillance was now to be taken over by another. Among the preparations for Bailly's arrival, was the briefing of William Herle, a prison spy in the Marshalsea, to which Bailly was destined. Herle was another of those swashbuckling Elizabethans who had pursued a colourful if hitherto unsuccessful career including piracy. Herle was not a common scoundrel. He was a man of education, had contacts with the court, and by 1584 had risen sufficiently in the ranks to be entrusted by Burghley with a diplomatic mission to the nobles of East Frisia.[38] Meanwhile he was still struggling to find a foothold on the bottom rung of the ladder. Whatever his shady past, he seemed sound in politics and religion so Burghley felt able to use him. He was put in the Marshalsea about a week before the arrival of Charles Bailly, with the commission of winning his confidence and that of Ross, arranging for correspondence between them and worming out secrets. Herle would not only manage the conveyance of their correspondence but provide the cipher for it.[39]

The most complete account of Bailly's arrival and arrest at Dover was included in a narrative by Cecil himself in which he set out how he came by knowledge of the duke's treasons.[40] There was another by Lord Cobham, warden of the Cinque Ports.[41] According to Cecil, 'about the 12 of April' Bailly was arrested with a portmanteau of books printed at Louvain, 'and certain letters also to the bishop of Ross'. So instead of leaving the letters at Calais as instructed, did Bailly bring them with him? Bailly, whose arrival was expected, was sent up to London to be interviewed by Lord Cobham, then at Blackfriars. According to Cobham, most improbably, at an urgent request from Cobham's brother, Thomas, the warden allowed some letters destined for Ross to be conveyed to him by Francis Barty: but only after Cobham had attached his own seal to the letters and attached the further condition that they must be opened in his presence. Francis Barty served the bishop of Ross, but he was also in the pay of the government,

37 Ibid., p. 38.   38 Ibid., p. 40. For Herle's mission to East Frisia, see Bodleian Library, ms Rawlinson, C. 424, f. 76.   39 *The m. c.*, pp 43-5.   40 William Cecil, 'The order in time how the matters have proceeded to come to the knowledge of the attempts wherewith the Duke of Norfolk hath been charged before before he was indicted of treason'; PRO, SP. Dom. Eliz., vol. 85., ff. 35r-38v. In Cecil's hand. Cf. *The m. c.*, p. 45, n. 2.   41 Ibid., vol. 81, ff. 117r-118v. The description of the

a fact not mentioned in Burghley's narrative. This meant, of course, that he and Walsingham could inspect the letters beforehand and add or subtract whatever they desired before they got to Ross. If no tampering had been intended, the obvious procedure would have been for Cobham to take the letters to the bishop himself or summon the bishop to him. There was no technical difficulty, it may be said in passing, about restoring broken seals.

Burghley himself claimed that he only learned of the letters by a process of gradual deduction. His narrative, 'The order in time ... ', states that after ordering Bailly to the Marshalsea as a result of discovering the books, visits by a secretary of the Spanish ambassador 'and one or two of ... Ross' men ... in the night by stealth' aroused suspicion that 'Charles had some greater matter in charge than the bringing of the said books.' After allowing a few letters to pass between Ross and Charles Bailly, 'it was thought good suddenly to attach Charles, and cause him to decipher those letters' – as if Burghley had no idea what was in them. 'In the end, after much ado with Charles, an alphabet was gotten' – presumably the one supplied by Herle – 'and about the week after Easter, it was perceived by those letters that Charles had brought over with him certain packets of letters from Ridolfi' and some of the exiles: 'and how the Lord Burghley was abused by having a wrong packet of forged letters delivered to him instead of Ridolfi's.'[42] Evidently, this account claims that Bailly did bring Ridolfi's letters into England. It also contradicts Cobham's 'Declaration' that the letters were taken from Bailly when he arrived at Dover. This source also says that Burghley wrote to Cobham 'the day after ... he had the books, that he heard there were also certain packets of letters brought with the books, and desired they might be sent to him. Whereupon was devised that another packet was counterfeited by the bishop of Ross, and so by the Lord Cobham sent to the Lord Burghley, containing certain letters of no moment.'[43]

Amid the contradictions and uncertainties, what is certain is that Cobham, his brother and Barty were working for Burghley not for Ross. Cobham was made to carry the blame for a contrivance whereby Burghley could claim that all that was known came from pressure to be applied to the wretched Bailly. We may be certain that if Cobham really had betrayed his trust in the way suggested, he would have been shown no mercy. As it was, Cecil wrote to Shrewsbury on 19 October, 'My Lord Cobham is in my house as a prisoner who otherwise should have been in the Tower. I loved him well, and therefore am sorry for his offence.'[44] His subsequent career showed no diminution of favour. It was all a blind. Evidently, the government was anxious for the bishop to receive the compromising letters alleged to have come from Ridolfi and the rebels in exile; but only after they had been examined first, and in such a way as to reas-

whole incident is marked by obscurities which were presumably intended to confuse.   42 'The order in time ... ', f. 36r.; *The m. c.*, p. 49 and n. 1.   43 Cobham's 'declaration' in Cecil's hand(?), SP. Dom. Eliz., vol. 81, ff. 117r-18v. Cf. BL, Cotton ms, Cal. C. iii, ff. 103f. Printed in Kervyn de Lettenhove, *Relations politiques des Pays Bas et de l'Angleterre sous le règne de Philippe II*, vi (Brussels 1886), pp 188-90.   44 *The m. c.*, p. 50 and n. 1.

sure the bishop that they had not been doctored or edited. Ross admitted that, as soon as he heard of Bailly's arrest he made every effort to get hold of any letters brought in, and also set on foot the counterfeiting of a similar packet to be passed to the English government; an effort furthered and indeed made possible by Thomas Cobham. For Charles 'at his first taking had ... so great fear that he uttered plainly ... he had brought letters which could cause himself to be hanged and many others; which was told unto the Council by his takers, and that moved them to take the sharp trial of him'.[45]

Ross, not being present, had no true idea of what happened to Charles at his taking. Charles was under irresistible pressure from the first to say in his own letters and narratives what he was told to say, at least for the sake of appearances. This was not to save him from the rack. So we have no independent witness of what really happened. It is unlikely that Bailly gave himself away so quickly and so completely. A question remains about the numbered letters, which were important in view of their bearing on Norfolk's case as it developed later. The letters may have been brought in by Bailly, defying the order from Ridolfi to leave them at Calais. It is also possible that no compromising letters arrived at all, and any that were, were concocted by Walsingham and Burghley in prior arrangement with Ridolfi to give or fortify the impression that the duke, Queen Mary and others had been involved with Ridolfi in his invasion plot. All our information here comes from Cecil and his henchmen, apart from Bailly who broke down, as well he might, under terrible pressure and came to say what he was told to say. Ross' examination of 26 October 1571 asserts that he received a letter numbered '40', identified as Norfolk, and another '30', identified as Lumley. There were also letters to de Spes, the Spanish ambassador, the queen of Scots, and Ross himself. Anything which came from Ridolfi presumably fortified the notion of a plot.[46]

The further adventures of Bailly, who was committed to the Marshalsea on 13 April, were described in letters of Herle to Burghley. It was Herle who suggested that heavier pressure should be brought to bear on Bailly who could be expected to give way easily, 'for he is fearful, full of words, glorious and given to the cup, over whom I have already won some good degree'.[47] On 14 May, on the strength of evidence claimed to have been found in correspondence, it was considered time to put Ross under house arrest with the bishop of Ely at his Holborn residence. Ross had not seen Mary since the beginning of December when he had permission to see her for further instructions. This, originally granted by Elizabeth, was now countermanded by Burghley. It was

45 John Leslie, 'Here followeth the discourse of the proceedings of the Queen of Scots' affairs in England since the XI of April 1571 to the XXVI of March 1572'; BL, Add. ms (Yelverton) 48, 027, ff. 45v-70v. For further comment on this source, see *The m. c.*, p. 51 and n. 1.   **46** Ross' identification of Norfolk as '40' and Lumley as '30' was replaced by Mary as '30' in the later stages. There was much byplay in this business of identifying the letters allegedly from Calais. Cecil never succeeded in producing a narrative which consistently described the whole incident: which supports the idea that no letters came from Calais. At one point Thomas Cobham told Hickford he had taken out the two letters numbered '30' and '40' at Dover while Bailly and Cobham were engaged in animated conversation. It is not likely unless it was done by contrivance. See *The m. c.*, pp 52-3; William Murdin, State papers 1571 to 1596 (London 1759), p. 23.   **47** *The m. c.*, p. 55.

essential for Burghley's overall plan to keep those accused of plotting out of contact with one another so that what each knew of another's alleged part in the plot could only come by way of communication through a government approved messenger.

Bailly was now committed to close imprisonment but Herle continued to have contact with him. At one time he was only able to talk to him through a hole in the wall, an arrangement reminiscent of one used many years later at the time of the gunpowder plot. Letters passed between Ross and Bailly were made part of the evidence for implicating Ross. Bailly was forced to admit that two of Ridolfi's letters were addressed to '30' and '40' but he insisted, no doubt truthfully, that he had no idea of their identity. He also admitted, 'The said letters be not written in the cipher with the alphabet he giveth now. For this alphabet he had from the bishop of Ross by William Herle when this examinate was in the Marshalsea.'[48] Herle was pretending in this to be acting for Ross!

Some facts seem clear. The correspondence between Ross and Charles was not only completely known by Cecil and Herle but from the beginning could have been altered, edited and added to at will by Cecil. Bailly could only suppose that Ross had the alphabet of Ridolfi's letters. One thing emerges above the surface of this morass. Nothing that passed between Bailly and Ross could fairly be regarded as evidence of high treason even if they had been subjects of the English queen. Ross replying to a letter of Bailly's on 20 April confirmed that the code for the numbered letters was not his and could only ask Charles to supply it.[49] In a word, the compromising letters, as they proved to be, at least in their general import, could only have come ultimately from Burghley.

About 20 April Bailly was transferred to the Tower. It was all part of Cecil's intention to make the discovery of the letters appear as something gradual and not in fact known by him from the beginning. Ross had been trying all this time to secure Bailly's release, but without avail. Bailly made a desperate appeal to Ross after a racking: 'Do not let them put me on the rack again or I shall be lost for ever.' Herle told Burghley on 30 April that the bishop had been reduced 'to such rages at home, that he would neither eat nor sleep for two days, not permitting any man within his gates'.[50] Burghley must have laughed heartily in the quiet of his study.

On May 2 Bailly capitulated completely. He wrote to Burghley, 'Putting all my confidence in your Lordship and assuring myself that you will keep it secret, as you have promised me, and cause me to have my libertywithout stain of mine honor and credit ... ' He proceeded to give an account not only of his own recent visit to Europe but also Ridolfi's and his plans for fomenting an invasion of England. It was never necessary for the Florentine to let Bailly into the real purpose of his European tour, which should have been secret, and it is reasonable to suppose, once again, that this was part of the plan prearranged with Burghley and Walsingham before he left.[51] Bailly was now ready

---

48 Ibid., p. 63.   49 Ibid.   50 Ibid., p. 73 and nn. 2 and 3.   51 Bailly's letter of capitulation of 2.6.1571 is Salisbury MS, v, No. 124. See also *The m. c.*, p. 75.

to return to Ross' service; but with the intention of betraying to Cecil any of Ross' affairs that came his way. Most important, it is in a letter of 5 May to Cecil, and again in a letter a few days later to Guerau de Spes, the Spanish ambassador, that Bailly insists he 'left a packet of letters at Calais in the hands of the captain, M.Courdan', and he adds 'not knowing anything of Ridolfi's letters'.[52]

Although he seems to have done so, it is not easy to see how Bailly managed to get a letter past Burghley's wall to the Spanish ambassador. Burghley could hardly have countenanced this. Ross may have planted a heavy bribe. In the letter to de Spes Bailly mentioned the fact that Burghley in at least one interview intimated that he already knew a great deal about Ridolfi's journey. Indeed he did! The Fleming concluded, 'In fact there is some important traitor or spy among you or in Flanders who gives information of everything. Here they have brought it to this traitor Herle who is sometimes at court.'[53] Perhaps Bailly had not capitulated so completely after all. And perhaps Burghley became aware of the fact. Far from being released, a letter from Bailly to Cecil of 12 October was addressed from 'The Little Ease', a dark and airless four-foot square cell situated between two dungeons in the White Tower.[54]

Burghley's treatment of Bailly, heartless as it was, had in it a method far from madness. It was essential that the appearance of government ignorance of what was in hand be maintained if the plot were to be used effectively against the duke, and for that matter the Scottish queen. Apart from Burghley and Walsingham, it is doubtful if any had a complete idea of what was afoot even in the council. Contemporary record, or absence of it, makes it clear that Leicester remained on the periphery. Elizabeth herself knew nothing of what her principal secretary was contriving. Certainly, Bailly's claim that Ridolfi's fateful letters were left behind in Calais helped neither him nor the government. The letters in any case have disappeared as surely as the casket letters, and it may be, after they had fulfilled a similarly useful role in discrediting intended victims. Some time in November 1572 Bailly was sent into exile. By that time the severity of his sufferings had affected his memory and rendered him safe enough to be discarded.[55] His task was done and his usefulness ended.

Four persons were mainly accused of complicity with Ridolfi in his wild scheme: Norfolk, Mary, queen of Scots, Guerau de Spes, the Spanish ambassador, and John Leslie, bishop-designate of Ross. Born in 1526 with a descent from the barons of Balquhain, and endowed with considerable native ability, it is not surprising that the bishop's career thus far had been fairly distinguished. After a doctorate in law from Paris in 1553 and ordination to the priesthood in 1559, he became professor of canon

---

52 Ibid., p. 77.   **53** Bailly to de Spes, 10.6.1571 is in the Vatican Archives, *Nunziatura di Spagna*, vol. 2, f. 497f. Spanish decipher endorsed 'translated from the French. Received on 31 May'; cf. BL, Add. ms. 26, 056B, f. 190; *Cal. S. P. Rome*, 1558–71, No. 774; *The m. c.*, p. 77-8.   **54** The phrase at the end of Bailly's letter of 12.10.1571, 'From the Little Ease' is omitted in Murdin, ibid., pp 15-17. For a description, see Sir George Younghusband, *The Tower of London, from within* (London, 1918), p. 9; *The m. c.*, p. 8 and n. 3.   **55** *The m. c.*, p. 80 and n. 1. An extant bill of charges for his stay in the Tower goes up to 29.9.1572; PRO, E. 404/118.

law at Aberdeen in 1562, an ordinary judge of the court of sessions in 1565 and a member of the Scottish privy council. In 1561 he brought back Mary from France to the throne of Scotland; joined her at Bolton castle, her first prison in England, in 1568. He became her confidential adviser and ambassador to the court of England from 1569. He was a man of integrity though not a saint, stained with the tar of politics but not completely corrupted. His was a diplomat's devotion both to the Catholic faith and to his queen. Consistently he tried to convince Sir Francis Knollys, keeper for a time of Queen Mary, that he had been 'always quiet in matters of religion'.[56]

Ross was the only character in the Ridolfi drama who left a personal narrative in detail of events as he saw them. It was perhaps an apologia rather than a chronicle. Nevertheless, it is probably the closest approach we have to the truth of these contorted events. There was no lack of confessions and examinations from him and others, but these were usually reported in other hands than the examinate's and produced under the kind of pressure which made even a semblance of objectivity unlikely. 'A discourse containing a perfect account given to ... Princess Mary, Queen of Scots, and her nobility ... of his whole charge and proceedings ... from his [Ross'] entries into England in September 1568 to the 26th of March 1572',[57] admits that Ridolfi discussed with him plans for invasion by foreign troops. They would assist an indigenous rising led by Norfolk, all to be paid for by the pope. Ross claimed that the aim of the enterprise was not to overthrow Elizabeth but to oblige her to embrace Catholicism, or at least to tolerate that religion, while approving the marriage of Mary and the duke. It is not likely that Ross, an ambassador, would have countenanced the destruction of Elizabeth, the monarch to whom he was accredited. His main aim was the release of his own queen, but foreign invasion was hardly an experiment that could have been controlled. By this time, it was already evident to the bishop that Mary would never be released by diplomacy. He was therefore ready to listen to counsels of desperation hoping that madness might somehow be excluded.[58] And it is one thing to listen and another to encourage or cooperate. Ross was an experienced and skilful listener, as became a good diplomat.

We must remind ourselves that from the beginning of March 1571 Mary, de Spes and Norfolk were kept in isolation from one another. Communication even by letter was known by them to be unsafe; and they could only communicate through persons allowed by authority. The most important of these was Ridolfi, and another, William Barker, Norfolk's steward, by this time tried but hardly trusty. Whatever was done or said on any matter by any of the other three, or by all of them, was known to the fourth only by what arrived by messenger. If the messenger was 'corrupted', or under instruction to deceive, the others could know nothing of it whatever they might suspect. They all reposed thus under the possibility of endless deception. So in considering their depositions and statements made later as part of the official enquiry, the only portion likely to be true and uncoloured was that which depended on the direct

56 *The m. c.*, pp 88-9.   57 'A Discourse ... ', *The m. c.*, p. 51, and n. 1.   58 Ibid., pp 91-2.

experience of the deponent. When one speaks of another, he or she is only conveying hearsay and not fact. So if the bishop claims that Ridolfi revealed his plot to Mary and Norfolk it does not follow that he did so but only that he said so. Ross claimed that Ridolfi told him that the duke accepted his scheme and approved of his further wanderings in Europe to drum up support. To accept this as true would be to deny all that we know from authentic sources about Thomas Howard.[59]

After Charles Bailly's admissions, Sussex, Burghley, Sir Walter Mildmay and Sir Ralph Sadler visited Ross in his house on 13 May to get more information. Ross, insisting on diplomatic immunity to cover his silence, was content to say that whatever Ridolfi had told Bailly, 'it was but an Italian discourse, and of no moment'. After this, all Ross' servants were removed save one or two to wait on him in a passing illness. Skipwith and Kingsmill, two courtiers, were appointed to keep close watch on the bishop.[60] The councillors searched Ross' study for compromising material. The next day he was committed to the bishop of Ely. All correspondence between Ross and Mary now passed through Burghley's hands. The bishop was examined five times between 13 May and 17 August. Even when his examinations were signed, this was not much of a mark of authenticity. Sir Thomas Smith, as ambassador extraordinary, later admitted to Catherine de Medici not only that he himself had writtem examinations with his own hand, which was usual enough, but later confided to Burghley that he and Dr Wilson had actually forged the signature of the duke of Norfolk to a statement he himself had refused to sign.[61] What could be done for Norfolk could be done for Ross. And Smith was in a position to do it. His political sense would have precluded scruple

On 13 May Ross admitted arranging for the reprint of the book maintaining Mary's title and sending cipher letters to Englefield for redistribution. It was only Ridolfi's word that he had letters from Mary for Alba, but this was for a landing in Dumbarton to help her cause in Scotland to which she had every right. This examination was unsigned by Ross and only endorsed by Cecil; so it was presumably Cecil's addition that attributed to Ross the identification of '40' as Mary and '30' as de Spes.[62] An identification only for the time being.

On 26 October Ross was reported as changing '40' to Norfolk and '30' to Lumley. This was an examination written by the flexible Smith even if it was apparently signed at the foot of each page by Ross. Evidently it took some time for the government to make up its mind what it wanted the numbers in the problematic letters to stand for. There must have been an intention at one time to get rid of Lumley along with Norfolk. On 6 November Ross produced an examination more resembling his hand which was apparently signed by him. This reaffirmed the meaning of the numbers as stated on 26 October. This also claimed the cipher used was Ridolfi's who used it for letters to Ross, Norfolk and the queen of Scots. It was written by Ridolfi's servant who gave a copy to Ross in the presence of William Barker. Ross admitted helping the

59 Ibid., pp 93-4. 60 Ibid., p. 95. 61 Ibid., p. 98. 62 Ibid., p. 99.

rebels of 1569 escape from Scotland to Flanders. By Ridolfi's advice he procured letters from Mary to the nuncio in France to help them with money, which might be done through Ridolfi's brother who was a banker in Rome for the pope.[63] But another account of Ross' examination of 13 May denies that there were any letters from Ridolfi for any English noblemen, although there was one for the bishop, another for Mary, which never came to her hands, and one for de Spes. Although it was endorsed, 'Probably written by the Bishop of Ross', it was even more probably written by Smith.[64]

Ross' examination of 13 May was made the pretext for informing Mary that Ross for his 'sundry practices with our rebels and fugitives ... to move new trouble in our realm' could no longer be treated as her ambassador and only as a private person and so would be 'restrained from his liberty'.[65] From this time Mary lost any voice to speak for her at the court of Elizabeth. Her enemies were closing in. De Spes was also examined on 14 May by Mildmay and Smith. While admitting correspondence with the Low Countries in matters of merchandize, he recalled nothing that touched the queen or her estate. Ross in subsequent examinations continued to deny that there were any letters from Ridolfi apart from those to Mary, de Spes and himself. There were no letters for English noblemen. Ross was careful to state more than once that as soon as he had smelt trouble he had burnt all correspondence which might be subject to misinterpretation. It was his practice to burn up dangerous matter every three months. Likely enough.

It was not surprising and not in itself compromising that Ross should have had relations with Ridolfi. Apart from the fact that he was a banker with Roman connections and lent extensively to English clients, Ross also hoped he would be able to get money from the pope to help the cause of the Scottish queen. Ross admitted at one point that he was hard put to it for money since nothing came to him from Scotland. With financial considerations in mind, Ross also carried on negotiations with the Spanish ambassador, an even more dangerous person. After his imprisonment in Walsingham's house, Ridolfi was allowed to tell Ross that he was the pope's secret agent. If it was true, it is curious that he did not make this revelation before; another good diplomat, he no doubt distrusted everybody as a matter of principle and basic political wisdom. Having sufficient problems on hand in Scotland, it is sufficiently unlikely that Ross, a careful professional, would have entertained the wilder aspects of Ridolfi's plot, although he may well have been told of it as a speculative venture. It is also certain that Ridolfi claimed that Mary knew of it and approved. In fact she would only have approved of foreign intervention for Scotland. This would tally with her later claims which were never disproved against her.

It was Bishop Leslie's recommendation, it seems, that secured Ridolfi an interview with William Barker, Norfolk's man. But Norfolk himself avoided any interview with Ridolfi, and still less agreed to sign any letters of recommendation for his imminent

63 Ibid., pp 99-100. 64 Ibid., p. 100, nn. 1, 2. 65 Ibid., p. 101.

continental journey. Ross understood this to be only a journey to help the cause of Mary in Scotland and the exiles of 1569. When Ross learnt in an interview between himself, Ridolfi and Barker that Norfolk refused to write or sign anything, if Barker's statement is to be believed, Ross committed the enormous indiscretion of writing for him. ' "Then", said he [the bishop], "though my lord do not write, I will write that Ridolfi cometh in his name ... " 'Ridolfi wanted something more compromising but this had to do. Later on, after receiving what appeared to be Ridolfi's letters from the continent, Ross protested to Barker, 'You see ... in how uncertain state we stand. Ridolfi is now gone to take a contrary course to that we have ever used, that is to leave France and trust to Spain. How ready Spain may be to help us, ye may see by this great preparation against the Turk.' Not only the king of France but the archbishop of Glasgow, Mary's ambassador in Paris, would think they had deserted tried and trusted friends for new who could only be taken as the enemies of France.[66] The French had recently promised a subsidy of 4000 crowns a month and this would now be jeopardised. But the bishop had not yet understood the half of it. Not only would the French be alienated, but the English regime have every excuse for proceeding heavily against the Marian cause when it became evident that Ridolfi was touring Europe to engineer an invasion of England. How can one doubt that all this was foreseen and planned ahead while the Florentine lay in Walsingham's house in the late autumn of 1570? Nothing else seems to make sense amid the cacophony of conflicting voices hardly amounting to evidence.

The exclusion of Ross from Mary's presence meant more than that she had lost the only voice at Elizabeth's court that might have done something, if not much, to counteract the influence of Burghley and other enemies. She could now be misrepresented to Ross as having agreed to the wildest of Ridolfi's schemes. Ross could likewise be presented to her as at least failing to wait for any instructions she might have given him to stay away from the Ridolfi imbroglio. Meanwhile Mary approached de la Mothe Fénélon, the French ambassador – not de Spes, be it noted – to work for Ross' release and reinstatement; and also for Charles IX's approval for his ambassador meanwhile to become her channel of information. De la Mothe referred the matter to Burghley. His position was embarrassing. He had been asked to work for a woman who had, as he had been told, schemed with her ambassador to promote a plot to dethrone Elizabeth, and in concert with the hated Spaniards. Burghley used all his considerable skill to insert the thin end of a wedge of doubt in what had been Fénélon's unquestioning assumption so far that Mary's cause was that of France.

After another examination on 16 June, which adds little enough to our understanding, Ross penned a letter to Elizabeth on 22 June which repudiated on his part and his queen's in unequivocal terms any intention to collude in foreign invasion schemes; unless it were in Scotland, and only then in the event of a failure to bring about a successful treaty with England which would send Mary back to her own coun-

66 Ibid., pp 104-6.

try. 'Whatsoever attempts or enterprises either foreign princes or private men, or any of your own unnatural subjects, against their duty, would pretend for troubling your estate or realm, I would not only forbear to assist them thereto, but also I promise faithfully, if I had any knowledge thereof, I would without any delay make your Majesty privy to all that I knew thereof.'[67]

We do not know if this letter reached Elizabeth; probably not.

On 8 August Ross was again examined before Burghley, Knollys and Sussex. This time he went further in repudiating any idea that he would feel bound to support an invasion of England even if it had the pope behind it. News allegedly from Rome claimed 'that the pope was soliciting other princes to invade this country, and also to stir up a rebellion by the subjects within this realm by means of the Catholics'. Ross affirmed, 'If any such matter were in hand, it was not for the queen my mistress' cause but rather proceeded of the pope himself, whom they know by experience to have an ardent desire to bring this country to his obedience, and without any doubt he will seek by all means possible to that effect. Therefore the same shall not be imputed to my mistress or me.'[68] There was nothing new in the idea of a good Catholic being at odds with the pope in a matter of politics.

What was Elizabeth's knowledge of what was afoot, if any? A new parliament opened in April and was dissolved on 29 May. At the beginning Elizabeth insisted that Ross be sent to his queen so that he could have no influence, even the remotest on its transactions. It was of course imperative, if the real plot engineered between Burghley, Walsingham and Ridolfi was to succeed, that the protagonists be kept apart from one another so that they could be given erroneous accounts of what the others had in mind. Had the queen understood what was being planned she would hardly have ordered Ross to join Mary. As Ross' diary informs us, it was Burghley who told Ross that although the queen had commanded him to depart, 'he had obtained licence for me to remain'.[69] Clearly, this was not done as a favour to Ross. Nor was it easy for Burghley, since the affair had become a battle of wills between two imperious ladies. Another dangerous moment for Burghley occurred in mid-July when Ross tried to get permission to go to his queen through Leicester. Burghley had gone to his house in the country and would not return for eight days. On 14 July de la Mothe went to Hampton Court to plead the cause of the imprisoned Ross before the queen. Elizabeth agreed to have Ross examined once again and then sent to Mary on the way to Scotland. Evidently Burghley was kept up to date with the news from court because although he was not due to return before the 21st, Ross recorded his return on 17 July. After this

---

67 Ibid., p. 111.   68 Ibid., p. 113. The limited obligations of a Catholic in following papal policy rulings were also indicated by Ross in an interview with the earl of Southampton soon after the excommunication of the queen in 1570. See *The d. q.*, pp 178-9. *Robert Persons* handled the same problem in 'A discourse against taking the oath in England; memorial for Cardinal Bellarmine, 1606'; see Edwards, *Robert Persons*, pp 323-4; T. Clancy, *Papist pamphleteers*, passim.   69 *The m. c.*, pp 116-17 and 117, n. 1. Ross' diary goes from 11.4. to 16.11.1571, original booklet in Ross' hand (?); BL Cotton ms, Cal. C. iii, ff. 2r-38v.

there was no further word of Ross being allowed to join Mary or to return to Scotland.[70]

The bishop of Ely was also instructed to prevent Ross from having any contact with external sources of information, leaving it to Kingsmill to 'have strait charge of him'. Nor was Ross to have any contact with de la Mothe beyond writing an open letter. However Ross was allowed to go with Ely into the country, his letters and keys being returned to him with a promise that full liberty would be restored at the end of the royal progress. Ross put it down to the subsequent discovery of the duke's alleged delinquencies in September as causing this permission to be cancelled. Meanwhile Ross had an enjoyable time at Ely in the company of the Anglican bishop, his wife and family.[71]

The arrest of Robert Hickford and William Barker, Norfolk's men, on 6 September heralded the arrest of Ross at Downham, one of Ely's houses, on 16 October and his transfer to London. As Ross understood it, the duke had also been arrested and examined, following 'letters found and gotten in the duke's house, and partly by their plain confessions, declarations and answers which was done in ... September and in the beginning of October'. It was all given great publicity, including books which had come to the bishop's hand even before he left Ely, 'wherein I was greatly burthened among others'. It was craftily presented to Ross that practically everything to do with the plot was already known from the confessions of the others. Furthermore, they had been very ready, especially the duke, to make the bishop the principal scapegoat and culprit. He had apparently been shamelessly misrepresented and betrayed. Indeed, the alleged contents of the confessions were made the pretext for a wholesale round-up of characters unacceptable to the regime. 'Upon hope of pardon every man did confess what he knew, and how far they had dealt with the queen my mistress or with myself, or [with] any other her ministers, or with the duke or his servants. In the which every man did excuse himself as far as he could, and laid the burthen upon others, as the use is of all those that are accused.'[72] So there was no reason for Ross to try to shield men who had been content to throw him to the wolves.

An examination before the council on 24 October, with Burghley present of course, left Ross in no doubt of his position. The 'most ancient', presumably the presiding earl of Bedford, assured him they had 'good proofs' of his dealings against the queen and her estate 'most wickedly of anyone that ever came into this land'. So Elizabeth would no longer regard him as an ambassador, as he had 'pretended, but for a private man and a wicked practiser for a pretended queen justly deprived from her realm. And our sovereign is determined to use you as a false traitor Scot, that no faith or credit should be given unto you, who hath dealt so craftily with the nobility and gentlemen of this realm under colour of papistry and other things that you have brought a great number of their houses to ruin.' Norfolk and others could only 'curse the time that they ever knew you. For you have been the chief author of all rebellion and sedition of this land.

70 *The m. c.*, p. 117.   **71** Ibid., pp 119-21.   **72** Ibid., pp 122-3.

For before your coming all was in quietness.'[73] The charges depended on Norfolk's answers to some fifty questions given on 10 and 11 October. These have been 'lost'. Surely too conveniently?

Ross, as he claimed, was neither cowed nor provoked into anger by the extravagance of the charges. He reminded his examiners, quite correctly, that since his coming into England he had been mainly concerned to devise conditions deemed reasonable by all parties which would allow his mistress and himself to return to Scotland, as they wished. He was sure that there was no proof that he had ever worked against the just interests of England; but he would only agree to answer questions about his relations with Mary in her presence. There was no point in questioning him about his relations with Englishmen since, since 'by the laws and treaties betwixt the two realms, the testimony of an Englishman is not admitted against Scottishmen, nor yet of a Scottishman against an Englishman. And so their confessions cannot hurt me more than mine can hurt them.'[74] Far from grateful for such reminders, the lords informed him he would be sent to the Tower 'where the pinches or racks' would make him tell another tale. True to their word, he was put in the Bloody Tower 'where no man of honest calling had been kept many years before, with close windows, and doors with many locks and bolts ... with a cockshot, as they call it, set up without, right against my windows to keep away all light and sight from me'.

On 26 October, at another examination before Knollys, Smith and, of course, Burghley, the latter told Ross that all was known about his principal part in the plot from the signed confessions of the rest including Norfolk and his servants. 'The discourse and articles for Ridolfi's dispatch ... [had] been gotten at the duke's house.' The bishop was assured that all those who accused him were within the Tower and would be brought to confront him to confirm their accusations. This, of course, was never done, nor could it have been on the present thesis. Burghley next assured Ross that if he freely declared the whole proceedings, on the queen's guarantee, nothing he said would be 'used to accuse any man'. If he refused to say what he knew, he would be treated 'as a private man' and subjected to torture.

Not surprisingly, Ross capitulated. 'Since matters are discovered by the principal persons themselves who did meddle therein, and are now in hand, I would not be so obstinate as to stand manifestly against the truth confessed by them, after that the same be shown unto me.'[75] He was shown interrogatories and the answers made earlier by Hickford, Bannister and Barker as well as the duke. After this he realised 'there was no man to conceal upon but myself'. All the same, Ross' admission amounted to little enough. 'I never spoke with [Norfolk] but once since his coming from the Tower,

73 Ibid., p. 124 and n. 1. The duke's important answers of 10, 11.10.1571 were 'lost' and seemingly do not exist even in copy in any collection. Ross' account appears to be the only extant indication of their contents. They dealt mainly with the projected marriage to Mary, Norfolk's relations with the northern rebels of 1569, an attempt to take the Tower, assist Mary's escape, and his alleged part in Ridolfi's last plot and accompanying events. See Ross' 'The discourse of the proceedings ... '(above) ff. 54r-56v.   74 *The m. c.*, pp 127-31.   75 Ibid., p. 131.

which was in September 1570, by the convoy of Bannister.' The reason for their meeting was Ross' desire for the duke's advice on certain articles proposed by Burghley and Mildmay as the basis of a treaty which would allow Mary to return to Scotland. Norfolk's advice was to agree to all reasonable conditions to ensure her liberation. Nothing else came up in their conversation and that was the only meeting.[76] Ross was careful to state, 'I cannot assure any way what the duke did agree unto, nor what was propounded to him by Ridolfi.' Acting on what he took to be Mary's instructions conveyed by Ridolfi, he admitted, 'I sent to the duke this discourse which hath been found in his house; and some letters from the queen my mistress by the convoy of Bannister, and desired that the duke would confer with Ridolfi and instruct him of his credit and dispatch conform to that which ... [Mary] had writ unto me.' Ridolfi was brought to the duke by Barker. What was it that Ridolfi showed him? Not the 'discourse' assuredly which outlined the invasion of England. The duke's too conveniently lost answers of 10 and 11 October seem to have denied all knowledge of such, as we would expect. Ross' evidence on what went missing is valuable. Norfolk 'had not confessed that he heard anything of strangers to come to invade the realm, or trouble the estate, or endanger anywise the queen's Majesty's person, for that he would never agree unto, but only for aid to relieve the queen of Scots.' In a word, what Ridolfi showed Norfolk as his 'discourse' and what Ridolfi showed Ross as having been approved by Norfolk as his 'discourse' were two very different documents. Norfolk signed nothing.[77] As we might expect, Ross' examination of 26 October, a long and flowing narrative in the hand of Thomas Smith, left out many key phrases such as 'Barker said' or 'Ridolfi said'. Consequently a superficial reading of the document makes it sound like the bishop's own witness and experience – as it was intended to. It was signed by Cecil, Knollys and apparently Ross. Certainly, Ross could not have known precisely what instructions Mary gave to Ridolfi, or if what he saw were those also shown to Norfolk. According to what Ross was told, Norfolk agreed that if she could not get satisfaction from a treaty with Elizabeth, then Mary could go elsewhere. A further unlikelihood was that Mary's instructions were supposed to have been written in French and in clear. Further examinations of Ross on 3 and 6 November add little to our knowledge of what he knew and only confirm the present thesis.[78] Ridolfi's claims as to Mary's and Norfolk's alleged reactions made it possible for him to send back from Europe a stream of compromising letters which they were supposed to be only too ready to receive.

On 6 November Ross was allowed to pen a letter to Mary 'it being first showed to the queen of England'. He gave her a fairly full account of events as they touched him

76 Ibid., p. 132. 77 Ibid., p. 133. 78 Ibid., p. 136. Ross' Examination of 26.10.1571 (Salisbury ms, 6, nos. 68-74) was printed in Murdin, pp 20-32 but with some twenty variations from the original, mostly insignificant, and some six erasures. But add to line 14 on p. 24, 'He saith those instructions which were sent for the queen were in French, but a long tr[anscript?] of a discourse.' If such a document was sent in French and in clear, it is another argument against Ridolfi. At the end, 'This examination aforesaid was written by Sir Thomas Smith ... and the bishop of Ross hath subscribed it with his own hand.' This need not be true of course.

especially since 19 October. He explained how he had been obliged to confess to her involvement with Ridolfi. 'A great part of your Majesty's letters sent from time to time to the duke, and likewise sundry letters sent by me to him of the greatest importance, was come to their hands, whereof some were produced before me, so that thereby they were made privy to the most secret matters that your Majesty at any time did treat with him, either by your ministers or otherwise ... [So] there was no further place left to me to deny or refuse to have meddled in those causes, in respect of so manifest proofs.' So he had plainly confessed to what he took to be 'the whole proceedings' between queen and duke. Ross had also seen what were no doubt genuine letters brought by John Hamilton coming from Alba with letters from the French nuncio for Mary in January 1571, and also letters brought by Andrew Beaton for Ridolfi at the same time, which promised armed assistance from abroad if Elizabeth refused to conclude a treaty. We do not know what reached Mary but it was as a result of some of these letters that she 'caused write a letter to me [Ross] bearing a long discourse, with certain articles in French to the duke of Norfolk' asking for his advice. 'And because none was more fit to take the voyage on hand nor Ridolfi, therefore in the same letters, your Majesty [Mary] did recommend him to the duke of Norfolk, willing him to confer with him at length, and direct to these princes with such credit and instructions as the duke thought most expedient for obtaining his demands – which letters, discourse and instructions hath been gotten in the duke's house, and are all in the Council's hands – and that thereupon Ridolfi did confer with the duke at length, and was fully instruct-ed and directed by his advice; and letters sent upon the duke's behalf, and by his own advice – albeit he would not subscribe them – to the pope, the king of Spain, and duke of Alba, of the which also since he hath received answer from the pope. And Ridolfi has made his whole voyage and is now in the Low Countries.'[79] Ross closed with a lament that such schemes had ever been entertained, and repudiated any idea that he had taken part in them. He came as close as an ambassador could to rebuking his own sovereign for giving ear to it all without even a word to him. Ross seems to have been completely taken in by Burghley's wiles. Or did he deep down realize the terrible con-sequences of not allowing himself to be convinced?

Mary received and wrote a reply to this letter of 8 November which was not allowed to come to the bishop's hands. Cecil, to complete the task of sowing discord between the two, informed Ross that Mary remarked on the letter that it was the voice of Jacob and the hand of Esau. 'For although that I had written the same, yet another had held the pen, and was the cause of the writing thereof.' In fact Mary's original letter sug-gested confusion of mind in the presence of what her ambassador had drawn her into without her knowledge. Burghley reported it as if she was angry that Ross could have betrayed what she was about to do for her own relief.[80]

It seems likely that Ross gave way to one of his well-known rages when he discussed these matters with Dr Wilson, master of the requests. 'The bishop seemeth to me ...

---

79 *The m. c.*, p. 142.   80 Ibid., p. 144.

very glad that these practices are come to light, saying they are all nought ... He saith further, upon speech that I had with him, that the queen his mistress is not fit for any husband. For first, he saith, she poisoned her husband the French king, as he hath credibly understood. Again, she hath consented to the murder of her late husband, the Lord Darnley. Thirdly, she matched with the murderer, and brought him to the field to be murdered. And last of all, she pretended marriage with the duke, with whom, as he thinketh, she would not long have kept faith.'[81] Well might Wilson exclaim, 'Lord, what people are these! What a queen, and what an ambassador!' It is hardly possible that a man so close to events had no inkling of the real nature of the plot. Certainly Wilson would know what to write and what to leave out. He himself supplied proof that he was used to shady business. He closed his letter, 'I do send your Honour enclosed so much as is translated into handsome Scottish, desiring you to send unto me Paris closely sealed, and it shall not be known from whence it cometh.' We do not know what this was about but it sounds less than aboveboard and well suited to the general context.

After this, Ross surrendered completely to Burghley. On 1 November he wrote to reassure the principal secretary that from now on he would hide nothing 'which were fit for her Majesty to know'. He described himself as 'always sorry from the bottom of my heart that either the queen my mistress, or others who seemed to favour her, should have given ear to such vain and unlikely designs and devices' favoured by malcontents everywhere. He protested further, 'whatsoever was used by me, was done as a minister, and by commandments, as I trust her Majesty doth consider'.[82] He found it easy to believe that Mary had not been able to endure longer Elizabeth's, or rather Burghley's, systematic procrastination. Writing to Cecil again on 16 November, Ross could have reflected that his own queen must have seen as well as he did the small likelihood that 'princes would so lightly put their hands to so great a matter, and so unlikely a war, when they would not send a small support for relief of her oppressed subjects in Scotland'.[83] He also apologised for the fact that he had told rather less than the truth as he knew it, or more correctly as Ridolfi wanted him to know it, in his examination of 24 October. But he then had reason to believe that the government knew much less about the whole affair than they did. Afterwards he realised that Cecil had information which could only, as he thought, have come from the duke and his servants. Ross even allowed himself to believe, or so he wrote, that Burghley would not 'affirm anything but that which is true'!

The duke's arraignment on 16 January 1572 urged Ross to exclaim, 'Lord God, how much it grieved me.' Even more grievous for him was Wilson's attempt, in spite of earlier council assurances that nothing the bishop said would be used in evidence, to get him to give evidence which in fact was used in court against the duke. Wilson wanted certain letters which Ross had received from Ridolfi. 'For they never have gotten any letters of any secret matters except those which were found in the duke's house.' Ross refused, giving a remarkable testimony to Norfolk. 'Nor yet that I ever

81 Ibid., p. 145.   82 Ibid., p. 145 and n. 2.   83 Ibid., p. 146.

heard him open his mouth either maliciously or traitorously against the queen or the realm.' And if he were forced to be present, Ross assured them he would declare this before the whole assembly.[84] He had in any case already destroyed any possibly compromising letters.

Not until 1573 was Ross allowed to leave for France. There had been an earlier project to exchange him with the Scots for Northumberland but they decided that money was more important than revenge. So the earl was sold south instead to be executed. Ross continued to work for Mary's release in France, describing her as 'put in prison by the trickery and calumnies of her enemies', and contrasting her treatment with the cordial reception given by James III to Henry VI when he fled to Scotland after his defeat by Edward of York.[85] The removal of the threat of the rack doubtless made it easier to tell more of what we may take as the truth.

It is perhaps evident by now that in order to tangle relations effectively between the various parties accused of complicity in the plot a great deal depended not only on Ridolfi but also on the duke's secretaries or stewards. The three concerned were Lawrence Banister, Robert Hickford and William Barker. Barker stands out as the man who cooperated most completely with the government and with Ridolfi in betraying Norfolk. This is indicated by the manner in which he was handled. His part in the plot was played down. At the end he received nothing less than a royal pardon for his significant contribution towards securing Norfolk's conviction. Barker, as Ross mentioned in his longer discourse, was old and infirm at this time. Wilson and Smith give the impression he was also infirm in mind – and therefore very suggestible and responsive to pressure. Whatever his true inclinations where Norfolk was concerned, there was always the threat of dire retribution to make him remember whatever was desired and in the manner desired. He had been in retirement and no longer enjoyed the confidence of the duke. Indeed, the latter declared at his trial, 'I would have trusted one Banister afore fifteeen Barkers'. Bromley tried to bolster Barker's credit to make his witness more cogent but the duke insisted, 'He was not of credit about me. For I used him not these fourteen years.'[86]

The other two were dealt with more severely, especially Banister who was subjected to torture. This is already a sufficient indication that they were faithful to Norfolk and told the truth. According to Ross, the Council 'caused Mr Barker, who was the principal mediator betwixt the duke and me at all times, and knew most of all other, to be brought face to face with me in the presence of the council to accuse me, as he did very extremely on divers points, where I asked him who did first open these matters to the council, considering no man was of counsel to the most part of them but the duke, Barker and I alonely. But he suddenly answered with these words, "Even I revealed them for the love I bear to my prince and country, and so will I do all that I know".'[87]

Lawrence Banister was a man trained in law and a justice of peace. Hickford and Barker were both gentlemen born. Barker was a man of longer experience than

84 Ibid., p. 149.   85 Ibid., p. 153.   86 Ibid., p. 202 and nn. 1, 2.   87 Ibid., p. 170.

Hickford which explains why when Hickford suffered a passing illness Barker was used again at this fatal time by the duke to handle his business and correspondence. Or so it was claimed. The duke did not destroy his own correspondence, surely the mark of someone who has little to hide. He left it with Barker. He was also an important messenger when from 1570 the duke was under house arrest. Barker, while having access to the duke's codes and ciphers, could see to it that more compromising tasks such as copying and deciphering dangerous letters, genuine or manufactured, could be left to Hickford. If the codes were used to forge letters and messages in the ducal name, it would evidently be difficult for Norfolk to clear himself by a plain denial, and equally difficult to provide something better by way of proof of innocence. Hickford would assume that what Barker did was by the duke's orders.

Hickford was the first to be arrested, on 1 September. Ross was given to understand that he it was who started the avalanche of subsequent accusation. Hickford admitted to having letters from Ross and the queen of Scots and others 'which he kept under the mats in the duke's bedchamber, and others in the tiles of the house, which then presently he caused to be found and delivered to the council, which was the deciphering written with his own hand of the discourse above-mentioned sent by the queen of Scots for the dispatch and credit of Ridolfi to the duke, with the alphabet and common ordinary cipher used between the queen of Scots and the duke.'[88] There were seventeen letters in all which Ross thought the duke had given orders to burn. 'But they were preserved, not without great suspicion that the same was done of industry and set purpose to betray him, as did well appear by the proceedings.' In answers to his examiners on 16 September, Hickford was quick to repudiate the idea that he 'was the only betrayer of my master and that by my means he came to the Tower'. It was Barker who was 'the only revealer of [his] master['s] secrets'. Hickford subscribed to his revelations only subsequently. Although at his trial he pleaded guilty, and made no brave showing, he maintained his innocence throughout of any treasonable matter. 'I did never know that any such thing was meant by my lord or any other. And whatsoever was by him or any other intended, I was not privy unto it.' He deciphered one letter of Ross to the duke at the latter's order. He knew nothing of the duke's alleged approval for Ridolfi's wilder enterprise. He had a cipher which was left behind by Ridolfi. This presumably he persuaded Norfolk to keep for future correspondence on financial affairs. If in fact Ridolfi saw fit to write to Norfolk in this cipher on other and compromising matters, it would be difficult for even a well-disposed jury to believe that the duke had not foreseen and even prearranged it. 'The alphabet was left under the mat hard by the window-side in the entry towards my lord's bedchamber where the map of England doth hang; whereof I made my lord privy.'[89]

88 Ibid., p. 172. The Edinburgh copy of Ross' 'The discourse ...' used by Anderson, has a curious tendency to exonerate Barker and substitute other names for his in compromising matters. So Banister is substituted for Barker in this ms as the man who was used by Norfolk to take three letters to Ridolfi. See ibid., p. 171. 89 *The m. c.*, p. 174.

Barker was probably drawn into the government toils from the summer of 1570 when correspondence between Mary and the duke was renewed since many if not all of these letters fell into official hands. It seems likely that Norfolk was encouraged by his false friends to take up again this dangerous connection with Mary. As he told his children in a letter of 4 February 1572, 'So that I, having been driven anew to have intelligence with the queen of Scots and her ministers contrary to my duty and my promise to her Majesty, I was enforced for fear that Barker or the bishop of Ross at any time should discover this my new intelligence; they having my head thereby under their girdle, to conceal those things which in the end gave those vehement presumptions against me to concur with their false accusations in divers material points.' [90]

It was an essential part of the Burghley-Walsingham plot that letters coming from Ridolfi should be firmly attached to the ducal household and by implication to the duke himself. Interception at the ports was a hazardous process, as the Bailly incident proved. The only effective way of making sure that compromising letters reached the duke and reached the council was to win the services of at least one in a position of confidentiality in the household. Barker was the man. He would hover about Hickford, receiving letters and writing replies not only as directed by the duke, but as directed by others. He wrote replies which were certainly not at the duke's dictation and may have been answers to letters which never existed or arrived. To ease the conscience of such a man, and to give a better motive for compliance than the threat of dire consequences if he refused, it was presumably put to him that the duke's fidelity to queen and state were merely being tested. If his intentions were sincere, surely he would reveal all matters to the council which he must see as suspicious. Then all would be well. If he did not, the duke must be held suspect. We need not suppose that Barker enjoyed his task. A cry of anguish which issued at his examination of 15 September seems to have summed up his basic attitude. 'Oh hard hap of servants! For beside the evil terms that are given them they are either thought evil of for their masters, or evil dealt with for themselves. And if they be faithful then be they asses perpetual, and must do as they be driven or else be beaten. In such sort of service I poor wretch have never been accounted of but in time of adversity, and then put to do what I did detest.'[91] Certainly, the duke was under no illusion as to the man who principally betrayed him. At his trial he declared, 'I chiefly challenge none but Barker in whom you may see what fear may do ... It is well known that Barker's stomach is nothing; he hath been known well enough. Fear hath done much in him.'[92]

90 Ibid., p. 186.   91 Ibid., p. 203, n. 1.   92 Ibid. Barker's confessions and depositions, most damaging to Norfolk's reputation, and much used in his trial, are very unsatisfactory as evidence. His answers in the examination of 9.9. are in his hand (?) but they are preceded by a page heavily scored through and in places completely obliterated. One can discern, 'I never dealt with the Spanish ambassador nor none of his ...' followed by obliteration. The confession of 17. 9. is in Barker's hand but the last two paragraphs are in another hand and seem to have been added after the last line of Barker's writing and before his signature. In the first paragraph, the original 'he thinketh' has been crossed through and replaced by 'he saith'. Other confessions, such as the 'last confession' of 19.9. are only signed 'Will Barker', and not oth-

Certainly Hickford and Banister were very much involved with the bag of money, some £600 in gold which was sent across the Scottish border to help those designated for forensic purposes as the queen's enemies. This money came not from Norfolk but from the French ambassador, de la Mothe Fénélon, under orders from France. Barker was the most likely channel of information for the government of French intentions. De la Mothe 'sent to know if I could help to convey it. I sent him word I could not tell yet, but I would see what I could do.'[93] Barker approached Norfolk but at first he was altogether opposed to any servant of his having part in it. Later he changed his mind, informing Barker 'there was come a merchant of Shrewsbury that had brought butter from Banister who might be a good messenger for the money.'[94] At his trial, Norfolk denied all treasonable intent or sending dangerous letters. The money was to go to Lord Herries by way of Richard Lowther. But too many people, at least half a dozen apart from duke and ambassador, somehow became involved in a transaction which should have been carried out by one or two at most.

Who was 'Mr Brown of Shrewsbury'? According to the attorney-general at Norfolk's trial, Hickford gave Brown the money which was to be delivered to Banister. He was supposed to have informed Brown that it contained £50, though why he should have bothered to give him this information is not clear. But Mr Brown was a man of more than ordinary sophistication and with a sense of destiny beyond ordinary mortals. His suspicions led him to think he was carrying not £50 in silver but £600 in gold. Not even bothering to open the bag to see what was inside, he 'went to one of the queen's privy council, and disclosed his suspicion so that he might learn what he carried'.[95] When the bag was opened, not only was the bullion revealed but also letters: among them a paper identifying Norfolk with the fateful Quarante, 40, the number chosen by Ridolfi, as we remember, for compromising letters to one otherwise unnamed. How can we fail to believe otherwise than that Brown, whatever his real identity, was a government agent, and that at the time of delivering the bag to the council, a letter was included to connect the duke, not only with the Scottish transaction but with Ridolfi's far more sinister activities on the continent? Is it likely that if Norfolk had been aware of what was going on, he would have chosen the same code number for himself on this occasion as that devised by Ridolfi?[96] Probably there never was such a letter. We have only the word of the prosecution which had to accept whatever was given it as evidence. The letter was not produced in court.

erwise in his hand. This confession states at the end that it was given without compulsion, but Smith and Wilson in their letter to Burghley, admit it was obtained with the threat of the rack. The confession of 22.9. in Smith's hand although signed by Barker has an addition between the lines. One page is unsigned of the deposition of 27. 9. while the joint examination of Barker and Hickford on 26. 9. nowhere has the signature of either. Most unsatisfactory is the examination of 10.10. which is signed at each pagefoot by Barker, but is not otherwise in his hand and and contains a great number of alterations and cancellations. All the examiners signed it on the last page. Similar additions if fewer were made to his confession of 11.10. A copying error (?) in this document makes Barker write 'the French king' although the context clearly calls for 'the Spanish king'. All these confessions are in Salisbury ms 158.   **93** *The m. c.*, p. 163. **94** Ibid.   **95** Ibid., p. 158.   **96** Ibid., p. 157.

De la Mothe tried to get the money back, and at first expressed satisfaction that it had been intercepted since he 'would write to the queen's Majesty to demand it'. But once again Burghley had legal friends to help him. Two such assured him that money sent to an enemy by a friend could still be kept as taken from the enemy. In any case, it could only be reclaimed in the court of admiralty where it would be 'controversum indeed'.[97] Charles IX and Catherine de Medici tried to recover the money through the English ambassador but apparently without success.

One of the most compromising letters sent to the duke, brought up at his arraignment, was received in the Charterhouse on 16 June 1571. He explained its provenance most effectively not at his trial, alas, when it might still have done him good, but in a letter to his children dated 4 February 1572. 'Barker brought me a writing, which he said was deciphered, being a letter from the pope to me; and that there were certain words in the said writing which did tend as though he had received a letter from the party that he wrote that unto. After no small heat with Barker, professing, I fear me with oaths, my detestation of him and his see, I said, "Here must needs be some packing, and that you Barker must be privy to it. For if the pope should send this letter and mean it to me, then of necessity it must fall out that there hath been some forged letter in my name sent unto him".'[98] Had Norfolk probed further, the whole plot against him might have come to light. As it was, Barker claimed, probably truly, 'that he was never privy nor consenting to any such letter. Marry, he said, he thought it might be Ridolphus his doing for his better estimation, and protested that after that he would never deal with him nor hear from him.' It was here that Howard made two fatal mistakes. He failed to probe Barker. Worse still, he failed to reveal the dangerous occasion to competent authority. The papal letter referred to Ridolfi's disastrous plot in unmistakeable terms. Even Burghley's dark ingenuity would have found it difficult to bring the axe to Norfolk's neck if the duke had got in his revelation first.

Howard later realized his mistake and also explained how the epistolary evidence was set up against him. 'This now doth not excuse my undutifulness that I would conceal any such letter, as I did both this, as he said, of the pope's, which was double-written, and also another, as he likewise affirmed which came from Ridolphus.' His instinctive loyalty to a servant, in this case the untrustworthy Barker, was his undoing. 'I wrote as Barker said to me, for ... I never had any cipher between me and any of those princes, or else with Ridolphus. And those letters which Barker showed me had neither hand, direction nor seal. They might be made in London for ought that I know. He showed me once a little packet undeciphered, which he swore he knew not what was contained in it till one Cuthbert, the bishop of Ross, his man, did tell him, which he said was one of those that he showed me. God knoweth whether it were or not.'[99]

97 Ibid., p. 162.   98 Ibid., p. 177.   99 Ibid., pp 177-8. John Cuthbert was Ross' principal secretary. He is not to be confused with Cuthbert Reid who described himself as a steward in Ross' household and had by this time only been in the bishop's service for a year. Reid was previously a scholar at Aberdeen university where Ross had also taught, 'black-coloured, low of stature, having no beard ... black-headed' and some twenty years old: cf. Salisbury ms 158, No. 74; *The m. c.*, p. 81. He disclaimed

One of the most damning letters kept for future use by Barker was a letter supposed to have been written by Mary to Ross on 8 February 1571. It amounted to a summary of the whole conspiracy, including the dethronement of Elizabeth, and was intended to show that the Scottish queen was every bit as guilty as Norfolk of what would have been taken in a subject as high treason. There is no good reason to believe that Mary wrote this letter. Over the period of the Ridolfi plot she wrote about a hundred letters. They all consistently push three claims when they deal with politics: her right to the English succession if Elizabeth failed to produce an heir; her right to the present throne of Scotland; her right to intervene in the politics of Scotland as she saw fit, and using force if necessary. This letter of 8 February exists only as an alleged copy in Robert Hickford's hand. It bears an attestation in the same hand: 'This copie being conferred word by word with the originall copie is agreing in all poincts with the sayd originall. This xth of January 1571[2].' One cannot believe that if there had been an 'original' of this extraordinary letter it would not have been preserved. What exactly is a 'copie' of an 'originall copie'?[100] It must amount to a certainty that the 'originall copie', copied again by Hickford, was in the hand of Cecil or Walsingham. Obviously, this would not have been preserved.

When the letter was read out in court, the duke showed signs of complete bewilderment – he was no actor. It was one of the letters claimed to have been found under the mats in the duke's apartment. Evidently, Barker's was the principal responsibility for the preservation of the letter and therefore its emergence in the trial. Norfolk was so taken off guard that he overstated his own case. 'What manner of man he was is no

any connection with the bishop's paperwork or messaging. According to James Cauldwell who described Reid above, John Cuthbert was 'of the age of twenty-eight, as I judge, palefaced, low of stature, a thin yellowish beard, a yellowish head, without any hair of the cheek, both steward and secretary of the bishop of Ross, and one that did all about here'. According to Barker, 'Cuthbert is the chief man that is able to disclose more than any other; if any such things have proceeded at any time' (Wm Barker, 'Cuthbert the Scot', 30.9.1571; Salisbury ms 158, No. 65, in Barker's hand and signed.) Ross admitted Cuthbert's importance in the work of ciphering and deciphering. He deciphered the 'first letters sent by Ridolfi'; Ross, examination of 6. 9.1571; Murdin, pp 46, 51. Ross managed to get John Cuthbert out of England under the nose of Burghley by about the end of August 1571. He may have passed into complete obscurity but he is the likely author of *A treatise of treasons against Queen Elizabeth and the crown of England, divided into two parts, whereof the first part answereth certain treasons pretended that never were intended: and the second discovereth greater treasons committed that are by few perceived ...* ', published in Antwerp in January 1572. It was a devastating attack on the regime of Cecil who sent Sir Thomas Smith to Flanders to find and identify the author but without success. The authorship question was dealt with by Conyers Read, *Lord Burghley and Queen Elizabeth* (London 1960), p. 95; T. H. Clancy, S. J. , 'A political pamphlet: the Treatise of treasons', reprint from *Loyola University Studies in the Humanities*, 1962 who tentatively names T. Gifford; Calendar of the Salisbury mss, ii, No. 120 suggests David Chalmers and John Gordon; the case for John Cuthbert is considered in *The m. c.*, Appendix 3, pp 391-7. See *The d. q.*, p. 100. For Mary to Ross, 8.2.1571, see *The m. c.* p. 178 and *The d. q.*, pp 391-5. *The d. q.* stated the letter was in Burghley's hand, but it was much more likely in Hickford's together with the signature and comment about the copy. Nevertheless there was a similarity between Cecil's and Hickford's hands. Cecil had more than one hand at his disposal. See photographs facing p. 400 in *The d. q.*   **100** *The d. q.*, pp 390-400.

matter to me, I know of no more, nor am to be charged with no more than I myself am privy to. I never dealt with him about any cause of mine.'[101] Evidently Norfolk was completely thrown for the moment. In fact the duke was related to Ridolfi as a creditor for quite legitimate lending and borrowing transactions. He was not Ridolfi's only client, nor Ridolfi the only banker with a financial hold on English aristocratic houses.

Much was made at the trial of the extraordinary providence of God by which vital evidence came to light – the merest chance, without which it would never have been discovered. As the attorney-general claimed at Norfolk's trial, 'the cipher in which these letters were written, having been hid in the tiles, was found by chance. And thus it will appear how things hidden will, by God's providence come to light.'[102] There was certainly some delay before the cipher-key came to light but this did not deter the sleuths Wilson and Smith. Soon after Hickford's arrest, he consented to decipher some letters. These came to Sir Henry Neville's hand, as far as he could say from memory. The result was promptly dispatched to Burghley. 'As much haste as we made, yet had the duke gotten away the alphabet of the cipher, who therefore hitherto thinketh nothing is known. Although your Lordship may perceive nothing will be long hid.'[103]

Elizabeth meanwhile was taking a great interest in the proceedings. She urged Norfolk's examiners to 'get the understanding by all means possible' of the letters in question. While an approximate decipherment of the letters would do for present purposes, it was clearly desirable that the cipher-key should be found for the accurate rendering of letters which could be expected to compromise Norfolk in the extreme. It is obvious that if the duke had been genuinely involved in treasonable correspondence he would have done nothing to assist the discovery of the cipher-key. Whatever the propaganda peddled at the trial, it was admitted by Smith and Wilson in their letter to Burghley of 9 September that it was the duke himself who gave the green light to Hickford to tell them where the cipher-key could be found. Out of loyalty to his master he had previously hung back. 'Talking with the duke heretofore, and charging him that he had the cipher which we missed, and which should lie under the mats, he cast out a word, and said that Hickford's memory might fail. It had been, and might lie betwixt tiles. We, calling Hickford before us, at the first he said that was before the house was full builded. Now it is ceiled there and took it to be surely under the mats. Yet after a night he remembered ... and said it might be in such a place, but he could not so demonstrate it that any man might find it. If he went himself he doubted not to find it if it were there. Whereupon I, D. Wilson went this day with him, and one of the Tower, his keeper, to Howard House, and found it indeed betwixt two tiles in the roof, so hid as it had not been possible to have found it otherwise than by unripping all the tiles, except one had been well acquainted with the place.'[104] So much for one more tale of marvellous chance !

With the cipher-key put in their hands by the unsuspecting duke, they were able to decipher Ridolfi's 'letter of discourse', whatever this was. The duke claimed 'he never

101 *The m. c.*, pp 178-9.   102 Ibid., p. 179.   103 Ibid., p. 180.   104 Ibid., p. 181 and n. 1.

saw nor heard of it'.[105] The 'letter of discourse', according to Smith and Wilson, seemed to be 'written in the Scottish queen's name'. It is not clear whether Smith and Wilson were consummate actors or whether they really believed in the duke's guilt. They admitted at one point that if, against all his protestations, he was guilty, 'then is the duke a devil and no proper man'.[106] If devils were involved they were surely to be looked for elsewhere.

The cipher-key was, in any case, an old one: given to Hickford at Howard House, as he claimed, in September 1570 a month or so after the duke's release from the Tower to house confinement. This code was known to few persons and so Cecil could have used it with impunity for coded documents of any date he chose. Norfolk wrote in code only to Liggons, Banister, Ross and the Scottish queen. Hickford who supplied the above information also insisted that Norfolk 'never sought to procure [Mary] to attempt anything against the queen's Majesty's person ... or the disquietness of this realm, but always advised her patiently to bear her afflictions; and that time was the only thing that should be her preservation'. He wrote to the bishop of Ross but only 'as the matter required answer'.[107]

Not that for all his naïveté in some respects Howard was without forebodings. He exclaimed more than once, 'How unhappy a man I am to deal with such persons. This trouble is enough to bring a man beside himself.'[108] This corroborates what he said at his trial. Needless to say, Hickford got no thanks for his candid defence of his master. All the same, while indicating Barker as having been 'the most doer betwixt the duke and other foreign practisers', and Banister as 'somewhat obstinate but little he knoweth', Smith and Wilson gave Hickford their own grudging testimony in writing to Burghley on 20 September. 'Hickford, as we can perceive, was only the writer or secretary of that which otherways was practised; no practiser, but rather repugning and misliking of more than allowing, but only for duty and service' sake, and therefore straight acknowledged his error, and confessed as soon as he was earnestly charged.'[109]

Much was made at the trial of Barker's evidence as the principal go-between for the duke and the main characters of the plot. Barker arranged a meeting between the duke and Ridolfi at which Ridolfi was supposed to have received the notorious instructions from the duke for his visits to the courts of Europe to stir up invasion. The duke was supposed to have received lists of names of knights and nobles who would assist or not the great design. The meeting lasted an hour but Barker was not present. It was never suggested that he listened at the keyhole. Norfolk did not deny the meeting but insisted more than plausibly that it concerned a 'recognisance' or guaranty offered for the extension of a loan. The duke did the Florentine no favours, not even when Ridolfi warned him 'that Walsingham had told him that the said duke should never come out of prison'.[110] Perhaps for a moment the Italian felt some pity for a man whose head, thanks to him, was already as good as on the block. A dangerous man to have dealings

105 Ibid., pp 180-1.   106 Ibid., p. 182.   107 Ibid., p. 183.   108 Ibid.   109 Ibid., p. 184, n. 1. 110 Ibid., p. 185.

with was Guerau de Spes; and Norfolk was careful to avoid him. But 'to please the curious Italian head of Ridolfi, they devised it among them to deal with the Spanish ambassador. As for me, I never heard from the Spanish ambassador in the matter. I never saw him but once at my lord treasurer's. I was angry with Barker for going to him in my name. And he excused it, and said that he could not otherwise content the bishop of Ross and Ridolfi. And so that affirming of the letters was Barker's doing and not mine.'[111]

What exactly were these 'instructions', so often referred to in the examinations and trial, as they came to Norfolk's hand? It will be evident by now that much depended on creating deliberate ambiguities when it came to producing documents which would compromise the intended victims. In his 'answers' of 13 October 1571 Norfolk gave his own account of how and what he received. 'Ridolfi was not with him before he had the "instructions", for Barker brought' them to the duke in the morning, 'the which he misliked and took them to Barker in the afternoon. And Barker said he would deliver them to Ridolfi. And that night Barker brought Ridolfi to [Norfolk] into the long gallery where the duke walked with Ridolfi. And Barker stood in the window. And when Ridolfi came to that point to require [Norfolk's] letter to the duke of Alba, [the duke] sought to break off; and ... by that token ... when Ridolfi and Barker went down the duke bolted the door after them. And the next morning the duke asked Barker whether he had delivered the "instructions" to Ridolfi. And he said, "No". For if he should be taken in the nighttime, he would not like ... [to] ... be found with those writings about him. But he had appointed a place where they should be delivered to Ridolfi that day.'[112]

It seems that Barker did not return these instructions to Ridolfi whatever they were. There is no reason to believe they corresponded with the instructions Ridolfi was peddling in Europe as coming from the duke and pushing the invasion plot. The duke insisted that what he saw was quite harmless. 'In the instructions in French delivered to him by Barker there was no such thing contained of a power to be sent into England and another into Ireland ... and yet he read the whole of that which was delivered to him by Barker.' Evidently, it was a very different document which was put into the hands of the attorney-general as evidence. He claimed at the trial, 'After this talk the duke delivered to Barker a paper, saying that Ridolfi left it with him; which paper contained the sum of the treason. And therein was also a paper of the names of divers noblemen, knights and gentlemen in cipher, whom they counted that they would take the duke's part. But they counted without their host; so that there was for every name a cipher of which "40" was for the duke, and "30" for the Lord Lumley. Barker received it of the duke and delivered it again to Ridolfi.'[113] Lumley would shortly be displaced by Mary.

Barker's story corresponded fairly well with Wilbraham's accusation. On 10 October he was reported as saying under examination, that he 'went with Ridolfi to

111 Ibid., p. 186 and n. 1.   112 Ibid.   113 Ibid., p. 187.

the gate; and in the way Ridolfi told [him] the duke did like well of the matter, and was willing that the queen of Scots should be aided, which Ridolfi trusted would shortly be. And the next day in the morning the duke told [Barker] that Ridolfi had left a paper with him, and said he had not read it, and bade [Barker] give it Ridolfi. And [Barker] saith he looked on the paper, and therein were written the names of many noblemen, knights and others, and on the side of every name a cipher in a number.'[114]

Bromley, the solicitor-general, also made Barker the conveyer of the letter taken from Bailly alleged to have come from Ridolfi which was directed to the duke under the number '40'. 'This letter ... was sent to the duke from the bishop of Ross by Barker. Barker delivered it to the duke from whence it was sent back again to ... Ross by Cuthbert; and by Cuthbert it was deciphered, and carried again to the duke by Barker. Upon this occasion Cuthbert was sought for. The duke conveyed him away; and this conveying away of Cuthbert the duke hath confessed.'[115] In fact John Cuthbert, Ross' servant, was successfully hustled out of the country by his master. Norfolk admitted that a decipher sent to him as "40" came to him but not that he had any prior arrangement for the receipt of any such letter. 'Where they say this message was sent by my privity, by reason that I was meant by "40", I deny it. I never wrote by Ridolfi. I refused to do it. I knew not that his letters were to me but as Barker said. And it was not likely they should be to me. For it was a matter that I was not privy of, and in a cipher which I had not. Ridolfi left no cipher with me. As for the taking of the packet, I knew nothing of it. The letter I never saw in cipher.'[116]

Norfolk's statement is clear, unambiguous and convincing. There was more. 'Barker brought me a decipher, telling me that '40' was for me and '30' for the queen of Scots. When he told me first he had the cipher, I asked what I should do with it and how I should read it having no cipher. Barker answered that it was left with Cuthbert. For Ridolfi at his departure told him that he would write answer of the money for the Scottish queen, and that he would leave the cipher with Cuthbert, and that he had done so. And in the letters deciphered did appear that the duke of Alba had promised aid of money for the Scottish queen for her necessities, but he could not yet do it for want of commission, but as soon as he had commission he would.'[117] It seems that Barker, or rather his employers, were hoping for an unconditional letter of approval from Norfolk which could be taken to approve not only financial assistance for Mary but for everything else Ridolfi had gone abroad to declare falsely as the plan of duke and queen. He did not oblige. It made no difference to his case.

Even the honourable not to say ingenuous Norfolk suspected by now that some kind of trap was being laid for him. 'When I heard of this I misliked this dealing with the duke of Alba, having before refused to write to him in the matter at Ridolfi's request. And I threatened Barker if he so dealt any more with me. The letters might be to me as Barker said, but I knew not so much.'[118] Bromley dismissed the duke's defence as 'a bare denying', making as much as he could of the fact that the duke

114 Ibid. 115 Ibid., p. 188. 116 Ibid. 117 Ibid. 118 Ibid., p. 189.

received the letter. 'Thus you see the duke confesseth the receipt of the letter. He only denyeth it was to this effect.' Bromley also insisted that there were two witnesses, not one as Norfolk claimed, namely Barker and Ross, or rather his factor, John Cuthbert. Norfolk pointed out, 'Barker and Cuthbert might make the letter themselves and put in and out what they list.'[119] Barker's examination of 10 October 1571 claimed that 'the effect of which letter was that Ridolfi had spoken with the duke of Alba and had had good audience, and that the duke did like well of the matter that Ridolfi came for, and willed in any wise that the matter might be kept secret, and promised to do his best therein.'[120] What Barker said, or was alleged to have said, at the trial, from which he was, of course, absent, pinned the worst on the duke. He 'willed that when a foreign power should enter into this land at the port which Ridolfi had named, that the friends of the enterprise here in England might be in a readiness with force between that port and London. And this was the effect of that letter, as far as he remembereth, which the duke ... did read in this examinate's hearing, and did deliver back again to this examinate [Barker] to carry again to the bishop of Ross. Which letter this examinate delivered to Cuthbert.'[121]

As Norfolk insisted, 'It may be that Barker received this letter as you spake of, and that Cuthbert deciphered it, and that it contained the matters that you might allege. It may be that they kept that letter still to themselves, and might bring me another letter containing only such matter as I was content with containing the private cause.'[122] There the duke had it in a nutshell. The solicitor-general had no adequate reply beyond harping on the fact that the duke acknowledged receipt of the letter – a letter – which letter? whose letter?

Barker, as the usual messenger between Ross and the duke, used the free field for invention, exaggeration and misrepresentation to blacken the character of Ross even more than that of his master. Ross, as he learned later, was supposed to have encouraged Norfolk not only in Ridolfi's wilder schemes, but even to raise rebellion in April 1571. 'There were a great number of earls, lords and barons which were assembled at the parliament that were offended with certain extreme laws that were to be made against [the Catholics]. For the which cause they would be glad that the parliament were stayed and broken up. And therefore in consideration that the duke was in disdain and discredit, and not suffered to come to the parliament, he had good occasion offered to take some enterprise [in hand] by the assistance of his friends then assembled ... and then was the best opportunity that ever he should have again. For it would be very hard to convoke thereafter so many friends so well-minded together as were then in the city without suspicion. And so he needed not to abide any forces from princes beyond the seas. For by this means he might easily be master of the country and relieve the queen of Scots and himself, and get what conditions pleased him best of the qeen of England.' Ross was accused of sending a mesage to Norfolk by Barker to this effect, offering a Scottish precedent by way of encouragement. The ducal

---

119 Ibid., p. 188.   120 Ibid., p. 189.   121 Ibid., pp 189-190.   122 Ibid., pp 191-2.

answer likewise by Barker, as it was claimed, was 'that the duke would attempt nothing before that he should hear from Ridolfi of the answers of the foreign princes. And Barker said when he told the duke's answer the bishop was very highly moved and offended therewith, and said he would never look for any further good to be done by the duke either to himself or to the queen [Mary] his mistress.'[123]

This did not depend simply on Barker's word since Ross admitted in the 'Discourse' 'that Ridolfi before his departing had at certain times discoursed with Barker and me what the duke might do by the assistance of friends, if he pleased, without any help of strangers; and what noblemen would take the part with him ... ' Barker's part in bringing all parties into discredit and causing confusion is clearest from Ross' 'Discourse'. 'And so Ridolfi was conveyed to him [Norfolk] by Barker and conferred with him at length upon certain articles of a device [and] plot which he had drawn. And at his returning he said to me that the duke had fully satisfied him, and that he would take his journey out of hand so being the duke would subscribe three letters which he had made for his better credit. And I sent the same to the duke with Banister, but he refused to subscribe them, and he said he should satisfy Ridolfi.' So Banister's honesty as a go-between and reporter seems proved. Barker, presumably under pressure from his puppet-masters, who would have kept a careful eye on every aspect of the situation, repaired the omission. 'And so he [Ridolfi] was conveyed again by Barker to the duke, and then was satisfied upon that point, as he said to me [Ross]. For upon the next day Barker passed to the Spanish ambassador, and there in Ridolfi's presence and mine, affirmed that it was the duke's pleasure that Ridolfi should use these letters albeit they were not subscribed according as Barker's deposition did bear.'[124]

The bishop's narrative also maintains that it was Barker who carried Bailly's letters to Norfolk, both the originals in cipher and Cuthbert's deciphering on a second expedition; although whether it was Cuthbert's or something else substituted the bishop does not presume to say. It was also Barker who carried the pope's letter to Norfolk. And Barker who maintained his charges in the presence of the bishop himself. '[T]he council caused Barker afterwards to come to their own presence face to face with me, where he avouched the same to be true as he had confessed and written before' especially as regarded the bishop's alleged encouragement of Norfolk to create a stir at the parliament time. 'By this it is easy', complained Ross, 'to judge how hardly I have been used, and what high points have been laid to my charge, as if I had been chief author and inventor of all these devices. But to say the truth ... I spake these purposes only by way of discourse to assay what the duke would do for the relief of the queen my mistress and himself.'[125] It would have been undiplomatic to reject Ridolfi out of hand since he could have been the channel of financial relief for queen and ambassador, but Ross could well have been disappointed that Norfolk refused more violent courses to

---

123 Ibid.   124 Ibid., p. 193. Barker's answer to the 29th interrogatory in his examination of 10.10 (see p. 187) mentions the letter to Norfolk from the Pope: drafted on 5.5. and ciphered on 16.5.1571; reproduced in translation in *Cal. S. P. Rome, Elizabeth, 1558-1571*, from Vatican Archives, Pius V, Ep. ad Princ., xix, f. 362.   125 *The m. c.*, pp 194-5.

resolve his problem. All the same, he insisted that he had never discussed such matters with any apart from Banister and Barker. He 'was not certain what Ridolfi did for he never told [Ross] that he had communicated the same to any man'.[126] Although Hickford was set to deciphering by Smith and Wilson, he plausibly maintained that he had no part in Ross' dealings with the duke. '[F]or this twelve months together he wrote little unto my said lord, but dealt altogether by Mr Barker who brought intelligence to and fro between them, both by word of mouth and sometimes by writings, whereunto I was never made privy.'[127]

Although Barker emerges as the man most obviously used as an agent provocateur in the duke's dealings with Ridolfi, Ross and Mary, his examinations under pressure exercised by Smith and Wilson show a proper initial reluctance on his part to open up. Some of this may have been genuine. As we have seen, his earlier confessions vindicated Norfolk's honour to a notable degree. Smith and Wilson must have known they were accepting a task which involved more than merely uncovering the truth. The 'truth' had to be politically correct. Burghley was working for posterity and not only for his own age. He realised the importance of having the right records to come to view at the right time in the future. Like all men of genius, Cecil had an eye for detail. If Barker had disgorged all he knew immediately, it would have been too facile and suggested contrivance. On 17 September Smith and Wilson wrote to Burghley suggesting impatience at the results so far achieved and announced their intention of bringing 'a couple of them to the rack' – if only because it was 'so earnestly commanded'.[128] After this Barker obligingly regurgitated the plot, as we have seen, providing further detail and elaboration in subsequent confessions. Perhaps he really needed the threat of the rack to overcome reluctance arising from some residual decency and regard for his former master.

A word on the unsatisfactory nature of the Barker documents is more than a matter for a footnote. His answers given on 9 September seem to be in his hand but they are preceded by a page of writing heavily scored through and sometimes completely obliterated. One such cancelled passage ran, 'I never dealt with the Spanish ambassador nor none of his ... ' followed by obliteration. The confession of 17 September may be accepted as in his hand but the last two paragraphs are in another hand, and appear to have been added after the last line of Barker's writing and before his signature. Other confessions, including the 'last confession' of 19 September, are only signed 'Will Barker' and are not otherwise in his hand. This confession claims to have been given without compulsion but must have been given under threat of the rack promised on 17 September. Smith apparently wrote the confession of 22 September, with an addition between the lines probably added after Barker's signature. One page of the deposition of 27 September is unsigned. The joint examination of Barker and Hickford of the 26th is nowhere signed by either. Most unsatisfactory, perhaps, is that of 10 October which is signed at the foot of each page by Barker but is not otherwise in

126 Ibid., p. 195.   127 Ibid., p. 196.   128 Ibid., pp 197-8.

his hand. It carries a great number of alterations and cancellations. The examiners signed it on the last page. Similar though fewer additions were made to the examination of 11 October. Whatever one may conclude as to the value of Barker's depositions as evidence, surely no impartial observer even in that generation could regard them as adequate grounds for bringing in a verdict of guilty on a capital charge unless there was a strong political motive. Which there was.[129] While Barker was pardoned, as we have seen, Banister was not only put to torture but suffered the confiscation of goods and estate.[130] The sentence was apparently carried out. Hickford was also tried and found guilty but does not seem to have ended at Tyburn.

Elizabeth, as we have inferred, knew nothing of the intrigue surrounding the pursuit of Norfolk. A fact attested by a singularly maladroit intervention in the trial. This time Thomas Bromley may be believed. Near the end of proceedings on the second charge, the solicitor general told the peers, 'I have ... one thing more to say from the queen's ... own mouth. The lords here of the privy council do know it very well, not meet here in open presence to be uttered because it toucheth others that are not here now to be named. But by her Higness' order, we pray that their lordships will impart it unto you more particularly. In Flanders by the ambassador of a foreign prince, there the whole plot of this treason was discovered, and by a servant of his brought to her Majesty's intelligence; the minister not meaning to conceal so foul ... a practice, gave intelligence hither by letters, and hath therein disclosed the whole treason in such form as hath been proved ... Wherefore I refer the more particular declaration thereof to the ... privy council.'[131] Although Burghley was most anxious for the duke's condemnation, it is difficult to imagine that he would have stooped to anything so artless. What happened to the letters? Who was the servant? Ridolfi? As Jardine commented, 'A more flagrant violation of the plainest principles of justice than this enforcement of evidence to be given in the absence of the prisoner, of which he could have no knowledge, and consequently no means ... of answering or explaining can hardly be conceived.'[132]

Burghley behaved, as one would expect, with great discretion and circumspection throughout the trial. He made the occasional intervention when a turn for the better in the duke's cause seemed to threaten. Before the trial, he was careful to make sure the main protagonists in the plot would not meet to compare notes; a necessary precaution emphasized by his cancelling permissions from the queen for Ross to join his mistress. Nevertheless, his most uncritical admirers could hardly doubt that essential rigging and scenesetting were due to him.

Why was Cecil so determined on the duke's downfall? The reason is not difficult to find. As we remember from his early brush with Sir Nicholas Bacon in the council, the great man was not prepared to brook opposition to his chosen way of doing things on the way to realising his blueprint for the new England: the England which was to

---

129 Ibid., p. 204. See also n. 92 above.　130 Ibid., p. 205.　131 Ibid., p. 236.　132 Jardine, op. cit., pp 233-4. Quoted in *The m. c.*, p. 236.

last for all time – and almost has! He warned the lord chancellor, as we remember, in clear terms of the danger of his opposition. Bacon gave way on a relatively trivial issue and all was well. In the duke Cecil found a rival who was not prepared to give way, and on issues much more important.

Towards the end of 1568, it was decided to seize a number of Spanish payships which had put in at Southampton to avoid the consequences of foul weather. The ships were on the way to Flanders carrying money to pay the troops of the duke of Alba. The seizing of the ships represented not only an advantage for Elizabeth who needed the money for her own purposes but also constituted a blow against the hated Spaniard in the cause of true religion.[133] But hatred of Spain was not yet ingrained in the English national character. Many might disagree with them in religion but the importance of maintaining trade and commercial links was evident, if not to all then certainly to Norfolk and his friends. Their wealth depended to a large extent on good relations between the wool-producing areas of East Anglia and the weaving and finishing industries of Flanders. The sequestration of the ships led inevitably to a strong protest from the Spanish ambassador, de Spes, who was not less determined than Cecil to secure a conclusion favourable to his own side in the long controversy that followed. Norfolk, the earl of Arundel and Lord Lumley strongly opposed the high-handed action of their opponents on the council. No doubt this was why Lumley at one point was supposed to correspond to the number on one of the compromising and problematic letters mentioned above. Leicester played a balancing game between the two sides, taking into account the need to prevent either side becoming too strong, and also the attitude of Elizabeth who was swayed by self- as well as national interest. She was willing to endorse the confiscation while her government could get away with it but when war threatened she drew back. So at first she supported Cecil; but as a threat of war with Spain and even France loomed larger, she began to waver. Her wavering began in earnest when on 29 December 1568 Alba ordered the detention of all English shipping in Antwerp.[134] Elizabeth, still following Cecil, decreed a suspension of trade and commerce with Flanders on 7 January 1569; and in the same month put de Spes under house arrest. Alba retaliated with a suspension of trade with England in mid-April.[135]

France saw an opportunity to settle its own score over English support for the rebel Huguenots. While Norfolk had no time for the religion of Spain or France, he had a great deal for the hardship inflicted on the good citizens of his own East Anglia by this suspension of trade. It also hit his own finances hard at a time when he was under bond to Ridolfi for £3000, with another £1000 for Arundel and Lumley.[136] There were stirrings in the country which were to explode in the northern rising of the autumn. By Lent 1569, even Leicester, hitherto a supporter of the Cecil faction, had passed to Norfolk's side. He expressed his opposition to Cecil in the council in no uncertain terms.

---

133 The fuller story of the payships question is set out in *The d. q.*, chapters 1 and 2.   134 *The d. q.*, p. 26.   135 Ibid., pp 26, 32.   136 Ridolfi's loan agreement of 28.8.1570 is in Simancas, Estado, Leg. 826, f. 131; Lettenhove, op. cit., vi, pp 19–20. Essential quotation in Latin in *The d. q.*, p. 299, n. 1.

Ridolfi and other Italian bankers who operated in England, and who provided the money to all sides in the first place, had nothing to lose apart from time and the trouble of drawing up new contracts. Whatever the outcome, it meant little more to them than some paperwork making them perhaps even better off than before. England, Flanders, what did it matter? So Ridolfi, siding principally with Norfolk and his friends rather than Cecil, was careful to keep his lines open to all. Ridolfi was also nuncio segreto for the pope but there is small reason to suppose he took his duties, if any, very seriously.[137] Roberto played a complicated game between the parties. At one time he even urged the council, if Benedict Spinola told the truth, to detain two Venetian ships for its own use. Alba had no use for him, regarding him as a man without principle and as having betrayed Spanish interests to the English.

For a time it seemed as if the omniscient and omnicompetent Cecil had overreached himself. According to Ross, no less than three attempts were made to arrest him during May and June 1569. It is likely that he had to kneel at the council table to receive a rebuke. Indeed, only the direct intervention of Elizabeth seems to have saved him.[138] Cecil was never more dangerous than when cornered. It is not difficult to imagine his inner feelings as he rose from his knees: a man some fifty years old and of long experience, put in his place by the young duke in his thirties. But there was more to it than wounded pride. Norfolk and his allies represented another kind of England; one with which Cecil had no sympathy; a Protestant England but not one which sought to drive the Catholics to extinction. Therefore an England, horror of horrors, which might one day return to Catholic faith. Toleration of religion could only hasten the day. As he knelt in humility, Cecil we may assume without rashness, had already condemned Norfolk to death. Only time was needed to bring about the desired effect.

Cecil was a past master in the art of dissembling. His first task was to make it seem that he had been converted to the other side and would work to further their intentions. He next detached Leicester from the Norfolk faction, convincing him that his true interests lay elsewhere. He even feigned friendship with de Spes who was released from house arrest in July 1569.[139] Indeed, so successful was Cecil in reinsinuating himself into the general confidence that he was able to take over Norfolk's pro-Spanish stance as though it was his own; not without the duke's resentment. By the summer of 1569 the danger of war had passed. The profit and loss account as calculated at this time showed that Elizabeth had gained somewhat over the Spaniards in the takeover. By February 1570 it was decided that the confiscated money and ships should not be restored to Spain.[140] Philip II and de Spes might fume but there was nothing they could do about it. By the time Hamburg became an alternative to Antwerp the atmosphere of crisis had passed to chronic stalemate.

Meanwhile the northern rising took place in the autumn of 1569. This altered radically not only Thomas Howard's significance in the total situation but also the part

137 *The d. q.*, pp 42, 43, 49.   138 Ibid., pp 59–60 and *The m. c.*, p. 23.   139 *The d. q.*, p. 65.   140 Ibid., p. 77.

that Ridolfi would play in it. The rising cast its shadow over both. The duke of Norfolk was sent to the Tower on 11 October 1569.[141] He would never again know full liberty. The first step to Cecil's full revenge was accomplished. Ridolfi under arrest in Walsingham's house, as we have seen, evidently threw in his lot with what instinct told him would be the winning side. It was the only alternative to his destruction, real or metaphorical. Apart from his eponymous plot, which came later, there was another important respect in which he seems almost certainly to have served Cecil while betraying the Catholic and papal cause. A movement for the excommunication of the recalcitrant Elizabeth had been gaining force in Rome for some time. Dr Nicholas Morton should have brought in a bull about the time of the northern rising, but when it was quickly extinguished by the ruthless competence of Sussex, it was too evident that such a thing was best forgotten. Ridolfi was set at liberty before mid-November 1569.[142] As the secret nuncio, it was surely his influence which promoted the re-opening of the excommunication process in Rome by Pius V on 5 February 1570.[143] Indubitably, none of the Catholic powers wanted it. They were not previously con-sulted and criticised the bull's subsequent promulgation in round terms. The interna-tional Catholic community was divided yet again: made a fool of by a seeming friend.

Ridolfi tried to get substantial compensation later from Gregory XIII for all his heroic if unavailing efforts on behalf of Catholic orthodoxy. In his address to the pope, he praised his own labours for uniting the English nobles under Norfolk, president of the council, who wished to marry Mary, queen of Scots and become king of England. He claimed further that Pius V 'sent an express messenger to me Ridolfi with perhaps eighty of the said bulls, some printed and some in manuscript, with explicit order that as I desired to do him service, and no less to the apostolic see and the whole of Christendom, so I should with speed see to it that the said bulls were distributed and promulgated in England, without having any regard whatsoever to purely personal interests of mine, promising me that the Holy See would see to my reward.'[144] Ridolfi

141 Ibid., p. 137.   142 Ibid., p. 168. Unfortunately the Ridolfi family archives have been dispersed which means that much that might have cast light on Roberto's contribution to the plot story has been lost. Cf. Karl Stahlin, *Sir Francis Walsingham und seine Zeit*, Heidelberg 1908, Band 1, p. 246, note. 'Die übrigen in Italien angestellten Nachforschungen , die vor allem darauf abzielten, Näheres über seine Schicksale im Hause Walsinghams zu erfahren, bleiben leider ergebnislos, da das Familienarchiv der Ridolphi gegenwärtig in alle Winde zerstreut sein soll'. Quoted in *The d. q.*, p. 174. This was confirmed to me by the present(?) Marchese Ridolfi whom I met in Florence.   143 It has recently been announced (December 1997) in the press that the Vatican intends to make certain categories at least of the Holy Office archives available to students. The late Fr G. Anstruther, O. P., found undated notes by Laderchi in the Fondo Albani (Vat. Arch.), 138, f. 227 to show that the 'processus' record of the excommunication was once in the Holy Office archives but the archival staff assured him that they were unable to locate it. This confirmed what J. H. Pollen attempted earlier. See his *English Catholics in the reign of Elizabeth* (London 1920), pp 147–52. It is likely that a 'pending file' on the subject grew over the years. Philip II twice held up the excommunication in 1561 and 1563: see Sir Charles Petrie, *Philip II of Spain* (London 1963), p. 195. Philip was much opposed to the bull. See the promulgation of the bull in 1570: see *The d. q.*, pp 169 and nn. 1 and 2, and pp 180–181.   144 *The d. q.*, p. 176. Ridolfi's memorandum to Gregory XIII writ-

claimed that he put the bull into execution speedily. Indeed, he himself nailed it to the bishop of London's door! Felton who did the actual nailing most likely got the bull and further instructions from the Italian. Unfortunately, Felton's answers and other records of his subsequent examination before his execution are more of the documents which have been too conveniently lost. They could well have included valuable clues to Ridolfi's part. Clearly, any share of his had to be kept hidden since Cecil and Walsingham were not supposed to know anything about it.

The bull Regnans in Excelsis, dated in Rome 25 February 1570, where it still resides complete with seal, was by no means speedily put into execution. This occurred at a time when its promulgation was calculated to do the maximum good for the Cecil faction. De la Mothe Fénélon reported a stormy meeting in the council in his dispatch of 11 June 1570. Cecil was doing his utmost to prevent his queen from allowing her sister-queen to return to Scotland even after a treaty. 'He dared to tell her in the presence of Leicester that she acted alone, and without the concurrence of her most effective ministers while she insisted thus on throwing herself into manifest and certain peril to her person and estate in contemplating the restitution and deliverance of the queen of Scots. The queen in anger asked him how he could be so sure. Up to that moment she had never heard anything from him on the subject which was not full of passion and hatred.' It is hard to believe that Cecil was without a reply but Leicester reportedly cut in, ' "See for yourself, Madame, what sort of man is the secretary. When we were all together yesterday at London, he assured us that he would advise you to restore the queen of Scotland. Now he says the clean contrary." She replied, "In the same way he often tells me many things about you which I find afterwards to be quite untrue. However it be, Mr Secretary", says she, "I want to free myself of this affair, and listen to what the king asks of me. I shall take no further notice of the rest of you brothers in Christ!" '[145] It was at this precise moment that the bull of excommunication was posted up on the bishop's door on 25 May, the feast of Corpus Christi for the Catholics.[146] It came only just in time for Cecil. On 15 May Ross had been released from imprisonment.[147] Worse might have followed; but the promulgation of the bull may be taken as the watershed in the history of this time. From now on the Cecilians prevailed and increased their dominance. Norfolk was already doomed.

Cecil always proceeded like a cautious huntsman keeping upwind from his prey. He always tried to prevent his enemies from thinking that he was the cause of their down-

ten some time later to secure compensation for all his efforts in the cause is in Archivio di Stato, Florence, Fondo Mediceo, filza 4185, f. 516. Printed in Cecil Roth, 'Roberto Ridolphi e la sua congiura', *Revista storica degli Archivi Toscani*, anno ii, April/June 1930, fasc. ii, pp 11-16. **145** *The d. q.*, pp 154, 176. Felton's confession produced under torture on 27. 6.1570, which must have contained important information on the circumstances of the posting of the bull, has been 'lost'. For the report of a showdown in the privy council, see de la Mothe Fénélon, *Correspondance*, iii, 2nd Instruction à part, 11.6.1570, pp 187f. **146** *The d. q.*, p. 153. It is likely that Ridolfi was responsible for a formal petition to the pope for Elizabeth's excommunication. A 'copia ad Summum Pont.' undated and with no indication of authorship is in Archivium S. J. Romanum, Fondo Gesuitico, capsa 651, No. 598 (ff. 61r-2v.); see *The m. c.*, pp 404-7. **147** *The d. q.*, p. 177.

fall. He never gave them overt reason to believe they were his enemies. After all, he could never be sure when he might need them. Writing in July 1570, he repudiated any idea that he was opposed to Norfolk's delivery from the Tower. Sure enough, Norfolk exchanged the Tower for confinement to his own Charterhouse on 3 August 1570. Cecil admitted publicly that, since Norfolk had abandoned his latest marriage plan, there was no reason why he should not come back to the queen's service; and in this he claimed the support and approval of Leicester.[148] Cecil reopened a friendly correspondence with the duke who, completely beguiled, responded with his usual candour and a readiness to let bygones be bygones. He hoped that Mr Secretary would help him to win back the favour of the queen. But Sir William had a much better idea. In October 1570 he made a visit to Chatsworth with Mildmay as part of the charade of reopening negotiations with the Scottish queen for her release. He mentioned the visit in a subsequent letter to Howard but said nothing of one particular.

Ross, who had no reason to lie, wrote, 'They [Cecil and Mildmay] have spoken to me of the queen of Scots' marriage by way of conference ... The secretary hath told me secretly he could like well of the duke of Norfolk marrying, but now is no time to speak of it. He sayeth that the queen of England fears that the queen of Scots and Norfolk would wax overgreat in that case. But yet he thinks that this surety that the queen of Scots makes to the queen of England shall put away that fear. And so the matter may be followed. I think he may be made to labour for that marriage if Norfolk do cause employ him; and in the meantime, I will deal with him as of myself to tie(?) the knot of sure friendship between Norfolk and the secretary. For he shows himself very plain to me in many things ... '[149] As a later Elizabethan wrote, 'the ministers of darkness give us truths; win us with honest trifles to betray us in deepest consequence.' It is somewhat astonishing that the bishop could have been deceived into thinking that Cecil meant him or his mistress any genuine good. But hope springing eternal in the human breast set Ross, Norfolk and Mary firmly on the path of final disaster. That correspondence between the duke and Mary recommenced from this time was confirmed by Hickford who wrote in answers at his examination of 1 October 1571, 'It is now almost a year sithence the beginning of such conveyance had between them.'[150]

So successful were the machinations behind the scenes that it was decided to use the occasion to eliminate Mary as well as Norfolk. At first the alleged numbers '30' and '40' occurring in Ridolfi's letters given to Bailly, as it was claimed, were made to refer to Lumley and Norfolk. Lumley, habitually on the side of the duke, was now targeted as a notable supporter of the marriage project. By the time of Norfolk's trial, however, '30' had been conveniently settled on to indicate Mary. It was a daring move; but by the end of 1570 Elizabeth was firmly back in the Cecilian fold and much could be presumed. But not as much as all that. Elizabeth could be shrewish and vindictive but she was not bloodthirsty. She delayed the execution of the duke of Norfolk no less than three times before the axe finally descended on his neck to Cecil and Walsingham's

148 Ibid., pp 191, 245.   149 Ibid., p. 287.   150 Ibid.

relief and joy on 2 June 1572.[151] But she could not be moved to kill her fellow-sovereign for all her hard words hitherto. No effort had been spared to achieve a double victory but it was not to be. Time, all the same, was on the side of her enemies.

Ridolfi went to the continent claiming to carry instructions from the Scottish queen as well as from Norfolk, and letters to Alba, Philip II and the pope for the invasion scheme. It was a bitter disappointment to the true organisers of the plot that Elizabeth refused to seize the opportunity offered her. Not until fifteen years later were Burghley and Walsingham able to rejoice in the destruction of Queen Mary after what one may fairly take to be another carefully contrived round of plot-making. Meanwhile, Mary continued steadfastly to maintain those three claims: first her present right to the kingdom of Scotland; second, the succession to the English throne if Elizabeth died childless; third, the right to intervene even by military force if necessary or possible in her own northern kingdon. She never countenanced any attempt on the life of Elizabeth or her present possession of the throne. She was consistent in her policy during the Ridolfi plot and subsequently, being well aware that she could afford to wait. Her health was fair even after the worst that a succession of Elizabethan prison houses could do to destroy it. The prospects of the English queen marrying, let alone producing a child, diminished by the year. And so did Mary's prospects of being allowed to live.

151 *The m. c.*, p. 245.

3

The Somerville plot

Before Mary's death, a brace of plots occurred between 1583 and 1584 which heralded the Babington plot. A word on the background may be helpful. After 1581 and the
execution of Edmund Campion, Alexander Bryant and Ralph Sherwin, the gauntlet
thrown down by the Elizabethan government was picked up by Robert Persons, Jesuit,
and other Catholic exiles and foreign governments whom they could persuade to support their cause. They set out with determination to assist and encourage Spain and
France to bring about a change of regime in England by armed force. Elizabeth's government by a policy of persecution thus created a problem for itself. It could only be
solved by force: and virtually was. The problem continued until the end of the century and ended in victory for the Protestant cause. The victory was real if Pyrrhic.[1] Spain
and France could not be brought to overcome their ancient rivalry even to support so
good a cause – as the militants saw it. The secrecy essential for success was notably
absent. Walsingham's superbly competent system of espionage usually knew everything before it happened. Hostile activity on the continent was taken as good reason to
discredit the papists further within their own country through their contriving, as it
seemed, an endless succession of plots against the state. Whose these really were is
what this book is about. There was no unanimity among the papists even on the continent for forward and aggressive policies. In England such policies were actively
opposed or not positively forwarded by any party among the Catholics. Even individual supporters of violence prove to be almost entirely agents-provocateurs.

Unlike the Huguenots in France, who showed no hesitation in trying to win their
way by force, the English Catholic community in England preferred the way of non-
violence. They had little alternative. They threw up no militant leader in the country
itself. The fact was emphasized by the one half-hearted attempt to improve the situation by force in the northen rising of 1569. There was no Condé, Coligny or Henry of
Navarre. Such a man would have been swiftly destroyed had he emerged. The only
hope of the papists was that by showing compliance and loyalty and repudiating the

---

1 For the various invasion attempts see J. Kretzschmar, *Die Invasionsprojecte der Katholischen Mächte
gegen England zur Zeit Elisabeths* (Leipzig 1892); A. J. Loomie, 'The Armadas and the Catholics of
England', *Catholic Historical Review*, 59, p. 300; F. Edwards, *Robert Persons* (St Louis, Missouri 1995).

warlike endeavours of their co-religionists on the continent they could eventually win acceptance. It was an argument from weakness and their enemies were well aware of it. Had the English regime been other than it was, they might in time, and not too much time, have made their point. The English are not by nature a persecuting race, and the claims of the ancient faith could not be lightly set aside in the mind and memory of the nation as a whole. But Cecil, Walsingham, Leicester and their closest supporters could only be content if and when Catholicism was uprooted completely from the land. In the contest there were no holds barred or underhand shifts which could not be used by government to bring the Catholic community into hatred and contempt. Much depended on the attitude of good Protestant neighbours, the majority. It took a long time to convince them of the essential wickedness and depravity of the aliens among them. Not until the gunpowder plot was the process set irreversibly in motion. Even now the smell of sulphur from gunpowder that never exploded still hangs in the atmosphere of the history of the times.

In the latest round of plots, we are often hampered by lack of evidence which would clinch certainty. As Dasent pointed out in masterly understatement, 'The loss of the privy council registers between June 1582 and February 1585 to 1586 is much to be regretted.'[2] Along with much else, as we shall see. Perhaps the clearest, if excessively succinct, account of these plot or plots, showing family connections clearly, was that given by Nicholas Sander in his history of the Anglican schism.[3] John Somerville, whose head was the first to roll in the next bloody encounter with the state, emerged as a well-chosen victim. He was the head of an ancient Catholic family with lands in Gloucestershire, and Warwickshire with the family seat at Edstone.[4] Born in 1560, educated at Hart Hall, Oxford, his wife was Margaret, daughter of Edward Arden of Park Hall, a Catholic family. There were marriage connections with the Grants of Northbrook, also Catholic.[5] In this way, if one came to be implicated in a serious fault then there was every possibility of besmirching a good many others. John Somerville gratuitously obliged the enemies of his faith. In the midsummer of 1583, he was reported as being 'affected with a frantic humour'. Indeed, he was reported as saying, 'I will go up to the court and shoot the queen through with a pistol.'[6] He hardly got beyond Banbury before he was arrested and taken to the Tower. He seems to have been the first and only unequivocally genuine example of a Catholic assassin in all these years. All agreed that he was deranged. What he said inside the Tower is not known. In fact after he crossed that dark threshold he disappeared from view if not from history. His examinations were not kept. He was tried at Guildhall on 16 December 1583 with those he was accused of having implicated along with himself.

2 J. R. Dasent, *Acts of the privy council of England:* new series, xiv, 1586-7 (London 1897), p. vii.   3 Nicolai Sanderi, *De Origine ac Progressu Schismatis Anglicani. Libri tres … Aucti per Edouardum Rishtonum, & impressi in Germania, nunc iterum locupletius & castigatius editi …* (Romae 1586). No pagination. Entries in form of a diary.   4 *Dictionary of national biography,* 58. Subsequently referred to as Dnb.   5 Ian Wilson, *Shakespeare and the evidence …* (London, 1993), p. 52.   6 Dnb and Wilson, ibid.

No record of the trial is known to exist. Those arraigned with him pleaded not guilty. Somerville pleaded guilty. All were convicted and sentenced to death. He and his father-in-law, Edward Arden, were removed to Newgate on 19 December for the last act. For Somerville it came sooner than was expected. Two hours after his transfer, his body was discovered in his cell. He was said to have been strangled. Suicide or murder? There is a parallel with the case of the eighth earl of Northumberland soon to follow. All the prisoners, it was recorded, were shut up separately so that a revenge killing seems unlikely.[7] Prisoners were usually allowed to say something on the scaffold before the final moment; contrition following confession of the crime was normal. Perhaps it was feared that Somerville might say too much and spoil the popular impression of his plain delinquency. So care was taken to see that the public ear would not be perplexed or offended. It is possible.

Going back a little, following Somerville's arrest, the priest Hugh Hall, who served as Somerville's chaplain and confessor disguised as a gardener, was arrested on November 4. Edward Arden, Somerville's father-in-law, was arrested on 7 November on the like charge of intending to kill the queen. On the 16th, Mary Arden his wife, and her daughter Margaret, John Somerville's wife, and John's sister, Elizabeth, spinster, joined the others in the Tower. A month later, the priest and the ladies were tried with their husbands and sentenced to death. The husbands were executed, the priest and the ladies were spared.[8] It is probable that Hall was spared to make him seem responsible for further descents on the Catholics following names actually or allegedly wrung from him in the course of examination. This 'mercy' would promote distrust of the Catholics for their priests. The government was well aware whom they wanted to destroy. Sander reported that at his execution with the others on 22 December, 'Edward Arden taken to the scaffold, had his hanging interrupted (suspendio interremptus est), and protested he was entirely innocent of everything of which he had been accused apart from his adherence to the Catholic faith.'[9] This is more than plausible. If there was a better case for the government in the documents than appears in the bald statement of facts known to us, their disappearance leaves it unproven. C. Stopes concluded that 'they had been deliberately destroyed'.[10]

---

7 Dnb. See also J. H. Pollen, S.J., *The Month*, 1902, p. 616.   8 Ibid. There is a date discrepancy between Dnb and Sander's account. Sander claims that on 21 December John Somerville, 'since he was scarcely sane (vix sanae mentis), was taken from the Tower to another prison, and was found strangled in his cell the following night whether by his own hand or another's is not clear'. Dnb refers us to the Visitation of Warwickshire for a source.   9 Sander, op. cit., entry for 22.12.   10 C. Stopes, *Shakespeare's Warwick contemporaries*, 1907, p. 107. Quoted L. Hicks, *An Elizabethan problem*, (New York 1964), p. 39, n. 100.

4

The Throckmorton plot

While the Arden-Somerville plot was under investigation another much more important and complex sequence of events revolved round Francis Throckmorton who gave
his name to another plot. This merged into the Babington plot which was used to eliminate perhaps the greatest potential obstacle to the success of the Protestant revolution,
namely the continuing existence of Mary, queen of Scots. Mary, a Catholic with a son
and heir, was the obvious successor to Elizabeth. Elizabeth, whose prospect of marriage and producing a Protestant heir diminished by the year as she advanced in age,
would leave the country facing a return to Catholicism when she died. If the Protestants succeeded in averting that catastrophe, there would still be a succession crisis.
Who would take over? Mary was aware of her right to the succession and of the
improvement of her own prospects with every day that passed. She was also aware that
she was the main obstacle to the distant prospects of the protestantising party who
could only see her as a menace. They could be expected to do everything possible to
remove her from the scene before Elizabeth died and her own succession was assured.
Mary was also aware that, as the captive of the English queen, however unjust her
imprisonment might be, there was little she could do to help herself. Her wisest course
was to accept the superiority of force majeure, avoid offering any resistance to
Elizabeth's present occupation of the throne, while continuing to claim the throne of
Scotland, and do all in her power to come to terms with the rival queen in a treaty
which would restore her freedom. Time was on her side. Elizabeth might have been
brought round. Her government could not be. Mary's best weapons, as she saw it, were
prayer, patience, and the limited degree of diplomacy open to her. Her progress in
spirituality was perhaps an inevitable concomitant of an increasing awareness that the
world could not do much to help her. Above all, she realised she must avoid any activity which might be taken as a reasonable threat to the existence of Elizabeth.

Her enemies, notably William Cecil, Lord Burghley and lord treasurer, Robert
Dudley, earl of Leicester, and Sir Francis Walsingham, principal secretary, and Sir
Christopher Hatton, vice-chamberlain, who between them now had most of Elizabeth's attention, were as well aware as Mary of her wisest policy. Their main fear was
that she might persist in it. Their main hope was that she might grow tired of waiting
patiently, so that aided by crafty diplomacy and the unscrupulous exploitation of peo-

ple and events in the next few years, and by plain misrepresentation, they might bring her down before it was too late. And even if she did not lose patience, it might be possible to manoeuvre her into a situation where it would be easy to make people believe she had. Not only the Protestant revolution but their whole careers, and perhaps their very lives, depended on it. Politics in this century was a game played literally for heads. As for Elizabeth, while she could not be unaware of the threat at least to the future represented by the Scottish queen, the Ridolfi plot showed she was not prepared to be unjust. She too in her time had been in mortal danger as a pawn on the board before the game made her a queen. There is no reason to suppose she approved of, or even suspected – certainly not fully – the methods used by her enemies to bring down Mary; any more than she had been aware of the true nature of the plot to bring down Norfolk. But she was prepared to be ruthless if the situation demanded it. There was nothing soft in the makeup of the Tudors. The problem would be to bring her to recognize a situation where ruthlessness was demanded. It would not be easy.

Undoubtedly, Mary's enemies were helped by the good intentions of some of her friends, or of those who had no wish to be her enemy. The dividing line among the Catholics could be traced back to 1582. When the English government decided that the group of priests, including Jesuits, which came from Rome in 1580, was not the peace mission it claimed and intended to be, but was the first wave of a new aggression, it reacted strongly. One could say, overreacted. The treatment of the priests was brutal even by the standards of a century which were nowhere notably humane. The rack and gyves, the Pit in the Tower, and needles under the fingernails in one case at least, were all intended to frighten off the wouldbe missionaries.[1] It succeeded in frightening off one bishop who came with the party, Thomas Goldwell of St Asaph, even before he crossed the Channel. It also succeeded in warning off a great many of the laity. The Marian clergy were still largely left to themselves as a withering survival on the margin of the new movement. The effect of persecution on many ex-patriates on the continent, including Allen soon to be a cardinal, and on Robert Persons, the Jesuit, who rejoined them, was to convince them that no business was to be done with the existing regime in England. The only argument they would respect was the mailed fist. The answer to the Catholic problem, which was taken to be that of the nation as a whole, would be invasion from the continent, ideally by a combined force led by Spaniards and French. The sooner the better.

The first plans were laid in 1582. But the difficulty of getting Spain and France to work together even for so lofty a cause, and the impossibility of bringing Philip II to commit himself, already overcommitted in the Netherlands and the Mediterranean, to

---

[1] See James Heath, *Torture and the English Law: an administrative, and legal history from the Plantagenets to the Stuarts* (Westport, Conn. and London, England, 1982). This includes 'A selected Bibliography on torture', pp 305-7. For our period, see pp 81 to 160. See also F. Edwards, *The Elizabethan Jesuits* (London and Chichester 1981), passim. Much has been written on the mission of 1580. See T. M. McCoog, S.J., *The Society of Jesus in Ireland, Scotland and England 1541-1588* (Leiden, New York, Cologne 1996).

yet another venture, revealed the scale of the operation: also the unlikelihood of its ever being able to surmount the practical difficulties.[2] The effect on the exiles was twofold. The difficulties merely spurred the militants to greater efforts. Much of the energy of Allen and Persons over the next few years was spent on urging and persuading the Catholic powers, including the papacy, to take up the English cause immediately and effectively. In the event, not until the Armada was any effort mounted which had a prospect of success. This spectacular fiasco is as much part of every islander's general knowledge as the battle of Hastings.

There was another and influential section of the Catholic community abroad, supported by the generality of Catholics in England, who had no desire to promote their cause by violence. They feared to be occupied by Spain; and to stir the English government to fiercer persecution by supporting wilder schemes abroad. They opposed the militant policies of Allen, Persons and other exiles wholeheartedly. Mainly passive during the abortive preparations of 1582, they adopted their own kind of aggressiveness in resisting the policies of Allen and his party from 1583. The principal exponents of this other view-point and policy were Thomas Morgan, Charles Paget and to a lesser degree, his brother, Thomas, third Baron Paget. Their background helps to explain their attitudes at this time.

Born in 1542 or 1543, Thomas Morgan came from a Welsh Catholic family. About 1560 he entered the service of the bishop of Exeter, and afterwards became secretary to Thomas Young, archbishop of York, until his death in 1568. The earls of Northumberland and Pembroke recommended him in 1569 as secretary to the earl of Shrewsbury, the Scottish queen's jailer at Tutbury. Sir William Cecil endorsed it. Morgan won the confidence of the captive queen and managed her correspondence. He passed on to her information from Shrewsbury's correspondence of what was happening at court. It was also claimed that 'whenever her rooms and boxes were to be searched, he had notice beforehand, and concealed her papers'.[3] We need not suppose that there was anything incriminating to conceal, and Mary, knowing what she might expect, would have been more than ordinarily cautious. She was not a fool.

Shrewsbury discovered that Morgan was conveying letters to Mary from John Leslie, bishop of Ross, her former ambassador, later an exile in France. The earl reported the fact to Cecil on 28 February, 1571/2.[4] Dismissed from the service, it was not until 15 March 1572, that Morgan was examined by the council in London. He was put in the Tower on a charge of acquaintance with the Ridolfi plot and kept there some ten months. Leicester may have been mainly responsible for his imprisonment but Cecil seems to have been responsible for his release.[5] Soon after, he left for France; and in 1573 Queen Mary directed him to Paris to join Charles Paget as a secretary for James Beaton, archbishop of Glasgow, her ambassador. Morgan became skilled in fac-

2 L. Hicks, *An Elizabethan problem*, p. 50 and n. 31. Philip II was willing to help Lennox in Scotland with 10, 000 crowns in 1582 but not military aid. Henri III was even more lukewarm. See F. Edwards, *Robert Persons*, chapter 5.   3 Dnb, 39, pp 31-3; L. Hicks, op. cit., pp 3-5.   4 Dnb, ibid.   5 Dnb, ibid., Hicks, p. 5. For Morgan's own account of himself at this time see Hicks, pp 81-5.

ing all ways so that it is difficult to determine in which direction he was really looking at any givem time.

The Pagets belonged to a landowning family in the midlands, substantial if not distinguished. Both Thomas, the third Baron Paget, and Charles his younger brother, were the sons, second and fourth respectively, of William, the first Lord Paget. Both matriculated as fellow commoners of Gonville and Caius on 27 May 1559. Thomas succeeded to the title, on the death of his elder brother Henry, on 28 December 1568. Thomas and Charles were both committed Catholics. Thomas spent fourteen weeks in prison for his religion before taking up the title. He remained in England until 1583 when he joined his brother in France after the discovery of the Throckmorton plot.[6] Charles soon established a close understanding with his fellow-secretary, Thomas Morgan. Mary trusted them if only because their opposition to the militant policies of some of the other exiles exposed her to less danger and compromise. While she was willing to be released, she was not willing to effect this through any serious threat to, still less the overthrow of, Elizabeth. But she was not averse to force of arms in advancing her cause in her own kingdom of Scotland.

Since 1581 Mendoza had been working for the overthrow of the Anglophil party in Scotland; which put him clearly in the sights of the English government. Early in 1582, William Crichton, the Scottish Jesuit, went to Scotland. He returned to France about 15 April with an invasion project sponsored by the duke of Lennox. This was overseen by Guise, the nuncio Castelli, the Spanish ambassador, de Tassis, Glasgow, Allen, Crichton and Robert Persons. Afterwards Crichton went to Rome and Persons to Lisbon to drum up support from the pope and Philip II respectively. Thomas Morgan and Charles Paget, whose eirenism already made them suspect, were not consulted. They subsequently repudiated the plan.[7] Beaton, Mary's ambassador, favoured the Guise party and the invasion project. Nevertheless, Paget and Morgan, his employees, secretly opposed him while they 'wrung from him the administration of [Mary's] dowry in France' which was about 30,000 crowns a year.[8]

As one would expect, the English government did not stand idly by. In July 1581, Walsingham went on special embassy to Paris. While there, he saw the use to which Paget at least could be put. He assured him that Elizabeth would now be ready to excuse his departure without leave. They agreed to continue correspondence after Walsingham's return to England in September 1581. Apart from religion, Paget agreed to follow Walsingham's advice in everything; and of course pass back information about anything of interest.[9] Inevitably there were those who wondered what was the real allegiance of men like Morgan and the Pagets. Were they no better than the spies who owed no allegiance except to their own need for a living and survival? But even a hostile critic such as the late Leo Hicks, a brilliant researcher, could not and did not hide the evidence which suggests that, after all, they meant what they said in their

6 Dnb, 43, for biographical details of the Pagets.   7 L. Hicks, pp 6-7.   8 For Mary's dowry and income, see ibid., chapter XI; cf. Dnb, 43, pp 46-49.   9 L. Hicks, p. 8.

loyalty to the Scottish queen, while she lived, and to their basic Catholicism all the time. Rejecting the notion of force, the only alternative was to work with the English government as far as possible. The hope was to convince them that the majority of Catholics at home rejected the militants almost to a man; and many even abroad. They wanted toleration for their religion. For the rest they owed all loyalty to Elizabeth and even her government.

They understood that they had to prove themselves. Formal expressions of good-will were not enough. They must go further and reveal not only all the designs of the militants, but also supply information on Catholics and their families in England even if they had no connection or sympathy with miscreants abroad. It was a tall order but they could only comply. Their hope and belief was that the government would become convinced of their sincerity and eventually extend the desired toleration to the Catholic community, excluding only those who were 'militant'. Evidently they had to adopt an attitude of friendship and cooperation not only with the English embassies abroad, notably in France, but also with men whom they knew to be spies or hostile to their faith. They also had to talk fair to the militants. The ruling junta in England never had any intention of openly tolerating Catholics of any kind. The only good Catholic was a dead one. Meanwhile, the Morgans and Pagets need not know that, and could be used to divide the Catholic community against itself, providing information about what was going on much more dependable than anything the professional spies could offer. For the most part, these, in any case, soon became known to everybody for what they were and so were of limited use.

The co-operators, who included in their ranks priests such as Christopher Bag-shaw, Edward Gratley, John Cecil and the Appellant priests at a later date, won for themselves considerable alleviation in persecution. But they were never accepted by those they sought to convince. And when it was understood by the 'militants' that they were passing information to the government about members of their own communion with whom they were in disagreement on matters of policy, they were regarded with distrust and even loathing by non-aligned Catholics. They were equated with the rest of the spies in Walsingham's service.[10]

Certainly spies and bona fide papist supporters of government used the same language of obedience and fawning adulation towards the queen and even towards Walsingham. It is often difficult to discern the true allegiance of writers from their letters since most at one time or another are pretending to be on the side of the addressee whoever it was in the hope of winning confidence; worming out larger secrets by betraying a few smaller. These may be genuine. And there was always the hope of picking up a few crowns from an ambassador. Lies and exaggerations abound. The task of historians is daunting. Small wonder unanimity can hardly be hoped for.

In spreading false propaganda, the government itself was never behind. Part of the motive was to keep the queen herself in a perpetual state of undeasiness, bring her to

10 Ibid., p. 220.

hate the Catholics and incline with less reluctance towards the Huguenot party in France. It was with this in mind that the government set the tone of an epoch by claiming to uncover a papal league directed against England in 1580. A large part of the intention was to discredit and misrepresent the mission from Rome of that year. And to give the maximum significance to a farcical 'invasion' of Ireland. It was important to represent this 1580 mission to England as the aggression it was not. The object was reconciliation. The missioners were warned to keep off politics. The celebrated bull of excommunication of 1570 was declared to be non-operative.[11] From the first the English government represented the mission as an attempt at subversion. In 1585 an official pamphlet[12] set out the details of a papal league against England which was supposed to have been set up in 1580. The attorney general, John Popham, assured a distinguished audience in the star chamber that there was a league between the pope and 'certain foreign princes' to send 20,000 men against England to depose the queen, and crown an English Catholic as king. The mission of 1580 was sent in to win support. The evidence was claimed to be in a letter sent to William Allen from Rome. John Hart, priest, was quoted as the authority who deposed on oath on 31 December 1580 that about February that year Allen received a letter saying that Spain and Florence were putting together a league against England. On 3 November 1581 Hart confessed that priests were coming in to win over the papists. Some 20,000 troops were supposed to be on the way. In fact this was the number projected for the invasion of 1582 as included in his plan by the duke of Lennox for that year. A Venetian report bumped up the threat of 1580 to 33,000 infantry, 2,000 horse and a number of German mercenaries.[13]

It was all pure fiction. R.B. Merriman established the fact that there was no evidence for it in the archives of the time; unlike the sources for the projects of 1582 and 1583.[14] It was unlikely on the face of it since Philip II had only just taken over Portugal and was much engaged in the Netherlands. There is nothing to confirm it in Hart's examination of 31 December which only mentions Gregory XIII's suspension of the excommunication.[15] This meant that Catholics could obey Elizabeth with a good conscience. They could have done so in any case even without the relaxation.[16] As for Allen's receiving a letter from Rome 'in February last', as he pointed out, he was still in Rome when the confederation was supposed to have been concluded on 18 February 1580. He only left Rome on the 25th. He also pointed out the absurdity of communicating any such scheme to Hart.[17]

11 T. M. McCoog, op. cit., Ch. 4; F. Edwards, *Robert Persons*, Chapters 3 & 4.   12 'A true and summary report of the declaration of some of the earl of Northumberland's treasons, delivered publicly in the court of the star chamber by the lord chancellor and her Majesty's ... privy council and council learned touching the ... most wicked and violent murder committed upon himself in the Tower of London, the 20th day of June 1585. Printed by C. Barker', *Somers Tracts*, i, 1809, pp 212-24.   13 Ibid., p. 215; *Venetian Calendar 1558-1580*, p. 649; L. Hicks, op. cit., p. 223 and n. 656.   14 R. B. Merriman, *The Rise of the Spanish Empire* (NY 1934), iv, p. 516, quoted L. Hicks, p. 224.   15 John Hart's examination, 31. xii. 1580, SP12/144, nos. 64, 65; Hicks, p. 225. Hart wrote to F. Walsingham on 1.12.1581; probably forged, but it says nothing of the league or of Hart's alleged intimacy with Allen. See Hicks, p. 227.   16 F. Edwards, *R. Persons*, pp 323-24.   17 Hicks, p. 226 and n. 668. See

Sir Henry Cobham, English ambassador in Paris, was busier than any in spreading the false rumour. He was the first to report on the league, and in January 1579 Elizabeth brought up the matter with Mendoza. Mendoza of course knew nothing of it, and realised that Elizabeth's ministers were anxious to disturb relations between England, Spain and Burgundy, and attach the queen to the French: and more particularly the Huguenots with whom Cobham was in close contact.[18] 'The supposed league, again, was frequently mentioned in Cobham's dispatches, bearing out Mendoza's earlier remark that he persisted in reporting it.'[19] Cobham claimed that the bishop of Ross gave him the articles of the confederacy who told him that Goldwell and the priests coming to England were to be its instruments. In the summer of 1580 William Eve from Devon published the articles in Waterford, claiming that they were well-known in England, and he had given out twenty copies of them. He seems to have been in no trouble with the Irish or English authorities on this account.[20] As Allen was quick to point out, it is sufficiently unlikely that the Catholics would have published beforehand the articles of a confederacy whose success depended on surprise and secrecy.

It is reasonable to conclude that the English government, notably Cecil, was responsible for the fabrication and dispersal of the articles. The truth of the situation was sufficiently conveyed by the spy Roger Bodenham who reported to Dr Wilson and to Burghley on 1 June 1580 from San Lucar that no preparations were being made in Spain for a descent on England.[21] As Ambassador Priuli reported to the Signory on 2 December 1580, with regard to the articles, 'these English are so artful in their negotiations that I cannot be sure that this story may not have been their invention, or if not entirely so, then at least to a degree.'[22] There was a similarly fictitious papal league in 1567 designed to prevent Elizabeth joining a league against the Turks. All the above was the prologue to set the atmosphere for an enquiry on another strange death, rather like Somerville's, but much more distinguished, namely that of the the eighth earl of Northumberland. The earl was found dead in mysterious circumstances in the Tower on 20 June 1585.

Some of the people who could not be fooled all the time had sufficient influence to oblige the government to set up a formal court of enquiry in the Star Chamber on 23 June 1585. This court consisted of key members of the executive sitting with tried and trusty members of the judiciary who could be expected to cooperate to the full in

W. Allen, *An Apologie* ... [for the 2 colleges] 1581, sig. 15r/v.   **18** Mendoza to Philip II, 27.1.1579; *Spanish Calendar 1568-1579*, p. 632; quoted Hicks, p. 229 & n. 672.   **19** Hicks gives a list of Mendoza's dispatches on p. 229, n. 677. For an account of Stucley's earlier ambivalent career, see John Izon, *Sir Thomas Stucley* (London, 1956); F. Edwards, *The marvellous chance*, chapter 5. The story of the papal 'Irish expedition' of 1580 under San Giuseppe, a fitting ally and protégé of Stucley, is still to be told. See *A new history of Ireland*, ed. T. W. Moody, F. X. Martin and F. J. Byrne, iii 1534-1691, Oxford 1976, p. 107f.; A. Kenny, *The Venerabile*, vol. 20, pp 91-98, 101-3, 171-5. There is much in the Vatican Archives; see F. Edwards, *R. Persons*, p. 50, n. 31.   **20** Hicks, p. 231 and n. 679.   **21** Ibid., and n. 684; *Foreign Calendar 1579-80*, pp 284, 285.   **22** Hicks, p. 232 and n. 649; *Venetian Calendar 155880*, p. 649 (No. 686).

bringing back a verdict desired by the powers that were. Burghley, Shrewsbury, Leicester, Hatton, Hunsdon and other leading members of government were there to witness the star performance put on by the men of law.[23] After Popham's preparation of the ground with his description of the papal league described above, and its avowed intention to depose Elizabeth, the court moved to the latest scandal of Northumberland's suicide. There were those who were uncharitable enough to suppose that the earl's death was murder and not suicide. It did not go unnoticed that shortly before his death, one Bailiff, a servant of Hatton, a man with a reputation among some hardly less sinister than Leicester's, assumed the keepership of the earl. The official reporter of the court, while admitting 'what suspicions the fugitives muttered' thought it 'not meet to insert anything upon mere hearsays and reports'.

Northumberland, accused of, and imprisoned for treason, proved by examinations and confessions, 'grew ... into such a desperate estate that he murdered himself'.[24] It fell to Sir Roger Manwood, lord chief baron of the exchequer, to describe the earl's death, and in no little detail. This was accepted 'by a very substantial jury'. Before his death, the privy council commission had 'thought necessary for the benefit of her Majesty's service' that servants Pantin, Palmer 'and the earl's corrupt keepers should be removed'. The plausible reason was given that it was feared the earl had been able to defeat his incommunicado by paying his keepers to overlook contacts with people outside, notably William Shelley. Thomas Bailiff, 'gent.', Hatton's man, was put to guard him instead. Without attempting to emulate Maigret or Morse, undeniably there were peculiar circumstances in the case. Unfortunately there seems to be only one account of the affair which begins to be comprehensive and comprehensible: that put out as the official story.

Bailiff, by lieutenant governor Hopton's command, was shut up with the earl from 2 p.m. on 20 June 1585. After bringing the earl his supper and other services, Bailiff came to an outer chamber 'where he lay part of the night'. During the night, the prisoner got out of bed to bolt his door on the inner side – a strange privilege for a prisoner – telling Bailiff he could not sleep unless the door was fast. About midnight Bailiff was woken up by 'a great noise'. He called to the earl but got no answer. Bailiff sent for the watch and Owen Hopton about 12.45 a.m. 'In the meantime, Bailiff heard the earl give a long and most grievous groan, and after that a second groan.' By this time Hopton was on the scene. There was no further sound from the earl so the door was broken open 'bolted ... on the inner side'. The earl was found dead in bed 'and by his bedside a dagge' – pistol – 'wherewith he had killed himself'. A rash assumption?

Hopton confirmed the story, adding that after entering, he turned up the bloody sheets to find a wound 'very near the pap' which he thought at first 'had been done with a knife'. He left to write his report for the court but not before bolting 'the door of the earl's bedchamber on the outside' – a curious system of double-locking. We are told that much violence had been needed to break open the door which had been

23 Somers Tracts, i: full title of article in n. 12 above.   24 Ibid., p. 214.

closed by 'a strong iron bolt'. But apparently it was still in good working order so that Hopton could relock it now to keep out the unauthorised inquisitive. Only after writing his report did Hopton return to make a proper investigation. This time he found a dagge on the floor 'about three feet from the bed, near unto a table that had a green cloth on it, which did somewhat shadow the dagge'. If he had not already mentioned the dag, this might have been taken to mean it had not been noticed before. Perhaps Hopton was simply a bad narrator. This time, after removing the bedclothes, he 'found the box in which the powder and pellets were, on the bed under the coverlet'. There was no other door to the earl's chamber apart from that which was broken open. Beyond that, the only other door gave on to a privy connected with no other exit or entrance. It seems worth noting that the lord chief baron later declared that the earl's apartment was part of the royal suite: 'all the daytime the earl had the liberty of five large chambers and two long entries within the outer doors of his prison ... The windows were of a large proportion, yielding so much air and light as could be wished.' For the rest the earl was well-treated and had no visible motive for suicide. He had been imprisoned for his alleged 'practice' to liberate the queen of Scots in 1569 at the time of the northern rising. Although the charge was capital, as he was assured, he had only been fined 5000 marks of which 'as it is credibly reported, there was not one penny paid, or his land touched with any extent for the payment thereof'. In fact Sir Henry Percy's conduct in the northern rising had been exemplary from Elizabeth's viewpoint. He not only actively opposed his brother the earl's part in the rising but had joined the royal troops in suppressing it. To say, as was now said, that he had subsequently been readmitted to honour and favour by Elizabeth about her court was more than misleading. But he was suspected to have lapsed grievously. Hence his present predicament.[25] The earl was awaiting trial on the charge of assisting the invasion of England intended for 1583, although he insisted strenuously on his innocence of any involvement. A trial should have acquitted him. So why suicide, which was taken as an admission of guilt and fear of subsequent disgrace?

Hunsdon, no doubt intending to make the mode of the earl's death more plausible, added more details which in fact only obscured it further. On 21 June, Jaques Pantin confessed that James Price gave the dag to the earl in Pantin's presence. Hunsdon claimed that the dag at the death-scene was charged with three bullets. Surely this meant that much more powder would have been needed than usual? One may wonder whether an Elizabethan pistol would have been able to withstand the force of such an explosion. At all events, Hunsdon deponed that when the earl was found, he lay on his back on the left side of the bed so that he was presumed to have taken the charged dag in his left hand and put the barrel to his 'left pap (having first put aside his waistcoat) and his shirt being only between the dagge and his body, which was burned away the breadth of a large hand, discharged the same, wherewith was made a large wound in

25 Ibid., pp 221-3. For Northumberland's rejection of his brother and the northern rising, see Hicks, p. 45, n. 114.

his said pap, his heart pierced and torn in divers lobes and pieces, three of his ribs broken, the chine bone of his back cut almost asunder ... the three bullets were found by the Lord Hunsdon which he caused the surgeon in his presence to cut out, lying all three close together within the breadth ... of an inch or thereabouts.'[26] If the earl was wearing his shirt and waistcoat he could hardly have been prepared for sleep. Was he expecting trouble? It is more likely that Hunsdon told more of the truth than Hopton. Clearly the kind of wound described by Hunsdon could hardly have been mistaken for a stab-wound as Hopton first claimed. Nor is it likely that the earl, after sustaining such terrible injuries involving his heart, would have had life enough left in him for groaning – twice. Without attempting further to unravel a whodunnit, one could ask what motive could there be for the government wanting to put Northumberland out of the way. It is not hard to find.

Amid the welter of conflicting loyalties, lies, half-truths and counter-lies, which turn the grounds of historical enquiry into a quagmire, one may discern from 1582 another subdivision of the loyalist papists. As we have seen, there were those like Allen, Englefield, Persons and other exiles who threw themselves wholeheartedly into the task of overthrowing the regime in England by military force from the continent. There were those others like the Pagets, Morgan, Ross, Owen Lewis and their friends who were determined to resist all efforts to move the English government other than by persuasion and the example of a loyalty which genuinely attempted to be unswerving. But some at least among the 'loyalists' were not averse to the idea of liberating the queen of Scots through outside foreign help, but not the violent sort that would have threatened Elizabeth in life, limb or throne. Morgan and the Pagets seem to have been among these. But their correspondence was careful, as they knew it must be. All sides were infiltrated by spies who spoke sweetly and unreliably to everyone. Many would say anything for their stipend from ambassadors abroad or ministers in London. Some like Giordano Bruno alias Fagot were simply consumed with hatred for every kind of papist.[27]

Even among themselves, the loyalists could not always trust one another. Morgan and Charles Paget never seem to have fallen out; but Thomas Lord Paget, who fled to France in 1583 after the 'discovery' of the latest plot, wrote to his brother Charles on 25 October 1583 to tell him that his stay in Rouen caused much misgiving because of the people there – many militants including Persons. Thomas reminded Charles of his duty to England and threatened to disown him if he forgot it.[28] The government contributed generously to the atmosphere of mistrust, as Camden admitted: 'counterfeit letters were sent in the name of the queen of Scots and left at papist houses', and spies and rumour-mongers of the right kind everywhere encouraged.[29]

---

26 *Somers Tracts*, i, p. 222. Ralegh assumed that Hatton was responsible for the 8th earl's death. See W. R. to R. Cecil, Feb. to Aug, [?]. 1600, Salisbury mss 90, no. 150; printed in E. Edwards, *Life of Sir Walter Ralegh*, ii (London, 1868), pp 222-3.   27 For Bruno's capacity for hatred, see J. Bossy, *Giordano Bruno and the embassy affair* (London, 1997), Vintage edition, passim.   28 Lord Paget to C. Paget, 25.10.1583, Dnb 43, p. 46   29 See G. Goodman, op. cit., pp 119-20.

Walsingham made use of the Catholic loyalists but had no respect for them. Willingly if not cheerfully, he used and misrepresented them for his own purposes. He wrote to Stafford on 16 December 1584, 'Charles Paget is a most dangerous instrument, and I wish for Northumberland's sake he had never been born.'[30] It is certain that the principal secretary had no affection for Northumberland. Charles Paget soon shed his illusions, if he ever had any, about the men who were employing him for their purposes while he served them for his. He wrote to the Scottish queen on 18 July 1585, 'But he [William Shelley] will, I fear, drink of the same cup the earl of Northumberland has done, and so shall I with many more. Such are the devilish practices of the earl of Leicester and his confederates.'[31] Paget was surely too intelligent a man to suppose Leicester was unique among his employers when it came to 'devilish practices'. The Cecil, Leicester and Walsingham axis was inevitably concerned to cause as much confusion as might be among the papists. In fact they hated the cooperators almost as much as the militants since they represented a dangerous body of sympathy towards Mary, queen of Scots. Morgan, Paget and many of their friends seem to have been consistent in their service and support for the captive queen.[32] It was important to weaken and if possible destroy this group as much as the militants. In fact, the militants were as much a danger to Mary as her Protestant enemies since, being less sensitive of the consequences of their militancy, albeit sympathetic, they gave the government a better excuse for proceeding to extremes against her. The militants could not be unaware of the danger in which they placed her by advocating moves for her release by foreign powers without reservation. The loyalists, while repudiating all idea of invasion from outside, were willing to consider means for the release of the queen and her reinstatement in her own kingdom by assistance from within England and Scotland. This could not be reasonably construed as treason since it did not in any way threaten Elizabeth. For which reason the government could only regard them as being more dangerous as being more insidious.

The Throckmorton plot was an attempt by government to bracket militants and pacifists and destroy them all, proving to the world in the process that there was no difference between them. They all had treason in view and the overthrow of Elizabeth. Northumberland, Thomas and Francis Throckmorton, allies and friends of Morgan and the Pagets, were patently influential supporters of Mary of Scotland. In the absence of real evidence, it is never clear what the loyalists intended with regard to Mary's liberation at this time apart from wanting it. The government had to bring pressure to bear to provide by hook or by crook the appearance of evidence required to prove the common iniquity of them all to justify their destruction. The pressure bore down more particularly on Northumberland and Francis Throckmorton.

30 Walsingham to Stafford, 16.12.1584, Dnb, ibid., p. 47.   31 C. Paget to Mary, 18.7.1585; quoted Hicks, pp 26-7.   32 T. Morgan and C. Paget seem to have been sincere in their service to Mary. Hicks thought they were government spies and adduces as evidence their intimacy with Walsingham and authentic spies such as Gilbert Gifford and Thomas Phelippes. But all parties kept in touch with all others as part of their daily work and duty to know what was afoot.

Although the evidence against them was, to say the least, unconvincing, they were caught in the net and paid the full penalty of noncompliance with the demands of statecraft. The hatred of the militants for the cooperators or loyalists never diminished at the sight of their misfortunes. This is attested to excess in the surviving evidence. Allen wrote frequently against them. Charles Browne denounced Morgan to Philip II. They were known to be in touch with Walsingham and that was enough. Assailed on all sides, Morgan was arrested in Paris in 1585 at the instance of Queen Elizabeth. A large list of accusations was drawn up against himn in Spain in 1590. He was imprisoned in the Low Countries by order of Parma for two years before release in 1592. Stafford frequently reported from Paris the loathing of the opposing party for the Morgan-Paget faction.[33]

Returning to 1583, Northumberland refused to confess to participation in any plot against Elizabeth as the government wished. The most probable reason for his refusal was that he was innocent. According to the official account, the privy council told Northumberland as from her Majesty 'to tell the truth of the matters so clearly appearing against him, either by letters privily to her Majesty or by speech to ... Hatton. Sir Christopher Hatton told him if he admitted all, he would be dealt with favourably in the mitigation of punishment due to him.' The earl refused to oblige; 'but resting upon terms of his innocency, having ... conveyed away all those he thought could or would any way accuse him, he made choice rather to go to the Tower', risk her Majesty's wrath and the extremity of the law.[34] There was a limit to the pressure which could be applied to a nobleman. Convention forbade the use of torture. Doubtless, convinced of his innocence, he realised that if his case came to judgment in a court of his peers, as also belonged to his rank, he would be completly vindicated. It would be astonishing if he played so completely into the hands of his enemies as to commit suicide before a trial which would have exonerated him, as he had a right to believe.

Less fortunate was the situation of his alleged partner in crime. Francis Throckmorton gave his name to the latest 'plot'. He was the son of Sir John Throckmorton of Feckenham, Worcestershire, a member of a leading Catholic family. Sir John was the seventh of eight sons of Sir George Throckmorton of Coughton, Warwickshire, and brother of Sir Nicholas Throckmorton. Queen Mary appointed Sir John chief justice of Chester and made him a member of the council of the marches of Wales. He was knighted by Elizabeth at Kenilworth in 1566. By 1579 the shooting star had fallen. In that year he was suspended from his office of chief justice and subsequently tried in the court of star chamber for maladministration of justice. He was found guilty and fined. He did not long survive his disgrace, dying on 23 May 1580. Richard Puttenham eulogised him in *The arte of English poesie*, published anonymously in 1589. *The Dictionary of national biography* adds interesting detail.

33 Hatred for the Morgan-Paget faction and its pursuit by their enemies is evidenced in Hicks pp 63, 73, 78, 87, 88, 90, 125. The whole of this work could be taken in one aspect as an indictment of the faction.   34 *Somers Tracts*, i, pp 223-4.

According to Godfrey Goodman, who was in a position to know, the true cause of Sir John's undoing was that, before he became chief justice of Chester, he had been instrumental in securing Mary's succession after Edward VI. Being close to the Dudley Northumberland of Edward VI's time, he had learned of a plot to put Mary out of the way before the king, then in extremis, died. Sir John warned Mary 'who presently took horse and rode sixty miles that day, and came to her servant Jerningham in Norfolk, where it pleased God to bless her with a prosperous success'. Shortly afterwards, Mary promoted Sir John to become chief justice. After her death, he 'did constantly in his grace after meat pray for the soul of Queen Mary. Truly, Queen Elizabeth did not much affect them who did belong to or did any way commend Queen Mary.' It was therefore not difficult for the earl of Leicester to have his revenge. He had never forgiven Sir John for his influence in preventing the crown passing to the Dudleys. Sir John's successor 'told me [Goodman] that he had done nothing but that which was legal and just, and very frequent and usual with all other judges; and that was, the mending of a record, which the earl of Leicester was pleased to term the changing, altering and corrupting of records; and for that he was turned out of his justiceship.' Leicester pursued the son, Francis, as a further instalment of his plan to bring this eminent Catholic family to final ruin.[35] It seems to fit in with Leicester's reputation, the earl of Sussex' 'gypsy'. The aspersion on gypsies is surely unjust.

The case against Francis as a plotter becomes on analysis flimsy enough. As Hicks observed, 'The central point of the Government case, it must be ... emphasised was that ... conferences at Petworth between the earl of Northumberland, Charles Paget and his brother Lord Paget, were concerned with traitorous practices connected with the invasion plan of 1583.'[36] The case rested primarily on the confessions of Francis Throckmorton. 'At his trial on 21 May 1584, however, he persistently denied the truth of these confessions, as they had been made under the influence of torture ... '[37] The importance of Throckmorton's confession in the case against Paget and Northumberland was admitted by Popham, the attorney general, in a paper in his own hand. 'The probability of this matter for the coming over of Charles Paget into Sussex to such intent as is set down, being the principal point to touch the earl of North[umberland] standeth only upon the confession of Fr Throckmorton.'[38]

35 Godfrey Goodman, *The court of James I*, John S. Brewer edition, i (London, 1839), pp 116-19. Goodman enlarges interestingly with quotations from Camden on the pursuit of Francis Throckmorton. Since his findings are not always to standard taste, Goodman is sometimes treated dismissively as a gossip. Brewer's introduction (ibid., pp vii-xvii) reassures us that Goodman, later bishop of Gloucester (1625), was a man of learning and integrity. He was educated at Westminster under William Camden and later at Trinity College, Cambridge. He believed that 'in the eye of the law we [the C. of E.] are still one with the said [Roman] Catholic Church' (p. ix). His convictions brought him into conflict with the Anglican authorities but he repudiated 'popery' (p. xii). He wrote his memoirs 'in the homely and easy style of one who had no enemy to malign and no party to gratify' (p. xvi). As a man of integrity, his observations on the politics of his time, with which he was in close contact, and especially on the numerous plots involving Catholics and others, give his original witness unique value. He is occasionally guilty of error. Who is not?   36 Hicks, p. 38.   37 Ibid., p. 39.   38 Ibid., pp 22-3.

Much is uncertain: but it is certain, after consideration of his previous career, that Charles Paget did not return to England in 1583 to sell the idea of the projected invasion to Northumberland or anyone else. We do not have to take Persons' word alone, which was widely corroborated. True, Paget was present at the meeting in Paris which adopted the Guise invasion plan of 1583, and gave the impression of accepting it. But when he went or was sent to England in September 1583, if he mentioned the matter at all to Catholic parties, which is unproven, it could only have been to advise them against it. These would have included Mary, queen of Scots. Samerie, the Jesuit, who made three clandestine visits to her at different times to persuade her to reject Paget's position, confirmed that she would, wise woman, have nothing to do with the Guise scheme or anything else of the kind. This was also the report brought to Mendoza and confirmed in 1586 by Pasquier, her master of the wardrobe. Persons reported Guise as saying that Paget volunteered to go to England to sell the scheme and on arrival did the exact opposite, advising all parties he met against it. Persons later reproached Paget by letter for telling the priest William Watts, as they were both 'walking upon the ... seaside', waiting for a sail to England, that this was his plan, and that he could destroy in a few days all that the Jesuits had been planning for long.[39]

A sufficient reason for Paget's business with Northumberland was to persuade him to let his sons come back to England and not let them go to Rome as Persons wanted. Percy had sent his agent Pullen to Paris to see how his four sons were faring with their education. Elizabeth wanted them back in England but Allen and Persons thought it best for the earl, to say nothing of his succession, to keep one or two of the older ones in France or even further afield. Since the boys were 'entrusted in some sort to Paget', he had the last word on their immediate destiny. They all returned to England and lost their 'good inclination' towards Catholicism. Persons thought the sons should have been sent to Italy whether the father wanted it or no.[40]

There is the usual difficulty, perhaps more than usual, with regard to the paucity of surviving documents to plumb the depths of the plot. The disappearance of evidence does not help to convince us of much truth in the government story. Of the confessions of Throckmorton, Shelley and Northumberland, none survive save one of Throckmorton's and one of Percy's, that of 11 May 1585. This does not support the government's case and was not referred to in Throckmorton's trial. There were some seventy examinations but 'well over twenty, and these the vital ones, have disappeared'. There are references to eleven confessions of Throckmorton but the only one surviving does not help the regime. Mention occurs of ten confessions of William Shelley. None survives. The surviving documents only touch the fringes: Paget's coming to England, a visit to Petworth, the departure of Lord Paget and Sir Charles Arundell for the continent. There is no indication in government sources of the real purpose or purposes of Paget's visit to England.[41]

39 F. Edwards, *R. Persons*, p. 91; Hicks, chapters 1–3, especially, pp 22–3 and nn. 69, 70.   40 F. Edwards, *Robert Persons*, p. 90.   41 Hicks, p. 31 , n. 89 and p. 39, n. 100.

An official account of Francis Throckmorton's trial was published as *A discoverie of the treasons ... practised and attempted against the queene's Majestie ... by Francis Throckmorton, who was for the same arraigned and condemned in Guyld-Hall ... on 21 May 1584.* It was claimed to be 'a letter sent from a gentleman of Lions-Inne to his friend' dated 15 June and published on 10 July, the day of Throckmorton's execution. In fact it was a pièce justificative based on a rough draft in the hand of Thomas Wilkes, Burghley's clerk.[42] As one would expect, it was heavily weighted against the accused, but if one reads it with proper distrust, it tells us something. To wring from Throckmorton sufficient evidence to put him on trial, he had been subjected to treatment that was savagely inhuman even by the standard of the times. On the day of his arrest, 13 November 1583, he was put in Little Ease in the Tower, a hollow cube in a wall some four feet by four. On 23 November, he was 'gravissime' tortured on the rack, and the same day thrown into the Pit, a deep hole in the ground without light or amenities. The same day Edward Arden was also racked and, on 24 November, Hugh Hall, the priest. We do not know how long Throckmorton was confined to the Pit but an earlier martyr, Alexander Bryant, treated with like brutality, was left there for fifteen days. On 2 December Throckmorton was racked again, twice in the same day.[43] Not surprisingly, he gave way and confessed what was wanted of him. Later he denied it. Presumably under threat of a repetition of his previous experience, he reaffirmed his first confession, giving reasons for his change of mind. One reason was obvious and sufficient.

According to Professor John Bossy, Nicholas Fagot alias Giordano Bruno, 'procured in so far as it was in his power to do so, the arrest, torture and execution of Francis Throckmorton, whom Castelnau said he loved as himself, and by whose fate he was appallingly harrowed. He did all this while buttering up Castelnau in three dedicatory epistles with fulsome professions of esteem, friendship and undying gratitude for looking after him and sticking up for him.'[44] As Bossy reminds us, although judi-

---

42 'A Discoverie of the Treasons practised and attempted ... ', *Harleian Miscellany*, iii, 1809, pp 190-9. Full title and alleged source on pp 190-1. T. Wilkes' rough draft of this is in SP 12/171, No. 86; see also Hicks, p. 31, no. 89.   43 Francis Throckmorton's rackings are mentioned in Nicholas Sander, *De Origine ac Progressu Schismatis Anglicanae ... 1586.* See above; under dates. For the torture of A. Bryant, see F. Edwards, *The Elizabethan Jesuits*, p. 130.   44 John Bossy, op. cit., gives a graphic account of Bruno/Fagot. One of Castelnau's household in Salisbury Court on the Thames, he acted as chaplain and as spy for Walsingham. He heard and betrayed the confession of at least one man, Pedro de Zubiaur. The queen did not approve of this (p. 167). 'He despised and detested Jesus, and had a special contempt for the Cross and for any form of the Mass or Eucharist'; p. 148. 'Romanism aside, [G. B.'s] venomous pasages on women, Jews, Protestants and Jesus demonstrate the catholicity of his victims and the pleasure he took in their discomfiture or worse. Fantasies of retribution seem to have been his daily bread' (p. 160). He was associated with William Herle in much of his spying (pp 101, 158). G. B.'s 'actions as a secret agent in England were in the first place dedicated to the frustration of English popery in so far as it covered a political movement designed to overthrow Queen Elizabeth and her government; to that end he had successfully exposed Francis Throckmorton, recruited Courcelles into English service, denounced, (if his story had been true),

cial torture was not supposed to be part of the English judicial system, since the sovereign was the fount of law it could be applied by special prerogative, and often was in cases of treason. Whether this was applied to discover the truth or to make sure that the victim supplied the 'evidence' needed for the purposes of policy and propaganda, the reader may judge. At all events, Bruno–Fagot was mainly responsible, it seems, for the further brutality inflicted on the wretched Throckmorton. Bruno would have heard from Castelnau of the victim's previous ordeal. But not satisfied with this, he passed on – a ghoulish example of the jokes for which he was famous? – the report that an Irish Catholic gentleman in the Fleet had dropped a hint that Throckmorton had not confessed even half of what he knew. Even Bossy, who wastes no sympathy on popish recusants and believes that what was wrung from Throckmorton was the truth, conceded, 'this was a perfectly needless invitation to Walsingham to have him tortured again, and perhaps the Irish gentleman as well'.[45]

Thus softened up, the accused was submitted to trial. It was claimed that 'secret intelligence' showed he had conveyed letters to Mary, queen of Scots and received letters from her. If he had, this would not have constituted treason. Although Mary had been treated as an enemy rather than a refugee after her arrival in England in 1568, this was quite unjustified in law. She had committed no act of hostility against England or Elizabeth. But the fact of Throckmorton's interest was presented by the prosecution as something sinister. He had been watched for months to collect evidence. Finally, two gentlemen 'of no mean credite' – was one of them Herle? – were sent to his house by Paul's Wharf where he was arrested and 'conveyed presently away' by one of them while the other searched his papers. In that search, two papers were allegedy found, one giving the names of certain 'Catholique noblemen and gentlemen, expressing the havens for landing of forraine forces, with other particularities'. One was in secretary hand which the accused confessed at the bar as his own; 'and the other in the Roman hand, which he denied to be his, and would not show how the same came unto his hands. Howbeit in his examinations he hath confessed them both to be his owne handwriting, and so they are in trueth.' They also 'found twelve pedigrees of the descent of the crown of England printed and published by the bishop of Ross in the defence' of the Scottish queen's title to the succession 'with certaine infamous libelles against

Pedro de Zubiaur, and planned to spring Thomas Morgan from the Bastille' (p. 157). But the value of G. B.'s information may be gauged from the fact that he alleged Henry Howard, a convert to Catholicism (?), was a priest and cardinal in petto, no less (p. 103). Bossy thought this was 'probably one of his jokes'; p. 103. If so, when is he to be taken seriously? Howard was G. B.'s pet hate. He secured his arrest and imprisonment for at least six months (p. 104). G. B. posed as a Catholic zealot to Girault, another of Castelnau's household, who betrayed the method of importing Catholic books into Englnd through the embassy (p. 147).   **45** Bossy, op. cit., p. 159, n. 63. In G. B.'s play, *Il Candelaio*, 'Manfurio cannot bear the pain of his whipping, as Throckmorton could not bear the pain of his torture; in both cases, Bruno's reaction was to inflict more'. On torture and its application to Throckmorton, see also Hicks, pp 31-2, n. 90. Bossy gives a useful short diary of events, with date correspondencies in O. S. and N. S. and a connection with W. Parry (p. 106).

her Majestie, printed and published beyond the seas'. They were not further specified. None of this amounted to much but the last was given a twist to appeal to the prejudice of the court: 'which being found in the hands of a man so ill-affected, comparing the same with his doings and practices against her Majestie, you will judge the purpose whereof he kept them'.[46]

Much was made of the two papers: the list of ports and the list of noblemen. One is reminded of the lists of noblemen on the person of Ridolfi when he went abroad for the last time. Shortly after his arrest, Throckmorton was questioned by members of the privy council about them. At first 'he most impudently denied with many protestations that he ever saw them; affirming they were none of his'. Knowing the system, he claimed at first they 'were foisted in (as he termed it) among his papers by the gentlemen that searched his house'. Perhaps he forgot them and afterwards remembered. As Hicks observed, 'the paper in secretary hand, containing the list of the havens was drawn up, according to his own statement, with the aid of his father, which would make it at the time of his trial on 21 May 1584 some four years old, and so, not made, as his accusers maintained, in view of the invasion plan of 1583'.[47] This would put it well before the date when any connection with an invasion plan was even plausible. After more insistent questioning, Throckmorton thought that the papers had been left 'he knew not how, in his chamber by a man of his, (who long before was departed out of the realm) named Edward Rogers, alias Nuttebie, by whom they were written'. It was claimed that Throckmorton tried to get three messages to his brother George telling him of the examination about the two papers with the names of noblemen and havens, asking him to confirm that they had been written in Edward Nuttebie's hand, known to his brother. The letters were intercepted, 'and this was taken to be a device to have his brother confirm his falsehoode'.[48]

Two torture sessions were admitted but only after he was 'persuaded in very milde and charitable maner to confesse the trueth' by the commissioners, pardon being promised if 'he would betray the depths of his practises'. The second time, he was hardly tortured at all but confessed 'before he was strayned up to any purpose'. The interrogatories put to him were 'for brevity's sake omitted' in the published version. The accused was allegedly forced to confess that 'some years ago' when he was at Spa and Liège he had conferred with Jenny, 'a notorious traitor', and Sir Francis Englefield about an invasion. As we have seen, the alleged time of this makes it altogether unlikely. Sir John was dragged in to make him the adviser for drawing up the list of Catholic gentry and acquainting him 'with the description of the havens for landing forces'. A simple exercise in demographic analysis and geography thus becomes the stuff of treason. Even less plausible was the claim that Francis' brother Thomas 'by letters and conference', and 'Thomas Morgan by letters', told him of 'a resolute determination agreed on by the Scottish queene and her confederates in France and other forreine

---

46 Charges against Francis Throckmorton, *Harleian Misc.*, iii, p. 192. **47** For the list of havens, see Hicks, p. 31, n. 89. BL, Stowe ms 1083, ff. 17-20 is given as a source. **48** *Harl. Misc.*, iii, pp 191-2.

partes, and also in Englande, for the invading of the realme'.[49] More plausible was the suggestion that Guise would head the invasion when it happened. But no one should believe the 'pretention' that it was only to deliver Mary and force Elizabeth to grant 'a tolerance in religion for the pretended Catholiques'. The real intention, 'the bottom whereof should not at the first be made generally known, should be, when Elizabeth resisted, to depose her'.

The bottom of the case was probably not even known to the principal law officers conducting the prosecution. As Hicks noticed, it is surprising 'to find that Mr Attorney (Popham) and Mr Solicitor (Egerton), a year after Throckmorton's trial and condemnation were still not acquainted with all the details of the case, as is clear from the phrase, "in Throckmorton's case you [Thomas Wilkes] did travail both honestly and diligently and may remember such parts thereof, which Mr Attorney and Mr Solicitor have not heard of" ... At all events it confirms the impression that the law officers were briefed by Wilkes and did not prepare their case from a study of the documents.'[50]

It was further charged that in August 1583 a special messenger was sent to England 'under a counterfeite name from the confederates in France' – this was Charles Paget, alias Mope – to push the plot in England. Thomas Throckmorton, when last in England, acquainted Francis with what was planned, who agreed to help with the aid of the Spanish ambassador, Bernardino de Mendoza, 'whom he instructed howe and with whome to deale for the preparing of a convenient partie heere within the realme'. An ingenious excuse was found for the fact that no proof of communication between Francis and anyone else for this formation of a party could be found. Francis 'woulde not be seene to be a sounder of men, lest hee might be discovered, and so endanger himselfe and the enterprise'. The ambassador, as 'a publique person' would be safe.[51] Thomas visited England, it seems, to persuade his brother to settle his affairs and put himself in safety in France, as he himself had done. If the release of the Scottish queen, by means which could only by adverse interpretation be taken as a threat to Elizabeth, were not speedily accomplished, Francis should risk no more time in perilous England.

As for Mendoza, who was supposed to have been informed of the latest invasion scheme by Paget and Francis Throckmorton, there is no evidence in the dispatches to suggest that the ambassador had knowledge of, and certainly not authority for, any

49 Ibid., p. 192.   50 Hicks, p. 41, n. 104. Popham made a summary of F. T.'s treason after he denied the truth of his confessions at his trial on 21.5.1584 (SP12/171, no. 79). Popham admits the alleged treasonable intent of C. Paget's visit to Sussex depended only on F. T.'s confession, but at his trial on 21.5., Popham invoked the 'alleged confession' of William Shelley of 19.12.1583 (Stowe ms 83). This confession is also referred to in 'The case of William Shelley', November, 1585 (Egerton MS, 2074, ff. 73-4). But Northumberland was never tried. 'Changes in the drafts, and the several manifest untruths that they contain ... make the official accounts given in the two pamphlets, the one concerning Throckmorton, the other' Northumberland 'quite unreliable'. Thomas Norton may have assisted Wilkes in preparing the case.   51 *Harl. Misc.*, iii, p. 192.

such thing. Philip by 1582 was only prepared to help Lennox in Scotland with some 10,000 crowns but not with military aid. Mendoza was supposed to have told Francis that Philip had promised to pay one half of the expenses of the English enterprise. It is certain that Philip made no such promise and that the failure between him and the pope to agree on the relative size of their contribution made the whole venture a nonstarter. Not even by the spring of 1585, which was supposed to be the best time for the enterprise, had these difficulties been resolved.[52]

In his defence, Throckmorton maintained that the matter contained in his confessions was 'false and feyned', made simply to avoid further torture. He admitted his postal contacts abroad with the expatriates. He 'haunted continually two ambassadours in London', visiting Mendoza twice a week when he was in the capital. Through all these he maintained contact by letter with Thomas Morgan and Thomas Throckmorton in Paris, although they were known to be 'notorious practisers, very inward with the duke of Guise, and contrivers of the treasons and devises for the invasion intended'.[53] But such contacts did not amount to treason. After breaking down at the end of his torture, Francis was reported to have said, 'Nowe I have disclosed the secrets of her who was the dearest thing to me in the worlde (meaning the Scottish queene), and whome I thought no torment should have drawn from me so much to have prejudiced, as I have done by my confessions; I see no cause why I should spare anyone, if I could say ought against him; and sith I have failed of my faith towards her, I care not if I were hanged.'[54] Thomas Dekker if not quite Shakespeare.

The accused, after 'charging her Majestie with crueltie, and her ministers with untruethes in their proceedings against him', moved by 'a vain conceite', appealed to a law of 1571 which specified that, in the case of certain treasons, no person should be arraigned for them unless he was indicted 'within six monthes next after the same offence committed, and shall not be arraigned for the same unlesse the offence be proved by the testimonie and othe of two sufficient witnesses, or his voluntary confession without violence'. But 'the lord chief justice and other of the judges in commission at his trial' told him he was being tried under the act of Edward III An.25, [AD 1302]. This 'admitted no such limitation of time or proofe'. The best way 'to redeeme his life' was 'by submission and acknowledging of his offence, which for a time after

---

52 Hicks (op. cit., pp 54, 50 and n. 131) for Thomas Throckmorton and Mendoza. He points out on pp 46-57 and in the notes, a number of inconsistencies in the dates mentioned in the official pamphlets. 53 For Francis Throckmorton's contacts with ambassadors, see *Harl. Misc.*, iii, p. 196. It includes a curious and unconvincing account of 'a casket covered in green velvet' which F. T. 'very cunningly conveied out of his chamber by a maid servant' although one of the gentlemen searchers was in the room at the time and did not notice what was happening. John Meredith, a friend of F. T., allegedly gave it to Mendoza. At his arrest, F. T. was interrupted 'writing to the Scottish Queen in cipher or a letter in cipher by him written unto her': an obscure phrase. F. T. was said to be anxious for the casket not to be discovered. It all sounds like a ruse whereby letters to and from Mary could and have been concocted for 'evidence'. In the sequel it was not considered necessary. There was already sufficient 'evidence' to send F. T. to the gallows. Cf. ibid., p. 194. At least part of the intention was surely to compromise Mendoza. 54 *Harl. Misc.*, iii, p. 195.

he had confessed his treasons, he was contented to followe, and nowe ... after his condemnation, by a new submission to the queen's majestie the 4th of June, hath resumed that course ... '[55]

Like everything else in the process, Throckmorton's alleged submission and declaration of 4 June raise difficulties which did not go unnoticed by Hicks. The two documents are printed near the end of the official account of the trial. But it is not clear how or where precisely they were presented, or what was Throckmorton's reaction to them and presumed objections. In presenting the submission, Popham seemed to imply that there had been an earlier submission; which made him wonder why Throckmorton went back on it. But no such submission has survived; if it ever existed.[56] There is an undated manuscript endorsed as 'ffraunces Throgmorton's submission to her Matie' but it is not in Francis' hand, though signed by him. It resembles closely the hand of Francis Mills, Walsingham's secretary.[57] Francis' signature can be verified by comparison with the only confession of his extant. The main point of this 'submission' was to withdraw the denial of the truth of his previous confessions and to throw himself in abject terms on the mercy of Elizabeth. Elizabeth is God's image on earth, and he begs from her 'remission and forgiveness'. But if she is not prepared to grant it, he begs improbably 'the trebling of the torment justly imposed upon me ... for the heynous cryme whereof I remayne ... justly condemned'.[58] As Hicks noted, 'a curious feature' of the signature 'is that it does not come immediately after the words "Your Majesty's most woeful subject ..." but at the end of the page, after one third of the sheet had been left blank.'[59] Examinees were usually careful to make sure their signatures came at the end of their confessions so that extra material could not be inserted by the examiners.

Hicks was not the first to notice another peculiar feature about this submission. The calendarer of the state papers was convinced that, although it was dated 4 June, it was originally enclosed in a letter from Owen Hopton to Walsingham of 1 June 1584. Hopton there stated that he had supplied the prisoner with pen and ink, but Throckmorton used it not to answer some of Hopton's questions, as he had wished, but to 'write a supplication to the queen's Majesty, which herein I have sent you'. Lady Throckmorton, Francis' mother, had been allowed to see him. She 'gave him good and motherly counsel to deal plainly and loyally with her Majesty, and to discover such practices as he knew'. In fact he was already supposed to have confessed these. Throckmorton avoided Hopton's further urging to state what he knew, and requested pen and ink and the opportunity of further private conference with his mother before he wrote anything down. Hopton, who had obliged on his own responsibility before, now refused to allow him the further use of pen and ink until he had Walsingham's specif-

---

55 Ibid., p. 196.   56 Did F. T. make an earlier 'submission'? See Hicks, op. cit., p. 41 and n. 105. For a source, see Holinshed, *Chronicle*, iv, p. 543.   57 F. T.'s 'submission' was in F. Mills' hand, SP12/171, No. 1 (i). See Hicks, pp 42, 44 and n. 105. Printed in *Harl. misc.*, iii, p. 196.   58 *Harl. misc.*, iii, p. 197.   59 Hicks, p. 44.

ic approval. Hopton made the peculiar plea that Throckmorton be obliged, 'for else he will speak slanderously of me at the hour of his death, for he is very angry, that I have sent the supplication to Your Honour, written to her Majesty ... '[60]

Hicks had a plausible explanation for Throckmorton's anger. While his mother was allowed access, Throckmorton was not allowed to see his wife. 'Could it be that Throckmorton was tricked into signing a paper which had been substituted for that mentioned first by Hopton, which might well have been a supplication to the queen to see his wife? ... Was [his anger] because Throckmorton had discovered that he had been tricked into signing the present "submission", in which the signature is so oddly placed, and that Hopton feared that he might say at the time of his execution that he could not have written the paper, for he had not had in his possession for a sufficient length of time the means – pen and ink – to do so? Certainly, these two documents, the submission and Hopton's letter, suggest that some trickery was practised. Nor must it be overlooked that the submission was only published after Throckmorton's execution, when he could not expose any such trickery.'[61]

As Hicks further observed, 'it is also to be noted that there is no mention in Hopton's letter of Throckmorton's declaration of his treasons, which is pages longer than the submission, and which the government stated the prisoner had penned the same day as the submission, viz. 4 June 1585. Nor is there any evidence apart from the government's assertion in the pamphlet, that he ever wrote such a declaration.'[62] This declaration seems to have been read out at the trial after the submission. It gave an account in some detail of Throckmorton's epistolary dealings with the Scottish queen through Godfrey Foljambe and others which began 'was two years' – 1581 or 1582? His dealings with Paris were through Thomas Morgan, not through Thomas his brother. Francis was altogether discouraging about any prospect of success for an invasion attempt. So far plausible; but then Morgan was supposed to have urged him to liaise with Mendoza who assured Throckmorton it would be 'verie easie to make alteration here with very little force' since men were used to peace. Mendoza sounds him out on the best place for making a landing, the probable cooperation of the Catholics, and the difficulty of rescuing Mary, to all of which Throckmorton gave properly discouraging replies. Evidently, the intention is to give the most sinister intepretation possible to the accused's contact with Mendoza. Throckmorton's most fatuous suggestion was that a small force should be sent into Scotland with the approval of James VI to conduct border raids until Elizabeth was worn down sufficiently to release Mary and grant the Catholics toleration.[63] One could reasonably conclude that the so–called declaration was a fabrication, and never used in the trial at all.

An attempt was made to cover or reduce the interval when the supposed lists of gentlemen supporters and possible landing-places were made. At one point Mendoza

60 For O. Hopton's letter to Walsingham of 1.6.1584, see Hicks' note on the calendarer, p. 42, n. 107; and *Cal. SP Dom. Elizabeth 1581–90*, p. 179. **61** For Hopton's trickery practised on F. T., Hicks, p. 44. **62** The 'declaration' was not in Hopton's letter: Hicks, p. 45. **63** The 'Declaration'; *Harl. misc.*, iii, pp 197-9.

urged Throckmorton to supply him with the lists so he departed to his country to arrange for the sale of lands prior to departing to France 'as also to fetch the draught of gentlemen and havens for the most part of England, which had been set down by me, above two yeares since, and left behind at Feckenham in my studio.' He did not find the draft at Feckenham so returned to London 'where I found the note of names in secretarie hand, which I carried to the Spanish ambassadour, and there drew that other in Romane hand, in his studie; putting down Chester to be taken, in respect of the easinesse, as I thought, and the rather to give him encouragement in the matter. I left it with him ... ' So by now Francis has passed from discouragment to encourage-ment. But the day before his arrest, he reports, Mendoza 'sent me backe the paper in Roman hand, desiring me to set downe the same at my leisure more exactly; which was the cause that it was not in my green velvet casket'. Otherwise the writings it contained were as he had already confessed.[64] Whatever was in the green casket, if it ever exist-ed, is as futile a subject for speculation as the equally problematic casket and its letters associated earlier with the Scottish queen. They too 'disappeared'.

As Hicks reminded us, there is no evidence 'apart from the government's assertion in the pamphlet, that the accused ever wrote such a declaration'.[65] Bishop Godfrey Goodman gave his own opinion of the case against him. 'There was found in his study a note of some harbours in England, what ships and of what burden they would carry, and how safely they might there abide; an observation which certainly many mariners and seafaring men do observe, but this being found with him, and he being known to be inclining to the Church of Rome, upon some pretence that it was for an invasion, he was found guilty.'[66] Goodman had more to say on characters we have already encountered. He pointed out that it was at this time that Lord Paget and Sir Charles Arundell, two Catholics with court connections, began to be wary of the regime 'through the subtle practices of Leicester and Walsingham ... Singular kinds of fraud were invented, privy snares laid, that they [the courtiers] might, whether they would or no, through improvidence, be entangled in the snares of high treason.'[67] Further-more, 'counterfeit letters were privily sent under the name of the queen of Scots and [of] the fugitives, and left in papists' houses'. Lord Henry Howard, the late duke of Norfolk's younger brother, received about this time a letter that had clearly been forged. The man who delivered it told him it came from the French ambassador. The ambassador denied it on oath to Elizabeth herself. Robert Beale visited Mary in the spring of 1584 and made a report which got back to her ears after due or undue manip-ulation by the councillors. Mary declared, 'I have never said these things as they have been taken. Walsingham has made, I believe, similar alterations in the matter of reli-

64 Ibid., p. 199.   65 There is only the pamphlet to prove that F. T. wrote the 'declaration': Hicks, p. 45.   66 G. Goodman, *The court of King James I ...* , p. 116. See note 34 above.   67 The departure of Charles Paget and Charles Arundell at this time was bound up with a court scandal involving Edward de Vere, 17th earl of Oxford. See B. M. Ward, *The seventeenth earl of Oxford 1550-1604* (London 1928); Charlton Ogburn, *The mysterious William Shakespeare: the myth and the reality* (New York 1984) passim.

gion: he has cut and falsified the text.'[68] All of which merged into the further developments which were exploited to bring the Scottish queen at long last to the scaffold in 1587.

Throckmorton was executed at Tyburn on 11 July 1584. His end was consistent with what we know of him before he became caught in the toils of Walsingham's statecraft. As in Norfolk's case, the Anglican, so in Throckmorton's case, the Catholic, we may be confident that they told the real truth as they knew it before they came into the presence of a court that would judge them mercifully only if they had told the truth. The Jesuit reported it as he heard it: 'they have put to death good Mr Throckmorton, although they had promised to spare his life. God has willed it so, for he made a very holy and edifying end. He would not ask pardon of the queen ... at the hour of his death, but said that she ought to ask pardon of God and the state for her heresy and misgovernment in allowing innocent men to be killed every day.'[69] Lord Hunsdon, the queen's cousin, corroborated this in his own way in a letter to Davison of July 23 1584. 'He died very stubbornly neither asking her Majesty's forgiveness nor would willingly have anybody to pray of them.'[70] It was customary for the condemned before death to appeal to the mob in attendance for their prayers. Evidently, Throckmorton was convinced they could not help him and that he had no need of their prayers.

68 John Paul, 'The queen's tragedy', unpublished ms, pp 199-201. See below. The ms was given to me about the time of Dr Paul's death. It is now in the BPA. 69 Hicks, pp 47-8 and n. 115. 70 Ibid., and n. 116. Hunsdon to Davison, 23.7.1584, SP 52 Scotland, 35, no. 58, from Berwick. The calenderer 'corrected' the 'original pray of them' to 'pray for them'.

5

William Parry's plot

In the early summer of 1583, William Allen and Robert Persons, leading Catholic exiles and exponents of 'forward' policies, went to stay with Thomas Morgan and Charles Paget in Paris. Although Paget and Morgan were known to be rivals and even enemies of the clerics, the meeting was an attempt to bring about some kind of unity in a common cause. Lord Paget, Charles' brother, and Sir Charles Arundell, also seen as ambiguous characters, came over from England about this time. Allen, the senior partner, and Persons did their best to convince Charles Paget and Morgan of their sincerity towards them. They shared all their 'affairs and secrets' with Charles, and he in turn with his noble brother and Morgan.[1] They also shared their confidences with William Parry who came to Paris towards the end of 1583.

Every effort was made later by authority to bury William Parry in oblivion and obloquy. So in an official account of his 'horrible treasons' he was described as 'a man of verie meane and base parentage, but of a most proud and insolent spirit, bearing himself alwaies far above the measure of his fortune'.[2] But there was more to say about his origins than this. According to a memorandum supplied by Parry to William Cecil and endorsed by Cecil, 'The family is known in fflyntshire by the name of Bethels. We beare for arms ... a chevron betweene three bores heades, sable, tusked or. For antiquity there is no fflintshire man can say more ... Next above my father was Ithell Vaughan, one of those that did homage to the prince at Chester in 29 Edward I. And so of these trifles sufficient.'[3] He was born at Northop, his father being 'a poore gentleman who was of no greater fortune then to be (as many gent of that country were) of King Henrye's garde, and appointed to attend upon queen Mary while she was

---

1 F. Edwards, *Robert Persons*, p. 87. For Charles Arundell and the Pagets, see Parry to Walsingham, Paris, 17.12.1583. He is sorry to hear of Elizabeth's anger at their departure from England; *Cal. SP Dom. Elizabeth, Additional 1580-1625*, no. 46. The English ambassador reported on their presence in Paris in his dispatch 2.12.1583; ibid., no. 44. According to Parry to Walsingham, 18.12.1583 (ibid., no. 47) from Paris, Arundell and Paget do not complain of her Majesty's government 'but that oppressed by their country they must either leave it or abide and suffer more disgrace than they were able to bear'. They speak admiringly of Walsingham, and 'they shun such company as might be offensive to her Majesty'. Parry had several meetings with them.   2 Holinshed, *Chronicle*, 1808 edition, iv, pp 561-8.   3 W. Parry's account of his origins, BL Lansdowne ms 43, No. 13, 3pp, a.l.s., from Fetter Lane, 2.8.1584, endd. by W. Cecil, 'D. Parry alias Bethell'. See also Dnb, 43.

princess.'⁴ The same source tells us his mother was a Conway of the house of Bodrythan, Flintshire. His father had thirty children, fourteen by his first wife and sixteen by William's mother. He died about 1566 at the age of 108. His land was very small, a lease of the parsonage of Northope 'wherewith he commonly mayntayned seven or eight at the schole'. William's father was named elsewhere as Harry ap David of Northop.

Parry went to London to seek his fortune. He began well by marrying a widow, daughter of Sir William Thomas, and found employment with William Herbert, earl of Pembroke. In 1570, he obtained a small appointment at court. Soon after this, he entered on a second marriage, again with a widow and even more substantially endowed, Catherine, formerly wife of Richard Heywood, an official of the king's bench. By his own account of 1584 William still had land in Flintshire worth 20 pounds a year 'of my own purchase'. His wife, the second presumably, had an estate worth 80 pounds a year 'whereof I have not handled penny for some years past'. When he wrote, 'my state at this time (by my ill husbandry and liberality) is no better than this'. But he had not lost out by treading the path of the prodigal. 'For unthriftiness I can truly say that dycing, carding, hawking or hunting did never cost me twenty pounds.' His fault, as he claimed, lay in overgenerosity. Besides his 'trouble and travaile', his main charge was two nephews one of whom was soon to be 'of the mynystery'. He maintained another in France, one in London and two at a county school in Flintshire. For ten years he has 'mayntained wholy ... a poore brother, his wife and a fifth sonne'. He also helped to support 'twelve poor folks in Northop'. So he needed Cecil's help.⁵

Although this information bears date 1584, something similar must have been addressed to Cecil before he got his foot on the first rung of the ladder. His plea was not rejected. But from a landowner of substance he was reduced to becoming a spy in government service abroad to escape from creditors. He visited Rome, Siena and other places. By 1577 he was back in England to ask Burghley for a post. But in 1579 Parry was forced once again to flee his creditors. He wrote his excuses to Burghley for departing, it seems, without formal permission. Whatever we might suppose from his record thus far, the shrewd Burghley concluded he was a usable kind of petty adventurer. He trusted him well enough to recommend him as a chaperon for Anthony Bacon, his wife's nephew in Paris. And Parry decided it would help his spying business to become a Catholic.⁶

4 Ibid.   5 W. P. mentions his wife in a letter to F. Walsingham from Paris, 6.12.1583. 'For myself I begin to despair of better fortune, my state, besides my wife's portion, which I will not impair, being brought to £20 in land. Fiat voluntas Dei, to whom I commit you'; *Cal. SP Dom. Eliz. Addenda*, no. 45 (p. 100).   6 See L. Hicks, S.J., 'The strange case of Dr William Parry: the career of an agent-provocateur', *Studies*, September 1948, pp 343-62, especially p. 344. There are a number of W. P.'s letters in *Cal. SP Domestic, Addenda 1580-1625*: to W. Cecil from Paris on 4.6.1580 (pp 6-7); 20.7.1580 (pp 9-10); 30.7.1580 (pp 10-11) with information received on 15. 7., 17. 7., 19.7, 20.7., 22.7., 25. 7., 27. 7., 29.7. Much on the alum trade will be found in Lawrence Stone, *Sir Horatio Palavicino* (Oxford 1956), pp 42, 46-52.

Returning to England, Parry became involved in an affray with Hugh Hare in the Temple in November 1580. This followed renewed friction with creditors. 'The evidence given against Parry upom his arraignment' on 2 November claimed that he entered the 'domum mansionalem' of Hugo Hare in the Inner Temple, Farringdon Ward, between 6 and 7 p.m. 'cum intentione ad felonice interficiendum et murderandum praefatum Hugonem Hare necnon ad felonie spoliandum etc.' (*sic*).[7] The 'evidence' produced in the same source relates that a Mr Towse 'went up presently before the hurte and found the nayle of the latche of the doore thrust out. He could not say that Parry did yt. To thentry and intente he sayth nothing. That Parry said he had no weapon. Neither entry nor intent proved. Mr Southerby deposeth that he was by at the speaches in the yard. He thought ... no harm had happened if Hare had not threatened to put Parry in a sacke. Mr John Hare deposeth as Mr Southerby. This maketh for the prisoner ... Hugh himself deposeth that Parry brake the dore. That he intended to kill. He urgeth the sending away of his man and bydding of Mr Vaughan in Welsh to be gone. Utterly denied by Mr Vaughan. He [Hare?] deposeth that Mr David Williams gave him warning that Parry would kill him. Mr Williams denyed yt upon his othe. It will be proved that the recorder spake with the jury. And that the forman did drinke.'

In spite of this unsatisfactory evidence as it has come down to us, it seems that Parry was found guilty on the murder charge. This might have cost him his life since he was sentenced to death but he received a pardon from the queen, no doubt at Burghley's prompting. The thought occurs to one that this bizarre episode was devised to put Parry in prison for a time as a spy, as happened earlier in the case of William Herle.[8] This could be the prelude to a good career in state service. Notable is the confidence placed in Parry at this stage by the queen as well as Cecil, both fair judges of character although Cecil may be taken as the more penetrating of the two. Doubtless she followed Cecil's advice. We will not be surprised to learn that the Hare episode cost Parry little. Sir John Conway was persuaded to act as surety for his debts, and in July 1582 Parry had permission to travel abroad for three years.[9] This was when he made the contact with Allen, Paget and Morgan indicated above. It gave him valuable information on the intentions of the exiles. In January 1584 he crossed to England and laid his findings at the feet of the queen's government.[10] Persons and Allen did not know or claim that this was done by the arrangement or connivance of their Catholic rivals although these could hardly have been averse.[11] However, in the summer of 1583,

7 BL Lansdowne ms, 43, No. 51.   8 F. Edwards, *The dangerous queen*, p. 215.   9 Dnb., 43; L. Hicks art. in *Studies*.   10 [Martin Aray], *The discoverie and confutation of a tragical fiction devysed ... by Edward Squyer ... by M. A. preest* ... [1599, no place given]. See Allison and Rogers, *Catalogue of Catholic Books ... 1558-1640*. Scolar Reprint 71 (1971), pp 4v, 5.   11 Hicks, p. 355. Parry in London to Morgan in Paris, 22.2.1583/4. *Cal. SP Dom. Addenda, 1580-1625*. 'Before my departure from Paris, I laboured by conference with a singular man on this side, to be fully informed what might be done with conscience in that case for the common good. I was learnedly overruled, and assured that it ought not to fall into the thought of a good Christian ... The service you know never passed your

Persons urged Lord Paget to 'overrule or temperate' his brother: but without avail. Nor did influence brought to bear by the exiled archbishop of Glasgow, Guise and 'other persons of quality' bring the rivals closer together.

Parry came to Paris in September 1582 to 'find credit with Allen and Persons',[12] but even after his declared conversion to Catholicism his reputation as a spy and agent-provocateur was already too well established to move Persons even to grant him an interview. He had better success with Allen, not to mention Paget and Morgan. Parry then decided to offer his services to Rome by way of the Paris nuncio, Girolamo Ragazzoni. His first letter was addressed to Como, papal secretary of state, from Paris on 10 December 1583. It went with a warning from Ragazzoni that Parry was not to be trusted. Parry mentioned his previous contacts with Campeggio, the Venice nuncio, and with William Crichton, S.J., then stationed at Lyons. He went on to beg 'for a full remission' – in writing – 'of all past offences and some testimonial by which I may know for the future that I am held and received as a member of the Holy Catholic Church, as I have ever wished to live and so hope to die, though I have somewhat vacillated in matters of state (which causes me intense grief)'.[13] He went on to urge Como not to listen to his detractors but to trust the favourable report of Glasgow, the bishop of Ross, Crichton, Paget and Morgan.

On 1 January 1584, Parry addressed the Holy Father direct. He had in mind 'an enterprise ... for the public good, the peace of the whole of Christendom, the restoration of England to its ancient obedience to the apostolic see, and the liberation from her long and weary sufferings of the queen of Scotland, the only true and undoubted heiress of the crown of England'. Parry had resolved to take upon himself 'this very dangerous enterprise without any promise in this world'. He only desired in return 'a plenary and absolute indulgence and remission' of all his sins, and to be considered 'an obedient and devout son of the Holy Catholic and Apostolic Roman Church' in which he ardently desired 'to live and die'.[14] Parry's letter did not indicate the nature of his

hand and mine, and may therefore, with more ease and less offence, be concealed and suppressed.' Morgan is exhorted at the end, 'read and burn !'   **12** F. Edwards, *R. Persons*, p. 96, n. 81.   **13** W. Parry's letter of reproof, 10.12.1583; Hicks, pp 351-2. John Leslie, bishop designate of Ross, was Mary, queen of Scots' ambassador to the court of Elizabeth. He was expelled from England in 1574 after being charged with complicity in the Ridolfi plot. See above and *The dangerous queen*, passim. For William Crichton's activities at this time see Edwards, *R. Persons*, passim with a short life on p. 63; T. M. McCoog, S.J., *The S. J. in Ireland, Scotland and England ...* , passim; T. M. McCoog, editor, *The reckoned expense: Edmund Campion and the early Jesuits* (Woodbridge 1996), passim, and art. by Francisco de Borja Medina, S.J., 'Intrigues of a Scottish Jesuit at the Spanish court; unpublished letters of William Crichton to Claudio Aquaviva, Madrid 1590-1592', pp 215-45.   **14** W. P. to the pope, 1.1. 1584; Hicks, p. 352. Cf. Edwards, *R. Persons*, p. 97, nn. 82 & 83. Hicks gives the full text of the letter. The date erroneously given in the letter printed on p. 352 as 10 December, is very clear in the official transcript preserved in the British Province S. J. archives as 1 January, from Nunziatura di Francia, 17, f. 286, original holograph with trace of small seal. At the foot of the same folio, 'Ego Annibal a Codreto, presbyter Societatis Jesu, testificor Guilielmum Parry, armigerum Britannum, hodie mihi esse confessum et communicasse in templo nostro. Primo Januarii 1584. Parisiis. Annibal a Codreto, manu propria.'

enterprise, but as he claimed later it was nothing less than the assassination of the English queen. Thomas Morgan, Parry's compatriot and 'infinite friend', introduced him to the nuncio in the first place, and it was his influence rather than Parry's presumably which moved the nuncio to send on the spy's letters to Rome. However, Ragazzoni still considered it necesary to warn Como that Parry was not trustworthy.[15] Morgan himself may have been the origin of the warning since he had intercepted two of Parry's letters himself, as he claimed. These letters also Ragazzoni sent to Rome.[16]

Parry visited Siena and Rome in the 1570s as an intelligencer for Burghley before returning to England in 1577. But it seems he never got as far as Rome after his further permission to travel came in July 1582.[17] According to his own story, outwardly reconciled to the Church in Paris after a lapse of twenty-two years, he moved to Lyons, a city on the route followed by English Catholics going to Rome. But there too he was 'suspected' so he moved to Milan where he got himself a bill of confessional health from the Inquisition before moving to Venice. In Venice he met the Jesuit, Benedict Palmio, who introduced him to the nuncio, Campeggio. The nuncio gave him a passport to go to Rome 'and to return safely into France'.[18] However, the careful Parry wanted something more secure. Without waiting for it to arrive, he moved back to Lyons. Was someone on his tail? A passport of the required kind reached Parry in Lyons, but after consulting 'some good fathers' there he was back in Paris by October 1583. It is likely that he received an order from Cecil to go immediately to Paris since, as he well knew, preparations were in hand for the 'empresa' or invasion of England, and a reliable and intelligent witness of events was needed near the planning centre.

With Cecil's permission, Parry returned to England in January 1584. Winter was not the time for war and the first phase of the 'empresa' had ended in stalemate.[19] Parry assured him that he had important matter to reveal. He brought with him a copy of his letter to Rome to impress and convince the privy council of his mission. On the way he met William Watts, a secular priest, at Rouen who managed to get from him an admission that he was going to England 'to oppose the Jesuits'.[20] He claimed that Paget and Morgan had encouraged him in this. It was quite likely. In an audience with the queen and Burghley, Parry claimed that he had been sent with the approval of the pope and the friends of the Scottish queen, including the Jesuits, to kill Elizabeth and put Mary on her throne.

15 Hicks, p. 353. For the correspondence of Girolamo Ragazzoni, bishop of Bergamo, with Rome see *Acta Nunziaturae Gallicae, Correspondence* ... (Rome/Paris 1962), ed. Pierre Blet, S. J. References to Parry, including Ragazzoni's warnings of his unreliability, on pp 26-30, 169-70, 175-6, 381-2, 383-5, 397-8. 'Non ho voluto mancare di mandar l'alligata lettera per S. Bne, da la quale però credo che sia ben conosciuto chi la scrive; qui per certo non se n'ha molto buona opinione' (p. 176). Cf. pp 169-70, and p. 176, n. 3.   16 Edwards, *R. Persons*, p. 97.   17 Hicks, p. 354; *State trials*, 1730 edition, i, p. 122, col. 2. 18 *State trials*, ibid., col. 1. From the confession of 13.2.1584/5. Other details of his life at this point are also from this source.   19 See Edwards, *R. Persons*, chapters 6 & 7.   20 *State trials*, i, p. 122, col. 1. For an account of the complex quarrel between Charles Arundel, Charles Paget, Edward de Vere, 17th earl of Oxford and others, which involved Oxford in charges of sodomy, see B. M. Ward, *The seventeenth earl of Oxford* (London 1928), passim. William Plumer Fowler, LL.B., printed Oxford's

Como, meanwhile, sent an answer to Parry's letter. The letter was only in general terms approving what had been an equally general proposition by Parry.[21] Como's reply, which was sent on to Parry, arrived in March 1584. Parry showed it to the queen.[22] It simply commended, on behalf of the pope, Parry's 'good disposition and resolution' with encouragement to persevere in whatever it was. He was granted the 'blessing, plenary indulgence and remission of all [his] sins' which he had asked for. The pope also promised to acknowledge his 'deservings in the best manner that he [could]; and that so much the more in that [Parry used] the greater modesty in not pretending to anything.'[23] The letter on Italian paper with an Italian watermark seems altogether genuine. But Parry now supplied lurid details which Burghley and the queen made no difficulty in believing if only because his claims fitted in with policy. On 8 June, Cecil sent a letter to the archbishop of Canterbury urging him to stir up his preachers to a proper hatred of Rome.[24]

Parry expected proper recognition for his efforts, and told Burghley so in a somewhat jaunty letter addressed to him in May 1584. If any doubts still remained as to his true religious affiliation, 'the particular inclosed favourably delyvered by your lordship or Mr Secretary to the quene's Ma: would undoubtedly remove all doubtful conceipts of me in religion and duety. Yt were a small matter for the quene to avow my service with the credite of an hospitall.' The hospital in question was St Catherine's in East London which would 'serve [his] turne. I cannot thinke it possible for Mr Roukeby or any of his coat to adventure more than I have done in her service. I would to Christ her Ma: would commaunde any further possible tryall of me.' Walsingham had told Parry he thought the queen would give him a pension. Parry thought 'St Catherine's is in truth no other upon the reconnyng ... Remember me my dearest lord, and thinke yt not ynough for a man of my fortune to live by meate and drinke. Justice yt selfe willeth yt should be credit and reward.'[25] These were dangerous words to address to the most powerful man in England. Very different in style were Parry's approaches now from what they had been in the apprentice years up to 1580. Cecil could scarcely smile at the thought that a mere suppliant like Parry made them both equals. Parry did not get as much favour by appointment or office as he hoped for but he was not badly treated. Her Majesty made much of him and granted him several audiences and a liberal pension. He was also returned to parliament as the member for Queenborough, Kent, in November 1584. Indeed, his stock seemed to stand so high that that Sir Edward

letters for 1563 to 1585 and 1590 to 1603 in *Shakespeare revealed in Oxford's letters* (Portsmouth, New Hampshire, 1986). Professor Alan H. Nelson of Berkeley produced for private circulation 'Letters and papers of Edward de Vere ... 1565-1604' (Berkeley 1995) as a prelude to a larger work, 'My monstrous adversary: an Elizabethan court libel'. De Vere's poems were published with a commentary by Stephen W. May in *The poems of Edward de Vere ... and of Robert Devereux, second earl of Essex, Studies in Philology*, 77, No. 5, 1980. De Vere is a subject awaiting fuller study and recognition.   **21** Como's letter of 30.1.1584/5; printed in Hicks, p. 353. Italian original, BL Lansdowne ms 96, no. 13.   **22** Edwards, *R. Persons*, p. 97.   **23** Hicks, p. 353.   **24** BL Lansdowne ms, 43, No. 9. Contemporary copy.   **25** Ibid., No. 7, a.l.s.

Hoby, Burghley's nephew, empowered him to solicit his business at court, asking his uncle to listen to him as he would to himself.[26] It was all a considerable advancement for a man who only a few years before had apparently seen the noose dangling before his eyes. Parry by now clearly saw himself on the way to becoming a power in the land. Perhaps after all Cecil could afford to smile – grimly.

Certainly by the end of 1584, it was due as much to Parry as any that England was in the grip of plotmania. There was no lack of voices to take up the hue and cry. It cannot be said that the general apprehension was absurd. The Old Testament examples of Judith and Holofernes and Jael and Sisara were ethical foundation enough for the morality of assassination. Duplessis Mornay had defended it for the Huguenots in his *Vindiciae contra tyrannos*. Elizabeth apparently directed her secretaries Walsingham and Davison to write to Paulet, the Scottish queen's jailer, to organise her murder.[27] Sir Amyas Paulet had no love for his charge but whatever else moved him, he must have been aware of the likely consequences for the 'fall-guy' who dared to carry it out. Pope Gregory XIII and Como had the will but not the availabilty of a suitable instrument to put it into execution.[28] It is impossible to believe they thought they had found the means to hand in Parry. He had been recognised for years as a government spy and nuncios had warned against him. The guarded language of the Roman letters is proof enough of their doubt. Inevitably, Persons' name was linked with Parry's plot but neither he nor any other Jesuit was involved in this theoretical solution of a real problem.[29] Parry by this time was too well known everywhere as one of Cecil's agents to be trusted by anyone even remotely acquainted with his background.

26 Hicks, p. 354.   27. See Sir N. Harris Nicholson, *Life of William Davison* (London 1823), pp 86, 273-6.   28 Edwards, *R. Persons*, p. 85. Pierre Blet was undoubtedly correct in thinking that Gregory XIII and Como were unconvinced by Parry and were only playing him along for information.   29 For R. P. and assassination, ibid. John Bossy in 'The heart of Robert Persons', in *The reckoned expense*, p. 155, refers to his own 'discovery that, during his major period of political activity, Persons advocated or, shall we say, did rather more than condone the assassination of Queen Elizabeth as a preliminary to the enterprise of England'. This conclusion on R. P.'s attitude is not justified by what Bossy offers as evidence. He discusses an obscure Latin passage from a reply of the Jesuit general, Aquaviva, dated 5 June 1583, to a letter from Persons no longer extant (pp 148-9, and n. 25). Bossy admits it is impossible to define exactly some obstacle arising in connection with the 'enterprise', the invasion of England, from the Latin. He is doubtless correct in supposing it was connected with this. A cardinal unnamed was also involved. Bossy suggests this was Tolomeo Galli, the Cardinal of Como. Galli was favourable, like Gregory XIII, to the idea of assassinating Elizabeth as a preliminary to invasion. 'If Gallio was the cardinal in question, we can surmise what Persons' dubious proposal was' writes Bossy (p. 149). Nothing less than the queen's assassination. He continues on the strength of his surmise, 'I am sorry to say I think there can be no reasonable doubt that ... what Persons was putting to Aquaviva, and Aquaviva stiffly turn[ed] down, was [Gilbert] Gifford's offer to assassinate Elizabeth' (p. 150). Unashamedly, Bossy refers to 'the discovery that, during his major period of poitical activity, Persons advocated or, shall we say, did rather more than condone the assassination of Queen Elizabeth as a preliminary to the enterprise of England' (p. 155). He sees Persons possessed by a spirit of revenge. By the end of the essay, a possibility has become 'the distasteful fact' (p. 158). Bossy admits, 'these may be untoward suggestions; but suggestions seem to be needed' (p. 157). Untoward

On the subject of papal reaction to the assassination idea, one must add in paren-
thesis to the mystery of Parry's sojourn abroad from July 1582 a further obscure dimension. On 2 May 1583 Giovanni Battista Castelli, papal nuncio in Paris before Ragazzoni,
reported to Como a meeting with the dukes of Guise and Maine who assured him that
a member of Elizabeth's entourage was ready to undertake her assassination. His
declared motive was anger at the death of a relative who had been killed in the queen's
persecution. This was very probably but not quite certainly George Gifford. He had
already approached the Scottish queen who, consistently, would have nothing to do
with it. Mary, knowing her vulnerable position, was always careful to play the game correctly *vis à vis* the rival queen. Paris was amenable enough to the point of placing a substantial sum with the archbishop of Glasgow to be paid when the deed was done.
Castelli told Guise that he was reluctant to pass on the offer to the pope, not out of consideration for Elizabeth but because he felt it was 'not appropriate that [Christ's] vicar
should bring it about' – that is, her death – 'by such means'. But Guise insisted that this
would be not only the easiest but also the cheapest way of solving the problem. 'Would
to God that with such a small sum' – 100,000 crowns – 'a kingdom so important could
be won.' The Holy Father agreed completely with Guise, it seems, as to the legitimacy
of a solution which would rid the world at one blow of a leading heretic and irreform-
able tyrant. Castelli received the papal approval by way of Como in a letter of 23 May
1583. The pope would contribute 20,000 crowns towards the enterprise. 'God grant',
sighed Como, 'that this be not another of those promises that are never kept'.[30]
    One is tempted to see in this an earlier effort on Parry's part, preceding the offer
made later through Ragazzoni. But there was no hesitation apparently on the part of
top Catholic authorities in responding, and without concealment of its purpose, to this
first overture. Parry nowhere mentioned it. Apart from George Gifford, this might
have been yet another exile with a score to settle with the queen – her entourage was
not small – or yet another exile with the same idea in mind as Parry for promoting his

suggestions are never needed. The question of assassination was controverted among Protestants and
Catholics. Gregory XIII approved; his successors did not. Persons spoke for himself in *A temperate
wardword to ... Sir Francis Hastinges ... who indevoreth to slaunder the whole Catholique cause and all
Professors thereof ...* (Antwerp 1599). 'He was never consenting, witting, inducing, yielding, nor privy
to any such personal attempt against her Majesty in his life.' He was well aware that 'English
Catholics themselves desired not to be delivered from their miseries by any such attempt' (Scolar
reprint, 1970, pp 66-72). The remote justification for assassination is, of course, founded in the Old
Testament: Judith and Holofernes and others.   **30** BL Lansdowne ms 43, No. 51. See Robert
Toupin, ed., *Correspondance du Nonce ... Giovanni Battista Castelli* (1581-3), (Rome and Paris 1967).
Four letters from Castelli to Como bear date 2.5.1583 on pp 539-45. A priest of the VEC, Rome, 26
years old, has been martyred at York for rejecting the royal supremacy (541). The dukes of Guise and
Maine have given the nuncio a plan for assassinating Elizabeth. A Catholic of her entourage will do it
for 100,000 francs. Guise will put up 50,000 and the rest will be deposited with the archbishop of
Glasgow. If it succeeds, Guise will go at once to England. Castelli told Guise he would not mention
this to the pope, only the projected invasion plan (pp 544-5). Como replied to C. on 23.5.1583
(Nunziatura di Francia, 16, ff. 305-6, minutes in cipher), pp 552-3.

career. It is unlikely that Walsingham, whose eyes and ears were everywhere, would have been unaware of such an attempt at least in general terms. We have considered another attempt on Elizabeth's life reported at this time. John Somerville, a Warwickshire papist, swore to shoot Elizabeth as 'a serpent and a viper'. He made no secret of his intention so that his arrest, transfer to the Tower and execution followed with mathematical precision and inevitability.[31] His case was unusually simple; the effort of an acknowledged lunatic.

We return to Parry at the point when fortune seemed to promise much. Hope soon turned to disillusion. He had become involved with an English spy, Edward Neville, who was working for Walsingham in Rouen at least until November 1583.[32] According to Martin Aray, 'there was sent over unto Roan[Rouen]', at a date not clearly specified, 'Maister Nevill to exercise the same office of spierie, which Maister Parry had donne before in Italy, and waxing also weary of his occupation, for that rewardes came out of England slowly, he made great meanes in like manner to speak with Father Persons, who by chaunce lay for a time in that towne, but secretly, and in the end obtaining the same, and proposing his miserie and affliction of minde, he received the same answere and counsel that Doctor Parry had donne before: to wit that the best way of remedie was to leave that trade of life, and to returne to a vertuous and and peaceable Catholique course, and to have patience if for a time he were not trusted by Catholiques, being known to have bin employed against them, and that as his credit had been erazed by woorkes, so must his reputation be restored by deeds also, and by time. Whereto Maister Nevil answered that he could not live without credit, and rather then he would live so or see men crow over him, he would adventure far, and so they parted; and Maister Nevil returned to England, and there meeting with Doctor Parry, who was now grown discontented again for missing of divers suites (but especially of the headship of St Catherins, which he pretended, as I have been informed) they two fell into new discourses about that which in my opinion neither of them ever ment indeed, I meane the murdering of her Maiestie; but the one preventing [forestalling] the other in accusation, it was the doctor's evil luck to be hanged, who yet tooke himself for the more conning man.'[33]

It is likely that Parry met Neville in Rouen about the same time that he met the priest William Watts whom we encountered earlier. Neville, like Parry, was a cut above the average worker in the muddy field of espionage. He claimed to be the heir to his grand uncle, the fourth and last Lord Latimer. His daughter Dorothy married Cecil's eldest son Thomas who succeeded to the estates. It is likely that Parry and Neville, accomplices or colleagues in the spying business, would also have regarded one a

31 J. B. Black, *The reign of Elizabeth*, 2nd ed. (Oxford 1959), pp 376-7. Biographical details from Dnb, vol. xliii. Bossy convincingly identifies the would-be assassin of 1583 as George Gifford. See *The reckoned expense*, p. 150 and n. 27.   32 Hicks, p. 362 and n. 77.   33 [Martin Aray], *The discoverie and confutation of a tragical fiction devysed by Edward Squyer ... by M. A. preest ...* [1599, no place given]. See Allison and Rogers, *Catalogue of Catholic books ... 1558-1640*, Scolar Reprint 71 (1971) pp 4v-5.

nother instinctively as career rivals. Burghley no doubt came to regard Neville, with his succession interest, as an encroacher on the rights of his own family. It is unlikely that Burghley would have taken Parry into his confidence in such a matter, but Parry would have been shrewd enough to sense that any move to discredit Neville could only help him to more of his patron's favour. And Burghley's genius would have seen how both spies, who were becoming increasingly presumptuous, could be set on one another to ensure their mutual destruction. One could presume that Burghley put Parry on to watching his fellow-spy and rival. Or perhaps he needed no prompt.

At all events, Parry came to denounce Neville to the queen as a disaffected person. Taking advantage of a claim of kinship, he proceeded to embroil him in treason. In the summer of 1584, Parry, playing agent-provocateur, claimed that he tried to convince Neville that the only way to improve his fortunes was to kill the queen. Even after several attempts at persuasion, Neville was not forthcoming.[34] It was a dangerous game that Parry was playing and in the end the petard intended to destroy Neville blew up in his own face.

Neville's side of the affair was set out in a signed 'declaration' of 9 and 10 February 1585.[35] According to this, Parry visited Neville in his lodging at Whitefriars in the summer of 1583. He had just been denied the mastership of St Catherine's, which was ostensibly sufficient pretext for stirring Neville to treason. Parry persuaded him to visit him in Fetter Lane next day, which he did, finding him in bed. Parry sent out 'his men' so that they were alone – no witnesses! Parry took up the theme of rebellion for the cause of religion, the Scottish queen's title, and justice in general; all to be helped by invasion by foreign forces and the taking of Queenborough castle. Neville kept silence. Parry went on to suggest assassinating Elizabeth. He alleged Allen's book as authority for it, which Neville had not read. Neville, in any case, did not recognise that authority. Parry claimed Rome's approval and that he had a dispensation for it. Neville replied, as he said, 'I shall thinke it very strange when I shall see one to hold that for meritorious which another holdeth for damnable.' Parry asked Neville to think it over. The next day, 'if one man be in the towne, I will not fail to show you the thing itself; and if he be not, he will be within these five or six days.' Neville must have wondered why Parry did not hold the claimed 'dispensation' himself.[36]

Neville was invited to come to 'Chanon Row; then we will take the sacrament to be true to each other and then I will discover unto you both the party and the thing itself.' Neville 'praied Parry to thinke better upon it, as a matter of great charge both of soule and bodie.' Parry could only hope that Neville would see it all as he did so that they could 'do God great service'. Eight or ten days later, Parry visited Neville in Heron's Rents in Holborn 'as he ofen used'. While walking in the fields, Parry renewed his determination to kill the queen and was surprised at Neville's scrupulosity since she

34 Hicks, p. 355.   **35** 'Edward Neville his declaration', 9, 10.2.1584/5; SP12, 176, ff. 47–8. Printed Holinshed, *Chronicle*, iv, 1808 ed. n, pp 561–88, especially pp 564–5. Hicks gives 8.2. as the date of Neville's 'declaration'.   **36** Ibid., p. 564.

had sought his own 'ruin and overthrow'. Neville admitted his case was hard but to redress it so could only redound on himself.[37]

If he told the truth about Parry's approaches, Neville's suspicions must have been roused to incredulity whether with regard to his sincerity or his sanity by his further desperate words. It must have occurred to him that Parry was simply trying to draw him into the mire. He assured Neville that killing Elizabeth would be easy. She often walked in her garden with a small train. A barge would be ready to carry them speedily down the river and overseas when the deed were done. But 'we shall never be followed so far. And as for mine escaping, those that shall be with her, will be so busy about her, as I shall find opportunity enough to escape if you be there ready with the barge to receive me ... If you are still afraid, let us wait till she comes to St James. Meanwhile we can provide ourselves with men and horses fit for the purpose. May ech of us keepe eight or ten men without suspicion.' Parry boasted, 'I shall find good fellowes that will follow me without suspecting mine intent.' Each would have 'his case of dags' so that if there were a hundred there to defend her 'they were not able to save her, you coming on one side and I on the other, and discharging our dags upon her, it were unhappie if we should both miss her. But if our dags fail, I shall bestir me well with a sword yet she escape me.' Neville replied, 'Give over this odious enterprise and trouble me no more with the hearing of that which in my heart I loth so much.'[38]

Determined not to give up, Parry tackled Neville yet again. Elizabeth was now in residence at St James. Neville was 'the onelie man of England like to performe it, in respect of my value as he termed it'. Neville now changed tactic, pretending 'to be more willing' in order to get Parry to repeat his project before another witness. This would have provided the two witnesses he took to be necessary and sufficient – indeed, one more than necessary – to secure a conviction for treason in a court. The two spies are now wrestling to get the other over the hip. Parry was too wily to be caught easily. His last attempt to bring over Neville was on Saturday 6 February between 5 and 6 p.m. when Parry visited him in his chamber to talk with him 'apart'. So 'we drew ourselves to a window' where none could oversee or over-hear. Neville reported the opinion of 'a learned man whom I met by chance in the fields' who assured him killing the queen would be 'most villainous and damnable'. Parry was scornful, but added, 'I hope you told him not that I had aniething from Rome. "Yes, in truth", said I. Parry replied, "I would you had not named me, nor spoken of aniething I had from Rome".' He then urged Neville to go overseas soon, promising him 'safe passage into Wales and from thence into Britaine [Brittany], whereat we ended'. At this point Neville resolved to confess all.[39]

On 8 February, 1585, Neville laid a formal information against Parry. The official account claims that Elizabeth instructed Walsingham as a trusted friend of Parry to call him to his house to inform him that the queen knew of 'somewhat intended against her own person' which he must know about. Parry must reveal his knowledge,

37 Ibid., p. 565.   38 Ibid.   39 Ibid. Neville added his signature at the end.

and whether he 'himself had let fall any speech unto any person (though with an intent only to discover his disposition) that might draw him into suspicion as though he himself had any such wicked intent.'[40] It is significant that Elizabeth showed her awareness of Parry as an agent provocateur, and intended to give him every chance of clearing himself. As it was reported, Parry denied that there had been any such speech. But he later declared – not under pressure, it was said – that he had discussed with Neville a proposition included in William Allen's *A true sincere and modest defence of English Catholics* of 1584 claiming that it was lawful to kill a prince for the furtherance of the faith.[41] In fact Allen's book stated no such thing.

The day after his interview with Walsingham, Parry was confronted with Neville. The best Parry could do was to say that it was only Neville's word against his. A few days later, on 11 February Parry was examined in the Tower by Hunsdon, Christopher Hatton and Walsingham who induced him to make a full confession. He 'did voluntarily and without any constraint, by word of mouth make confession of his said treason, and after set it down in writing all with his owne hand in his lodgings in the Tower, and sent it to the court the 13th of the same, by the lieutenant of the Tower.' It was signed by Parry as of the 11th. The confession, which was used in the trial and there reported, contained enough to convict him of treason. A trial was now inevitable.[42]

Before we come to the trial, another incident must be considered which helps to suggest that Parry was playing a game which tried to be oversubtle and which put too much reliance on a credit with Burghley and Elizabeth which was not, and could not be, inexhaustible. On Thursday 17 December 1584, Parry rose in parliament to protest vigorously, at its third reading, against a bill proposing yet further penal measures against the Catholics. He was committed to the serjeant for his pains and confined in an outer room. When he was brought back to the house he was made to kneel. Instead of retracting or apologising, he repeated his objections and said he would justify them not to the house but to the queen herself. He was remanded in custody. Significantly, the queen declared to the house the day after by Sir Christopher Hatton, the vice-chamberlain, that while she approved of the reaction of the house, Parry by her appointment, and going some way to satisfy her, had revealed his reasons to some of the lords in council. Presumably Burghley was included. The house should therefore be content with a humble acknowledgement of his fault. This was given. Parry on his knees confessing his fault, excused himself for his rashness as a new member unacquainted with the proper way to behave in the house. The apology was accepted and the miscreant resumed his seat. 'The reasons for his protest were never made public.'[43] It seems likely that Parry was trying to vindicate publicly the sincerity of his attachment to the Catholics so that after whatever lay ahead he would be able to return to his spying practices as a man with a good record with the enemy.

It is not possible to take Parry's conversion to Catholicism seriously. Typical of many of his generation, as a consequence of all the changes and U-turns in religion,

40 Hicks, p. 355 and n. 84.   41 Ibid., pp 354-5.   42 Holinshed, op. cit., p. 565.   43 Hicks, pp 354-5.

he was left with no settled convictions. This was probably equally true of the members of Elizabeth's government. For the purposes of his spying work Parry was quite prepared to pose as a Catholic – or anything else had it been demanded. He wrote earlier in terms that were poliically and religiously correct from Burghley's viewpoint. His most important espionage for Burghley could be said to have begun in April 1580 when he wrote to him from Paris to allay the adverse effect that his 'departure and demeanour here' had caused at home. He expressed his readiness to return whenever the lord treasurer commanded it. Meanwhile, he was always ready to serve.[44] Evidently he was not discouraged since he wrote rather more confidently to Burghley on 1 May 1580. 'I do finde my credite and favour to be such with the best of the English and Scottish nations in Rome and Paris (by the hope conceaved of my redynes and abylyty to serve theym) that I doubt not within few monethes to be well able to discover the deepest practices if the same may be nourished with her Ma: resonable charge to be bestowed as occasion shall serve in trifling giftes (rather of pleasure than price) and frendly enterteynement, the true maner whereof shall alwayes appeare to your lordship.'[45]

At this stage Parry was properly cautious. He was careful to insist in this letter of 1 May that he would make no overtures until he had Burghley's full approval. 'Good my Lord, begynne to look favorably upon me and I will ende in doying you service ... but so as my service may be secretted from every creature (except her Ma: and your Lordship).' Parry is formally polite but already avoids subservience. 'As I said before, so I say agayne; if I be lesse ceremoniouse then I should be in writing unto you, I trust you will pardon me, who had rather serve you in dedes than please you in wordes.'[46] His services on the continent were evidenced in letters to Cecil from Paris between June and July 1580. On 4 June 1580 he reported the arrival in Rheims of Thomas Goldwell, bishop of St Asaph, and his party, which included Edmund Campion and Robert Persons, on the way to England. He also mentioned Strong, an Irish bishop, and Welsh, a priest. Letters to Parry from Rome of 16 May claimed that the Catholics were 'greatly comforted' at the thought that Elizabeth was writing to Rome 'as she did lately to Cardinal Sforza and Cardinal Como, and promised monsieur to write to the pope in favour of Palavicino'. This is an interesting reminder that the Elizabethan government needed to trade with the enemy to make sure of a supply of alum, the best available, for the English textile trade. 'The cardinals have command to satisfy her for the manner and cause of Palavicino's imprisonment.' If 'he is discharged, it is meant he shall be forthcoming upon sureties, until the pope and his farmers for the alum are satisfied in their demands'.[48]

On 20 July Parry reported on Copley, heir to a barony, another religious exile now anxious to come home. He is sorry the queen dislikes him, but he is ready to serve her

44 Parry to W. Cecil, Paris, 7. 4.1580. a.l.s.; BL, Lansdowne ms 31, no. 1.   45 S. to s., Paris, 1.5.1580; ibid., No. 3, a.l.s.   46 Ibid.   47 S. to s., Paris, 4.6.1580; Dom. Eliz. Add., 27, no. 17; Hicks, p. 359, n. 17.   48 Ibid. For the Rome/England alum trade, see L. Stone, *Sir Horatio Palavicino*, above, passim.

and will obey her whether she wants him to leave foreign service altogether or to go to some other Catholic country either for service or retirement. He is well regarded by Parma.[49] On 30 July, Parry urged Cecil to write 'by ordinary means', since letters sent by other ways were more closely watched and subject to interception which could turn to his danger. He preferred to deal only with the queen or Cecil. This letter of the 30th contained a number of items of information, each dated, until the end of the month of July. Cardinal Sforza 'secretly discovered his great desire to please her Majesty, and will, if he be well followed, do the same grateful service.' So while the pope was willing to encompass her assassination, at least one cardinal was prepared to be her secret agent. Meanwhile, a slanderous book had been 'secretly printed' in Paris: the bishop of Ross' *De titulo et jure Mariae Reginae Scotorum* was sold openly since he went to Rouen. Allen claimed to have no interest in matters of state, only in the seminaries, but his influence in Rome was minimal. The earl of Westmorland was another exile ready to make his 'humble submission with repentance of his error'. Parry thought this might be accepted if it were not 'offensive to her Majesty, nor contrary to the policy of the times'.[50] There is nothing in all this to suggest that Parry was other than the honest spy he seemed.

Three years later, Parry does not conceal his triumphalism. A letter to Burghley from Lyons of 10 May 1583, after telling him that he had been obliged to leave Venice where otherwise he had lived contentedly, reassures him: 'I have shaken the foundation of the English seminary in Rheymes and utterly overthrowne the credite of the English pensioners in Rome ... My instruments were such as pass for greate, honourable and grave. The course was extraordynarye and straunge, resonably well devised, soundly followed and substantially executed without the assistance of any one of the English nation.'[51] He does not conceal the fact that his known acquaintance with Elizabeth's ministers has not helped. 'Your honourable favour and Mr Secretary hath overthrown my credite with our countrymen on this side.' Inevitably came the spy's

49 S. to s. Paris, 20.7.1580, original, 3pp ; *Cal. SP Dom. Eliz. I/James I, Addenda 1580-1625*, pp 9-10. Parry writes in jaunty style recommending once again a character whom Cecil must have found as irritateing as his sponsor. Copley has a title to a barony. He is glad of Cecil's 'friendly mind' towards him(Parry's idea?) but sorry Elizabeth does not accept his professions of loyalty. He is ready 'to withdraw from foreign service, or confine himself to any Catholic state either for her public service or to pass a retired life.' Parry writes, 'I find him sufficient for the one as the other.' Elizabeth should be clement since 'it would be a pity by rejecting his suit to drive him to despair of returning, and strange to see such a man lack whose credit on this side for anything needs no repair'. He is well in with the prince of Parma who has given him twice the sum asked for to go to Spain in connection with his eldest son's illness and funeral expenses. 'If these or any other considerations may move you to procure his happy return, her Majesty will never repent her grace, nor you your pains and travail.' Cecil's reaction may be imagined.   **50** S. to s., Paris, 30.7.1580, a.l.s., Lansdowne ms 31, no. 9.   **51** BL, Lansdowne ms 39, No. 21. Parry to W. Cecil from Lyons, 10.5.1583, a.l.s. Two foolscap pages. A triangular section about 3½" by the width of the leaf has been cut off from the bottom of the second leaf. This indicates confidential matter cut off and presumably destroyed. Examples of this may be found in SP Dom. Eliz., vol. 83, f. 10 and vol. 139, no. 17. See F. Edwards, *The marvellous chance*, p. 19, n. 1.

plea for more money: ' ... if I were well warranted and allowed, I would either prevent and discover all Romayne and Spanish practices against our state, or lose my life in testimony of my loyalty to the queen's Ma: and duety to my honourable friends that have protected me.' One cannot assume without more ado that someone prepared to undermine the reputation of the exiles and the existence of the seminaries abroad was necessarily anti-Catholic. The Pagets and Morgan seem to have had this mind. The priest John Cecil and his associates were prepared to help the English government with their destruction some years later.[52]

Parry made continued efforts for eminent exiles weary of exile, not least the reconciliation and return of the earl of Westmoreland who fled abroad at the time of the northen rising. On 30 July 1580 Parry wrote from Paris asking Burghley to intercede with the queen for him: 'his life and liberty alone reserved, he is redy (with greatest repentance of his error and fault comytted in his youth) to fall at her Ma: fote.'[53] But Parry was already prepared to add his own comment on policy; which Burghley would not have found amusing unless as an example of humour decidedly wry. 'I know not whether the reclayming of desperate men do agree with our state and pollicy. And yet it is dayly sene that the kinges Christian and Catholicke do yt. Yea sometimes with advancement. The case is so greate that I dare not adventure to speke much in yt. And therefore do wholy referre it to your lordship's wisdome and grave consideration. Yf the motion be seasonable (as in trueth I do thinke it to be) and the service not offensive to her Ma:, it may be delivered unto my lord embassador's hande, who (as the earle tould me) by one Calvi, an Italian, did offerre to deale in yt, and within fewe dayes to dispatch yt.'[54] Parry claimed that the earl had spoken to him often about it, 'but Her Ma: plesure or your Lordship's opinion (as in everything) shalbe my rule in this'.

In September 1580, Parry presumed to air the grievances of another late servant of the English crown in a letter written to Burghley in London. Guido Cavalcanti, a name occurring often enough in English records, sent his commendations and a good excuse for absence since 'his goute and other griefes greatly increasing he was advised to remove to some warmer clymate ... He did mistrust that he hath had somme hynderers to his credite with her Ma: and did not stick to name whome he suspected. He did think his pension inferior to his desert and service to this crowne so many yeares, having spent in journeys to and fro much more than would have brought such a living ... He and his name have lyved under and served this state above eighty yeares; so ... would he die a faithfull servant to her Ma:.'[55] The lord treasurer, the object of Parry's own declared love and esteem, must certainly have smiled grimly to learn that 'both Catholique and Protestant on this side and that side have in this later tyme (for the best and greatest part) spoken much honour and good [of you]. Truly my lord yt cannot be that you do know in what estimation you live.'[56]

---

52 Ibid. See also Edwards, *R. Persons*, especially under John Cecil.   **53** S. to s., Paris, 30.7.1580, a.l.s.; BL Lansdowne ms 31, no. 9.   **54** Ibid.   **55** S. to s., London, 16.9.1580, a.l.s.; ibid., no. 13.   **56** Parry to W. Cecil, n. d., a. l. not signed, endd. on f. 69v. 'Mr Parry from Venice'; BL Lansdowne ms

But the passage of time made Parry less careful in disguising a critical attitude towards the system he professed to serve. He wrote to Burghley from Venice in March 1582 giving advice which could not have been welcome. 'The new booke printed at Rome, dedicated to the Cardinall S. Sixti, and intituled de persecutione Anglicana hath raised a barbarouse opinion of cruelty. I could wish that in those cases it might please her Ma: to pardon the dismembring and quartering.'[57] Again he was ready to put in a word for the dubious stray sheep anxious to return to the fold. 'Sir Richard Shelley is very desirouse to returne and promiseth very greate services if he be not disquieted for his conscience.'

Parry was aware that for the most part his reports and news items now were not of any great significance. He was keeping himself in reserve 'for such special service as I shall thinke fitte for the Qu:Ma: and gratefull to your lordship and Mr S[ecretary]'.[58] This, of course, was to be the plot which gained for him lasting notoriety and a traitor's death. In this same letter of 10 March from Venice, Parry made it clear he was aware of the perilous game he was playing and how much depended on the continuing trust placed in him by the queen and Burghley. 'I have presumed that your lordship hath ever estemed me for a true man to my prince and countrey so much whatsoever do come to your eares.' This sentence was underlined by Parry himself. 'I besech you to promise for me and I will not faile to performe yt God willing.'[59] There were further underlinings here to emphasize salient points. But Parry, with ample justice if small political wisdom, was still prepared to pass on criticism of English policy and politicians. 'I pray you tell Mr Sec. that here is so greate speech of his persecution and cruelty that your lordship (sometyme in the same predicament) is almost forgotten. My lords of Huntingdon and Leycester and Mr Sec. are the men most wondered at.'[60]

Parry had no doubt as to the significance of his service and career. Writing to Burghley from Venice on 28 January, 1583, he began by renewing his plea for 'the good knight' – presumably Sir Richard Shelley – who wanted to come home 'so as he might be warranted by passeport to comme and goe saulfely'. He claimed that 'his intent is (as yt hath bene alwayes) honorable and duetyfull to his prince and country'.[61] So Parry put his shoulder to the wheel of a man who had matters 'which he may not write or commyt to any man', and who no doubt hoped by this bait to get the required permission to return. Meanwhile Parry offered airy excuse for his own remissness in writing. 'I have purposely forborne to be too busy in wryting. And being greately looked upon, yt doth greately import me to looke how and what I write. I find yt a matter very unpleasant to be troubled or tyed to thadvertisement of ordynary occurrents.' No longer is he purveying the small but useful items of information typical of his earlier service. 'And yet if anything happen that I shall thinke of importance, I will not fayle to advertise your lordship.' The writer could use a subsidy. 'This place is very plentifull of good and badde but the best is hardly had without charge; which I coulde thinke

37, no. 32 (ff. 68r-9v.).   57 S. to s., Venice, 10.3.1582, a.l.s., ibid., No. 33.   58 Ibid.   59 Ibid.   60 Ibid.   61 S. to s., Venice, 28.1.1583, a.l.s.; BL Lansdowne ms 44, No. 24 (ff. 55r-6v.).

well bestowed to looke into men's proceedinges in this towne.'[62] Clearly, by this time
Parry sees himself as exchanging confidences with an equal. And in the circumstances
of the time an equal might come to be a rival. By now, if not before, the need to preserve Dr Parry must have come very low on the list of Burghley's priorities.

From the above it will be evident that Parry was genuinely critical of the rabid
extremes of Protestant zeal, and even of aspects of the queen's religion. But in a long
letter addressed to her from the Tower on 14 February 1584/5, he made admissions
which he could not have expected the queen or Burghley to have seen as other than
damning. It will be more convenient to consider this letter more in detail later as part
of the evidence presented at the trial.

The flashbacks above surely cast much light on the trial of William Parry, which
took place in Westminster Hall on 25 February 1585, and also on the verdict. He had
a double task: namely to play the part of the traitor caught redhanded and deserving
no mercy. At the same time, he must seen by the discerning to be more than he seemed.
What he had done was with the connivance of the state. But he could not for obvious
reasons say so. The aim of the trial was to bring the papists into disrepute through a
misguided convert, and Parry's villainy must be evident for all to see. But Parry could
not in the end bring himself to trust the directors of the scenario so fully as to play a
part completely unequivocal. It might have gone better for him if he had; sticking simply to the role of villain caught in the act. Undeniably, he was caught, fairly or unfairly, in a web of his own making whatever he did or said.

The indictment included the charge that on 31 August 1584 Parry had conferred
with Edward Neville to bring him into his plot to kill the queen. But before pleading
to the charge, Parry begged leave to say something. He claimed that the matters with
which he was charged were 'done so secretly as none can see into them except they had
eyes like unto God'. Nevertheless he was ready 'to confess the indictment'.[63] In fact,
he went so far as to say, 'I do confess that I am guilty ... and further that I desire not
life but desire to die.'[64]

The documents constituting the evidence in the case were Parry's confessions of 11
and 13 February taken before Baron Hunsdon, vicechamberlain Hatton and Francis
Walsingham: the letters of Como, of Parry to Burghley and to the lord steward were
read. The accused agreed that all the letters were authentic and, most important, his
confessions were made freely and not under duress. He even admitted there was 'no
treason that hath been since the first year of the queen anyway touching religion ...
wherein I have not much dealt, but I have offended in it.' He had also presumed to
state in writing who should be the queen's successor. This also was treason.

The confessions were mainly a rundown of his life as a spy or traitor to whoever's
side since his contact with the court from about 1570. He made no secret of his contact with several Jesuits during his time in Europe, especially from 1582, and with the
Paget-Morgan faction, their opponents. Morgan hoped he would do 'some service for

62 Ibid.   63 *State trials*, i, p. 122., col. 1.   64 Ibid.

God and his Church'. Parry replied, he would do it 'if it were to kill the greatest subject in England', evidently this time meaning William Cecil. But Morgan rejoined, 'Let him live to the greater fall and ruin of his house.' What he had in mind was nothing less than the death of the queen. Parry wanted further reassurance. 'Dr Allen I desired; Persons I refused; and by chance came Master Watts, a learned priest, with whom I conferred, and was overruled.' Watts said it was unlawful, 'to whom many English priests did agree, as I have heard'. Indeed, Parry admitted the existence of many 'quiet and obedient Catholic subjects in England'. This could have done nothing to help the defendant's cause with his judges. However, he agreed to kill Elizabeth if the pope approved and granted him 'full remission of [his] sins'.[65] In Paris, Parry also claimed he got the advice of the Jesuit Anibal a Codreto in confession. Subsequently he was 'lovingly embraced, commended, confessed and communicated at the Jesuits' at one altar with the Cardinals Vandosini and Narbonne. He got a 'certificate' to prove this, which he enclosed in the letter which was left with the nuncio Ragazzoni, as we have seen, to forward to Rome.[66]

Obscurely, the assassin further required of Morgan 'that some special man might be made privy to the matter, lest he dying, and I miscarrying in the execution, and my intent never truly discovered, it might stick for an everlasting spot in my race.' Meaning presumably that he wanted it to be known at some time that he had never seriously intended the death of Elizabeth. In fact no man was found trustworthy enough to know the full truth. Meanwhile, as part of the charade, Morgan told Parry, as he said, that Lord Ferniehurst would go to Scotland as soon as the death of Elizabeth was known and enter England at the head of twenty or even thirty thousand men 'to defend the queen of Scots'.[67] So far so good, but once again, Parry puts in a strangely true word for an enemy of state. Neither the Scottish queen nor her son had any 'privity, liking or consent to this, or any other bad action, for anything that I ever did know'.

When Parry got back to England, he interviewed the queen at Whitehall 'and very privately discovered to her Majesty this conspiracy much to this effect though covered with all the skill I had'. Evidently he clarified his role as an agent-provocateur as he had already done to others in authority: or else he would not have been allowed anywhere near her presence. 'She took it doubtfully' – wonderingly – 'I departed in fear'. The queen promised that 'never a Catholic should be troubled for religion or supremacy so long as they lived like good subjects'.[68] As Parry said he saw it, the situation had improved but was not yet good enough. It was while he was at Greenwich, 'suing for St Catherine's' that Como's enigmatic letter of 31 January, 1583/4 arrived giving approval for the unnamed enterprise. Parry was, moreover, absolved of all his sins and urged to go forward in whatever it was. He showed the letter 'to some in the court, who imparted it to the queen'. Parry did not know what she thought of it but 'it confirmed my resolution to kill her ... And yet I was determined never to do it', if it could be avoided by 'policy' or parliament. However, 'I feared to be tempted, and therefore

65 Ibid., p. 123, col. 1.   66 Ibid., col. 2.   67 Ibid.   68 Ibid.

always when I came near her, I left my dagger at home.'[69] He left the court on this occasion 'utterly dejected, discontented'.

Allen's book was mentioned, *A true sincere and modest defence of English Catholics*, published in 1584. According to Parry, 'it taught that kings may be excommunicated, deprived and violently handled ... while all wars undertaken for religion are honourable.'[70] In fact, as we have seen, the book taught no such thing. However, the defendant thought the queen should read it to see it 'is a warning and a doctrine full dangerous'. He lent the book to Neville with whom he conspired for some six months. It was claimed that Neville suggested to Parry in August 1584 that they should release Mary, queen of Scots, and take Berwick. Parry countered with the equally absurd notion of taking Queenborough and the navy, but this was only 'to entertain him with discourse'. Parry had 'a greater matter' in mind which he revealed to Neville only after swearing him to secrecy on the Bible. This was to kill the queen. He did not wish to kill her but if she failed 'to take compassion on her Catholic subjects' he would have done it. After further deliberation, Neville, as we have seen, decided enough was enough and told all to the authorities. 'I joy and am glad in my soul that it was his hap to discover me in time though there was no danger near.'[71] Thus reacted Parry. Neville's change of heart was attributed to the fact that the earl of Westmorland died about this time making him a possible successor to his estates.

Parry's letter to the queen from the Tower of 14 February 1585 contained many damning admissions. The copy of the letter in the Lansdowne collection is a draft altered in places, and endorsed by Cecil, 'Parry accuseth Nevel'.[72] The version printed in *State trials* shows many omissions as compared with the original which was reproduced in full by Strype.[73] Did the letter used in the trial also include the omissions, or was the truncated version considered sufficient for the edited, printed account? There seems to be no way of knowing. Likewise there seems to be no way of knowing whether this letter was the spontaneous effort of the spy or whether Burghley or Walsingham helped with further suggestions. It is likely that Parry was encouraged to make his own statement since it contained items that neither Walsingham nor Burghley could have been expected to include, even for the purposes of statecraft, in a trial intended to ensure Parry's destruction. However, they must have been well pleased to see the extent to which Parry made his longer life impossible. By this time he could be trusted to hang himself with his own rope. This letter was all the rope that was needed. It is significant that it was addressed to the queen and not to the council or Burghley. Parry was no doubt convinced in his heart that his relationship of trust and understanding with the queen would be sufficient to save him from the consequences of the more damning parts of his letter. Along with the more artificial inventions making Parry an assassin, at least as past intentions went, we may discern, maybe,

---

69 Ibid., p. 124, col. 1.   **70** Ibid. Cf. Hicks, p. 362, n. 84.   **71** Ibid.   **72** BL, Lansdowne ms 43, no. 47; 14.2.1584/5, draft altered in places.   **73** Parry to the queen, 14.2.1584/5, endd. by W. Cecil, 'Parry accuseth Nevel'; BL, Lansdowne ms 43, No. 47. This is a draft in W. P.'s hand, altered in places. The full transcript is given in J. Strype, *Annals of the Reformation* (London 1728), iii, pp 102-4.

the genuine mind of Parry in several areas. Although it was not used in its entirety in the trial, it will be useful to consider here the complete contents of the letter as they have come down to us. This helps to explain his end.

Parry began with a plain admission of past guilt. 'Your Majesty may see by my voluntary confession the dangerous fruits of a discontented mind, amd how constantly I pursued my first conceived purpose in Venice for the relief of the afflicted Catholics; continued it in Lyons, and resolvedly in Paris to put it in execution in England': all to bring about the restitution of England 'to the ancient obedience to the See Apostolic'.[74] All of which was clearly false. The popes fully approved, 'and some great divines'. But this was spoilt by, 'though it be true or likely that most of our English divines (less practised in matters of this weight) do utterly mislike and condemne it.' Parry admitted that it was Neville, his 'kinsman and late familiar friend' who revealed the plot. 'Whereof I am heartily glad. But now sorry (in my very soul) that ever I conceived it, however comfortable or meritorious soever I thought it. God thank him and forgive me; who would not now ... attempt it (if I had opportunity and liberty to perform it) to gain your kingdome. I beseech Christ that my death and example may satisfy your Majesty and the world, as it shall glad and content me.'[75]

After a kind of testimonial to his fellow-conspirator, Thomas Morgan, 'a Catholic gentleman, so beloved, trusted and protected in France as you shall hardly be able to touch him by any ordinary course ... and having no letter or cipher of his wherewith to charge him', the queen was advised, 'Leave him therefore to God and his amendment'. Perhaps the genuine Parry was coming through when he exhorted Elizabeth, 'Give some ease to your Catholic subjects'. Also when he averred, 'the indignities past between your Majesty and the King Catholic are many. You have disquieted his state, maintained his rebels, and do bear with such as have robbed him and his subjects. Many merchants are undone: some few are enriched. Some bad humours pleased, and yourself dishonoured. It may cost you dear. Look to it in time. There is possibility to repair all.'[76] Very cool!

Significant, not to say explosive, references to Mary, queen of Scots, followed Parry's advice that, as the queen's prisoner, she should be honourably treated while surely guarded. 'She may do you good. She will do you no harm, if the fault be not English. Satisfy her reasonably in her keeper ... It may else prove dangerous ... A new governor and a new guard may breed new doubts. Impulsion may do harm ... It importeth you much. So long as it is well with her, it is safe with you. When she is in fear you are not without peril. Cherish and love her. She is of your blood; and your undoubted heir in succession. It is so taken abroad and will be found so at home. The prince, her son, hath been illy handled by his subjects; troubled with inlet heretic practices, and often endangered in person. Now you have him protect him. He is your kinsman and second saufty.'[77]

---

74 Strype, pp 102-3.   75 Ibid., p. 103.   76 Ibid., p. 103. The contents of this paragraph are printed in Strype; not in *State trials*.   77 Ibid. Apart from the exhortation to treat Queen Mary well, the

Parry's last word was no less unacceptable, at least to Elizabeth's principal courtiers, as trampling rather than treading on the delicate corns of religion. 'Last of all forget the glorious title of supreme governor. Trouble none that refuseth to swear it. For that cannot agree with your sex. Luther and Calvin did not allow it. The Puritans smile at it and the Catholic world doth condemn it.'[78]

There was a final assurance of loyalty. 'With my heart and soul I do now honour and love you; am inwardly sorry for mine offence, am ready to make you amends by my death and patience. Discharge me a culpa, I beseech you, good lady, but non a poena.' Elizabeth was 'the best natured and qualified queen that ever lived in England'. The fuller version concluded, 'Remember your unfortunate servant' – this word was crossed out – 'Parry; chiefly overthrown by your hard hand. Amend it in the rest of your servants. For it is past with me if your grace be not greater than I look for. And lastly and ever, good madam, be good to your obedient Catholic subjects. For the bad I speak not.'[79]

Nothing could have alienated Burghley more completely than Parry's support for Mary, and his advocacy of toleration for the Catholics, if this was, indeed, his true mind. About this time probably Cecil wrote a masterly memorandum for the queen on the whole range of policy entitled, 'An antidote against Jesuitism written by the lord treasurer Burleigh [*sic*] to Queen Elizabeth concerning a pretended peace with Spain'.[80] It included an eloquent plea for intolerance. The treaty deals with 'factious subjects' and 'foureigne enemies'.'Your strong and factious subjects are the papists. Stronge I discompt them because ... by number they are able to make a great dinne, and by their naturall and mutualle confidence and intelligence they may soone bring to passe an uniteing with foureigne enemies. Factious I call them because they are discontented, of whom in all reasons of state your Majestie must determine if you will suffer them to be stronge to make them the better content, or if you will discontent them by making them weaker ... To suffer them to be strong with hope that with reasons they will be contented carryed with it in my opinion but a faire enamyling of a terrible danger. For first man's nature is not only to strive against a person's smarte but to revenge a bypast injurie ... When opportunitie shall flatter them they will remember not the after slacking but the former bynding, and so much the more when they shall imagine this relenting to proceed from feare rather than favour, which is the poison of all government when the subject thinks the prince doth anything more out of feare than favour.'

One is confirmed in the view that Cecil owed more to his classical education than to Christianity: 'therefore the Romans would rather abide the uttermost extremities than by their subjects to be brought to any conditions.' Furthermore, if Elizabeth tried to please the papists, this could only mean alienating her 'faithfull subjects, and to fasten a reconciled love with the looseninge of a certaine love is to build houses with the

---

rest is only given in Strype.   78 Ibid. The passage as given in part in Lansdowne 43, no. 47 differs slightly from Strype's printing but not substantially.   79 Strype, op. cit., p. 104.   80 'An antidote against Jesuitism ...' See Chapter 1, n. 12.

sale of lands. So much the more in that your Majestie, imbarqued in the protestant cause as in many respects by your Majestie it cannot be with any safetie abandoned, they having bine so long time the only instruments both of your councell and power.' All the same the idea of genocide or holocaust still lay in the future. 'It sufficeth to weaken the discontented, but there is no way to kill the desperate, which, in such number as they are, were as hard and difficult as impious and ungodly.' After a lengthy consideration of the ways in which the English papists could be weakened, Burghley held up Spain as the example of strength to be imitated. Philip was a prince whose 'whose closett hath brought forth greater victories than all his father's journies, absolutely by making his subjects a people all one hearted in religion ... '[81] So there could be no place in Burghley's commonwealth for a loose cannon like Parry who, to make matters worse, evidently had some influence over the queen.

To return to the trial. After the reading of Como's letter of 30 January 1584/5 in English, and Parry's to Cecil and the lord high steward of 18 February 1584/5, the court could at least agree with Parry, 'My case is rare and strange and ... singular'. That there was garbling, or excessive editing, is to be presumed in the official report of this as of all treason trials. But it shows through the latter part of his trial that Parry believed that the influential men present, who really knew what it was all about, would see to it that he was spared the death penalty. While he admitted he might now 'be punished by death', he clearly envisaged the possibility, rather probability, 'most graciously (beyond all common expectation) to be pardoned'.[82] He reminded the court his death could 'do no good'. So 'pardon poor Parry and relieve him, for life without living is not fit for him.' But if he had to die let it be soon. At this late stage before sentence was passed, he insisted he was guilty of 'persuading ... and yet never intending to kill Queen Elizabeth'.[83]

Hunsdon and Hatton, summing up, could only emphasize his admission of guilt. He had confessed the treasons, and admitted to planning it all with the assent and approval of the pope. How could he now say he never meant it? At this point Parry seems to have become aware of the hostile reaction of the court to all his admissions of guilt, and how they might be used against him. The top people from the queen downwards might know that it was all a propaganda exercise in which Parry must appear not as an agent provocateur but *tout court* as a popish assassin. Perhaps he now sensed the danger that the appearance of his guilt might be worth more to public policy than the truth of his kind of innocence. He began to lose his nerve at the prospect of impending disaster and real death. He dared to inform the court, contradicting what he had said earlier, 'Your Honours know how my confession upon mine examination was extorted'. Hunsdon and Hatton retorted, 'there was no torture or threatening words offered him.'[84] Parry now claimed they said that if he did not confess, he would be tortured. While denying this, they admitted that if the accused had not confessed, they would have been obliged 'in ordinary course to take [his] examination'.

81 Ibid.   82 *State trials*, i, p. 126, col. 1.   83 Ibid., col. 2.   84 Ibid., p. 127, col. 2.

This did not quite contradict Parry. Popham reminded him that in his examination of 20 February, 'he acknowledged that he was most mildly and favourably dealt with in all his examinations'. Parry did not deny it.

Hatton, no doubt unintentionally, conceded an important point to Parry in admitting that it was remarkable that Elizabeth was 'so far from all fear' when she heard his intentions from his own lips that she would not 'so much as acquaint anyone of her ... privy council with it'. They only heard of it when it was 'made manifest' generally. The queen was not stupid or unable to recognise a genuine villain. If she trusted Parry it was by a sound instinct that he meant her no harm: indeed, quite the reverse. Neverthelss Parry had admitted that he felt he ought to kill the queen when he saw her at Hampton Court. He now raged his denials at Popham. 'I never meant to kill her.' Incoherently he added that 'he must die because he was not settled.'[85] Hatton and Popham both took him up on this this, but he had nothing further to say. No doubt he told the truth. He was not 'settled' in the role he was supposed to play, more particularly in the courtroom; whether he was indeed an assassin, or merely the servant of the government as an agent-provocateur. To have said more on this angle could not have helped him, as no doubt he realised even in his confused and frightened state. So he was found hopping from one leg to the other with every prospect of overbalancing completely.

Without attempting to explain why Parry did not kill the queen when he met her privately, and it is sufficiently unlikely that he ever intended to do so, the lord chief justice summed up before pronouncing the inevitable sentence. 'Thou making show as if thou wouldst simply have uttered for her safety the evil that others had contrived, didst but seek thereby to credit and access that thou mightest take the apter opportunity for her destruction.'[86] There followed an attack on popery as a school of disobedience and king-killing. Popham also added a consideration which explained why government could welcome the presence of such as Parry in the commonwealth. If he had intended to relieve the Catholics in this way, they 'were most likely amongst all others to have felt the worst of it if [his] devilish practice had taken effect'.[87] After hearing the inevitable sentence, Parry, a man now consumed by fear, could only continue to rage – hysterically. 'I here summon Queen Elizabeth to answer for my blood before God!'

On 2 March 1584/5 Parry was delivered by the lieutenant of the Tower to the sheriffs of London and Middlesex at Tower Hill to be drawn on a hurdle to Palace Yard, Westminster, for the last scene. 'Where having long time of stay permitted him before his execution, he impudently denied that he was ever guilty of any intention to kill Queen Elizabeth.' In a life of subterfuge, on this occasion one may take it that he told the truth.[88] A report of his final speech shows that Burghley himself was present, some indication of the importance attached to this last appearance of Parry in public. He was given the opportunity, like all in his position, to make a suitable exit. He declared that he was brought to the place of execution 'not to preache but to die and to avowe

85 Ibid.   86 Ibid., p. 128, col. 1.   87 Ibid., col. 2.   88 Ibid.

his own innocencie, which he had declared at the barre after his judgment, and would there seale it with his blood'. He admitted two offences: reconciliatiion to the Church of Rome 'both at Milan and Paris (contrary to a positive law only); and 'entering conference' with Neville, 'and in concealing what passed between them, which he did upon confidence of her Majesty, to whom he had before bewraed what he had been sollicited to doo'. Topcliffe, also present at the execution, accused him by Como's letter of promising to destroy the queen, 'and was by him as from the pope animated thereunto'. Parry told Topcliffe he was mistaken. 'I denie any such matter to be in the letter, and I wishe it might be trulie examined and consydered of.' It is likely that Parry had cherished some notion that, in spite of his own declaration, the fact that the written evidence made no reference to assassination might have been enough to get him off the capital sentence. If the lawyers had been otherwise instructed, it might have done.[89]

The sheriff called on him 'to cease to purge himself synce the lawe had passed against him'. But Parry persisted. 'I die a true servant to Queene Elizabeth; for any evil thought that ever I had to harme her, it never came in my mynde. She knoweth it. And her owne conscyence can tell her so ... I die guiltles and free in mynde from ever thinkinge hurt to her Majestie. And I know her to be the annointed of God, not lawfull for any subject to toche her royall person ... If I might be made duke of Lancaster and have all the possessions belonging thereto, yet I would never consent to shedde the least droppe of blood out of the top of any of her fingers.' Burghley now intervened. He asked Parry what he thought of the proceedings of law against him. Parry 'answeared the same to be most just and honourable, pleadinge still his own innocencie of mynde'. There are echoes of the scene at the last moments of the fourth duke of Norfolk in 1572. Parry told 'Mr Treasurer' to tell the queen 'he died her faithful servant'. He appealed to the Catholics to 'serve her, obeie her, honour and reverence her'. She swore to Parry that if they obeyed her she would 'never trouble any of you for your conscience'. 'Mr Treasurer' urged Parry to admit his guilt. But he insisted, 'I praie God Elizabeth do not fynde that in taking awaie my life she hath killed one of the best keepers in her park.' A preacher called on him 'to be sorie for his synnes' and beg God's mercy. 'I will', said Parry, and recited the Lord's prayer in Latin and 'other private prayers to himself'. Sometimes the condemned by their final speech managed to evoke the sympathy of the volatile mob. But not Parry. The mob called out repeatedly, 'Awaie with him.'[90]

It is evident from the sparse account of his execution tacked on to the end of the trial – a fact borne out by the memorandum in Burghley's possession – that Parry expected to be saved from the gallows and the knife at the last moment. This happened to certain of the key characters spared from execution after the main and bye plots of 1603. But it was not to happen yet. Nevertheless, Parry tried hard and held up pro-

---

89 'A report of William Parry's speech at his execution', 2.2.1584/5, in secretary hand endd. in W. Cecil's hand. Unsigned. Printed in Camden, *Elizabeth*, p. 308. Given here from BL, Lansdowne ms, 43, No. 53. 90 Ibid.

ceedings as long as he could. 'After this a pause being made of his execution, he said he had written to the queen and councell who was lawful successor to the crowne of England' but it was not then 'fit' to name the party. There were further interjections to delay the fatal moment. Doubtless, he hoped for some last minute intervention to reprieve him from death. But none came.[91] 'And so without any request to the people to pray for him, or using any outward prayer himself, he was turned off [the ladder] and executed according to the sentence.'[92] He left by the hardest way. 'After one swing [he] was cut downe when his bowelles were taken out and he gave a great groanc.'[93] We might have learnt more about it all, with significant clues to Parry's death as well as his life, if the register of the privy council from June 1582 until February 1585/6, like other documents, had not somehow gone missing.[94]

91 Ibid. 92 *State trials*, i, p. 128, col. 2. 93 BL Lansdowne ms, 43, no. 53. 94 J. R. Dasent, *Acts of the privy council*, new series, 1586-1587, 1897, preface, p. vii, 'The loss of the council register between June 1582 and February 1585-6 is much to be regretted.' So there are no references anywhere in this important source to Parry. It is curious that a similar loss of the original registers occurred during the vital periods of the Ridolfi conspiracy and of the gunpowder plot.

6

Anthony Babington's plot

For much of the time the real contrivers of the plots of this period, designed to bring opponents of the regime, and more particularly papists, into discredit, kept themselves fairly carefully in the background. In the case of the Babington plot, however, no historian of any colour could deny that the principal contriver was Francis Walsingham, with the full approval of Burghley and the earl of Leicester. Leicester, whatever his previous or general reservations with regard to the lord treasurer and the principal secretary, was well content to work with them for the overthrow of the largest threat to the continuance of the regime – Mary, queen of Scots. Undoubtedly the Scottish queen represented a threat large enough to unite many conflicting interests. She was the obvious successor to Elizabeth, and many abroad would have been content to see her succeed before the natural death of the present incumbent. Furthermore, she was not only Catholic in religion but uncompromisingly so; and to make matters worse had a son who might succeed her in the southern kingdom and in the profession of her faith. True, James VI in the 1580s showed none of his mother's unswerving loyalty to the old religion. He was in any case, still very young, and still very much at the mercy of the noble factions. These had an influence not seen in England since the wars of the roses. Indeed, kidnapping the king was at this time a political pastime in which France and England exercised more than a remote interest and influence. The problem for Cecil, and Elizabeth under his influence, was to stabilize the situation for all time to come. James must become committed to the Protestant regime without ever being tempted to turn back. While Mary lived, and continued to claim at least a share with her son in the government of Scotland, there could be no stability of a kind welcome to England. Meanwhile the future of the Protestant regime in England under Elizabeth was precarious. Even if she married, which was now altogether unlikely, it was even less likely that she could produce an heir. The future of the Protestant regime was thus by the middle of the decade under serious threat. Cecil, Leicester, Walsingham and the rest, whose present and future depended on it, could not be expected to reject any effective remedy. Nor was it likely that Elizabeth could or would stand out against them. The great lever on her compliance was fear. Mary had to die.

Undoubtedly, the Protestant establishment had reason to fear from 1580 onwards. The arrival of the mission of seminary priests and Jesuits in the summer of 1580, noted above, presented a new threat by the old faith. The pioneer from the seminaries was the secular priest Cuthbert Mayne who entered England as a missionary in 1576. He paid for his temerity with his life. But the threat showed a new strength in the delegation from Rome in 1580 which included the Jesuits Edmund Campion and Robert Persons, two of the most remarkable men of their generation in the religious field. It must be re-emphasized that the original intention of the newcomers was not to constitute an aggression but to bring about a reconciliation with Rome. And if there could not be reunion then at least the Catholics might be tolerated. But this, the only human and practicable solution to the religious problem, would have to wait for another two and a half centuries of persecution and misunderstanding to run their course: until 1829 in fact.[1]

The incoming missioners did their best to get an understanding with the regime by way of negotiation and public debate. But from the first they were regarded not merely as an intrusion but as an enemy force working for Spain, the irreconcilable enemy abroad. The official rejection of the mission was uncompromising and brutal. Persecution and torture became the order of the day for the mission and all who supported it. Many managed to escape but not such as Campion and Alexander Bryant who were treated with inhuman cruelty.[2] In consequence many who went abroad, Persons included, became what the regime in England had forced them to become, as they saw it, the supporters of Spain for armed invasion as the only remedy left to meet the intransigence of Elizabeth's government. A distinction was made between Elizabeth and her ministers. She was seen as the prisoner of her court. The papists in England continued uniformly loyal to her even if they were given no credit for it by her ministers. Even among the more extreme spirits on the continent there was no proven desire for Elizabeth's assassination. Certainly not among the Jesuits and their allies. It was part of the propaganda adopted by Elizabeth's government to claim otherwise.[3] The plot we are about to consider was built on experience already acquired and showed points of resemblance.

The Catholic seminaries abroad founded by William Allen and Persons, notably in Rome, Flanders and Spain, ensured a stream of missionaries and martyrs to preserve what was left of the old faith when it soon became apparent that there could be no question of religious reunion with Rome. But almost from their beginning the seminaries produced not only heroes of the faith but also a significant number disillusioned by exile, bored by the tediousness of study, and ready for almost any employment that offered an alternative to the debased status of the usually penniless exile. Some start-

1 For the intentions of the mission of 1580-1, see T. M. McCoog, *The Society of Jesus in Ireland, Scotland, and England 1541-1588* ... ; F. Edwards, *Robert Persons*, especially chapters 3 and 4; for an adverse view, see M. L. Carrafiello, *Robert Parsons and English Catholicism 1580-1510* (Selinsgrove, USA), 1998.   2 For the brutal treatment of Campion, Bryant and Sherwin, see F. Edwards, *Robert Persons*, passim; *The Elizabethan Jesuits*, passim.   3 F. Edwards, *Robert Persons*, pp 84-6. John Bossy in 'The heart of Robert Persons' (T. M. McCoog, *Reckoned expense*), tried to argue that Persons advocated assassination, but see chapter 5 above on Parry's plot, n. 29 above.

ed out with the best of intentions in the Catholic sense, sons of ancient Catholic families which had suffered much for the faith. Some of these and others, as we have seen, were not convinced that the Cecilian regime in England was irreconcilable. The alternative to fomenting invasion from abroad to force a change was to throw oneself on the mercy of the regime. This meant offering 'service'. This might include spying on 'forward' elements among fellow papists. The return for this was grudging and unofficial toleration. For some it was not enough and they gave up the faith altogether. A few never had it; but going as far as ordination to the priesthood, they made themselves in this way more effective spies for Walsingham. These two classes were those most useful to the government but others could be utilised. The ordained or trained unbelievers were most effective for fomenting false plots. The former class, believers, more confused, might be inveigled and compromised and hang on the gallows as the victims of their own folly and the cynical shamelessness of the agents-provocateurs. It was a group of such youthful dupes who formed the ostensible core of the Babington conspiracy. The real core was a group of undercover agents working for the government. When their work was done, these continued to work under cover as before in the preparation of new plots for the master plotters on the council.[4]

The destruction of Mary, queen of Scots, was unfinished business left over from the Ridolfi plot of 1571. Elizabeth could scream and swear at those who crossed her but this was an almost necessary ploy for dealing effectively with a court that contained so many Renaissance bravos. Underneath the hard exterior, however, was a nature that did not accept easily the idea of shedding blood, and certainly not the blood of her own courtiers and kinsmen. It was only after two changes of mind that she eventually acceded, after pressure from Cecil and parliament, to the execution of the fourth duke of Norfolk in 1572. She had in spite of the opportunity offered her refused to execute the Scottish queen at that time to the bitter disappointment of Cecil, Walsingham and no doubt Leicester. Thanks to Elizabeth's reticence, the elimination of Mary had still to be achieved. With the threat of invasion, a resurgent Catholicism, a Scotland not yet wholly under English domination, and a future wholly uncertain, one prime factor making for instability must now be removed. Pressure must be brought to bear on Queen Elizabeth of a kind she could no longer evade.

To bring about the Scottish queen's death, she must be involved in a plot to murder the queen of England, and in a manner for all to see. Usually the organisation of such things was left to agents-provocateurs and workers in the penumbra. Direct evidence of connection with supreme power is not always easy to come by. But this was so important that it had to be in the hands of a master from the beginning. In any case, the phenomenal success of previous manouevres of the kind gave the regime a confidence to proceed further. There was less need to be surreptitious or even guarded. The plot which has come to be known by the name of Anthony Babington could more

4 For the seminary priests, see Godfrey Anstruther, *The seminary priests*, see above; M. A. Tierney, Dodd's *Church history of England*, 5 vols. (London 1839-43).

accurately be known as the Walsingham plot. And the evidence of its connection with the principal secretary is there for all to see.

An important factor in unravelling the plot is the surveillance which Cecil and Walsingham exercized over diplomatic correspondence. This was supposed to be privileged and inviolate. The privilege belonged not only to ambassadors but also to Mary, queen of Scots, as a sovereign in her own right, and to her agents, notably Thomas Morgan and the archbishop of Glasgow, in Paris. At least as early as 1579, however, correspondence between them both had been intercepted when Sir Henry Cobham, ambassador in France, showed clear knowledge of information contained therein.[5] By mid-May 1582 Burghley knew about hostile developments in Europe when the Spanish ambassador, Bernardino de Mendoza's, dispatch to Philip II by special courier of 21 May 1582 was intercepted. The pretext for this violation of diplomatic immunity was that 'his passport was only signed by a counsellor'. So they conveniently assumed is was forged.[6] Walsingham had seals for all the main states of Europe, it seems, so that passports could be forged for any occasion.[7] Mendoza on this occasion fondly imagined that his dispatch had not been tampered with. Arthur Gregory, an expert forger, was skilled also in opening letters without breaking the seals, or in remaking them. The correspondence of the French ambassador in Scotland, de Mainville, had certainly been intercepted in March 1582 although it was returned to him with the seals unbroken. He complained to Robert Bowes and William Davison, the English agents, but it had no effect.[8] More effective was Bowes' corruption of Rosco Benetti, who conveyed de Mainville's letters to de Mauvissiäre, the French ambassador in London.[9]

Apart from interception, which indicated only a certain mild beginning in double-dealing, there were even more dubious ways ways of handling correspondence. In

5 Interception of letters: see William Murdin, *A Collection of State papers relating to Affairs 1571 to 1596* (London 1759), p. 543. 'There was the occasion in 1579 when Palavicino arranged for the theft of a letter belonging to Mendoza, the Spanish ambassador in London. A few days later, a Spanish agent stole Palavicino's correspondence, and to his disgust and fury Mendoza found his own letter among the pile': L. Stone, *Sir Horatio Palavicino*, see above, p. 234. Cf. *Cal. SP Spanish 1568-79*, no. 577. William Cecil, to the English ambassador in Scotland, 20 February 1589, sent him a packet of intercepted letters; BPA, 46/4/3/27. Robert Beale and William Davison wrote to Walsingham on 18 March 1582 giving evidence of interception; *Bowes Correspondence*, Surtees Society, 1842, pp 382, 390-2. The Salisbury mss, foreseeably, contain many examples. One may note, *Sal. cal.*, iv: the effect of a letter from the duke of Parma to Philip II intercepted by the mayor of Lingres, 17 January 1591/2, p. 185: R. Cecil writes to Sir Thomas Heneage, vice-chamberlain and chancellor of the duchy of Lancaster, that the mayor of Sandwich has sent up Catholic books and letters taken off a Fleming, 23 May 1592; ibid., pp 199-200. A letter from Hugh Owen to John Owen 10 May 1593 ns, p. 306, and five letters from Rome of June 1593, pp 327-9, ibid. According to T. Fitzherbert, letters were sometimes sent from the English government to prominent Catholics abroad with thanks for services, with the intention they would be intercepted and compromise the recipients; see T. F., *An Apologie of T. F. in defence ...* , see below, Scolar reprint, no. 146, p. 10.   6 Mendoza to Philip II (London, 21.5.1582; *Cal. SP Spain*, iii, p. 375.   7 See confession of Thomas Harison of uncertain date but not earlier than 1587. He worked for some time in the secretariat. *Cal. SP Scotland*, ix, 530.   8 For de Mainville, see F. Edwards, *Persons*, p. 83, and n. 2.   9 For de Mauvissière, see ibid. p. 83, n. 3.

early March 1583, the Jesuit William Holt was taken. They took at least one cipher from him 'confessed to have been given forth by the Scottish queen'. This with copies of 'all the ciphers taken with him' was sent to Walsingham in London.[10] It was thus possible to forge letters in cipher, whether to cause confusion in the enemy, provoke further revealing replies, or manufacture compromising evidence. But not every sinister intention can be dismissed as government contrivance. From information forwarded by Bowes and Davison, it was evident that an invasion project was still in hand: and also a project to assassinate Elizabeth as a preliminary to liberating the queen of Scots. She would presumably have been put on Elizabeth's throne. But there is nothing to prove that Mary had any part in, or approved of, irresponsible proceedings of this kind. While Mary was anxious to regain her liberty, her first choice was always to effect this, if she could, through agreement with her captors. She died still trying. This was only common sense since this was the only way to liberty that could be safe and certain. She came to realise that negotiations to this end with Elizabeth's ministers were only intended to keep her dangling in suspense for diplomatic and political purposes. She therefore became less averse in principle to schemes for her release from captivity. But she was careful at all times to avoid any scheme for her release which would involve the death of Elizabeth. The object of the Babington plot was to prove that this was no more than lying subterfuge.

Certainly an attempt on Elizabeth's life was being mooted in Paris at this time by George Gifford, one of Elizabeth's gentlemen pensioners. Whatever his motivation and the genuineness of his offer, it was entertained in Rome by Cardinal Galli, secretary of state, although the Paris nuncio, Castelli, disapproved while passing on the information, as we have seen. It is important to remember that while tyrannicide was discussed and occasionally practised, even the theory was regarded as controversial. If Gregory XIII was by no means opposed to this answer to the English problem, Sixtus V, his successor, was very much opposed. While the subject was discussed theoretically in the schools, as it had been since the days of John of Salisbury, it was rejected as a practicable alternative by the Jesuits, as by most others, and notably by Robert Persons. In fact from 1614 it was even forbidden as a theoretical subject for public lectures in Jesuit institutions.[11] Meanwhile George Gifford claimed to have approached the Scottish queen, who would have nothing to do with it. This at least was plausible.

It will be evident from much that has gone before that even before her closer confinement and the confiscation of her letters and papers, the correspondence of the Scottish queen needs to be treated with much reserve. One cannot suppose that, considering the urgency of their problem, Cecil and Walsingham would have entertained any scruples in the matter of forging documents in her name if they could get away with it. There was no particular difficulty in acquiring her ciphers. Thomas Morgan was her decipherer and correspondent in Paris. He has been suspected as a double agent; but even if he were faithful to Mary, he was the good friend of others who may

10 For Holt, ibid., p. 83, n. 4.   11 *Jesuits and assassination*: ibid., passim. See n. 3 above; William V.

not have been; at least in the sense of being ready to believe some of the evil said about her. These did not include William Lord Paget and his brother Charles, who were in agreement most of the time. But from 1582 both began to do the work of spy for Walsingham. In September, soon after the arrival of the new ambassador, Sir Edward Stafford, Charles lost no time in offering his services.[12] So even before Mary's removal to Chartley in December 1585, in the whole of this final phase her correspondence needs to be treated very cautiously.

Surviving correspondence in Queen Mary's own hand may be taken as genuine. Alleged ciphers and deciphers, obviously, must be treated with reserve. If they contradict what was said above about her honourable intentions towards Elizabeth, they may be taken as spurious. From authentic letters and statements four main aims emerge consistently after her imprisonment in England from 1568: her liberty, her claim to the throne of Scotland at least jointly with her son, and her claim to the English succession as a legitimate descendant from Henry VII; but only in the event of Elizabeth failing to produce an heir. She also claimed the right to exercise such influence as she had left in her own kingdom of Scotland. At all times she repudiated any attempt, or association with any attempt, to come to the throne by way of Elizabeth's murder. Quite apart from her claims of honour as a sacred and annointed person, which she took very seriously, she was well aware of the fact that she was surrounded by enemies and traitors even among her servants. She knew she was hemmed in by the intentions of those reigning round and with Elizabeth who wanted her out of the way for her religion. So Mary was nothing if not careful at all times. Her destruction would not be easy.

The prelude to the final attack on Mary was the Throckmorton plot of 1583 to 1584. With his brother, Thomas, Francis Throckmorton got to know the Parisian scene from 1580. He was also a friend of the Spanish and French ambassadors in London and acted as letter carrier for Morgan and the Scottish queen. In November 1583 he was arrested on suspicion of bringing treasonable letters to Mary. As we have seen, no evidence of treason was produced; nor that he had brought in these particular letters. He was subjected to torture at least twice, and as Walsingham admitted, it was severe. He made eleven confessions but only one survived. Tried in 1584, he denied their truth, his admissions being made when he was maddened by pain. As we have also seen, the only authentic incriminating papers found in his possession were a list of havens around England and a list of noblemen. Hardly treason. All this was was a pretext for expelling Mendoza in January 1584, the last Spanish ambassador in

Bangert, *A History of the Society of Jesus*, 1986 ed., pp 117, 126; T. Clancy, *Papist Pamphleteers* (Chicago 1964), pp 96-106.   12 See John Paul, 'The queen's tragedy', unpublished ms given to me, now in BPA, 48/6/6, pp 36-40. Paul's is the best study of the plot to date. Regarding the doubtful authenticity of Mary's correspondence at this time, see also F. Edwards, *R. Persons*, Chapter 5. For the Pagets and Thomas Morgan and their contacts with Walsingham, see L. Hicks, *An Elizabethan problem* (New York 1964), passim. For spies in the French embassy, *Cal. SP Scotland*, vii, pp 6, 35, 472, 650 for the opening of Mary's letters.

England before 1605. The French ambassador, Mauvissière, was now Mary's only advocate of weight among the foreign envoys. Henri Fagot and Cherelles, important members of his staff, and through whose hands passed ciphered letters from Morgan and others to Mary from France, were in the pay of Walsingham.[13]

Before Mary could be finally disposed of, it was necessary to organise the Scottish scenario. In 1583 this appeared more favourable to Mary. James VI, held for ten months by the Protestant party after the raid of Ruthven, gained his liberty by August 1583. Walsingham went to Scotland to pressurise him into accepting or continuing the English connection. The bait was the promise of the English succession. Meanwhile, in November 1582, Mary made a new plea for her liberation. There could of course be no question of acceding to her request but in the spring of 1584 Robert Beale, Walsingham's brother-in-law and secretary, was sent to stage a negotiation. Mary offered to ratify the treaty of Edinburgh. Walsingham stalled. There was correspondence between Elizabeth and the rival queen. Meanwhile the situation worsened for England with the failure of the Gowrie conspiracy which was intended to bring James back firmly under Protestant and therefore English control. In May 1584 Gowrie was executed for his share in the murder of Rizzio, and Mary encouraged James to oust his pro-English councillors. By July, it was evident to Mary that she could look for little from Elizabeth but she was still her best hope however slender. Mary continued to press for more liberty. Her optimism even extended to asking leave for a visit to Scotland!

A new dimension was discernible in October 1584 when Patrick, master of Gray, on the recommendation of Lord Hunsdon, warden of Berwick, went to London to negotiate for James VI. While in Berwick, Gray went to church with Hunsdon, taking an active part in the service. Gray, while assuring Mary of his devotion to her cause, was able to convince Elizabeth that his true allegiance was to her when he came to London. The queen was not gullible; but it was evident where Gray's true material interests lay. So he could be trusted to betray the Scottish queen who was virtually penniless and powerless. Reassured by Gray, in spite of his previous assurances to Mary of which she may have had knowledge, Elizabeth allowed Nau, Mary's secretary, to come to her with propositions from his mistress for a settlement.[14] While in London Nau saw Gray once. He used the occasion to rebuke him for double-dealing.

Nau presented twenty-seven articles from Mary, farseeing and far-reaching. She would look on Elizabeth as the 'juste vraye et légitime royne d'Angleterre', renouncing any claim to her throne while Elizabeth lived and revoking any previous claims she had been obliged to declare in obedience to her late husband Francis II. She repudiated the papal bull of 1570 in so far as it could be turned to her favour or profit. She would not deal directly or indirectly with any English subject in England or abroad to

13 For Walsingham's infiltration of the French embassy in London, at this time, see John Bossy, *Giordano Bruno and the Embassy Affair*, New Haven 1991.   14 For Gray's mission to England, see Kervyn de Lettenhove, *Marie Stuart*, ii, 1889, p. 169; Alexandre Labanoff, *Lettres ... de Marie Stuart* ... , vi (London 1844), p. 28f.; Cal. SP Scotland, vii, p. 360. The J. Paul ms deals with this on pp 60-

promote foreign war against England or civil war within it, whether on the pretext of religion, or for civil and political ends. She would not support Elizabeth's subjects in rebellion or convicted of treason. In the autumn of 1584, following the murder of the prince of Orange, a Bond or Band of Association had been formed in England among a group of noblemen. This aimed to destroy anyone who plotted against the queen in favour of a third party. Even if the third party had had nothing to do with it, it should still be regarded as guilty. Mary offered to sign this bond herself although she asked for a prior revision or explanation of certain clauses as they had been indicated to her at Wingfield. She could hardly be unaware that they were directed against herself although she had as yet received no proper copy of the Bond.[15]

The twelfth article undertook to support Elizabeth if attacked from abroad or at home, and to enter into a league defensive with England. Mary would persuade James VI to do the same while respecting the ancient league between France and Scotland. But as a condition she wanted a secret assurance guaranteeing her right to the succession. If she returned to Scotland, she would make no changes in the religion there established, and oblige no Scottish subject to change; but she would require the free exercise of her own religion and that of her entourage until she returned to France. The principle of religious toleration was not of course accepted or understood in London. Once the principle of her queenship and joint sovereignty with James VI was recognised, she did not envisage taking any part in government or staying on in Scotland. There would be an amnesty for all past offences committed against her, although any provision which touched her honour should be 'revoked and annulled'. She would try to satisfy (contenter) Elizabeth with regard to the banished lords then resident in England provided they duly submitted to 'leurs princes', and if Elizabeth promised to take the side of Mary and James if they lapsed into their old ways. She would accept Elizabeth's advice when it came to arranging James' marriage. Meanwhile she wanted him to be joined with her in the treaty about to be signed. She also wanted some immediate relaxation in the harsh terms of her captivity in recognition of her willingness to enter into the treaty.

It was a fair and generous offer. But this was not a time for fairness or generosity on the other side. A Mary at large could simply not be trusted. Mary wrote to Elizabeth on 8 December asking her to see Nau privately and to let her know her will by him. She made another plea for her release. 'Would to God I could talk to you for a couple of hours.' This was the forty-second year of her life and the eighteenth of her imprisonment.[16] She wrote an accompanying letter to Walsingham next day thanking him for his favour and courtesy to Nau, asking him to give her packet to Nau which contained letters for the queen and to let her have a speedy reply.[17]

64.   15 For Mary's treaty terms presented by Nau, see Labanoff, *Lettres ...* , vi, pp 58-65, from PRO, *Mary, Queen of Scots*, xiv, contemporary copy, 28.11.1584, from London endd. 'Articles propounded by Monsieur Nau'.   16 Mary to Elizabeth, 8.12.1584, from Wingfield, minute in PRO, ibid.; printed Labanoff, vi, pp 66-7.   17 Mary to Walsingham, 9.12.1584, from Wingfield, a. l. s; PRO, ibid.;

On 14 December she wrote to the master of Gray. The letter was peremptory, beginning simply 'Gray'. It was mainly to insist on her close association with her son which Gray should take into account in all his dealings with the south. 'I want no division between me and my child, and I desire voluntarily, leaving all government to him, to assure him of his just possession, and only to ask that the 'auctorité' due to a mother be observed.' There was almost a threat. 'Let him not further disavow our association, if you do not wish to put his title in doubt, and force me to proceed in another way.' She wanted James to share with her in the treaty but not that he should simply treat for her or himself alone. 'Whoever has suggested that to him is nothing but a fool (sot) and a traitor ... I aim to depend entirely on the queen of England ... as her nearest relative, and to make a perpetual league between her and our country.' It was always understood that her son would follow her initiative in all important affairs and this was the most important. She was sure he would not wish to disobey her or see her grievously wronged.[18] The letter is only known in copy so we do not know what Mary really wrote. But if the copy corresponded to the original we can see Gray curling his lip in scorn as a helpless captive tried to play the part of a reigning monarch giving him orders.

Gray returned to Scotland in January 1585 to inform James of his achievement. The foundations of an alliance between Elizabeth and the young king had been firmly laid in London. James and his mother would never be associated in government. Mar and the exiled Scottish lords were to be allowed to return to London at James' request. This was something Gray had pressed for especially. Back in Holyrood, he thanked Walsingham for his help in getting James on to the right path and promised loyalty to Elizabeth 'to the disdvantage of the common enemy'.[19]

Mary got to know of Gray's double-dealing in the spring of 1585 and complained to Elizabeth. The English queen merely pointed out that Gray had acted on James' instructions. By this time the Parry plot was in full bloom, and added to Throckmorton's provided the excuse to break off negotiations with Mary. A definitive treaty between Elizabeth and James VI was concluded on 5 July 1586. This included a pension of £4,000 per annum for the king and envisaged a league offensive and defensive. The business was concluded by Thomas Randolph, chancellor of the exchequer, who was able to see to it that James' councillors were adequately paid to give their young master good advice. Gray suggested that the time had now come for the Scottish queen

printed Labanoff, ibid., pp 68-9. **18** Mary to Gray, 14.12.1584, from Wingfield, contemporary copy; BL, Cotton ms, Cal. C. viii, f. 462; Labanoff, ibid., pp 70-3. **19** See Paul ms, pp 66-8. While in England, Grey 'contrived, with the approval of Elizabeth and the assistance of Walsingham, a plot for the destruction of Arran; and Bellenden, the justice-clerk, who had recently visited England had been prevailed upon by the queen to join it'. Sir Edward Wotton, the new English ambassador in Edinburgh, was put in charge. Wotton found the master of Gray deliberating with his fellow-conspirators whether it were better to seize and banish Arran or assassinate him. Elizabeth sent a letter to Gray by Wotton telling him to desist from the grosser violence. Grey submitted, but as Wotton told the queen, 'they mean to make short work with him'; P. F. Tytler, *The history of Scotland* ... (Edinburgh 1866), pp 221-2.

to be poisoned. But England eschewed such crudities. Cecil and Walsingham already had in mind a better way: a plot against Elizabeth in which Mary would be involved, after which she would be condemned in a carefully staged treason trial and brought to the block.[20]

A Bond of Association had come into being as a semi-official popular reaction to the murder of the prince of Orange on 11 July 1584 and to the well-founded rumours concerning preparation for invasion from the continent. The bond had been inspired by Cecil, Walsingham and their supporters. It was an association aimed to take revenge on whoever should strike at the throne of Elizabeth and on whosoever it was meant to advantage. It was now contrived that a mere threat should be forged into an effective weapon. At the end of November 1584, the Puritan chancellor of the exchequer, Sir Walter Mildmay, presented to the commons a bill for the queen's surety, or safety. It was based on the provisions of the oath of the Association. After this, for Mary to be brought within the lethal intent of the act it was only necessary that she should be proved to be privy to a plot: not that she should approve or encourage it. As Sir Francis Englefield observed to Como, 'Naught can be looked for but the murder of that good queen.'[21]

'That good queen' was moved to Tutbury castle in Staffordshire in 1585, and in April, Sir Amyas Paulet, a Puritan more than ordinarily dour, privy councillor and

---

20 Mary wrote at length to Elizabeth from Tutbury on 23.3.1585. She complained of not being allowed to send letters to her son or even to have access to those who came from Scotland recently to negotiate on his behalf. She wanted her liberty and a chance to retire overseas to 'quelque lieu solitaire et de repos'. She was ready to renounce for herself and her posterity all claims to Elizabeth's kingdom. She was appalled that her only son should not only be prepared to deprive his mother of her state and crown but should be prepared to do this with the assistance of her rebellious subjects. Her reaction was angry in the extreme. '[A]sseurez vous que, dès aussitost, je le désadvoueray pour mon filz, et lui donneray ma malédiction, le déshéritant, non seulement de ce qu'il tient, mays de tout ce que par moy il peut prétendre ailleurs, l'abandonnant à noz propres sujects de luy fayre comme il a été instigué de fayre contre moy, mais aussi à tous estrangers de l'envahir et faire ressentir sa faulte.' However effective her curse, she made one true prophecy. '[I]l n'en jouyra jamais sans trouble.' For the rest she was still ready to conform to every reasonable demand of Elizabeth. Almost her last word was to repudiate any connection with the Parry plot with which Morgan, as Mauvissière had heard, had been connected. She was opposed to anthing of the kind. 'Je ne puis pancer que ceux qui attempteront à vostre vie, n'en fissent autant à la mienne, et quasy aujourd'huy la mienne semble despendre de la vostre': Mary to Elizabeth, 23.3.1584/5, from Tutbury, a.l.s., Salisbury mss; Labanoff, Lettres ... , vi, pp 132-40. As for James, 'in the midst of these intrigues, all was bustle and pleasure at the Scottish court.' Well aware of his position as a shuttle between opposing players, he kept his mental balance by making the most of pleasure, especially hunting, and developing a cynical sense of humour. After one such hunt, he called for a cup of wine and drank to all his dogs. 'And in particular, selecting and taking the paw of an old hound, named Tell True, who had greatly distinguished himself, he thus apostraphised his favourite; 'Tell True, I drink to thee above all my hounds; and would sooner trust thy tongue than either Craig or the bishop'. Craig was the royal chaplain, and the prelate, Montgomery, bishop of Glasgow. ': Tytler, ibid., pp 223-4; David Hume to James Carmichael, 20.3.1584/5, from BL, Calderwood ms, f. 1528.   21 Paul ms, p. 111. Mary wrote to Elizabeth on 5.1.1585 to join the Band/Bond of Association (une association générale) formed by some 'principauls seigneurs' to protect the Queen against assassination attempts of which she had heard. It was a gesture intended to assure the sister-queen of Mary's good faith and regard for her life:from Wingfield, a.l.s., Labanoff, vi, pp

friend of Walsingham and Leicester both, was appointed to be her gaoler. He could be trusted to make her captivity as unpleasant as might be. He began by ordering the removal of her cloth of state; but this seems to have been rescinded. She was not allowed to give alms lest this bring her friends or even liking in the locality. From now on her servants were closely guarded and accompanied by soldiers at all times. Everything she wrote passed through the hands of Paulet or his servants before reaching the French ambassador, the only man in high place she could trust. But Henry Fagot, vere Giordano Bruno, a chaplain in the French embassy and Walsingham's agent, assured him in 1583 that he would befriend Cherelles, the secretary in the same place. He would use him to find out out what was in Mary's correspondence. A new ambassador, Guillaume d'Aubespine, baron de Châteauneuf sur Cher, in Berry, and member of the royal council, arrived in England in August 1585. He did not take over from the previous ambassador, Michel de Castelnau de Mauvissière until September. The former officials stayed on. Walsingham continued to know all that was afoot. By 1584 Mary was aware that the ambassador's house was infested with spies. In any case, by December 1584 all her correspondence from abroad ceased. In the spring of 1585, Walsingham instructed Paulet to open all her letters. If Mary complained she was to be told, quite falsely, that this was Elizabeth's order. Most of her letters were now held up in the French embassy since they could not be transmitted freely to the prisoner.[22] Châteauneuf found a heap of her letters waitng for him undelivered since 1584.

Apart from the company, the new prison itself was intolerable. The dampness of Tutbury brought a serious decline in the Mary's health so that even Elizabeth was brought to relent. A transfer to Chartley was arranged in December 1585. This was to be the scene of the last act. We are about to enter a labyrinth leading to a morass of intrigue of which Walsingham was a past master. For her undoing Mary was to be led to believe that by an arrangement with a local brewer, set on foot by Gilbert Gifford, Walsingham's agent, she was able to send and receive letters secrctly through the

76-7. Further additions to the act for the queen's safety were proposed in January 1584/5: see *Cal. SP Dom. 1581-90*, pp 223-5.   22 Mary left Wingfield on 13.1.1585, arriving at Tutbury on 14.1. Paulet arrived on 19.4. Something like a contest, admittedly unequal, developed between Nau and Paulet. 'Paulet opened every letter and packet which was addressed to Mary or any of her household, and having read and copied them, he resealed them in the hope that the process of inspection ... would escape detection. But it did not.' (Stevenson, *Nau* ... , p. xxv). Paulet wrote to Walsingham, 'Nau is very curious to observe seals; and finding that things have been opened, hideth not his mind, but is as well answered': ibid., and PRO, *SP Scotland, Mary queen of Scots*, fxv, f. 70). Paulet made it clear to Walsingham in a letter of 6. 6. that he wanted Nau out of the way (ibid. and BL Harl. 6993, f. 90). Same to same, 14.7.1585, 'Nau hath a French busy head, more fit for France than for this country. This queen would be governed with quietness and to her good contentation if his ambitious nature did not interrupt it ... all his cavilling and quarrelling tends to none other end than by finding faults with this and that to win credit with his mistress, which no doubt he hath obtained in so great measure, as whatsoever she shall speak, write or do, it must be said to come from him and not from her ... ': ibid., and PRO *SP Scotland*, ibid., 16, f. 10. A seemingly complete list of Paulet's letters was drawn up by John Morris, S. J.; BPA 46/1/2/4.

French embassy. Her letters, after she had delivered minutes to her secretary – usually Nau who dealt with her French correspondence – were put into cipher. They were then put in a leather bag which was placed inside the bung of a barrel. Apart from the brewer, a man well known to Paulet since he had previously supplied beer to Tutbury, and Gilbert Gifford, the system was unknown to all except her own secretaries and those in the embassy. The correspondence whether coming, by way of Cordaillot, the new secretary, or by Cherelles, or going, by way of her own secretaries, was put in Fagot's hands at the French embassy in London. It then passed to Thomas Phelippes who deciphered incoming or outgoing letters and presented the results to Walsingham who masterminded the whole. Robert Poley, Leicester's agent, had preceded Gifford as the letter carrier and he it was who in December 1585 carried to Mary, with official permission of course, the bundle of letters from the French embassy which had been held up for a year or more. Mary was overjoyed, we are told, at the prospect of renewed contact with the outside world. About this time Gifford was allowed to take a cipher letter from Châteauneuf to Mary, and on 1 January 1586 visited the ambassador with a new cipher from her. Cherelles also visited Chartley about this time and received Mary's new cipher although Châteauneuf already had a copy.[23] Walsingham had only to wait. But he did rather more than that.

In December 1585 Gilbert Gifford came to London with Morgan's letter of introduction to the Scottish queen. In the event she never met him, but the document made an impression on the embassy. Over Christmas Phelippes went to Chartley to prepare Paulet for Gilbert Gifford's arrival. Mary noticed his presence. Although he promised to do her service she did not trust him and warned Châteauneuf against him. How much else did she suspect? The new plot began to crystallize when Gifford, residing with Phelippes in London in January 1586, made contact with Walsingham. He also made the acquaintance of Anthony Babington and other Catholics.[24]

Gifford replaced Poley for the Chartley letter run, being considered more adept. Both Poley and Gifford had been recommended to Mary by Thomas Morgan as men

---

23 Paul ms, p. 136. For the situation in the French embassy in London, at this time, see John Bossy, *Giordano Bruno and the Embassy Affair*, above. A brief overview of the events of 1585-7 is given in J. B. Black, *The reign of Elizabeth*, 2nd ed., (Oxford 1959), pp 375-89. Bernard Sepp, *Maria Stuarts Briefwechsel mit Anthony Babington* (Munich 1886), pp 7, 8, says that Cordaillot dealt with Mary and other Catholics but Paul shows that Nicolas de Cherelles was still an agent for Walsingham. He had been introduced to Walsingham by Fagot. J. H. Pollen, *Mary queen of Scots and the Babington plot* (Edinburgh 1922), remains essential reading, especially for the printed documents, pp 1-175. For spies in the French embassy, see also *Cal. SP Scotland*, vi, p. 431; 7, pp 6, 35, 472. For the opening of Mary's letters, ibid., vii, p. 650. 24 Paul ms, pp 127-32. Morgan's correspondence to Mary and other important documents from Hatfield were published by Murdin, op. cit., pp 434-588. He wrote her a long and informative letter from the Bastille, where he was imprisoned, on 9.4.1585: pp 439-446. Same to same, 15.10.1585, introduces Gilbert Gifford as the carrier of his letters to her. An account of his antecedents makes it clear why Morgan was prepared to trust him, and for that matter why Mendoza accepted him. At the same time Morgan warns her to be suspicious of Phelippes: 'he may perhappes be wonne to your service. But I dare not assure you of him as I wold I colde',

who could be relied on. This need not be taken to mean that Morgan too had been corrupted although it says little for his judgment that he should have been deceived by two such men. The Jesuit Samerie, alias de la Rue, no light judge of character, did not trust Morgan. But then Samerie was a man of the opposing party – a militant. Undoubtedly, Gilbert Gifford was a rogue of more than ordinary plausibility, much helped by an excellent background. He belonged to an old Catholic family of Chillington, Staffordshire. Paulet had known his uncle who lived near Tutbury. Gilbert's father, John, had suffered for the recusant cause and was in prison when Gilbert turned up in England. Meanwhile Gilbert went overseas in 1577 and after a stay in Paris went on to Rome in 1579 at the age of nineteen to study for the priesthood in the Venerable English College. At least from this time, another side of his nature prevailed. Rome, God's proverbial kitchen, was not a hothouse of vocations for those beyond the Alps. For some reason he was expelled. After further wanderings he presented himself at Allen's college at Rheims. Allen knew of some conduct unbecoming, but perhaps considering the background, decided to be forgiving. So Gifford was ordained deacon at Rheims by the cardinal of Guise, Mary's cousin. In 1583 he contacted Walsingham and offered his services. The betrayal of Mary to her death was to be his greatest work for Cecil and the principal secretary.

It was in the course of a shared dinner in Paris that Morgan learned from Phelippes of Mary's transfer to Tutbury; and that a 'secret post' had been organised with Gifford filling a key role. After the Parry plot Morgan had been imprisoned in the Bastille at Elizabeth's request, as we have seen, but significantly was now free again as the result of her further intercession. He offered 'to discover all the conspiracy of the queen of Scotland'. Which does not necessarily prove more than that he knew how to talk the language of diplomacy. The Spanish did not trust him. At liberty in France, he was forbidden entry into any Spanish dominion.[25]

It will be evident by now that the likelihood of Mary being able to transmit anything abroad that was not known to Walsingham was nil. It will also be evident that she

---

Murdin, pp 454-5. More on Gilbert G. is in Lettenhove, op. cit., i, pp 150-51; Allen, *Letters and Memorials*, passim. For R. Poley, *Cal. SP Scotland*, viii, p. 11; Hicks, op. cit., p. 159; for all the spies, see Pollen, *Babington* ... , pp xxxv-xlii.   25 Paul ms, p. 132. Morgan's case is dealt with in detail by L. Hicks, *An Elizabethan Problem*, p. 104 and passim. An important document is 'Sobre el negocio de Morgan' in Simancas, E. 607, f. 117; cf. Hicks, pp 88 and 78, nn. 223-4. Hicks rejected Morgan's bona fide. A final judgement seems impossible but the indications are that he and the Pagets were fundamentally loyal to Mary although they may have slipped on the black ice of intrigue laid down by Walsingham. Morgan is suspect for his friendship with Gilbert Gifford who he knew was in Walsingham's pay (Hicks, p. 89 and n. 254; *Sal. Cal.*, iii, pp 346-9). Parma kept him in prison for two years after which he was exiled not executed because 'parecia al duque de Parma que dandole el castigo que merecia todos entendrian que vengava los agravios particulares que le havia hecho' (Hicks, p. 90 and n. 256. Arrested at Elizabeth's request on 1.3.1585, he was in the Bastille until 13.8.1587. Waad went to France 14.3–17. 4.1585 to get his extradition (ibid., p. 152). Morgan informed Mary of something Ballard had in hand but warned her to keep away from it (ibid., p. 150). Mary knew through Phelippes of the 'secret channel' at Chartley from Christmas 1585, but he and Charles Paget knew enough about the people she was dealing with, whether professed friends or known enemies, to make it extremely unlikely that she would trust herself to any plan which could bring her within even the possibility of an action for treason. As a sovereign princess, she was above the law of another country, to say nothing of her own, but the act of 1585 showed clearly what was intended. She knew as well as Cecil and Walsingham that there was still no other remedy for her but time and patience. Elizabeth was a barren oak now visibly withering on the trunk. Whatever the degree of exasperation she might feel, a waiting game, as always, was Mary's best and only remedy. Even if her health had suffered by being placed in conditions which were presumably foreseen and intended by her captors, she was still young enough at the age of forty-five to outlive Elizabeth. But did she allow her patience to fail?

She yearned for liberty above all else. Did she now conclude that since this was unlikely to come from Elizabeth, it would most likely have to come by foreign help even if brought about immediately by the intervention of Englishmen? Would she allow herself to countenance a foreign invasion whether of England or Scotland to this end even if it threatened the life and certainly the continued reign of the present monarch? Letters of 6 and 8 April 1582 to Mendoza before his expulsion from England seem to suggest she acceded to plans being hatched on the continent for just this. It would have been very human. But some of the contents of the letters indicate forgery. What we already know of the ways of the English government does not make it absurd. Robert Persons learned later from Henri Samerie/Samier, a French Jesuit who visited Mary in disguise three times in 1582, 1583 and 1584, that Paget and Morgan had persuaded her to have nothing to do with the invasion scheme. She wrote herself to Henry Percy, earl of Northumberland, that he should 'be sure not to associate himself with the duke of Guise or the Spaniards in this project'.[26] If the queen's correspondence cannot be trusted during the earlier period, its contradictions make it even more problematic in the period of the Babington plot. How much that passed

threatened to leave her service if she negotiated with Guise, *Allen and the S.J.* (ibid., pp 115-116). In 1583 Morgan and Charles Paget tried to persuade Mary to rely on Guise for her release, excluding the Spaniards, but this was when they were admitted to the counsels of Guise and the Catholic party, which they apparently sabotaged (ibid., pp 116, 133). See also Edwards, *Persons*, passim.   **26** For the authenticity of Mary's letters, see Edwards, *Persons*, pp 72-4, 76, 83-4, 92, 109, 116, 122-3; Hicks, op. cit., 107, 114, 115, 123, 124. The possibilities of deception were increased from some time after 13.1.1584/5 when Hugh Owen wrote Mary a letter only known in a transcription or decipher in Phelippe's hand. 'Father Parsons thought convenient to give me a copy of his cipher by which I should directly from henceforth advertise your Majesty of some things.' Referring to a recent council of war, 'I will not molest your Majesty with any further discourse what passed, and was resolved, all concluding in fair promise; but of performance I see small appearance.' Parma, 'considering the danger' Mary was in, 'concurs with many of us in opinion that it were convenient to do your best to get out of their hands by escape, for that there is no present means to do it by force, and in England no place of strength to carry your Majesty to, where you might remain till more forces came.' Parma would assist with money and horses. Owen thought a winter escape would be best since the world would be indoors out of sight coping with the English weather. They would need two months notice on the continent: Cal. SP Scotland, vii, pp 536-7. As M. Philippson has shown (*Philipp II von Spanien*

through the so-called 'secret post' may be taken as the invention of Walsingham, in collaboration with Phelippes and Arthur Gregory, shamelessly doctored by the misuse of her own ciphers? It is surely significant that, although the government had access through Morgan and Charles Paget, if no others, to her authentic correspondence, it was found necessary to make her 'guilt' depend on one or two very dubious letters allegedly addressed to Babington and not to Châteauneuf, her usual channel. These letters were intercepted at the end of a series otherwise uncompromising.

We have considered the group of renegade Catholics, including at least one priest, who worked for the government in the operation of the plot. We now have to consider those who were more or less bona fide Catholics. Some were certainly less rather than more. Those who were later executed for complicity may be taken as bona fide, but no easy categorisation is possible since those executed had been infiltrated by the agents provocateurs. Intelligent Catholics everywhere knew that their best hope lay in a future which might not be far away. All in England were even more ready than before to show loyalty to Elizabeth, knowing they could look forward, and soon, to the probable succession of the Scottish queen and the beginning of emancipation. They would have been happy to see Mary released, but there is no evidence that they were prepared to see Elizabeth displaced by violence and even less by assassination. The topic of assassination must have been discussed at least quietly abroad though hardly in England. There were dramatic examples of its use in contemporary politics, already noted, which could not have been passed over in silence. But Robert Persons no doubt spoke not only for himself but also for the great majority of his Catholic contempo-

---

und die letzten Lebensjahre Maria Stuarts), although Mary sent a secret agent to Madrid in May 1580 with a view to negotiating her liberation, Spain always showed itself lukewarm to her cause (p. 432). Philip was apparently ready to sell Mary's cause about this time for an English alliance: not surprisingly since her roots were in France (p. 437). In 1583, when Charles Paget was sent to England as Guise's agent, his 'instruction' made it clear that the main aim of the impresa was to get the English crown for Mary and the supremacy of French influence in England. Not surprisingly, Philip held back, and rejected a plan in November 1583 which had papal support. Paget, frustrating the scheme in England, returned to tell Guise that nothing was ready there (pp 451-2). In September 1584 Crichton was captured with plans for invading England under the late Lennox (p. 456). Mary was reported in Taberna's dispatch to Rome of 8.1.1585 as sending a war plan to Englefield in Spain while negotiating for her liberty in England (p. 457). But by this time Mary's correspondence cannot be trusted. As McCoog says, 'throughout Elizabeth's reign, besides plots concocted for political reasons by William Cecil, there were – and this is too often ignored in Catholic investigations of plots – real conspiracies involving Catholic powers to liberate the imprisoned Mary ... and to place her on the throne occupied by her heretical cousin'; *The S. J. in Ireland, Scotland and England* ... , p. 6. Even if we allow the word 'conspiracy', were not projects to liberate Mary, unjustly held, altogether reasonable, especially by foreign powers? The puzzle in the Babington conspiracy is to know if there were any 'plotters' in England who really wanted more than Mary's release, and if they wanted more, who inveigled them into it, and how. There is no reason to think Mary wanted more than her freedom. For Mary and invasion projects, see also, Edwards, *Persons* ... , pp 72-4, 89-92, 115-116. By 1585 Philip had virtually abandoned Mary's cause. Lettenhove, op. cit., i, p. 105, citing de Taxis to Philip II, 27.10.1585. This letter is not in the *Cal. SP Spain*. See also Guise to Mendoza, 1.10.1585, ibid., p. 106.

raries when he declared, 'He was never consenting, witting, willing, inducing, yielding, nor privy to any such personal attempts against her Majesty in his life.' And he
was well aware that 'English Catholics themselves desired not to be delivered from
their miseries by any such attempt'.[27]

Among the group that was later indicted and executed for treason, the most forward in promoting the English queen's assassination was Walsingham's agent, Gilbert
Gifford. All the bona fide Catholics had to be spurred over the hurdle of initial reluctance to accept the idea. Some refused to be driven. Gifford's first success was with
John Savage. He resided at Rheims from 1581. Leaving in 1583, he soon returned to
study for the priesthood. He was then contacted by Gilbert Gifford who persuaded
him, after three weeks of effort, to overcome his moral misgivings to take an oath to
kill Elizabeth.[28] Did Savage go along with this merely to have something worthwhile
to offer Walsingham? See on! He was told that Dr William Gifford, a professor at the
seminary, approved. Walsingham was kept informed from the beginning of all developments, of course. Gilbert Gifford returned to England in 1585 to become Mary's
letter carrier at Chartley but the carbuncle continued to fester satisfactorily in his
absence at Paris as well as Rheims. John Ballard, ordained priest in 1581, introduced
John Savage to Anthony Babington. Ballard, a highly eccentric character, became an
informer for Walsingham some time after his ordination. He reminds one of Parry.
Calling himself Captain Fortescue or Foscue he entertained fairly lavishly and made it
his business to know the expatriates including Anthony Babington, Thomas Morgan,
Charles Paget and Anthony Tyrrell, another priest-informer decidedly unstable.
Ballard met Babington at the end of 1585 or in January 1586. He clung to him for more
than one reason. Socially ambitious, Babington gave Ballard the entreé to a social circle higher and wealthier than anything known to him hitherto.

Anthony Babington came from an affluent and distinguished recusant family in
Dethwick, Derbyshire. His age was about twenty-five. Not mentally agile, he was too
young and inexperienced to be a leader in a major enterprise unless pushed or captured
by an older and more forceful man such as Ballard. Ballard did not find it easy to draw
him in the direction he ostensibly desired. In mid-Lent 1586, Ballard got to know of
Savage's plot. Did this association come to resemble the Neville-Parry axis? This
seems to have been the beginning of amalgamation: although Ballard's project was
probably from the first less a private enterprise to curry favour or toleration than yet
another iron in Walsingham's fire. At all events, from this time there was only one plot.
After a dinner at Temple Bar with Babington and his friends, Ballard went to Paris to
consult Thomas Morgan and Charles Paget. Ballard now dominated the Babington
connection. Babington, meanwhile, at Morgan's urging, became the carrier of his letters to Mary.[29] Whatever Morgan knew about what was going on, and he would have

---

27 *The Despatches of Courcelles*, Bannatyne Club 1828, p. 25, mention a proposal to poison Mary. See
also, L. Hicks, op. cit., p. 95 and n. 267. Edwards, *Persons*, p. 85   28 Paul ms, pp 156-7; Hicks, ibid.,
pp 156-7.   29 Paul ms, pp 159-60.

made it his business to know without necessarily approving, there is no reason to believe Mary knew anything of any attempt on Elizabeth's life; or that Morgan changed his whole policy hitherto by encouraging her even to listen to plans for invasion which could involve the death of Elizabeth. When the invasion plans of 1583 were under discussion, Paget and Morgan, as we have seen, both warned her to have nothing to do with Guise or the Spaniards.[30] Morgan listened to everybody and said the right thing to keep in touch with what was going on, but if it did not adversely affect his own interests, it is likely and even probable that he was faithful at least in his own fashion to hers. Putting Mary in danger could not have helped him since he depended on her resources in France. The whole tendency of the loyalists or cooperators with the English government was to avoid unnecessary risks arising from cloak and dagger schemes. This was self-interest at least as much as loyalty.

We may take it that Mary knew of a design or designs to release her and reestablish Catholicism from 1583 but was not given the full account of what was intended. What she learned was garbled. All Mary's letters from about 1585 were addressed to Châteauneuf with the exception of two noted above which she was supposed to have addressed to Babington.[31] Through Cherelles they would all have been known to Walsingham. Any of them, as ciphers, could have been manufactured in the secretary's office. Among those coming to her were more letters supposedly from Charles Paget who, carefully avoiding mention of any attempt on the life of Elizabeth, gave her false information falsely declared to have come from Ballard. These letters claimed that Ballard, who was acquainted with all the best Catholics in England and some in Scotland, assured him that the Catholics would rise in her favour if they had support from abroad. Paget had taken Ballard to Mendoza in Paris and assured him of the same. Mendoza, who might have been tempted by the prospect of revenge against an old enemy, was said to have listened. If so, it must have been very critically. Perhaps he took into account the possibility that Paget by this time was Walsingham's man; or perhaps it occurred to him that his letters were forged. Mendoza sought further information from England; but it was Gilbert Gifford who was sent to get it. Certain it is that Mendoza was opposed to assassination. Writing to Philip II about this time, he insisted that while no means of bringing England to heel should be neglected, 'he would never advise Elizabeth's subjects to conspire against her life, she being their sovereign and a woman.'[32] The thought of a chivalrous Spaniard.

---

30 Edwards, *Persons*, p. 91.   31 Mauvissière left England in September 1585. Mary addressed her first letter to him and Châteauneuf jointly on 6. 9.1585. Before he left, Mauvissière got from Elizabeth a promise that she would be transferred to more salubrious quarters. She complains that the promise has not been kept, and of other matters. Nevertheless, she wrote to Mauvissière on 16.11.; Labanoff, ibid., pp 214-27, 233-5. Before he left, she gave him letters for the queen of France, Catherine de Medicis and the duke of Guise. 'Mais toutes ces lettres passèrent par les mains de Walsingham'; ibid., p. 227. Sepp, op. cit., pp 16-17, lists Mary's letters to various at this time most of which have been printed in Labanoff. For information on the 1583 attempt coming from Samerie and Pasquier, see Edwards, *Persons*, p. 91.   32 Paul ms, pp 161, 212.

Back in London on 22 May 1586, Ballard told Babington of his visits to Mendoza and Paget and that the impresa was imminent; a combined effort of French troops under Guise and Spanish under Parma. This was quite untrue, of course. Gilbert Gifford corroborated Ballard's story on another occasion. But the essential condition for the success of such an expedition was the prior murder of Elizabeth. This was the opinion of the agents-provocateurs among whom one has to include Ballard. According to his second confession, produced later under torture and therefore of little value, Babington, though still dubious about the morality of the action, thought that if the assassination took place, it should be by six men and not Savage alone. The six men were never decided on but the 'evidence' was made to suggest that the six men would have been Babington, Ballard, Chideock Tichbourne, John Savage, Charles Tilney and Edward Abington. Abington was the youngest son of the under treasurer of the royal household. His example would teach Elizabeth to be more careful of those she had about her. Apart from Ballard, they were all young men of good Catholic families. Their religion was enough to make them choice targets for the government. The valuable properties to which they were heir made them even more interesting. After attainder, it would all come to the crown. Also to be implicated were Robert Barnewell, whose family had sheltered Campion, and Robert Gage of a notable family in Sussex. Thomas Salisbury, with estates in Wales, was totally opposed to assassination. Edward Jones' father had been keeper of the royal wardrobe in Mary's reign. All in all they provided a spectacular example of treason and promised a most satisfactory settlement of old scores in their retribution.

Bernard Mawde and Robert Poley, two of Walsingham's most trusted beagles, were now to join the hunt, such as it was.[33] In fact the 'plotters', a covey of young blades, thoughtless, foolish and easily led on by men set on to destroy them, could have had no serious intent of carrying out what was never even as much as an overgrown schoolboys' prank. They made no serious attempt to observe secrecy. Certainly, 'none of the graver sort of Catholics, or those who were esteemed wise, should have any notice of their [the plotters'] intents, because they doubtless would have smelt the fraud and train that were laid for them.'[34] It is significant that Ballard allowed himself to be persuaded – he could not have needed persuasion – not to inform priests of more experience of what was going on since they would have 'hindered the course that was intended, to all their undoing'. William Weston, the Jesuit, met Poley through Babington, warning the latter to do nothing he could be ashamed of. When Weston's distrust of Poley became evident the Jesuit was seized and imprisoned in the Clink. Meanwhile

33 The plotters: Paul ms, pp 162-3. For Mawde and Poley/Pooley, see J. H. Pollen, *Queen Mary and the Babington plot*, passim. Babington's second examination at Ely House on on 20.8.1586 claimed, 'the sixe for taking awaie the queene were never named nor sounded, nor in my owne determination resolved uppon': ibid., p. 75. For Savage, see Pollen, *The Month*, vol. 110, p. 250; Morgan's letter recommending Gilbert Gifford, Murdin, p. 454; Gilbert Gifford's association with Walsingham's spies and Morgan, Lettenhove, i, p. 207, Labanoff, vi, p. 291.   34 Paul's quoted comment, ms, p. 165.

Burghley himself ordered a house to be made available where Robert Poley could meet the conspirators and keep them to their purpose.[35]

Babington himself visited Walsingham three times, the last being on 13 July 1586. On this occasion the secretary even told Babington he had been warned about him. A week before, on 7 July, egged on by Poley and Gifford, Babington had written to Queen Mary describing the plot to kill Elizabeth by six gentlemen 'all his private friends'. The murder would be followed by an invasion from abroad assisted by a rising in England, to be followed by Mary's accession. Babington, unlikely enough, wanted her advice. Walsingham knew all that was going on through the 'secret post'; not least the fact that she presumably never received it. Babington told Mary he would be at Lichfield on 12 July to execute her orders. Phelippes, of course, had the cipher key for her reply and no doubt wrote it. His letter to Walsingham on the eve of the great dénouement, included the notorious phrase, 'we attend her very heart in the next'. Mary's alleged reply was the so-called 'bloody letter'. It was dated 17 July. An alleged deciphered copy of this letter was sent to Walsingham with a drawing of a gallows on the outside. The only inaccuracy in Phelippes' safe prophecy was that Mary in the event was to be beheaded not hanged.[36]

Poley continued to visit Babington in his London lodgings in Heron's Rents. The spy, by the 'plotter's' carelessness, got hold of Mary's alleged reply of 17 July. Babington caught him taking notes from it. At this point Babington offered to take the letter himself to Walsingham the next day. The most reasonable explanation seems to be that he penetrated at last Poley's true role and saw that, like himself by this time, he was working for Walsingham. In any case, his best hope to escape a highly compromising situation for himself and his friends – one hopes he thought of them – would be to make it as public as possible that he was only trying men's allegiance, and none of his associates had ever had any serious intention of murdering the queen. Babington all this time, we may take it, was led on to believe by Walsingham that he was working for him in the role of informer. May one discern a resemblance between Barker, Parry

35 Paul ms, pp 169-71. Poley's house provided by Burghley, Strype, *Annals* ... , pp 4, 233. Weston was certainly arrested at the appropriate time. He described interviews between Walsingham and Babington, which took place on 25 June, 3 and 13 July, as if the latter were known to him and summoned. 'All these particulars Babington narrated to me with his own lips, and profound was my sorrow when I heard him. I knew full well what a master in the art of deception this Walsingham was.' Evidently Weston took it that Walsingham was trying to turn Babington into an agent, or perhaps he already was. Weston told Babington, 'I cannot tell you in what manner you can escape out of his snares. If you yield, you give up your religion ; if you decline his offers, you inevitably incur the peril of death. If you waver between the two, you will still risk your life and lose you reputation among Catholics.' Babington repudiated any idea of relinquishing his Catholicism. Quoted from Weston's Memoirs in J. H. Pollen, *Babington plot*, pp cxxvi-xxix. Pollen challenged Weston's statements on a prioris which do not seem to hold water. Weston wanted no more to do with Babington and never saw him again, as he says, no doubt because he feared a Catholic who was trying to play both ways.   36 Paul ms, pp 172-3. For Phelippes, and Mary's alleged correspondence, *Cal. SP Scotland*, viii, pp 53, 523, 531. This includes the 'bloody letter' of 17. 8.1586 and Phelippes' alleged decipher.

and Babington? At his last meeting with Walsingham Babington seems to have had some misgivings as to who were the real plotters and his own real part in the plot-scene. Typical of the dim-witted young man faced with new and frightening possibilities, he seems to have had no idea what to do – and did nothing. True, there was by this time nothing he could have done. The fly was caught in the web. His confused state of mind seems to be sufficiently indicated in a last letter to Poley. He was ready to suffer whatever fate had in store for him. He begged Poley to be true to him. 'Farewell, sweet Robyn, if as I take thee, true to me; if not adieu.'[37] Words of a man without resource and little understanding even now of the true situation: though fearing the worst.

The round-up of the conspirators was done without haste. The first arrest was not of Babington but Ballard – on 4 August. Although he feigned an act as if he expected the government to swoop on him, and ostensibly arranged for his escape abroad from Sussex from a Gage property on the coast, he returned inexplicably to London. He was arrested in Poley's garden. All of which confirms his 'double-agency'. His first resting place was the Counter. Walsingham meanwhile advised Babington to stay in London until he received a passport for which he had made previous application: a clear indication that Babington thought he was one of those on the right side – Walsingham's. He had presumably been acting under Walsingham's directions from the beginning but another spy, Scudamore, was deputed to keep watch on him.[38] A normal arrangement. In the next few days all the plotters were arrested except Edward, the brother of Lord Windsor. He got away. Like Tilney and Abington he was a gentleman pensioner. Poley and Mawde were arrested and imprisoned for a time to protect their cover. They were intended to live and fight another day; and they did. Gilbert Gifford, who by this time knew the system too well to have any trust in it, fled to France, needless to say without Walsingham's permission. Ordained priest in 1587, he was caught in a Paris brothel in December 1590. He died in the archbishop's prison not long afterwards.[39]

It was now Queen Mary's turn. After Phelippes went to Windsor to expound the latest scandal, Elizabeth gave orders on 9 August for Paulet to search Mary's quarters in every nook and cranny. She had to be got out of the way so that she would not have time or temptation to destroy anything usable as evidence against her. Any evidence manufactured against her would not seem plausible if she had had time and opportu-

---

37 The letter to 'sweete Robyn' is known only in an undated, contemporary copy, BL, Lansdowne ms. 49, no. 25. Printed in full in Pollen, op. cit., p. clxx. *Cf. Cal. SP Scotland*, p. 658.   38 Paul ms, pp 177-8. For R. Gage's and Ballard's movements, Morris, p. 235; search for Ballard and arrest, *Cal. SP Scotland*, viii, pp 584, 588; proclamation against Babington et al., ibid., p. 581; account of the hue and cry by Burghley, PRO, *SP Dom. Eliz.*, 192, f. 22; and by R. Southwell, *An humble supplication to her Majesty*, ed. R. C. Bold (Cambridge 1953). For the arrest of Babington, Gage, Charnock, Dunne and Barnwell, Pollen, op. cit., pp clxxi-clxxiii. For the public reaction in London, Strype, *Annals*, 3, I, p. 607 and Morris, *Troubles* ... , ii, p. 171.   39 Paul ms, pp 180-6. For Gilbert Gifford's end, see Pollen, op. cit., pp ccii, 118, 125, 127, 130 and 98n. on his correspondence.

nity to destroy it. She was sent to Sir Walter Aston's estate at Tixall on the pretext of a hunting expedition. Paulet went with her. Nau and Curll were turned away and kept incommunicado from one another in another house. They never saw Mary again. Only Bourgoing, her physician, and her two maids of honour, were allowed to remain with her. The rest of her staff were sent away. Meanwhile Chartley was systematically ransacked under the competent supervision of William Waad. The sack included not only her own closets but those of Bourgoing and of course the two secretaries. All papers and records allegedly found were packed up and sent to London. Mary returned to Chartley at the end of August under a guard of a hundred soldiers. She was now treated as close prisoner. From this time she was denied her priest.[40]

What was found in Mary's correspondence? As in the case of the Ridolfi plot, the only incriminating evidence against her existed in alleged copy: at that time two letters. Likewise in this plot there was nothing that could be called original evidence to compromise Mary. Dr John Paul, a careful scholar, established the fact that the original of Babington's letter of 6 July, which called forth Mary's reply of 17 July, has disappeared. As for Mary's reply, this survives only in eight contemporary copies. 'Not even that copy which Babington himself authenticated exists.' It was later established that a postscript was forged to bring forth more information from Babington. None of the contemporary copies include this postscript. The original drafts of letters from Mary at the end of July to Mendoza, Paget, Glasgow and others survive but they contain nothing incriminating. From these dubious copies of the letter of 17 July we learn that Mary was glad to renew correspondence with Babington, and praised his efforts to organise relief of the Catholics by invasion from abroad. Foreign help would be necessary for any kind of rising in England. The English government should be overthrown but Elizabeth maintained as queen. Babington should beware of spies and false brethren especially among the priests. Detailed suggestions were offered for her rescue. Although such a letter could have been concocted in its entirety, Dr Paul thought that 'apart from the passages most probably interpolated', the letter was substantially genuine. Certainly, she wished to be released and was a consistent upholder of Catholic faith. References to foreign invasion and armed rising may be taken as interpolation. It is more than plausible that she was willing to consider a plan for her own escape. But since nothing is certain as coming from her in this document it seems a waste of time to attempt further analysis.[41]

As we have seen from the Ridolfi and Throckmorton plots, Walsingham and Cecil would have entertained no scruples in manufacturing evidence where it seemed nec-

---

40 Paul ms, pp 191-5. For the Chartley search, *Cal. SP Scotland*, viii, pp 585, 607, 608. Chanteleuze (v. supra) printed the 'Journal de Dominique Bourgoing' on pp 465-582 of his *Marie Stuart*.   41 Copy of Babington's alleged letter to Mary in *The Bardon papers*, Camden Society, 3rd series, xvii (1909), edited for the Royal Historical Society by Conyers Read, p. 28 f. 'The letter is undated but the generally accepted date is 6. 7.1586' (Paul ms, p. 363). Included is a copy of Mary's alleged letter to Babington. For the latter's examinations, see BL, Yelverton mss, Add. 48027 f., printed in Pollen, op. cit., p. 49f. *Cal. SP*

essary and unlikely to be challenged. A glimpse of what presumably happened on a more extensive scale was provided later by the prototype of establishment historians, William Camden. To promote a politically correct history of the times, Burghley persuaded Camden to begin a history of Elizabeth's reign and provided him with documentation: 'whole masses of writing'. Camden also 'sought all manner of helps on every side'. On the whole, working on the material given, he produced a result which could only have been pleasing to those who wanted a history which would put Mary and the papists in a properly bad light. All the same, his Annals could hardly have been published until well after Elizabeth's death. Camden discovered, and admitted to his credit that, regarding the notorious letter of 17 July, 'there was cunningly added a postscript in the same characters that he [Babington] should set down the names of the six gentlemen' mentioned in Babington's lost letter of 6 July as being ready to kill the queen. According to Dr Paul, 'Camden's clear statement was for long unknown or ignored; but in the earlier part of last century the matter was placed beyond dispute by the discovery of a draft in the handwriting of Phelippes; it bore the superscription: "Post script of the Scottish queen's letter to Babington". It ran, "I would be glad to know the names and qualities of the six gentlemen which are to accomplish the designment; for that it may be I shall be able, upon knowledge of the parties, to give you some further advice necessary to be followed therein. *And even so do wish to be made acquainted with the names of all such principal persons, as also who be already as also who be.* As also from time to time, particularly how you proceed; and as soon as you may, for the same purpose, who be already, and how far everyone, privy hereunto." The giveaway is, of course, in the passage in italics above, which was cancelled in the draft.' If the postscript could have been forged, how much of the rest? Camden not only admitted that the postscript was forged but added, 'if not other matters also'.[42] Walsingham in a letter to Phelippes feared 'the addition of the postscript hath bred the jealousy' – suspicion – which caused Babington to delay a reply. The fact that he admitted the addi-

Spain, iii, p. 497 mentions Babington's torture reported by the French ambassador. 'Pollen says that Babington's accounts of Mary's letter were "so excellent" that he must have committed the letter to memory. He also says, in commenting on Babington's false authentication, that ′Babington is in a mood to oblige the government as far as possibleᵃ. This is naive ... Why was he in such a mood? The answer is almost certain that he was either being tortured or threatened with torture.' (Paul, p. 364). For Nau's minute and the ciphering of the letter, see *Cal. SP Scotland*, ix, p. 30; Cotton ms, Caligula C. ix., ff. 381v, 382. For Walsingham's anxiety, see *Cal. SP Scotland*, viii, pp 666, 673. For the probable destruction of the minute and drafts, see Morris, Paulet ... , p. 280f.; Pollen, op. cit., p. 29. The first admissions of Nau and Curll, A. F. Steuart, *Trial of Mary*, p. 162. Curll's admissions of August 1587, are in BL, Cotton ms, Cal. D. i, f. 90v. For the defence of Mary re her alleged letter to Babington, see Morris, op. cit., p. 228. This brings out the contradiction in the 'received' letter. Paul's 'restatement of the text' is based on Morris and the terms of Mary's letter. Cf. Pollen, pp cxlii and 33. For interpolation, Labanoff, vi, p. 397. See also Conyers Read, Walsingham ... , III, p. 40. Mary's statement at her trial is in *Cal. SP Scotland*, ix, p. 102.   42 Mary to Babington, Chartley, 17/27. 7.1586, PRO, Mary q. of Scots, xviii, no. 53. This is the crucial document in the whole case. What did Mary actually write, if anything, as distinct from her secretaries, especially Nau? The 'textus receptus', a discussion of the 'authentic text' and also the forged

tion of the postscript strongly suggests that he was responsible for the rest. Not until 3 August did Babington relieve Walsingham's anxiety by acknowledging Mary's alleged letter of the seventeenth. After which matters moved swiftly. Did Babington hesitate about playing a part even if it was allotted to him by the principal secretary?

The desired corroboration of the worst possibilities indicated in the 'bloody letter' above were wrung out of John Ballard by a racking so extreme that he was unable to stand at his trial and had to be carried to the bar and then placed in a chair for the arraignment. Not surprisingly, Ballard confessed that Mary had agreed to the assassination of Elizabeth. Babington was likewise tortured somewhere in the series of nine examinations before different councillors to bring him in line with Ballard's confessing to the letter of 17 July. Babington knew by now he was only a pawn in a game where he was at the mercy of queen, knights and castles. He told a certain Father Davis, a missionary priest staying with the Bellamies at Uxendon, that Walsingham was 'the contriver of the plot'. Babington was also in refuge there before his arrest. Nau and Curll, the secretaries, were not put on the rack but they could not have been under any illusion as to what their fate would be if they did not cooperate fully.[43]

Babington's second examination was laid before eight councillors headed by Burghley. Certain clauses, but not the whole of the 'bloody letter' in Phelippes' copy,

postscript, is in Pollen, op. cit., pp 26-46. Labanoff found eight contemporary copies, four in the PRO, three in the BL and one in France. Of the copy in France Labanoff says, 'the passages underlined in red about the assassination, present an evident contradiction with those that immediately follow. I am convinced that these are interpolations by Phelippes made in the original cipher' (*Lettres*, vi, p. 390, n. 1). Pollen was the first to use the Yelverton material (vol, 31). 'He concludes that the text in the copies of the letter which have come down to us is genuine. Yet he rightly points out the fraudulant way in which the text was made up by the government, but says of the postscript that was forged: 'I believe (my italics) that the postscript was the only forgery which Phelippes [the forger] was allowed' (p. 32). What is the evidence for his belief?' That the postscript was a forgery was proposed first by Camden, *Annales ...* , p. 479: 'Quibus subdole additum eodem charactere postscriptum, ut nomina sex nobilium ederet, si non et alia.' Lingard, a keen-eyed critic, accepted this, 'though the postscript does not appear in any of the deciphered copies. As Babington returned no answer, to have deciphered the postscript could have served to no other purpose than to provoke suspicion of its authenticity.' But Tytler discovered in the PRO 'a scrap of paper in cipher, on which was endorsed in the hand of Philipps, 'The postscript of the Scottish quene's letter to Babington'. It has been deciphered by Robert Lemon, and corresponds exactly with the description of the postscript left by Camden. It is not, however, a copy of that postscript, but, in my opinion, an original draft of it; for about the middle a certain passage is scored out with a pen, and a correction substituted for the line scored out. See it in *Tytler*, viii, p. 287; *Lettres de Marie*, vi, p. 395.' And Lingard, *History of England*, vi, p. 421, n. 1. Paul did not find Pollen's rejection of the Lingard and Tytler conclusion convincing but Paul pointed out Pollen's failure to notice 'the vital letter' of Walsingham to Leicester, of 9.7.1586; *Leicester Correspondence*, Camden Society, p. 341. This should be construed with 'the equally important letter' of Lord Henry Howard to Thomas Morgan, Cotton mss, Titus C. vi. f. 66. Nowhere is it evident to what exactly Mary gave her consent, if she did. Pollen, while rejecting the theory of interpolation, admits that nowhere in the letter does she approve of Elizabeth's assassination. Lingard as a historian has been vindicated in Edwin Jones, *The English nation: the great myth* (Stroud 1998).   43 Paul ms, pp 198-9, 220. He accepted as indisputable the evidence that Babington was tortured. By the fact of being in the Tower, the fear of torture was present and doubtless influenced the production of Babington's

were put before Babington as being attested by the other plotters. This was false but was a common trick. Babington not only accepted these but apparently signed a copy of the whole letter, but without the postscript. In his first examination he had acknowledged this too. He now wrote, 'This is the very true copy of the Queen's letter last sent to me'. It was not, but the eight councillors obediently countersigned it.[44]

nine confessions; Pollen, op. cit., pp 49-97. He accepted the probability of its application. Southwell in the *Humble supplication* (pp 17-18) made Walsingham and his agents mainly responsible for the Babington plot being 'both, plotted furthered and finished by ... Walsingham and his other complices, who layd and hatched all the particulers thereof, as they thought it would best fall out to the discredit of Catholiques and cutting off the Queene of Scots.' Challoner, *Memoirs of missionary priests* (1741), i, p. 214, quotes the priest Davis as saying 'Walsingham was the chief actor and contriver, as I gathered by Mr Babington himself, who was with me the night before he was apprehended.' See also William Weston's life in Morris, *Troubles* ... , ii, pp 181f. Quoted in A.G. Petti, ed., *Verstegan papers*, CRS 52 (1959), p. 19.   44 Paul ms, pp 202-4. Babington's 9 examinations between 18-20.8 and [8.9.1586] are in Pollen, op. cit., pp 49-97. 'Babington's first confession', on pp 49-66, meaning the first surviving, was probably the 2nd(?) although Pollen calls it the first. Regarding that of 18-20.8., taken at Ely House, although Pollen correctly calls it 'by far the clearest and fullest contemporary source', it is very unsatisfactory as evidence. It was 'derived from the official record of the trial' in *Cal. C.* ix, ff. 456-9. The 'complete text', as Cotton gives it, is in Yelverton ms xxxi, ff. 218-23 (BL Add. ms, 48, 027). 'Its date is about 1600' in an 'ordinary clerk's hand ... and the copyist errors are numerous ... sections and paragraphs are inserted.' The collector of the papers was Robert Beale, a clerk of the privy council, faithful to his employers as an editor, no doubt. More one could not say.

According to this, Babington went to France 'without licence' in 1580 and in a 6-month stay was contacted by Morgan who led him to Glasgow. Both enlisted him for Mary's service. After his return to England, they recommended him by letter to Mary who wrote 'a letter of congratulation' which came to him by a Mrs Bray of Sheffield. After coming to London, de Courcelles of the French embassy, gave Babington a letter from Morgan enclosing a packet which Babington was requested to deliver to Mary. Anthony Rolston and Mrs Bray became the means of conveyance 'of all such packets as I sent unto the Quene', some five times in two years. Realising the danger of the service, Babington broke it off in May 1583. Mary was removed from Shrewsbury's to Ralph Sadleir's custody on 25. 8.1583. 'The letters from Morgan, then forwarded, cannot now be identified' (Pollen, p. 50) The Caligula ms was edited to invert the sense so that 'Mary is represented as wishing to send packets to Babington which she has received from Morgan '(ibid., n. 3).

In July 1586 (Caligula, Yelverton gives June), Babington 'received by a boy unknown ... letters in sipher' asking him to send by that bearer letters which he had received from Morgan in April, as he remembered, directed to her. Babington refused but kept these 'in safety'. On a previous occasion he returned to Morgan another packet because he did not wish to become reinvolved in a dangerous business. He wished to go abroad but could not get a licence. In London, he was drawn with others 'our mishap ... into these cursed courses by the persuasion of such as abused our zeal in religion, and ... youthful ablity ... ambitious of honour and fame.' Ballard, fresh from Paris, approached him about May 1586 with a cock-and-bull story presented as coming from Mendoza: all was in place for an immediate invasion by the legendary Catholic League that summer without further delay. Savage's version of this manifestly inspired rumour was that the 60, 000 men would be recruited in England! (Pollen, p. 53 and n. 2). According to Ballard, Savage would be the principal assassin of Elizabeth. Although Babington claimed plausibly that he did not believe Ballard, he admitted discussing the apparent dilemma with his friends Salisbury, Tichburne and Barnewell. The Catholics in England stood in danger of an English Barthololomew. They agreed the best remedy would be to escape abroad, with or without licence. Babington tried for a licence through Poley 'which he had undertaken and had brought me to Mr Secretary once before,

Soon after their arrest, Nau and Curll were lodged with Walsingham, not as 'guests', like Ridolfi, but as prisoners. The government pressed Nau as to the whereabouts of a minute of Mary's reply to Babington which he had made in French from Mary's dictation. From this Nau had drafted a letter which he read back to Mary. Curll put this into English and then into cipher and sent it off. As Dr Paul observed, 'What therefore seems clear is that Nau wrote something down from Mary's oral directions to form the basis of a reply and that there was no authentic text [of this] in her hands. A kind of draft consisting of notes by Mary there may have been, but there were beyond any doubt the draft letters made by Nau and Curll. What happened to them?'

unto whome I made proffer of service in generall tearmes, and with many honourable speeches was dismissed.' The first interview with Walsingham was late in June (Pollen, p. 56 and n. 2). It could not have taken the experienced Walsingham long to sum up Babington as the ideal leader of his plot: young, green, garrulous, unsure of himself, easily overborne by older men and too ready to believe them. Poley is the main agent, Walsingham's trusty, but Savage and Ballard, possibly flattered and persuaded to play a role of testing men's allegiances, are the catspaws. Petti wrote, 'Poley's part seems to have been underestimated in recent works on the plot, and the fact has not been taken into account that ... on Burghley's orders, a house was placed at his disposal which he used for playing the part of a generous host to Catholics, and in particular to his fellow-conspirators. Among those to whom Poley offered the full use of his house was Fr. Weston' (*Verstegan papers*, p. 20, n. 16). But Weston was too old a hand to be caught. Ballard had the task of drawing Babington closer in. He resisted. 'I told him there were sundry other more fit, of greater age, authoritie, conscience and experience; and that it would be held extreme of presumption for me or any younge man to undertake the managing of so great an accion' (Pollen, ibid.). It seems that Babington only agreed, or thought he was agreeing, to a scheme to release Mary assisted by foreign forces. 'I advised [Ballard] that Savadge should surcease from prosecuting his intention, which he said was to kill her Majestie' (ibid., p. 57). Edward Abington was reported to favour abducting Elizabeth and oblige her 'to graunt toleration of religion if not reformation' taking 'care of the preservation of her health and life, removing from her such as should be thought meet, and placing other Catholiques in their room' (ibid.). This is curiously reminiscent of the bye plot of 1603. So far it is all fairly plausible. The spiders crawling across the web to the flies already struggling in its toils. But at this point the confession becomes obscure. One suspects contrived editing. Babington admits conferring 'with the three aforesaid gentlemen', seemingly Salisbury, Tuchburne and Barnewell, 'concerning the action of the Queene's person', which queen? – and also discussion with Tilney and Abington. These but not Salisbury 'were disposed to undertake the exploite for the Queene's person, if it were holden lawfull, whereof Mr Barnewell doubted, and some others, but for the invasion and surprising of her person they made no doubt'. The word 'invasion' is ambiguous and need not be taken to refer to a military operation. One suspects that Beale was busy with his editing. A little later, Babington says he 'never spoke' with Tuichburn [*sic*] 'touching any part of the practise neather did I knowe whether he was privie thereunto or no' although 'we recommended him ... whome in our intention Balard and I reconed one of the sixe with Mr Abbington, Tilney, Tichborne [*sic*], Barnwell and Savadge' (ibid., p. 58). Taking Poley into his confidence, who promised to follow Babington whatever he wanted, the latter thought they should stay away 'from all practises daungerous to the Queene person or the state', go abroad and take up the contemplative or studious life. Poley was opposed to this, of course, and since Babington could not get a passport for himself and friends, by the persuasion of Poley and Ballard 'I still enterteyned the practyze, but with suche extreme delayes as might well bewraye the repugnance which was in my nature' (ibid., p. 59). What practice exactly did he entertain? Beale's (?) skilful editing leaves the possibility that, in spite of Babington's rejection of assassination, it might be to kill Elizabeth. Ballard reproached him for his tardiness, fearing 'I would discover it unto the Queene herself' (ibid.). He would have done if he could hope

They must have been among Mary's papers seized at Chartley.[45] If they disappeared they could have contained nothing remotely incriminating.

Walsingham wrote to Phelippes on 3 September that the two secretaries could not yet be brought to confess they were acquainted with the letters that passed between Mary and Babington. It was all very correct. 'I would to God those minutes were found.' On 4 September Curll was reported to have acknowledged sending Mary's letter but 'he charges Nau to have been the principal instrument'. The minute was not extant. But Walsingham thought 'some extraordinary favour' shown to Curll might get him talking. To say what? Waad now came on the scene. He claimed that Nau told him the vital drafts or minutes in French and English would be found in Pasquier, master of the wardrobe's, chests. It was supposed that Phelippes had overlooked them. A few days before, Nau was certain these had been taken by Elizabeth's agents with everything else. As Paul observed, 'the documents were never found and it requires little imagination to surmise what may have happened. Were the draft letters and the minute not produced because of the forged passage ... and almost certainly because of other forged passages? Did Phelippes destroy these documents because they would have proved an embarrassment? Moreover, if no drafts or minutes were forthcoming, was there not still the decipherment of Mary's authentic letter which Phelippes had made and carried to Walsingham? ... The decipherment was not produced at Mary's trial.'[46]

for 'pardone for the rest.' They debated 'obiter' various dangerous themes to play for time and delay decision. Poley no doubt led the discussions since he suggested Leicester be killed 'by poison or violence' adding in Burghley and Walsingham for good measure (ibid., p. 60). According to this, it was Gilbert Gifford who finally edged the unwilling conspirators to their doom. He made two journeys abroad and two returns in the summer this year. His feigned plot only began after his first return in early June. Now he pushed it forward after a return between 26. 6. and 11.7.1586 (ibid., and n. 3). The only plot to which Babington subscribed was to rescue Mary. He mentioned Savage, Gifford, 'and one as I remember said to be nere Sir Walter Rawley' as wanting to kill Elizabeth, and threatened to denounce them to the lady if they did not desist (ibid., p. 61). 'Having the meanes to send to the Queene of Scotts by the boy that came for her packet [this was Phelippes' servant] I writt unto her touchinge everye particuler of this plott, unto which she answered xx or xxx dayes after accordinge as in my former confessions is declared' (ibid.). Perhaps the earlier confession conveniently 'lost'? made it too clear that the object was not to overthrow Elizabeth or help a massive foreign invasion but simply to free Mary. Babington's letter to her of about 6/16. 7.1586 from London, n. d. (see Pollen, pp 18-23) is only known in an 'official copy'. Contradicting all the above, it accepts Ballard's claim that a foreign invasion is imminent, and preparations must be made to receive and help it. Its objects are not only 'the deliverance of your Majestie' but also 'the dispatch of the usurping competitor' (ibid., p. 20). One must take it as a concoction to provoke Mary's likewise concocted reply of 17/27. 7. from Chartley. 'The unknown boy' who figured largely in Babington's letter carrying to Mary 'was of course Phelippes' messenger' (Pollen, p. 63, n. 3).   **45** Paul ms, pp 204-5. The question of the drafts for the letter of 17/27. 7.1586 by Nau and Curll is discussed in Pollen pp 27-29. Letters of Nau and Curll are given in 'The secret correspondence of Thomas Barnes, Gilbert Curll, Queen Mary and Anthony Babington', Pollen, op. cit, pp 1-48 passim. There was nothing in Mary's own hand to compromise her.   **46** Paul ms, pp 205-6. Letters to Phelippes from Walsingham of 8.1586, Pollen, op. cit., pp 131-5. S. to s., 3.9.1586, *Cal. SP. Scotland*, viii, p. 466, no. 748. Walsingham sends enclosed copies of a letter from D'Esneval and one from Châteauneuf, which have been intercepted, and of which he wants an account of the contents. 'Take care to find out such minutes as have been

Burghley now entered the scene to pressurise Nau and Curll into saying that Mary had committed crimes. They were assured they would escape punishment if they provided the confirmation of 'evidence' nessary so that the blow fell on Mary 'betwixt her head and the shoulders'. In the beginning of September and in mortal terror, Nau signed a statement 'as he can remember' that the letter, which had already been subscribed by Babington, in copy and without the postscript, was the letter written by Mary. When Curll was shown Nau's subscription, he too agreed: it was 'the like, I think, was written in French by Mr Nau and translated and ciphered by me'. Paul noticed the similarity between the technique used on this occasion and that used after the Ridolfi plot to get witnesses to assent. 'First, Babington's subscription was extorted. Nau saw it and himself subscribed. Curll saw Nau's subscription and assented.' Nevertheless pressure continued on Burghley's insistence. On 21 September, Nau made a lengthier subscription and on the 23rd Curll swore to the truth of his former statement. They would have been helped to agree by the knowledge that on 20 September Babington and six of his associates had been executed in St Giles' Fields with a barbarity that shocked even the Elizabethans. In August 1587, shortly before returning to France, Curll declared that the interrogators had shown him 'the two very letters' which Mary had written to Babington, one dated 25 June which had no bearing on the present issue, and the other of 17 July. They also showed him the 'true decipherments' word for word. On this evidence he had to confess, as he did, that he received Mary's answer from Nau, and that 'he put it in a cipher as it was sent to Babington'. This was much more than the cautious admission of nearly a year before. Mary was well aware of the pressure which had been applied to the secretaries to make them say the right thing, although she was in error in supposing they had actually been tortured. The thought and sight of the rack was enough.[47] Understandably.

drawn by Nau, who is not so deeply charged as Curll is, who wrote the letters to Englefield and Charles Paget.' Curll admits the letters were in his hand 'but that the minutes were first drawn by the queen their mistress. Both he and Nau are determined to lay the burden upon their mistress. By no means they will be yet brought to confess they were acquainted with the letters that passed between Babington and her. I would to God those minutes were found.' If the secretaries knew nothing of the latest letters between Babington and Mary, it could only mean they had been forged outside. By this time Phelippes had forged the postscript to the 'bloody letter'. Is Walsingham urging him, in effect, to produce some drafts in the same way? For the use of forgery by government, see Camden, *Annals ... 1635*, p. 261; *Cal. SP Scotland*, vi, p. 675. For Mary's experience of it, Labanoff, op. cit., v, p. 475.   **47** For the search at Chartley, see *Cal. SP Scotland*, viii, pp 585, 607-8; Chanteleuze, op. cit., pp 465-582. For the examinations of Nau and Curll, see Pollen, pp clxxxv-cxcv. Nau and Curll were in the presence of the rack, but compliance was made easier for them by the fact they were shown letters purporting to be found in Babington's lodgings which one may safely assume never existed. As Nau later apologised to James I, 'C'est affaire ayant esté approfondy et avoué en leur proces [the conspirators] tant par lettres, chiffres, mémoires, instructions et aultres papiers, qui furent pris en leur logis, ou il se trouva aulcuns de sa Majesté, que par leur propres adveus, recognaissances et confessions': quoted Pollen, p. cxc, from Cotton ms, Cal. B. v, f. 233. Curll made a similar testimony. As Pollen commented, 'To all who have studied the collection of papers which have come down to us from Phelippes these words of Curll will seem quite incredible.' Ibid. As the French ambassador wrote, 'Ces beaux conseillers d'Angleterre ... jamais ne produisent les

It would be erroneous to compare Nau with Barker and Bannister, the duke of Norfolk's honest servants, leaned upon in 1571. Nau had been in the service of the English government at least since 1584 when he received a secret service payment of £73. Some little time before the first batch of plot executions, Nau wrote fawningly to Walsingham asking him to intercede with Elizabeth for his freedom. 'I protest that after her I shall have my chief obligation to you, to be repaid by me with all humble service.' Although he was not freed until the autumn of 1587, he was well-treated by government. Richard Verstegan, a highly competent newsgetter, claimed that Walsingham 'hired' the two secretaries with £7,000 to betray Mary 'as was found in a bill in his [Walsingham's] study after his decease'. According to Paul, 'when Nau left for France he had with him 10,000 livres and had to leave as much behind'.[48] The sum of £7,000 seems enormous and unlikely, but it may be that this was to make it worth his while to ensure his silence on many details of the plot after he left England. This could have been coupled with a threat of retribution if he reneged. Elizabeth at one point in the failed attempt to secure the extradition of Morgan and Charles Paget apparently declared to Châteauneuf and Bellièvre in December 1585 'that the said Paget had promised Monsieur de Guise to kill her, but that she had means enough in Paris to have him killed if she wished'. Robert Persons, not a man to scare easily, went in fear of assassination himself on more than one occasion.[49]

The trial of the conspirators took place on 13 and 14 September. They were charged with assenting to a plan to assassinate Elizabeth, attempting to stir up a rising of English Catholics with the help of foreign forces, of plotting to release Mary and put her on the English throne. Their confessions and depositions produced before the pressure became extreme showed that they were by no means unanimous in their

mesmes pièces originaulx des procédures mais seulement des copies, lesquelles ils adjoutent ou diminuent ce qu'il leur plait.' Quoted in Pollen, p. clxxxviii from F. H. Egerton, *Life of Thomas Egerton*, p. 101; Lingard, op. cit., p. 435, n. According to Southwell, 'It is further known that the coppie of that letter which Babbington sent to the Queene of Scots was brought ready penned by Poolie from Mr Secretary, the answere whereof was the principal grounds of the Queene's condemnation.' Quoted from the 1600 edition of *The humble supplication*, Petti, *Verstegen papers*, p. 20, n. 20. 48 Paul ms, p. 210. Southwell(?) to Verstegan, December 1591, says, 'Naw, her secretarie, and Curle having been by [Walsingham] hyred with £7, 000 to betray their maistresse, as it was found in a byll in his study after his decease, as hath bene credibly reported. ': *Verstegan papers*, p. 3. A slightly extended report occurs in *The humble supplication*, edition above, p. 21, on Nau and Curll who, 'being the Queen's secretaries, framed such an answere as might best serve for the ditty of a bloudy rhyme, and fit his intention that rewarded them with soe liberall a fee.' A payment was made to Nau by the English goverment of £73 and 2d, which proved that he was 'long before the fatal catastrophe ... the paid agent of Queen Elizabeth.' See Agnes Strickland, *Letters of Mary queen of Scots*, iii, 1843, p. 249. The 10,000 livres, apart from another 10,000 left in England, and also a fortune of 100,000 livres amassed during twelve years in England, are mentioned in *La Mort de la Reine d'Escosse* (1588), pp 143-4. See also Petti, op. cit., p. 21, n. 21. Nau had easy opportunity to make up his own dispatches in 1586 since as Mary claimed, 'qu'il y avoit plus de xii mois que Nau n'escripvoit plus en son cabinet [Mary's] et qu'il se cachoit de tous et faisoit ses despesches en sa chambre pour sa commodit-té, comme il disoit, et pour estre plus à son ayse. ': Chantelauze (Bourgoing), op. cit., p. 525. 49 See Edwards, *R. Persons*, p. 106.

intention to kill the queen or came to accept the idea without persuasion by outside influences. John Savage seemed to have been so persuaded. Thomas Salisbury took it to be a deed 'most damnable'. The rest only seemed to agree that the liberation of Mary was the desirable end. Where they had been driven to the more extreme conclusion, it was under the influence of Walsingham's agents. For the purpose of the trial they were taken to be guilty of serious intent on all charges. The prosecution was conducted by lord chancellor Bromley, vice-chamberlain Hatton and attorney general Popham. The speeches added nothing to what we have seen above. Hatton went out of his way to attack the Catholic clergy and make them responsible for the plot and the corruption of the young plotters. The erstwhile Catholic clerics who were under the influence of Walsingham were, of course, the only ones who had pushed the cause of treason with any enthusiasm. The sentence to death for treason was inevitable. The condemned were executed in two groups, one on 20 September and the other the day following. The singular brutalities of the first day were not repeated on the second. Elizabeth, acting under the influence of extraordinary fear, had demanded the utmost cruelty in inflicting the sentence on the first day. To correspond to the finer feelings of her faithful subjects, she ordered the public entertainment of the second day to be muted. It was all a preliminary to the main show, the trial and condemnation of the queen of Scots.[50] On 25 September Mary, too unwell to go on horseback, arrived by coach at Fotheringhay for the last act of her tragedy. Paulet accompanied her in his own coach. By the end of September or the beginning of October, it was decided that she should be tried under the act for the queen's safety of 1585. A royal commission of forty-three members was appointed. Attorney general Popham supervised the drawing up of the indictment with the advice of Sir Thomas Egerton, solictor general, formerly a prosecutor at Edmund Campion's trial. She was tersely described as 'Mary, daughter and heir of James V, late king of Scotland and dowager of France'. Burghley, true to form, would have been content to hover in the background but Popham required his presence at the trial. Otherwise it might 'work great prejudice to the whole thereof'. Bromley, Hatton, Walsingham were present together with Sir Christopher Wray, chief justice of the king's bench, Sir Roger Manwood, chief baron of the exchequer, Sir Thomas Pickering, the queen's serjeant, Sir Walter Mildmay, chancellor of the exchequer, and others who could be trusted to support the action fully. Only a number of 'safe' persons from the neighbourhood were invited to assist. Elizabeth thought it 'a matter needless' that Nau and Curll should be present. Cecil and Walsingham agreed wholeheartedly.[51]

50 Paul ms, pp 223-34. The plotters' views on killing Elizabeth, *Cal. SP Scotland*, viii, p. 68of. See also Burghley to Hatton, J. Hosack, *Mary, queen of Scots and her accusers*, 2, p. 395. For the trials, *State trials*, i, editions of 1776 and 1809; *Cal, SP Scotland*, viii, 687; 9, pp 16, 17. For Elizabeth's plea for special cruelty, *Bardon papers*, Camden Soc., Series III, vol. I, (1909), p. 45. The executions: BL Add. ms, 48027 (Yelverton xxxi), f. 263v.; *State trials*, i (1730), ; *Cal. SP Scotland*, ix, p. 25. See also George Whetstone, *The censure of a loyal subject*, 1587 (ed. Payne Collier, 1863). Elizabeth's instructions for the second batch of executions, *State trials*, i, (1730), p. 134.   51 Paul ms, pp 236-66. Drawing up

Châteauneuf was Mary's only active friend and supporter in this final phase. He wrote to Elizabeth to point out that Mary as a sovereign person could only be judged by God, a sentiment with which Elizabeth could hardly disagree, so she could not be answerable to English laws. Elizabeth hid behind bristling hauteur. Through William Davison she told him, 'she could not but marvel that a man in his position should take upon himself the schooling of her Majesty and council.' The matter concerned only the English queen and her state. The ambassador's interference was intolerable since he must be aware that Mary was 'living under the protection of another prince [Elizabeth] and where no marks of sovereignty belong to her'. She had offended against the laws of England and must be tried by them. Elizabeth put on even more indignation when Châteauneuf claimed that Mary should have counsel, and warned him to 'intermeddle no further in those things which do in no way appertain to him'.[52]

On the evening of 12 October Mildmay and Paulet read Mary a letter from Elizabeth which made it clear that the English queen had already prejudged her before the trial. Maintaining her innocence of the charges against her, Mary resented the fact that she was addressed as a mere subject. She would not 'give so prejudicial a precedent to foreign princes as to answer to the effect of such a letter.' She enjoyed no protection from English statutes and she was not subject to them. She could only place herself and her cause now in the hands of foreign princes. She refused to come to any 'trial'. After a visit from Hatton on the 13th, however, a courtier with the smoothest of tongues, which he had used hitherto to good effect on Elizabeth, Mary agreed on the 14th, in an interview with Burghley, Walsingham and Bromley to a trial. It was to be on one point only, the charge that she had assented to an attempt on the life of Queen Elizabeth.[53] It was considered enough.

On the first day of the trial, 15 October, Bromley began the proceedings with the charge that she had 'conspired the destruction of her [Elizabeth's] person and of England and the subversion of religion'. There was no counsel for the accused, as was by now customary in English trials for treason. She had no notes, papers, letters or memoirs to assist her. All this she emphasised as she protested to the court she was a free and sovereign princess. God alone was her superior. The commissioners had been evilly informed about her. What she did now was for the maintenance of her royal

the commission, *Cal. SP Scotland*, ix, pp 73, 77, 80. The charge against Mary, Cotton ms, Cal. C. ix, f. 340f., partly in Latin, partly in English. For the question of a preliminary conference of the commissioners with Mary, and Nau and others in attendance, *Cal. SP Scotland*, ix, pp 88.89, 91. A full list of the commissioners is given in Chantelauze, op. cit., pp 496-8.   **52** Paul ms, pp 241-2. For Châteauneuf, *Salisbury Calendar*, 3, p. 182; *Cal. SP Scotland*, ix, pp 91-3. Elizabeth to Mary, ibid., p. 72; Mary's reaction, ibid., pp 96, 97. Cf. Chantelauze, op. cit., pp 499-502. Elizabeth's dismissal of Mary as 'her murtheress', ibid., viii, p. 657 and Morris, op. cit., p. 268. For the visit of Burghley and Bromley to Mary, Cotton ms Cal. C. ix, f. 340f., Camden, *Annales* (1625), p. 148. Chantelauze (Bourgoing), op. cit., pp 503-9.   **53** Paul ms, pp 243-8. For Hatton's visit to Mary on 13 October, see Chantelauze (Bourgoing), op. cit., pp 510-13. See E. St John Brooke, *Sir Christopher Hatton* (1946), p. 305; S. L. Motley, *The United Netherlands*, i, p. 408. Mary's first refusal to appear before the comissioners, *Lettenhove*, op. cit., 2, p. 27; *Cal. SP Scotland*, ix, pp 99, 100.

honour and dignity. She did not appear before the court as a subject of the queen of England. Her sole purpose was to show that she was innocent of the charge of implication in an assassination attempt against Elizabeth. This was the only matter on which she would answer. She required her protest to be drawn up as a formal document and each commissioner to sign it. Bromley answered that her protest would be recorded but it had no legal significance. Resident in England, she was subject to its laws and could be charged with any offence whatever her rank. The commission was then read out. She reasserted, as before the trial, that it was formulated under a law passed expressly against her – the act for the queen's safety of 1585. 'I well perceived', she said, 'when the instrument (or bond) of association was digested what way they meant to take with me.' Bromley and the other commissioners present had been signatories to the bond.[54]

Mary gave a moving speech recounting the hardships of her imprisonment and her right to justice. She no longer wished to govern but only to spend the rest of her life in peace. She would undertake nothing against the good estate of her sister queen. The assembly knew its duty too well to be much moved. All the same Burghley thought it good to intervene with a reminder that she had taken the arms of England and so aspired to the English crown. She pointed out that the arms were taken by order of her father-in-law, Henri II. She only insisted on her right to the succession, not to present occupation. In answer to Francis Gawdy, the queen's sergeant, accusing her of complicity with Babington, she not only denied the charge outright but claimed that she had not received any letters from Babington, and so could not have answered them. Alleged copies of Babington's letters were produced. She said, 'Let it be proved that I received them.' One of the official copies of her 'bloody letter' to Babington of 17 July was then read out on which the whole case depended. She asked to see the copy just read out. After due inspection she denied writing 'any such letter'. She protested that she was not to be charged 'but by her word or by her writing, and she was sure they had neither the one nor the other'. Nau's minute, his French draft of the fatal letter and Curll's translation were not produced, and as we may fairly presume, never existed in the compromising form claimed. So they were destroyed. One thinks of the observation made by Châteauneuf some two months later in another context. 'Those fine councillors of England had forged, falsified and composed all such writings as they pleased ... For it must be noted that they never produce the actual original documents of the proceedings signed by the parties but only "copies", wherein they add and take away what pleases them and serves them in their usual inventions.'[55]

54 Paul ms, pp 251-4. Sir James Mackintosh, *History of Scotland*, iii, p. 317, for an opinion on the trial proceedings. Lord Campbell, *Lives of the Chancellors*, ii (1845), p. 127, for the charges against Mary; Camden, op. cit., p. 153; Chantelauze, pp 514-17.   55 Paul ms, pp 254-8. Mary denies receiving Babington's letters; alleged copies are produced in court; *Cal. SP Scotland*, ix, p. 268. 'Après que sa Majesté eust respondu qu'elle n'avoit jamais parlé à Bainton et que, combien qu'elle en eust ouy parler aultrefois, toutefoys, elle [ne le] cognoissoit et n'avoit jamais trafficqué avec luy; qu'elle ne sÂavoit que c'estoit de ces six hommes dont l'on parlait. ': Chantelauze (Bourgoing), p. 517. Châteauneuf's

Mary was now reminded that the alleged copy of the letter had been subscribed not only by Babington but also by her secretaries. She was ready with her answer. 'If they have written anything prejudicial to the queen, my sister, they did it without my knowledge ... I know for certainty that if they were present they would clear me in this case, and if I had my manuscripts here I could answer all this particularly myself.' She pointed out that it would be a parlous state of affairs if the guilt or innocence of princes had to depend on the depositions of secretaries. Nau could have been bribed or pressurized to commit perjury, and Curll could have done little else but follow him. Anything she had dictated had been only for her deliverance. In these circumstances it mattered little if, as the prosecution insisted, the witness of the two secretaries agreed. They also insisted that Babington had confessed 'freely and voluntarily' and that Nau and Curll had not been constrained. None of which was true, of course. Mary's insistence that Nau's testimony was worthless provoked the commissioners to fury. 'Like madmen they went on, sometimes altogether, sometimes one after another, in order to bring in the queen as guilty.'[56]

Presumably when some kind of order was restored, Mary dealt with Walsingham. She had learnt that he had 'practised' against her son's life as well as her own. She had been warned to beware of Ballard who had an understanding with him. But at this point, giving way at last to the relentless pressure, Mary broke down and wept. Walsingham's reply was sklfully ambivalent and expressed what could be taken as a kind of truth. 'I take God to record I have done nothing unbeseeming an honest man, nor anything in public, but that becomes a person of my rank.' He had only been diligent in uncovering conspiracies. 'If Ballard had offered me his service, I would not have refused it, but rather have recompensed him for his pains. If I conspired with him, why betrayed he it not, to save his own life?' The accused might have asked to

allegations about copies of letters, *Cal. SP Scotland*, ix, p. 268.   56 Paul ms, pp 258-9. For Mary's repudiation of the 'bloody letter', see *State trials* (1809), i, p. 475; Pollen, op. cit., p. 30. Labanoff reproduces the following at the end of the 'contemporary official copy' (PRO, *Mary queen of Scots*, 18, No. 51): 'P. S. Ne faillez brusler la présente quant et quant. Au-dessous est éscrit ce qui suit: C'est la copie des lettres de la Royne d'Escosse dernièrement à moy envoyées. Anthonie Babington. Je pense de vray que c'est la lettre éscripte par Sa Majesté à Babington, comme il me souvient. 6 September 1586. Nau. Telle ou semblable me semble avoir esté la response en françoys par monsieur Nau, laquelle j'ay traduict et mis en chiffre, comme j'en fais mention au pied d'une copie de la lettre de Mr Babington, laquelle monsieur Nau a signé le premier.' Gilbert Curle 5 September 1586. 'Au dos, de la main de Phelippes: Queen of Scots to Anthony Babington. 17 July 1586.' Although Mary denied any knowledge of the letter, Tytler's discovery of Phelippes' forged postscript in the PRO in 1842 see his *History of Scotland*, viii, p. 326 led Labanoff to detect two further forged interpolations in the text which alone made it compromising. 'Il n'entrait nullement dans mes intentions d'admettre dans ce Recueil aucune pièce apocryphe; mais comme ce faux postscriptum me semble une des preuves les plus convaincantes des interpolations introduites dans la lettre même de Marie Stuart ... que j'ai signalées ci-dessus ... '; op. cit., vi, p. 395, n. 1. After three probable interpolations on pp 387, 389-90, in italics, he notes (p. 390, n. 1), these passages 'relatifs au projet d'assassinat, présentant une contradiction évidente avec ce qui suit immédiatement, j'ai la conviction que ce sont les interpolations faites par Phelippes dans le chiffre original. '

whom could Ballard have confessed since there was no third party independent of those who had him in their power. In fact she merely asked him not to take offence at what she said: virtually an apology. Walsingham's hatred was implacable, unrelenting and altogether intelligible. As he wrote to Cecil at the time of the Ridolfi plot, 'So long as that devilish woman lives neither her Majesty must make account to continue in quiet possession of her crown, nor her faithful servants assure themselves of the safety of their lives.'[57] Walsingham's public career would certainly have ended with Mary's accession. And presumably Burghley's. And others'.

To make sure that any residual sympathy for the accused should not affect the outcome even remotely, Burghley, a most skilful performer, took on the direction of the second day of the trial. The proceedings largely repeated those of the day before. Cecil, putting on the ponderous as he well knew how, assured Mary they had not come to censure her but only to follow the demands of justice. Whoever was impressed, Mary, of course, was not. The whole charade had become as wearisome to her as to the assembly: indeed, we are told that most of the earls and barons present were booted and spurred, hoping to make a quick getaway after the formality of an early conclusion. Ignoring their impatience, Mary recounted some of her recent history and her contant efforts to secure a treaty with Elizabeth. Burghley insisted that if Mary had been released she would only have continued to plot. Indeed, her persistence for deliverance was nothing 'but a plot against the queen, for even when it was adoing, your

---

57 Paul ms, pp 258-9. The frenzied behaviour of the court comes in Chantelauze (Bourgoing), op. cit. p. 526. The testimony of Nau and Curll was made much of. It is important to remember that nothing would have come to her except through the hands of either, more especially Nau as her principal secretary. As we have seen, he had been corrupted for some time. They were not permitted to confront her in the court, as she wished. 'Curle she acknowledged an honest man, but not a meet witness to be against her. As for Naw, he had been sometimes a secretary (said she) to the cardinal of Lorain, and commended unto her by the French King, and might easily be drawn either by reward, or hope, or fear, to bear false witness, as one that had sundry times rashly bound himself by oath, and had Curle so pliable unto him, that at his beck he would write what he bade him. It might be that these two might insert into her letters, such things as she had not dictated unto them. It might be also that such letters came to their hands, which notwithstanding, she never saw.' She exclaimed, 'The majesty and safety of all princes falleth to the ground if they depend upon the writings and testimony of secretaries. I delivered nothing to them but what nature delivered to me, that I might at length recover my liberty. And I am not to be convicted but by mine own word or writing. If they have written anything which may be hurtful to the Queen my sister, they have written it altogether without my knowledge ... Sure I am, if they were here present, they would clear me of all blame in this cause. And I, if my notes were at hand, could answer particularly to these things.' (*State trials*, i, p. 145). Chantelauze (Bourgoing), p. 526 for Nau's insolence. Since her letters went out in cipher, it seems disingenuous at first sight that she should insist on matter in her own hand as being the only form of admissible proof. However, minutes and drafts would have been in her hand for the secretaries to put in cipher. Which is, no doubt, why Walsingham made a great show at one point of looking for the drafts. For a compromising letter from Mary to Charles Paget of 17. 7.1586, clearly envisaging invasion, which rings false throughout, see Labanoff, vi, pp 400-4. For Walsingham's self-defence, ibid., col. 1; for his hatred carried over from the Ridolfi plot, see Edwards, *The marvellous chance*, p. 268. See also, *SP Foreign*, 122, ff. 151-2.

man Morgan lured Parry to kill the queen', and afterwards she gave him a pension. 'You give pensions, madame, to murderers.' Mary was reportedly content to reply, 'My Lord, you are my enemy'. Burghley retorted, 'No. I am enemy to the queen's enemies.' She reminded the lord treasurer that it was only honourable to help Morgan, her Paris agent who had lost all for her sake. She reminded him further that the English government had given pensions to her own enemies in Scotland, and bought her son into the bargain. Burghley could only reply that James had been given money for his 'engagements', and Elizabeth liked him. When the performance was over at last, the queen, passing out of the hall, addressed the commissioners with dry good humour. 'You have behaved severely with your charges and have treated me rudely for a person not learned in the laws of chicanery. May God forgive you – and keep me from having much to do with you.'[58]

Elizabeth had ordered that no sentence be passed at Fotheringhay so the court was adjourned till 25 October to the star chamber. Now that the die was cast Mary seems to have experienced no further fear or anxiety. Paulet, happy in the knowledge of how it must end, treated her with a little more courtesy; though not for long. Walsingham wrote to assure Leicester the case was sufficiently proved by the evidence of her secretaries under oath and their writing. Mary's only defence had been a 'plain denial'. This had also been thrown at the duke of Norfolk in 1572, and for that matter at Hermione in *The Winter's Tale*. On the 25th, Nau and Curll were brought before the star chamber but not face to face. They were reported to have testified against Mary once again 'without hope of reward or fear of punishment'. As Paul pertinently observed, 'At Fotheringhay the accused was heard without the vital witnesses; in the star chamber there were two witnesses (separately called) without the accused.' Inexorably, sentence was passed against Mary. Camden admitted, 'the sentence bred divers doubtful opinions amongst men'. In the star chamber Lord Zouche had the courage to declare that while Mary may have been privy to the plot, there was nothing to prove her 'compassing' or 'imagining' the queen's death. He seems to have said something in her favour at the previous trial but, not surprisingly, it was inadequately reported.[59]

58 Paul ms, pp 260-3. The second days' proceedings and the confrontation with Burghley are in *State trials*, i, p. 146, col. 1 to p. 148, col. 1; see also, BL Cotton ms, Cal. B. v. f. 174 and Cotton Cal. C. ix. f. 580. Chantelauze, op. cit., chapter 11, pp 235-60: Mary's criticism of the trial procedure, pp 235-7. As Hosack observed, neither the attorney nor solicitor general, nor the queen's sergeant had any part in the second day's proceedings. Cecil's obvious animosity towards Mary was altogether unworthy of a judge (op. cit., ii, p. 427). While the trial was in progress, Cecil had a memo passed among the commission summarising the 'indignities and wrongs committed by the Queen of Scotland against the Queen of England', a shabby device more worthy of a statesman than a judge, as J. F. Meline saw it (*Mary queen of Scots and her latest English historian* ... , 1871, p. 291. Mary's final comment on leaving the assembly, Chantelauze (Bourgoing), op. cit., p. 254.   59 Paul ms, pp 264-6. The star chamber meeting of the commissioners, *State trials* (1730), i, p. 148. Nau and Curle 'by oath, viva voce, voluntarily without hope of reward, before them avowedly affirmed and confirmed all and every the letters, and copies of letters, before produced, to be most true' (ibid.). Sentence was passed on the absent Mary that 'pretending title to the crown of ... England. [she] hath compassed and imagined ...

The Scottish queen's execution was not rushed. A new parliament was summoned at the end of October to deal with the issue. Hatton, Mildmay and Sir Ralph Sadler delivered themselves predictably and goaded the assembly almost unnecessarily to what reads like slavering bloodlust. Lords and commons confirmed the sentence of the star chamber and a joint committee of both houses presented a petition to Elizabeth on 12 November urging Mary's execution. Elizabeth replied suitably to the occasion but guardedly. She sent Thomas Sackville, Buckhurst and Robert Beale to Fothering-hay to acquaint Mary with the sentence passed in star chamber and confirmed in parliament. Elizabeth herself wanted Mary out of the way but did not relish being, as she must be, the prime instrument of her destruction. Perhaps she remembered that her own mother, Anne Boleyn, had died by the axe. She appealed to the faithful lords and commons for a solution which would avoid the death sentence. But they were adamant. Burghley pressed her for the solemn proclamation of the sentence. Leicester returned from campaigning in the Low Countries to join his voice to Burghley's on 24 November; the day when the stalling Elizabeth gave an 'answer answerless' to the parliamentary petitioners.[60]

It was about this time that Elizabeth bethought her of an answer to her problem which could have been effective but was highly controversial and fraught with unseen consequences. It seems she directed her secretaries Walsingham and Davison to write to Paulet to have the rival queen killed. Since Pope Gregory XIII and the cardinal of Como had been ready to entertain this solution for their Elizabeth problem, one cannot presume to censure the English queen for such a thought. Gregory's successors, faced with the problem, rejected this solution: so did the Jesuits, be it noted once again, as a practical alternative though it might be discussed in the schools as a thesis. It had been put in practice to further both Protestant and Catholic causes abroad. Paulet refused to entertain any such idea, hardly out of sympathy for Mary, but because, apart

divers matters tending to the hurt, death and destruction of ... our Sovereign Lady ...' This official report noted that the sentence 'depended wholly upon the credit of the secretaries, and they not brought face to face ... [So] much talk there was, and divers speeches ran abroad ... Nau's apology to King James, written in ... 1605, wherein laboriously protesting, he excuseth himself, that he was neither author, nor persuader, nor the first revealer of the plot that was undertaken, nor failed of his duty through negligence or want of foresight; yea, that this day he stoutly opposed the chief points of accusation against his lady and mistress: which' as the official account drily observes 'appeareth not by records.' No further comment on Nau seems necessary. For Walsingham to Leicester, 15.10.1586, see *Cal. SP Scotland*, ix. Lord Zouch's song outside the choir is reported in Hardwicke, *State papers*, i, p. 225; J. Morris, op. cit., p. 300.   60 Paul ms, pp 268-79. For proceedings in the parliament and plea for Mary's execution, *State trials*, i, 148-50, including the petition by the lord chancellor and the queen's reply; D'Ewes, *Journals of the Parliaments of Queen Elizabeth*, pp 393-5. The substance of the lord chancellor's speech in the lords, and Puckering's speech to the commons, pleading for Elizabeth's decision to execute, and her reply on 24.11. are in State trials, i, 150-3: 'And now for your petition, I pray you for this present to content yourselves with an answer without amswer.' Ibid., p. 153. See also J. E. Neale, *Elizabeth I and her parliaments*, 2, pp 116f., 126. Leicester no less than Burghley was most anxious for her execution; see *Leicester Correspondence*, see above, pp 431, 447.

from any question of personal honour, he realised the invidious position in which he would be left after the deed. He told William Davison flatly, who had been tipped off by his masters, 'he would not liberate her [Elizabeth] from her embarrassment by the assassination of his prisoner'.[61] The queen was not pleased.

Under the act of 1585, proclamation of the sentence was essential before further action could be taken against a guilty party. The sentence against Mary was proclaimed in London on 4 December amid scenes of public rejoicing; and elsewhere at later dates. James VI made a perfunctory attempt to save her life if only because there was a good deal of opposition in Scotland to the killing of a Scottish queen by the English. A delegation arrived in London in the first week in November. The fact that the lightweight and inexperienced William Keith, master of the wardrobe, was joined to the serpentine Archibald Douglas as the senior member, is a sufficient indication of the superficiality of the lifesaving aspect of the mission. Keith made his plea without guile and mainly for Mary's life. Douglas made it his business to see that the first consideration, James' succession to the English crown, should be assured, even if it meant sacrificing Mary. Douglas understood the real intentions of his king better than Keith. But to save appearances, and to meet the continuing demands of some of the Scots and Courcelles, the French ambassador to Scotland, a second ambassaage comprising the master of Gray and Robert Melville arrived in London at the end of December. Elizabeth, whose irritation and even anger had to be overcome on the previous occasion, was scarcely welcoming.[62]

The French court was correctly and even sincerely insistent on Mary's reprieve from the death sentence. Nevertheless, political considerations rather than family ties or any others were uppermost in the minds of Henri III and Catherine de Medici. Mary's death could not serve French interests and could seriously disturb the balance of power. But word was that the Scottish queen had threatened to transfer her succession right to Spain if James persisted in his heresy.[63] A Spanish conquest of

61 For the projected assassination of Mary, see BL Add. ms 48, 027 (Yelverton xxxi), f. 49; *English Historical Review*, 40, pp 234-5; Sir N. Harris Nicholson, *Life of William Davison ...* (London 1823), pp 86, 273-6.   62 Paul ms, pp 280-92. For the proclamation of the death sentence, see Holinshed, *Chronicle*, 3 (2) (1589), p. 1586. For pressure for Mary's execution and Scottish reactions, see R. S. Rait and A. J. Cameron, *King James' secret* (London 1927), passim and p. 34; Cal. Salisbury mss, 3, pp 175-6; *Cal. SP Scotland*, ix, p. 171f. James' care for the English succession is in *The Warrender papers*, vol. B, f. 337, quoted in Rait and Cameron, pp 96-7. For the correspondence of the master of Gray to Archibald Douglas, 8.9. and 29.9.1586, showing James' coolness to his mother's cause, see Murdin, op. cit., pp 568-9; s. to s., 10.11., 27.11., 25.12.1586 for a further account of this negotiation, ibid., pp 571-6. See Tytler, op. cit., viii, pp 332-40. For Leicester's views, see Rait and Cameron, op. cit., pp 127-9 (citing *The Warrender Letters*, p. 135).   63 Paul ms, pp 293-5. For the French reaction, see Teulet, *Rélation ...* , v, p. 420; Lettenhove, op. cit., ii, p. 137; Alphonse Goovaerts, Bernard Mawd, Ballard, Gifford et Gratley ... un document inedit, annoté et commenté, (Bruxelles 1896), pp 7-20. For the question of Mary's will, see *Cal. SP Spain*, iii, p. 641; 'The will of Mary Stuart', art. by J. D. Mackie, *Scottish Historical Review*, xi, (no. 43 April 1914), pp 338-44. A 'projet de testament fait par Marie Stuart' (see Labanoff, 4, p. 352, from BL Cotton ms, Vespasian c. xvi, f. 145) was drawn up in

England which might follow Mary's death could only be seen as a disaster for France. Ambassador Stafford was urged to send a plea to London for Mary's safety. Elizabeth by way of reply sent Sir Edward Wotton to France to convince the court of Mary's flirtations with Spain. Wotton took with him ten parcels of documents to underpin his audience with Henri on 14 October. This was after Mary's trial but before her sentence. A counter-request was made for the extradition of Thomas Morgan, then living comfortably in the Bastille, but it was claimed that the political and religious situation made this impossible. Charles Paget, who was also asked for, had made himself scarce. Their surrender could only be seen as a betrayal of the Catholics. It was also objected that Elizabeth was giving aid to the Huguenots and Navarre. So Wotton returned to England with only a gold chain for his pains. As if to emphasize his failure, Pomponne de Bellièvre was sent to England to plead Mary's cause in person.[64]

Bellièvre and Châteauneuf were received in audience at Richmond on 7 December. Bellièvre admitted he could not know the truth of the accusations against Mary but she was a sovereign ruler and so not subject to any other sovereign prince. The laws of England could not apply to her. The most severe measure permissible would be to return her to her own country. For the rest he was certain that she would not have so far forgotten her royal dignity as to encourage others to meddle in English affairs. If she were a prisoner of war then she should be judged by the law of nations not by the law of a country not her own. If, against all reason, Mary were killed, there would be a day of reckoning for 'an act so strange and extraordinary which would be committed against all the laws of the world [and] against the person of a sovereign, anointed queen'. Elizabeth replied in measured terms. Mary had 'so many times conspired against my person and the state'. Mary was not her equal. 'One must know what is due to the royal dignity and to the rank I occupy where she is only an inferior ... I know how much the blood of princes is precious, but from the inferior to the superior there is no appearance of right.'[65] One can hardly fail to note the arrogance. One important point she made which may well have expressed a certain truth. She claimed that she herself was not free and in truth was but a prisoner. Perhaps every successful monarch

2.1577: original draft in Nau's hand with many corrections in Mary's hand. James remained Mary's heir if he became Catholic. Otherwise, with papal consent, the right should pass to the king of Spain or others of his family. This will was never put into formal shape. Angry with James, she wrote to Mendoza on 20.5.1586, promising sub conditione to make Philip her heir (Labanoff, 6, p. 309). She made a will the night before her death but it touched only personal matters (Mackie, p. 340). **64** Paul ms, pp 296-300. For Wotton's embassy, see Teulet, *Rélation* ... , v, p. 420; *Lettenhove*, op. cit., ii, p. 137; *Cal. SP Spain*, iii, p. 641. Wotton made much of the will (see n. 63) to discredit Mary in France. When Mary's servants arrived in Paris in 1587 they brought no will with them. But Philip II told Mendoza to keep the autograph letter in which she referred to the will. Elizabeth claimed she had the will and burnt it, no doubt a ruse to cover its non-existence. Philip and Elizabeth both maintained its truth for the opposite ends of their propaganda. Curle claimed to have seen the will in Phelippes' house. Mackie took this to be the 'projet' of 1577. For the rest, 'the story of the completed will was the invention of Spanish statecraft' (op. cit., pp 342-4). **65** Paul ms., pp 301-5. For Bellièvre's negotiation, see Labanoff, vi, p. 473; Egerton, op. cit., p. 89; his first speech with Elizabeth on 7.12., Teulet, op. cit., iv, p. 46.

is a prisoner of the court. Those like Mary, and later Charles I, who try to be independent must expect to come to grief.

Bellièvre had two more audiences with Elizabeth but they accomplished nothing. Elizabeth felt herself even more constrained than before to see to the removal of the main cause of her embarrassment not only at home but also abroad. Her credit stood low in France to say nothing of Spain. Ministers saw her difficulty and decided that the best way of restoring lost sympathy, astonishing as it must seem at first sight, would be to concoct another plot. Nothing succeeds like excess. The prisoner of her court, shackled by circumstances she now feared to control, Elizabeth felt bound to acquiesce. The plot was arranged to be discovered at the beginning of January 1587. Its principal object was to discredit and effectively silence, at a dangerous time for those who wanted Mary's death, the French ambassador Châteauneuf. Inevitably, Burghley was behind it. He reported in his own hand all the statements that were made. Bellièvre's report made later and Châteauneuf's dispatches tell a different story, and no doubt the true one.[66]

Early in the new year, Châteauneuf was summoned to Burghley's house for examination before himself, Leicester, Hatton and William Davison. His secretary, Des Trappes, had been arrested because a 'manifest occasion' had occurred giving the queen reason 'to think otherwise of himself than was belonging to an ambassador sent hither by the king, his master'. After his initial angry reaction at this slur on his honour the ambassador was persuaded to listen to the charge. William Stafford, brother of Sir Edward in Paris, claimed that, in the course of a recent visit to the embassy to get assistance for a passport to France, Châteauneuf had asked him if he knew anyone who might be ready to murder Elizabeth. Stafford knew such a man, Michael Moody, who was then in Newgate for debt. He had the reputation of a rakehell and would do anything for money. Stafford also claimed that Des Trappes had approached him to the same effect, promising Stafford not only the friendship of all the princes in Europe favourable to Mary but a pension of 100,000 crowns from the pope! [67]

Stafford took it further and visited Moody in jail on New Year's day. Moody was eager to cooperate. Stafford and Des Trappes visited Moody again together to settle details. But the Frenchman had a sudden attack of conscience. Stafford must return to the prison to tell Moody that were it not for the honour of Stafford's family, Des

---

66 Bellièvre's second audience, Egerton, p. 91, and Lettenhove, op. cit., 2, p. 164. See also a letter to Brulard, Egerton, p. 92; *Cal. SP Spain*, iii, no. 529. Bellièvre's third interview with Elizabeth, Egerton, p. 101. Elizabeth wrote to Henri III (Egerton, p. 98) and to Catherine de Medicis (Lettenhove, ii, p. 219). For Catherine's comment, see ibid., p. 220, n. 2.   67 Paul ms, pp 312-20 for the 'bogus plot'. For the official story see Murdin, op. cit., pp 578-83. See also L. Hicks, *An Elizabethan problem* (v. supra), pp 153, n. 418 (Bellièvre and Châteaunef to Henri III from London, quoted from Agnes Strickland, *Letters of Mary, queen of Scots*, 1843, ii, p. 192) and n. 420, quoting Stafford to Walsingham from Paris, 24.3.1587; cf. *Cal. SP Foreign, 1586-1588*, p. 203. It was designed to shame Mary in the eyes of France and impede further intercession on her behalf. See *Cal. SP Scotland*, ix, pp 249, 268, 421 et alibi.

Trappes would reveal all immediately to the queen. By way of corroboration, Moody himself had confessed to all this. Des Trappes had previously visited the prison on his own to ascertain the extent of Moody's debts and to assure him that his debts would be paid if he undertook this latest commission. Des Trappes now left for France, meaning to join Bellièvre at Dover, but was arrested at Rochester. Burghley made it clear at the interview that there was no charge against the ambassador but the charge against his secretary was just. Châteauneuf was reasonably incensed at hearing this farrago of nonsense. At first he refused point blank to listen to what a brace of villains such as Stafford and Moody had to say, but in the end he was persuaded to listen to Stafford. Stafford, in contrast to Moody, had a cultivated tongue. He was quite prepared to swear to the truth of what he said. The ambassador rejected everything for the rubbish it was, but Burghley now used a trick which had served on previous occasions to retain the initiative. Des Trappes had told him of the activities of the other two but the ambassador had not informed the queen as he should have done. This put him clearly in the wrong. Châteauneuf bridled, and reminded Burghley he was responsible only to Henri III, his master.[68] The delaying tactic succeeded.

The further disabling of Châteauneuf's influence for Mary was assured by placing him under house arrest. Des Trappes was put in the Tower so the two could have no contact. Sir William Waad was sent to France to complain about the harm done to the good relations between the two crowns by this latest conspiracy. Burghley was nothing if not thorough. Waad wasted no time in France. He poured out against Mary what Bellièvre described as 'calumnies, falsehoods and tricks'. Burghley's latest plot was the last straw for the folks at home, young and old, proving beyond popular doubt that while Mary lived, Elizabeth was in constant peril.

The dénouement of this latest plot occurred somewhat unexpectedly on 6 May 1587. At Elizabeth's request Châteauneuf went to visit her in the old palace at Croydon. The talk came round to the latest plot. A moment arrived when she ordered Walsingham to join them. She then admitted to Châteauneuf quite lightheartedly, 'Here is the man who wished me to be killed'. Whatever his true thoughts, the good diplomat smiled. The queen enlarged. The Des Trappes conspiracy was something she had never credited, and the proof was in a dispatch she had sent to Henri III. She had always regarded the ambassador as the soul of honour. He sent his own report of this bizarre interview to the king on 13 May. Elizabeth further asserted that the plot was concocted by the two knaves. Moody was dismissed as a man who would do anything for money. Of Stafford she did not wish to speak out of respect for his family. His brother was her ambassador in France. His mother was a member of her court. She retracted anything she had previously written to Henri against his ambassador. She wanted Henri's friendship, as she said. Certainly, the death of Mary brought for-

68 Paul ms, pp 315-16. For Cecil as the presumed author of the plot, see Hicks, op. cit., p. 154; B. W. Beckingsale, Burghley, *Tudor statesman* (1967), p. 163, n. 8. For details of Moody's career, Alan Haynes, *Invisible power*, (1992) (see above), pp 80, 82, 92, 95, 132, 133, 136.

ward the threat of an alliance between France and Spain for her revenge. Stafford had no doubt been rehearsed in his part of the plot by Walsingham under Burghley's stage direction. He was well content to prove his loyalty and regard for his career by this subterfuge. Châteauneuf was content to ask that Des Trappes be allowed to return to France so that the affair 'could be clarified for the contentment of his Majesty and for my discharge'. Elizabeth was also ready to clear Des Trappes as well in order to allow him to return to France to pursue his legal career. She was sorry she was responsible for what had happened but insisted that the ambassador use his influence with his secretary so 'that he will never plead a process at Paris for revenge on account of the wrong I have done him'.[69] The whole sordid little tale reminds us that she, no less than Catherine de Medicis, was a princess of the late Renaissance.

Elizabeth had already shown her deviousness in the final handling of Mary's execution. After the death sentence and its approval in Parliament, a warrant was drawn up for Mary's execution and left in the hands of secretary William Davison. Elizabeth signed the warrant when Davison presented it to her, with the further instruction to take it to lord chancellor Bromley for sealing. The secretary was further told to keep all secret. While Elizabeth seemed to be in more determined mood, she was still hankering after someone to remove the responsibility from herself for the necessary deed. According to Davison, as he was leaving her presence on this occasion, 'she fell into some complaint of Sir Amias Paulet and others that might have eased her of this burden'. She wanted him to write to Paulet and Sir Dru Drury, who was about to share the jailership with him at Fotheringhay, to 'sound their disposition in that behalf'. Davison told her it would be useless to write 'knowing the wisdom and integrity of the gentlemen', but he promised to consult Walsingham. Her Majesty was not amused. Nevertheless, letters were sent. Foreseeably, Elizabeth was left with her problem. When Davison saw her again, 'with a great oath she swore that that it was a shame the deed were not already done'. Far from admiring their integrity, the queen could only complain irritably of the 'niceness of the precise fellows'. According to Paul, 'Three times over the years the English queen had had parleys with Scottish regents for Mary's deliverance to them, provided that she was killed as soon as possible after her arrival in Scotland.'[70]

At his last visit to the queen – after the warrant had been signed and sealed – she intimated to Davison that there was no hurry; indeed, there should be delay 'for the form'. The secretary observed that the course taken was the safest. The queen said no more. Davison shared his latest experience with Hatton and Burghley. They and some key councillors at a special meeting, being aware of the queen's reluctance to shoulder

69 Paul ms, pp 318-19. Châteauneuf got a letter to de Trappes and a reply through William Crichton who occupied an adjacent cell; see Pollen, op. cit, p. 166, from Crichton's *De Missione Scotica Puncta Quaedam Notanda Historiae Societatis Servienda* (Chambéry 1611). For Châteauneuf's interview with Elizabeth on 6.5.1587, see Teulet, op. cit., 4, pp 195f.   70 Paul ms, pp 321-53. For the warrant episode, see 'Davison's Discourse', *Cal. SP Scotland*, ix, p. 287. See also P. F. Tytler, op. cit., 8, pp 340-7. After the sealing of the execution warrant but before its dispatch to Fotheringhay, Walsingham

the burden, and the possible consequences, decided to send the warrant to Fothering-hay on their joint responsibility. Davison assured them that, at his last meeting, she had made it clear she did not wish to be troubled again. Robert Beale carried the warrant to Fotheringhay on 4 February accompanied by letters to Shrewsbury and the earl of Kent.[71] Beale read out the death warrant to Mary after dinner on Tuesday, 7 February. A comment by the puritan Kent made it clear, whether he intended it or not, that she was dying for religion and not for alleged plotting.

One of Mary's last acts before the last of all was to swear on a bible 'that she had neither sought nor attempted the death of Elizabeth or any other person'. She made similar protestation on the scaffold a few hours later. The commissioners merely remarked that an oath on a popish bible was of no account. They even refused her the ministrations of her priest at the last, although Préau was still in the castle.[72] Her last

and Davison wrote the same evening 'recommending to her keepers the secret assassination of their royal charge at the queen their mistress' special request' (ibid., pp 342-3); the letter to Paulet follows in extenso on pp 343-4, Elizabeth taking 'it most unkindly that men, professing that love towards her that you do, should in any kind of sort, for the lack of discharge of your duties, cast the burden upon her; knowing, as you do, her indisposition to shed blood, especially of one of that sex and quality, and so near to her in blood as the said queen is.' See also, N. Harris Nicolas, *Life of William Davison*, pp 108-9. Paulet did not burn this letter, as directed, and sent back a clear answer. He was sorry to live to 'this unhappy day in the which I am required by my most gracious sovereign, to do an act which God and the law forbiddeth.' (Tytler, pp 344-5). 71 For the execution warrant, see *Cal. SP Scotland*, ix, pp 262-3 (Harl. ms 290, f. 203). The letter to Shrewsbury of 3.2., addressed to him as the 'principal commssioner', was delivered to him by Kent since his house was on the way to Fotheringhay. Shrewsbury's letter was endorsed, 'brought by Mr Beale to the commission the 6th of February ... with him came Sir Drew Drury, and the 7th went to Fotheringhay, and the 8th ... exe cuted the Scots Queen according to my commission' (ibid., p. 264, from BL Lansdowne ms 982, f. 78b.) The letter to Kent, also of 3.2., told him, ' ... And in the meantime your lordship shall under-stand by this bearer how needful it is to have the proceeding herein to be kept very secret, and upon what occasion no more of the lords in commission are at this time used herein' (ibid., p. 264, from Cotton ms, Cal. C. ix., f. 204). 72 By this time Mary looked for nothing better than death. Her last letter to Elizabeth was dated 19.12.1586. It received no reply and in the circumstances it was alto-gether remarkable that it reached her at all. Mary was sorry she had been denied any opportunity to show Elizabeth 'ce que j'avoys sur le coeur, tant pour ma descharge d'aulcune malveillance ou envie de commettre cruauté ou acte d'ennemye contre ceulx à qui je suis conjoincte de sang, comme aussy pour charitablement tous pouvoir communiquer ce que je pensois vous pouvoir servir tant à votre salut et préservation que por l'entretien de la paix et repos de ceste isle.' (Labanoff, vi, pp 473-480). For the rest it was a declaration of her unswerving Catholic faith. She accepted the warning conveyed by Buckhurst and Beale to prepare herself for death. She only desired that after her enemies had 'assuaged their black desire for my innocent blood' she might be allowed Catholic burial in France (ibid., p. 476); to send a jewel, a blessing and a farewell to her son; that her servants should keep her small bequests to them; and that she be executed publicly lest her enemies claim she had committed suicide. Nowhere did she ask for mercy since doubtless she realised the other queen was too much in the grip of her ministers to be able to grant it even if she wished. Elizabeth was not unmoved by the letter. Leicester admitted to Walsingham, 'There ys a letter from the Scottish queen, that hath wrought tears; but I trust shall do no further therein; albeit the delay is too dangerous.' Quoted in Lingard, op. cit., vi, p. 451, n. 2, from Ellis, *Original Letters*, iii, p. 22. Apart from inspired rumours of invasion, destruction, the escape of Mary etc.

letter was to Henri III, written on the day of her execution, 8 February, in the early hours. 'I am to be executed like a criminal at eight in the morning.' She had 'suffered much for almost twenty years' at Elizabeth's hands. At the end she was not allowed to have her papers even for the purpose of making a will. 'I scorn death and vow that I meet it innocent of any crime, even if I were their subject. The Catholic faith and the assertion of my God-given right to the English crown are the two issues on which I am condemned, and yet I am not allowed to say that it is for the Catholic religion that I die, but for fear of interference with theirs.' She asked the king as her 'brother-in-law and old ally' to pay her 'unfortunate servants the wages due to them' and to have prayers said for her. 'As for my son, I commend him to you in so far as he deserves, for I cannot answer for him.' In the end it was Philip II of Spain who authorised Bernardino Mendoza, his ambassador in Paris, to pay the wages and pensions of Mary's servants.[73]

It is unnecessary to describe yet again the scene painted in many places of Mary's poignant end in the great hall of Fotheringhay.[74] While her closest councillors could only have felt profound relief at the news that the unfinished business of fifteen years was now completed, Elizabeth's feelings may have been mixed. Certainly, she did her best to escape the fact of her responsibility. Undoubtedly, she feared the wrath of foreign powers, notably Spain and France, and their support of any reaction in Scotland. Davison and to a lesser extent Burghley were therefore made the public scapegoats for the regicide.

there was always the magisterial memo of Burghley on the whole subject to keep the queen in line: 'was anything ever devised abroad or at home to the trouble of her majesty's state, but this gentlewoman' – he avoids the word queen – 'was the only way, means and cause? Were it not then more than time to remove that eyesore?' ('The policy and justice of the proposed execution of Mary', *Cal. SP Scotland*, ix, p. 253 from PRO, SP12/45, no. 106, 9 pages in the hand of Burghley's clerk.) Cecil makes a pious appeal, 'The Church whereof her Majesty is a defender, mother, nurse, craves it at her hands' (ibid., p. 256).   **73** Paul ms, pp 337-8. Mary wrote to Elizabeth again on 12.1.1587. See Chantelauze, op. cit., pp 579-81. It did not of course reach her. One of Mary's last letters, of 7. 2., was to Préau, her chaplain. She had wished to make her confession and receive the Sacrament but this had been 'cruellement refusé'. She asked him to pray and keep a vigil for her that night; Labanoff, vi, pp 483-4. She also made her will, mainly concerning small bequests to her servitors: see Labanoff, vi, pp 484-91. For its receipt by Mendoza, see *Cal. SP Spanish*, iv, p. 158. The original of her last letter, to Henri III is in the National Library of Scotland, Adv. ms 54.1.1, published in facsimile in 1977; also in Labanoff, vi, pp 492-4. It seems the letter passed from the royal archives in France to the Scots College, Paris, where it remained until the revolution and the dissolution of the college. It came to the Advocates' Library in 1918.   **74** There are many accounts of the death scene. The official account is in *State Trials*, i, pp 155-6. See also, T. F. Henderson, *M. Q. of Scots, her environment and tragedy* (1905), pp 612-13; Cotton ms, Caligula C. ix, f. 580; Teulet, op. cit., iv, p. 154 (La vray rapport de l'exécution); BL Lansdowne ms, 51, art. 46, printed in Ellis, op. cit. 2nd series, 3, p. 112; Camden, *Annals ...* (1625), p. 202; A. Fraser, *Mary, queen of Scots*, 1971 edition, pp 615-52. At the end she insisted once again on her innocence of plotting against Elizabeth's life (*Cal. SP Venetian*, viii, p. 456f.) She took an oath on the New Testament to the same effect. Her accusers merely said that an oath on a popish bible meant nothing; Chantelauze (Bourgoing), p. 573 and Jebb, ii, p. 616f.

One cannot believe that there was ever any serious danger that the unhappy Davison, as loyal a servant as she ever had, might be executed himself, although it seemed to threaten for a time. The queen took legal advice on the matter but it may be taken as part of the charade. True, Davison was put in the Tower and fined, but he was released in 1589 and his fine remitted. All the while he continued to draw his salary as secretary of state, and a few years later he was granted land worth £200 a year. No doubt Burghley had much to do with all this, as was just. Perhaps knowing the sequel, and the force of raison d'état, none of the councillors came to Davison's rescue or even made serious protest to the queen. In many respects it showed itself once again to be the court of Rigoletto's duke. Burghley was publicly ostracised for a time and professed great distress. But when the decent interval had elapsed, some three months later, foreseeably, he was taken back into full favour. France did not react beyond the demands of political correctness. King James' face was saved by a letter from Elizabeth which deplored the 'miserable accident', with a further assurance that he never had 'a more loving kinswoman or a dearer friend'. The important thing for him was that the English succession seemed safe and secure. Philip II was not so acquiescent. Indeed, he concluded that the time had come to put into serious operation once and for all the 'empresa' which had hung fire since 1583.[75] But whatever the future had in store

---

75 'An intelligence in France to Walsingham', 1.2.1587, warned the English authorities, 'if she [Mary] be dead, the thing must be handled with severity, with show of grievous offence towards those who had charge of her, and search throughout the realm' so that not even a milkmaid would be overlooked; *Cal. SP Scotland*, ix, p. 263, from BL Harleian ms 290, f. 213. It is not clear if the warning had assassination or execution in mind, but Elizabeth wrote to James VI on 14.2. 'I would you know, though felt not, the extreme dolour that overwhelms my mind for that miserable accident, which, far contrary to my meaning, has befallen ... I beseech you that as God and many more know how innocent I am in this case ... so will I never dissemble my actions but cause them to show even as I meant them' (*Cal. SP Scotland*, ix, p. 285; from Cotton Cal. C. ix., f. 212). Whether this was spontaneous or rose from what she had learned from Burghley, who could say? He too came in for her wrath. She would not have known how justified in fact it probably was. He protested to her on 17. 2., 'though for this late fact which so deeply offends your Majesty I am no more to be charged than others, yet I find by report that you do more bitterly condemn me than others, because you have not yet heard me as you have others.' He went on to catalogue his infirmities to rouse her sympathy: *Cal. SP Scotland*, ix, p. 286 from Landsdowne ms 115, f. 89, one page, corrected holograph draft, endd. 'My second letter to her Majesty. Sent by Mr Wolley.' Davison was the principal scapegoat in all this. There is no reason to doubt the accuracy of his 'discourse' (see above) which gives in fine detail events between 1.2. when Elizabeth signed the warrant and 13.2. when he was committed to the Tower. On 2.2 she summoned Davison to know if the warrant had passed the seal. Told that it was, 'she asked, "What need that haste?"'. Davison answered, he 'mad no more haste than herself commaunded. But methinkethe, saithe she, "that it myghte have been otherwise handled for the forme." The vice chamberlain admitted in conversation with Davison immediately afterwards, 'doubtful speeches of hirs bewrayenge a disposytyone to throw the burden from herselfe yf by amy meanes she myghte.' The vice-chamberlain reminded Davison that something similar had happened in the case of the fourth duke of Norfolk. They both went to Burghley who saw to it that the warrant was executed forthwith. On 10.2. Elizabeth in audience with the vice-chamberlain 'disavowed the said executyon as a thinge she never comaunded or intended, castynge the burden generally uppon them all, but chiefly uppon my

Burghley, Walsingham, Leicester, and no doubt Elizabeth, could only conclude that the Babington plot had been a huge success. It boded well – or ill – for the future, depending on the point of view of the onlooker.

showlderes, because as she protested I had, in sufferinge it to goe out of my handes, abused the truste she reposed in me.' No doubt in the bitterness of his grief while in the Tower, Davison vented his feelings in a poem some twelve verses long, 'The ritch find freinds, the poor stand post alone, They wealthe and honour gayne, the poor get none.' From *Cal. SP Scotland*, ix, pp 234-5, from Harleian ms 290, f. 266. One is reminded of similar outbursts in poems by Sir Walter Ralegh and Edward de Vere, the 17th earl of Oxford.

7

Richard Hesketh's plot

It was not until 5 July 1596 that Robert Cecil was formally sworn in as principal secretary. Nevertheless, his father had groomed him for the post and used his service in state matters appropriate to the office since 1591. The plots which preceded 1596 could not have escaped his interest and even influence. Although less important than the spectaculars of 1571 and 1586, two or three plots which preceded those of 1603 are important enough to call for some treatment before the conspiracies of the latter year which constituted the final runup to the gunpowder plot.

The Hesketh plot of 1593 to 1594 was convincingly handled by Christopher Devlin and Ian Wilson.[1] It comprised the usual mix. An eminent person taken to be inimical to the regime becomes tangled in a web of intrigue which brings him to the inevitably nasty end. There are agents provocateurs who flit on and off the scene, a fall-guy who likewise meets his doom, a recusant enclave which is clearly part of the target, and a dearth of reliable manuscript evidence of what really happened. Important documents have been 'lost' and others tampered with. The gods outside the machine seem to be – we will not be surprised – the Cecils, plural this time to include the rising star, son Robert. They preside over another scene of Walpurgisnacht wierdness. Leicester had left them by his death in 1588. Camden set out the basic details of the plot in his *Annals* as they were intended for popular acceptance. There were to be two versions of the story, both dictated, we may believe, by the demands of political correctness. Cokayne's *Complete peerage* continued the tradition based on the worst possible reading of events from the viewpoint of recusants and Jesuits. Making no immodest claim for himself, Devlin pointed out that no previous historian thought it worthwhile to challenge the time-honoured interpretation of events. As this told the story that everybody was content to hear, why challenge it? The question is by now presumably superfluous.

---

1 Christopher Devlin, *Hamlet's divinity and other essays, with an introduction by C. V. Wedgwood* (London 1963); 'The earl and the alchemist', pp 74-114. This was a reprint of three articles from *The Month* for 1953 under the same title on pp 25-38, 92-104, 152-166. See also Ian Wilson, *Shakespeare: the evidence* (London 1993), chapter 11, 'Murder most foul', especially pp 171-8: William Camden, *Annales or the history of the most renowned ... Princesse Elizabeth late queen of England* (London 1635) (English edition), pp 423, 436; Gillow, *Bibliographical dictionary of the English Catholics*, iii, 1887, pp 286-7; *Calendar of the Salisbury mss*, iv, v, see below.

Beginning with the man and his family who gave his name to the plot: according to Devlin's revised genealogy, there were at the time in question three branches of the family descended from the Heskeths of Rufford. Sir Thomas of Rufford and William of Poulton faced across to Bartholomew, Thomas and Richard of Aughton – three brothers who constituted the Aughton branch. The Ruffords of Rufford and Poulton were strongly popish recusant. The Ruffords of Aughton by this time were firmly Anglican.[2] Unexpectedly it was these and not one of the Catholic branches that became involved in the plot. However, spiritual allegiances could be loose: more often than not a matter of temporal advantage. The eldest of the Aughton clan, Bartholomew, described by Devlin as a temporiser, hardly enters the story. Thomas, more decidedly anti-Catholic, a lawyer, became an attorney in the court of wards. He would have had at least some notion of the Cecils' way of doing things. He would certainly have known that any discernible sympathy with papists would have effectively blighted his career.

Richard, the youngest brother, who gave his name to the plot, was also for all intents and purposes Protestant; but as a merchant, and especially from 1581 when he occupied the post of agent at Antwerp, he had many Catholic contacts. This must have included Richard Verstegan, the intelligencer, who resided there many years. One significant contact was the queen's astrologer, Dr John Dee. He mentions in his diary for 12 August 1581 the fact that through the 'diligence' of his 'friend Richard Hesketh, agent at Antwerp', he had received a letter from another student of occult philosophy and an astrological work of reference.[3] Verstegan described Hesketh as 'sometime a merchant' but 'fallen into decay by dealing with alchemists'.[4]

Whatever Hesketh's movements over the next few years, he was in England in 1589. Not for long since he was forced to to decamp once more. At his home in Over Darwen, he was the tenant of Thomas Langton of Newton who held most of the land

---

2 Ibid., p. 78. Devlin sets out a genealogy of the Heskeths which corrects the old Dnb according to E. K. Chambers, *Shakespearean gleanings* (Oxford 1944), p. 55. See also the Hesketh pedigrees from the *Visitations of Lancashire* 1613 ... etc. [*sic*] 1869. Rev. W.G. Procter, 'The manor of Rufford and the ancient family of the Heskeths', *Transactions of the Historic Society of Lancashire and Cheshire*, vol. LIX, pp 93-118: for Richard Hesketh see pp 106-7. Note 1 on p. 107 says W. Holt, S.J., 'offered Edmund York 40, 000 ducats if he would murder the queen [Elizabeth] quoting H. Foley, Records ..., i, p. 355 as his authority. For the relations between R. Persons and Ferdinando, Lord Strange, see Edwards, *Persons*, pp 146-7. Procter, op. cit., p. 106, n. 2, 'an entry in the Derby household book ... shows there was a considerable intimacy between the Derby and Hesketh families at this time.' Quoted from *Stanley Papers*, ii, Chetham Society XXXI. After Christmas 1587, 'On Saturday Sir Thomas Hesketh players went away ... On Sundaie [11.10.1587] Mr Robert Hesketh at dinner and manie others. On Thursdaie my Lord and Lady Strange went to dinner at Rufford. The church book at Great Harewood has the following ... 1593. Thomas Hesketh, Esq., a recusant, did notify his coming to the Martholme to dwell with his mother, to me, W. Harris, curat of Harwood, [4. x.] Elizabeth 36.'   3 Ibid., p. 112, n. 1, quoting Ewen, *Witch-hunting and witch trials*, p. 110. Dee refers to R. Hesketh in his diary under 1581: quoted Devlin, pp 78-9.   4 Cf. Edwards, *R. Persons*, passim, especially pp 146-8. R. Verstegen on R. Hesketh, quoted Devlin, p. 79.

between Bolton and Blackburn. Langton with some eighty of his tenants became involved in an affray to recover some cattle from the lands of Thomas Hoghton of Lea. Hoghton was killed, and Walsingham, as chancellor of the duchy of Lancaster, reacted strongly. Langton and forty of his tenants were arrested and charged with murder. No jury in Lancashire could be found to try them, but Hesketh who was very near them if not actually with them, thought it prudent to flee abroad.[5]

Hesketh went to Prague to join the entourage of Sir Edward Kelley. Kelley had his knighthood not from her gracious Majesty of England but from the emperor Rudolf II for his services to alchemy. Rudolf's interests also included the occult which made his capital a magnet for every sort of charlatan as well as men of calibre. Dee had been at Rudolf's court where Kelley was his 'medium' for a time in magical forays until the pupil outshone the master. The master returned to England in 1589, the year of Hesketh's departure. Kelley was happy to stay where he was. He had suffered the cropping of his ears in Lancashire for coining and had no wish to run the risk of further loss in his own country whether to body or estate. While in Prague he graduated from mere assistant to Dee's sorcery to the lucrative and even more honourable profession of transmuting base metals into gold. His profession suddenly became very honourable indeed when he succeeded, as he claimed, in turning something into gold. Whatever lay at the bottom of the crucible, Rudolf was ready to believe the best. He awarded the magician with a knighthood. Even the hardheaded and distant Burghley was taken in. Or said he was. He tried to coax Kelley back to England to serve his own sovereign. She was by now ready to withhold retribution for any past transgressions. Kelley's fame, which had spread to the English court, found an important advocate in Edward Dyer, poet and courtier. In Prague Kelley became the patron of such as Henry Leigh, steward of the Dacre estates. Leigh had also found himself obliged to seek a better fortune abroad. Meanwhile English government agents such as Thomas Webbe were keeping an eye on Kelley, and on Dyer, for a time also in Prague, and on one another as was by now standard practice.[6] No doubt Hesketh too was being carefully watched.

The bubble of Kelley's fame burst in the spring of 1591 when, unable to maintain his goldmaking claims, Rudolf committed him to prison. Left like mistletoe without an oak, the English community in exile looked for another protector. This proved to be Thomas Stephenson, Jesuit. Stephenson had no interest in the pseudo-scientific activities of Kelley and his circle but he felt it his duty to do his best for his compatriots as a matter of apostolic mission. This was the usual policy of English Jesuits abroad, including Robert Persons. They did not, as a matter of pastoral policy, confine their helpfulness to fellow-papists.[7] Father Stephenson found lodgings for Hesketh with a

5 Ibid., see index references under 'succession'. D. H. Willson, *King James VI and I* (London 1956), chapters ix and x. For Hesketh's flight after the Hoghton affray, Devlin, p. 80.   6 Devlin, p. 85. Hesketh goes to Prague and Kelley, ibid., pp 79-80.   7 Ibid., p. 88. The English community in Prague look to Thomas Stephenson, S.J., after Kelley is jailed: ibid., p. 80.

friend, fellow-Lancastrian and goldsmith, one Abraham Falcon. Falcon described Hesketh as 'yellow-haired ... a stout man, fifty years of age, clothed in yellow fustian with lace after the English manner'.[8]

Standing in the wings in England was the most distinguished victim of the present plot, the fifth earl of Derby. Ferdinando Stanley succeeded his father, Henry, at his death on 25 September 1593. He belonged to the literary circle of courtiers, notably Edward de Vere, seventeenth earl of Oxford, and the earl of Rutland. They none of them enjoyed the favour of the regime. When he was still Ferdinando Lord Strange, Henry's heir, he married Alice Spencer, daughter of Sir John Spencer of Althorp, in 1579. Spencer was one of the richest men in England. Some of the wealth flowed out to the happy pair and through them to an important circle of poets, writers and actors. After the death of the earl of Leicester in 1588 Ferdinando took over the patronage of the Burbage company of actors. Writers as diverse as Robert Greene and Edmund Spenser were glad to acknowledge his support.[9] While none of this impressed the Cecils, they did notice that Lathom, the family seat, was a focal point for popish recu-

---

8 Falcon's description of R. Hesketh, quoted Devlin, p. 81. An important source for the Prague circle was provided by Henry Leigh's long and detailed justification of a letter directed to him by Thomas Stephenson, the Jesuit, presumably brought back by Richard Hesketh and taken from him. Stephenson wrote to Leigh from Prague on 28.11. /8.12.1593 referring to 'our old acquaintance' and marvelling at Leigh's sudden departure without warning. He was informed from London, that Leigh had 'become a good subject for the current time'. Abraham [Falcon] was 'in good health and like to be wealthy'. Stephenson mentioned mutual friends, Thomas L[awson] and 'Mr K' Kelly? whose letter he had received from his house in Lancashire. (*Sal. Cal.*, iv, pp 424-5, cf. p. 451.) Stephenson wrote to Hesketh the same day, acknowledging R. H.'s letter to him of 20.9. (O. S.): (the day that R.H. had his interview with Derby). R. H.'s letter was delivered by Abraham Falcon. Stephenson is glad to know R.H. got home safely. 'Your letters sealed with the two floures are safely delivered to Abraham, together with my letter to you, and to my very beloved Mr Leigh. What you have signified to be writtten to my Lord, his Grace, shall be performed with speed. As yet I hear no word from him ...' – seemingly a nobleman in Prague: items of local political news follows, and cryptically, 'Our lord send us a king, and some more comfort after so many surging waves.' R.H. was asked to deliver Stephenson's letter to Leigh. 'Farewell, good, loving and beloved Mr Hesketh' (ibid., p. 424). Leigh was called upon some time in December 1593 to explain his embarrassing letter from Stephenson. After he 'overspent' his 'whole estate in her Majesty's service without any recompense, he was forced by circumstances to go to Prague to get help from Sir Edward Kelly at whose house he met Stephenson and Richard Tankard. Soon after 'the surprising of ... Kelly and all the Englishmen that were then at Prague' Leigh met Stephenson by chance 'upon Prague bridge' who offered to help him in 'so dangerous a time for all Englishmen.' He could not do other than accept his help but always with a view 'to do her Majesty's service'; indeed, 'notwithstanding the extremity of my want, God never suffered my heart to slide.' The rest is a fulsome repudiation of Stephenson and all his works, an assurance that he does not keep company with recusants, and 'no day passeth but divine service is said twice in my house '(ibid., pp 450-2). Leigh had been in dangerous places, met the wrong kind of people and made a friend of a Jesuit. He too could have been another Hesketh.   9 For Ferdinando, Lord Strange's patronage of the arts, see Devlin, p. 85; Ian Wilson, op. cit., pp 105-6; E. K. Chambers, *The Elizabethan Stage* (Oxford 1974), 1974, ii, pp 118-126, iii, 394, 402, 450; for Countess Alice, i, p. 174, iii, p. 434, iv, pp 67, 112; Andrew Gurr, *The Shakespearean Stage, 1574-1642* (Cambridge 1970), pp 24-9, 76, 163, 165, 167, 170, 173.

sancy even if the senior Stanleys were formally correct themslves in religion. Ferdinando's cousin, Sir William Stanley, had fought with distinction at Zutphen, where Sir Philip Sidney was killed, and at Deventer, during Leicester's 1586 expedition to the Low Countries. Leicester then described Stanley as 'worth his weight in pearl'. On 29 January 1587 William Stanley and his aide Sir Rowland Yorke, apparently disgusted with Leicester's conduct of the war and general incompetence, gave back Deventer to the Spaniards and defected with some 600 men out of a troop of 900 to the enemy.[10] Meanwhile Sir Edward Stanley in London harboured priests, while the family in Lancashire looked benevolently on Catholic families and families with Catholic connections on their demesne – Hoghtons, Savages, Halsalls, Gerards and, of course, Heskeths. It all cried to Burghley and son for cleansing action. The need was emphasised by the fact that in 1590 over 700 Lancastrians had been indicted for recusancy.[11]

With the death of Mary, queen of Scots, the Derbys emerged not only as plausible but as possible claimants to the English throne. Ferdinando was descended from Henry VII through his mother, Margaret Clifford, daughter of Eleanor Brandon, a granddaughter of Henry VII. 'It was well known that, by the terms of Henry VIII's will, the dowager Countess of Derby and her two sons were the only unquestioned legitimate English heirs to the throne.'[12] Burghley would have known all this. The recurrent danger of a Catholic successor to Elizabeth, or of someone not unfavourable to Catholics, was brought home to him by the agency of two Catholic priests. John Cecil and John Fisher, or Fixer, were two priests who by 1591 had become altogether disillusioned with the policies of Father Robert Persons, S.J. It cannot be said they had no reasons for their revision of attitude. The situation in the Jesuit seminaries founded at Valladolid and Seville at times approached the scandalous.

Founded for English students, the seminaries were funded from Spanish alms and the superiors were Spanish. At first, only men of firstrate abilities were appointed, but as the work of the Society of Jesus extended so did recruitment. The later intake was often inferior to the Jesuits of the first generation. There were also the bandwaggoners who jumped on for a ride that could be comfortable if not notably profitable. The Spanish Jesuit authorities, not surprisingly, kept the best superiors for their own institutions. One result of all this was that in day-to-day affairs the Spaniards could show pettiness and jealousy. The basic cause was that these English seminaries had to be kept going from Spanish resources when alms were in chronically short supply.

10 The surrender of Deventer: see Wilson, op. cit., p. 107. See Cardinal Allen, *Defence of Sir William Stanley's surrender of Deventer* 29. i. 1586/7, ed. Thomas Heywood, Chetham Society, xxv, (1851). The introduction pp i-xcic is still useful but overtaken in many places by more recent research; Geoffrey Parker, *The army of Flanders and the Spanish road 1567-1659* (Cambridge 1972), pp 8, 214-15.   11 Recusancy in Lancashire c. 1590: Wilson, p. 106; Christopher Haigh, *Reformation and resistance in Tudor Lancashire* (Cambridge 1975), especially pp 124, 293.   12 Derby's claim to the throne: I. Wilson, pp 106-8; for Henry VIII's will of 30.12.1546, *Rymer's Foedera*, Hagae Comitis 1741

The prospect of sharing limited resources with members of a hostile nation, whatever their religion, sometimes put a severe strain on Christian charity and generosity. Unfortunately, a few men appointed as superiors used the colleges as the means of a good life for themselves and even secular friends while the students had to go without. Persons meanwhile had the unenviable task of trying to beg money from an overburdened Spanish treasury; money which could thus be wasted.[13]

John Cecil and John Fisher decided by the spring of 1591 that enough was enough. Due to return to England, the two priests wrote to Persons on 5 April to get information which would help in ingratiating themselves with the English government. This now seemed to offer the only hope of a way forward to a better life for all papists. Replying to his model students on 13 April 1591, the unsuspecting Persons gave them useful information on the movements of two priests, William Warford and Oliver Almond, which they were able to give to Burghley as part of their peace-offering. More significant in the present context, they had been commissioned to sound out the possibilities of Lord Strange being adopted as the preferred candidate of the Catholics to follow Elizabeth.[14] Persons' references to the whole affair were such that if the letter had been intercepted, which happened fairly often, nothing could be proved without someone to explain and identify. Cecil and Fixer must investigate 'the man my *cousin*'. 'The form in which you may advertise me may be this ... "Your *cousin* the baker is well inclined and glad to hear of you, and meaneth not to give over his pretence to the *old bakehouse* you know of, but rather to put the same in suit when his ability shall serve ... " ' Further, 'I request you that my *cousin's* matter be dealt in secrecy, lest it may turn the poor man to hurt, but great desire have I to hear truly and particularly of his estate.'[15] The phrases in italics were in cipher in the original, deciphered in mar-

---

(George Holmes ed. n), VI, Parts I&II, pp 142-5; Lingard, *The History of England*, 1849, V, pp 212-215; J. J. Scarisbrick, *Henry VIII* (London, 1968), pp 488-94. Ferdinando, 5th earl, G.E.C, *The complete peerage* (London 1916), iv, pp 212-13. Spenser referred to him in 'Colin Clout'. 'He whilst he lived was the noblest swain/That ever piped on an oaken quill/ Both did he other, which could pipe maintain/ and else could pipe himself with passing skill.' In appearance, 'The build is light, the complexion fair and the hair dark brown, the beard peaked, and like the moustache, sandy. The eyes are blue. The expression is singularly amiable and intelligent.' His right to the crown came through his grandmother Eleanor Brandon (ibid., p. 212). He married shortly before 1580 Alice, daughter of Sir John Spenser of Althorpe, Northants. After Ferdinando's death, she married on 20.10.1600 as his 3rd wife, Thomas Egerton, 1st Viscount Brackley (= lord chancellor Ellesmere) who died 15. 3.1516/17. She lived, and died at Harefield, Middlesex, on 28.1.1636/7 aged about 81.   13 For the troubled state of the Catholic seminaries overseas c. 1590, see Edwards, *Persons*, p. 148.   14 John Fisher, John Cecil and Lord Strange. See Devlin, op. cit., pp 82-5; Edwards, *Persons*, pp 146 and n. 60, 147-9. For Persons to John Cecil and John Fixer, 13.4.1591, (n. s.), see *Sal. Cal.* iv, p. 104.   15 The 'bakehouse': Wilson, p. 108, Devlin, pp 84-5. Wilson following Devlin thought the authenticity of Persons' letter was doubtful since it is not in his hand. However, Persons was unable to write in his hand at this time: see Edwards, *Persons*, p. 146. He had been scrupulous hitherto in not involving Jesuits and seminaries working in England in political matters. But by this time it was evident that the government made no distinction in its persecution of priests, assuming for its propaganda purposes that all were

ginal notes. The key to their meaning was provided by John Cecil, now to be known as John Snowden, and Fisher, now to operate under the name of Thomas Wilson.

The 'cousin' in the cryptic passages was Lord Strange. 'Baker' and 'bakehouse' referred to the title and property Strange could inherit when the queen died – her realm. Some doubt has been cast on the authenticity of the letter as coming from Persons but there is no reason why it should not have been genuine. The fact that he was most probably part author of the Book of Succession of 1594, indicates his inevitable interest in Elizabeth's successor. He would make sure, if he had anything to do with it, that it would be someone at least favourable to the Catholics.[16] Persons' letters and other information were delivered by John Snowden to Burghley in an interview on 21 May, if not before.[17] He also gave details of the latest batch of priests from Valladolid including himself and Thomas Wilson alias Fixer. Persons was reliably described as not wanting a Spanish occupation of England but only a reformation of religion. Snowden's task was to ascertain who in England would be ready to help an invading army. Names and positions of Persons' correspondents in Europe were also supplied. An important part of his task was to contact Lord Strange and persuade him to get in touch with Allen.

Wilson made his report to Burghley the following day. Burghley was too shrewd to have them talking together. Wilson gave details of three Jesuits still at liberty in England, Robert Southwell, Henry Garnet and John Curry, along with information on pensions and pensioners. Much of what he said duplicated Snowden's account but he had more to say on Sir William Stanley. From this time Persons may be taken to have slipped into the role of public enemy number one. As Burghley commented, 'Persons doth prevail with them all, and in fine nothing is done there in English affairs but what he will.'[18] It was evident that something needed to be done to knock Ferdinando out of play. A note of July 1591, apparently referring to Snowden and Fixer's joint commission, referred to their being charged 'by means of John Garrat [Gerrard], a priest, to make trial of my Lord Strange, and see how he was affected to that pretence of the

engaged in politics and the overthrow of the regime. Furthermore, the question of Elizabeth's successor was now pressing. It could not be foreseen that she had another ten years to run.   **16** For the succession question, see D. H. Willson, *King James VI and I* (London, 1956), chapters IX and X; for the 'Book of Succession' of 1594 in which Persons had a hand, see Edwards, *Persons*, passim. For a recent hostile view of Persons, see Michael L. Carafiello, *Robert Persons and English Catholicism 1580-1610* (Selinsgrove/London, 1998) pp 33-55. English Protestants were also interested in the forbidden topic. Burghley wrote to son Robert on 6.1.194/5 informing him of the 'apprehension of a vicar in Oxfordshire and a servant of Sir Henry Lee's, for publishing a pedigree publishing sundry titles to the Crown, with an exposition endorsed upon the same pedigree, declaring the obstacles of all the titularies thereon saving my Lord of Huntingdon.' This was 'directly against a special Act ... (13 Eliz.), by which, as I remember, the first offence is to be punished by one year's imprisonment and forfeiture of all their goods, and the second offence as in praemunire. Sal. Cal. v. p. 80). T. Clancy, *Papist pamphleteers*, pp 16, 44-78.   **17** Cecil/Snowden's first interview with Burghley, 21.5.1591, Edwards, *Persons*, p. 147.   **18** Fisher/Wilson's interview with Burghley, 22.5.1591, ibid. and nn. 61-3. For Burghley on R. P., ibid., n. 63, from PRO, SP12/238, no. 161.

crown after her Majesty's death. The matter he would not communicate to any but Garnet and Southwell ... I brought this letter that my Lord [Burgley] might not think that what I told him of Lord Strange was a chimera.'[19]

English spies managed to pick up, if not always facts, then usefully inspired rumours which Burghley knew how to use. One of the spies, Barnes alias Robinson, informed Phelippes from Brussels on 13 June 1592, 'There is certainly intelligence between Strange and the cardinal [Allen]'. Next year, William Goldsmith spying in Rome, managed to procure 'some strictly non-committal letters of introduction from Cardinal Allen and his secretary to Sir William Stanley and to Dr Worthington, a Catholic divine in Brussels. Armed with these and with some gossip about Catholic hopes for Lord Strange, he hastened back to England, to Sir Robert Cecil, confident of a not unfriendly reception.'[20] Burghley incorporated this into his story of the plot as burgeoning in the summer of 1593. Always aware of the importance of giving precise dates to make an invented story sound plausible, he claimed that Hesketh, by this time in Brussels, was instructed by Stanley and Worthington to offer 'a hallowed crown' to Lord Strange while inciting him to rebellion and the dethronement of Elizabeth. Between April and September, Hesketh, in communication with Allen in Rome, received from him further directions and encouragement. Hesketh then allegedly set out from Hamburg for England. This was more plausible than Brussels as a port of embarcation for someone from Prague. As for the charge against Allen, Devlin, a cautious researcher, assured us, the only known letter addressed from Rome to the Low Countries by Allen at this time – a letter intercepted by Burghley – had to do with 'a report of a treaty between England and Spain to endeavour a liberty of religion for the Catholics. 14 August 1593'. This was merely a political ploy furthered by the English government for its own ends. The fact that Robert Poley was involved as a messenger, whom we met earlier in sinister circumstances, does not suggest otherwise. Poley had very recently been involved in some way with the murder of Christopher Marlowe at least as a witness.[21]

---

19 I. Wilson, op. cit., p. 108. Another letter seemingly to John Cecil or Fisher affirmed from another source some kind of connection between Strange and the succession: quoted from Charles Nicholl, *The reckoning. The murder of Christopher Marlowe* (London 1992), p. 229.   20 For spy rumours on expatriate papists and Strange, see Devlin, pp 85-6. William Goldsmyth to R. Cecil, 11.7.1593, report on Philip Woodward, priest, who said inter alia 'that Lord Strange, though he were of no religion, should find friends to decide a nearer estate than all these titles.' (*Sal. Cal.* iv, pp 335-6). For Barnes/Robinson, spy, see L. Hicks, *An Elizabethan problem*, pp 80, 84 and n. 240, 92, 161 and n. 446, 221 and n. 655.   21 Allen was not involved with Strange: Devlin, pp 8687. 'The only known letter that Allen wrote to the Low Countries', known to Burghley because he intercepted it, dealt with a 'report of a treaty between England and Spain to endeavour a liberty of religion for the Catholics. August 14 1593.' Burghley set the plot in his first version in the summer of 1593 'a year after Hesketh's execution and six months after Ferdinando's death.' According to this, Hesketh's mission from Stanley and Dr Worthington was to offer Ferdinando 'a hallowed crown' inviting him to depose the queen. Camden's later story had none of this (*Annals* ... , 1635, pp 436-7). 'There is a very clever, ambiguous propaganda version' of about 1596 'which may well be the intermediary between

Hesketh entered at one of the Cinque Ports on 9 September 1593. It is obvious in view of subsequent developments that he had been predestined to play a part by higher authority of which he could not have been aware. Although he had fled four years earlier to escape the homicide charge, his entry suggested someone who had now nothing to fear and was not in need of money.[22] He was evidently supplied at some point with a passport or at least with a written assurance that his entry would not be challenged. He also needed to have at least a provisional pardon for the murder charge. It is likely that the warden of the Cinque Ports, Lord Cobham, supplied both, no doubt with the full approval of Robert Cecil, his brother-in-law. Cobham Hall lay on Hesketh's route to London between Rochester and Gravesend. His recorded journey began at The Bell in Canterbury where he engaged one, Trumpeter Baylie, a young man lately from the wars, as his servant.[23] From Canterbury Hesketh travelled to Gravesend by way of Rochester and thence by river to London. The two spent a night at Paul's Wharf and another night at Hampstead before proceeding to The White Lion at Islington.[24]

On the morning of 16 September, as they were leaving the White Lion, a highly significamnt incident occurred, described by Hesketh in detail. 'A boy of the house named John Waterworth, in presence of the rest of the servants, as I remember, did deliver me a letter endorsed and directed to my late Lord of Derby, deceased, which they told me was from one Mr Hickman, my Lord's man, which letter, together with my passports, the next day after the death of my old Lord [on 25 September] were delivered to this lord at my request and for my discharge of the same letter.'[25] Hickman was the name of a government servant and agent: but more than one of this name was in state service and it is not clear who is indicated here. Some ten years earlier, Richard Hickman, protégé of Sir Christopher Hatton, introduced two nephews, Bartholomew and William, to Dr Dee. Devlin thought they were used in 'confidential employmant about the law-courts'. Perhaps they continued in the employment of Sir John Puckering, the lord keeper who succeeded Hatton in 1591. Bartholomew Hickman became Dr Dee's 'skryer' or medium. Dee was a close friend, or at least consultant of Puckering. He and the Hickmans, notably Bartholomew, all lived at Kew. Dee's diary contains a number of references to the Hickmans, Bartholomew and William, as well as Puckering. The sorcerers or apprentices seem to have been no more impressive than the other circle in Prague. 'Dee later discovered that all Bartholomew's spiritualist prophecies were drivel and deceit' (Devlin). In 1594, William Hickman offered Robert Cecil £1,000 for the receivership of wards. He was refused. Doubtless he did not help his cause by offering an extra £100 for Lady Burghley. Like Robespierre, Burghley did not

Burghley's first version which asserted Ferdinando's guilt and Camden's later account which denied it.' See *Sal. Cal.*, v, pp 58, 59; *Sadler papers*, iii, 20; Devlin, p. 86, n. 2.   **22** Hesketh's return to England on 9.9.1593: Devlin, pp 87-88. The sources are, the examinations of Bartholomew Hesketh on 4.11.1593, of Richard Baylye on 5.11., and of Richard Hesketh 7.11. (*Sal. Cal.* iv, pp 408-9).   **23** Devlin, p. 88; Baylye's exam, Sal. Cal. IV, p. 408.   **24** Ibid.   **25** Devlin, p. 89; R. Hesketh's exam, *Sal. Cal.* iv, p. 409.

object to a little bloodshed when the cause was right but at certain levels he was incorruptible. Certainly, with his student days well behind him, he no longer played for small sums. Another of the Prague circle who was now in London was Thomas Webbe, the agent.[26]

The fact that Hickman was never investigated in the mystery that blew up over Hesketh's letter makes it clear that he was an important subsidiary factor in the employ of government. There is likewise mystery as to what the letter contained which he handed to Hesketh. It was certainly enough to give the new earl of Derby cause for concern. Two more mysterious letters, apparently commissioned from Cecil or Cobham, mediately at least by the former, were written under order by Hesketh. He was called upon to write them presumably at an interview with the great man soon after his coming into England. They were addressed to Fr Stephenson and Abraham Falcon in Prague. Hesketh was thus firmly connected with the recusants in exile who could be taken to be interested in Derby's succession. The government saw to it that the passage of the letters was not interrupted. The adressees replied without delay, Stephenson, at least, obligingly adding the date of Hesketh's original. 'I received your letter ... dated the 20th of September according to your count' – the 30th on the continent. By the 20th, old style, Hesketh was well on the way to Lancashire so that there was some deliberate confusion intended by the dating of the letters. Not until 15 October O.S. did Hesketh write 'To Lord Cobham or Sir Robert Cecil', beginning, 'I

26 Only Hesketh in his examination of 7.11. mentions 'Mr Hickman' who was also 'my lord's man' which in the context and the usage of the time could only mean Burghley or perhaps his son, Robert. The Hickmans, Richard, Bartholomew, William and his brother(?) Walter were at least on the fringe of an influential circle residing at Kew which included at different times chancellor Hatton, Sir John Puckering and Dr Dee. Bartholomew was Dr Dee's 'skryer' or medium for his occult dabblings (Devlin, p. 90). The influence of the Hickmans, or at least the height of their aspirations, was shown later when William had it in mind to apply for the receivership of the court of wards. He had put aside his first request when he learnt the queen intended it for Sir Henry Killigrew but when he knew Sir Henry had withdrawn his suit, he asked for Sir Robert's favour (letter of 13.5.1594) 'and his father's good liking and allowance thereof' (*Sal. Cal.*, iv, p. 529). 'Mr Fleetwood' was given the preference. When William's brother Walter heard of it, he bearded Sir Robert in terms which were only just respectful and certainly not reverential. His letter of 15.5. reminded Sir Robert 'Mr Fleetwood is not of Lord Burghley's choice' but her Majesty's. So 'as it hath pleased his Lordship to signify Mr Fleetwood to be sufficient, so it might please him to allow of his brother's sufficiency' and get him appointed. If his brother were preferred, 'you shall have £1,000, and my Lady Dixie, my brother's wife, will with many thanks send unto ... your wife £100 to buy her four coach horses' (ibid., p. 531). Sir Robert made it clear that the request 'was not to his honourable liking, by the utter denial of his favour.' Undeterred, Walter discovered that since the queen was considering Lady Edmunds, 'he has thought good once more to be a suitor for his favour, with assured promise that Lady Edmunds shall have £1,000 if by her help it be obtained, and unto himself all duty and service which shall lie in his brother's power to perform' (s. to s., 16.5.1594). More lettercarrying perhaps for special addressees? There is frequent mention of Bartholomew Hickman in Dee's diary (James Orchard Halliwell, *The private diary of Dr John Dee*, Camden Society, 1842). Basil Fitzgibbon thought he might have been the Hickman who gave the letter to Hesketh in the White Lion, Islington. Dee destroyed all his papers on 29.9.1600 (*Diary*, p. 63).

have hereinclosed sent your Honour the two letters I promised.' These were presumably the two answers from Prague. In fact Hesketh was in close confinement by this time so there may have been further deliberate confusion over dating.[27]

Hesketh proceeded, as his companion Baylie makes clear, without haste due or undue to deliver Derby's letter. Before going to Lathom he turned aside to enjoy a long weekend with his wife. On Tuesday 25 September he set out for Lathom still accompanied by Baylie. This was the day the old earl died. It was not a time to disturb the household. Hesketh therefore turned aside to stay a short time at his brother Bartholomew's house at Aughton. On Thursday the 27th Richard went over to Lathom to hand in Hickman's letter and show his passport to Sir Edward Stanley. Ferdinando, the new earl, also saw his passport, as did the bishop of Chester who happened to be staying there.[28] In the ordinary course of events, Hesketh would have returned home, as he

---

27 R. Hesketh to Lord Cobham or Sir Robert Cecil, 15.10.1593 (*Sal. Cal.* iv, pp 389-390) is not easy to interpret. 'I have hereinclosed sent your Honour the two letters I promised', which, when they reached a certain factor in Nuremburg, he should send them on to a foreign Catholic an Englishman would arouse suspicion and he would receive the answer from the 'goldsmith or the father' Falcon or Stephenson? Hesketh asks if Dyer should know of his imprisonment. If he and 'his men or followers' knew of it, they would write to 'my lady Kelly or Mr Thomas Kelley, in respect of what I told your Honour the other day.' And then 'this goldsmith' would know it, Stephenson and the cardinal through the grapevine. 'So shall your honour never have them, which would be a great hindrance to the satisfaction of your Honour in my behalf.' Certain 'notes' were ' 'with the father' (Stephenson?) 'When they come I doubt not but the whole substance, abbreviated, is in mine your Honour has, saving a persuasion to speak with a priest, which now I remember ... and there will be found much more in mine than in them.' He had had an interview with 'Sir William', which could only be Burghley, of which no record remains. Hesketh, whatever he had been up to before, was now fully prepared to go all the way with the government. He had supplied notes from memory and had written two more letters to Prague, Falcon and Stephenson to elicit from them more information which would include 'a note of my own hand'. The rest of the letter suggests that he was a man changing sides and making up for dubious activities in the past. So he regards it as a distinct possibility that her Majesty might not consider him worthy of the 'favour of life' and he does not blame her. He asks Cobham or Cecil to put in a good word for him. 'I would be glad to live to make amends in some part although fully never shall be able.' He offers excuse for his wife, 'a poor gentlewoman' with 'many children'. She was 'never reconciled', that is, converted to Catholicism, any more than he was before his 'going over'. She had never helped him with money so that whatever happened to him, she should be left to enjoy the little she still had. 'She was born on her Majesty's lands, twice her living hath been taken over her head, and now she hath but four years to come, if she live so long.' Devlin thought it likely that Hesketh dealt with Cobham rather than Cecil since Cobham Hall was on Hesketh's route between Rochester and Gravesend while Cecil at this time was with the court at Windsor. But Cecil could have left the court for a time to deal with a matter as serious as Hesketh's. Moreover, he would already have known that his brother-in-law was not of the calibre required for such a delicate operation (cf. Devlin, pp 94-5). **28** Hesketh hands in the Hickman letter: Devlin, p. 90; cf. *Sal. Cal.*, iv, p. 381; ibid., p. 408. The letter was never used in evidence and its contents, while evidently compromising in view of the new earl's reaction, are unknown. It was of course intended for the fourth earl who died on Tuesday 25.9., the day Hesketh set out from Over Darwen to find the fifth earl (Devlin, p. 91). As Devlin emphasizes, the Hickman 'letter was the only sure evidence of any communication between Hesketh and the earl' (p. 93).

was eager to do. But from this point the course of events for Hesketh was to be no longer ordinary. Earl Ferdinando had evidently read the letter and passed it to Sir Edward, a recusant, to deal immediately with Hesketh. Sir Edward assured him that the letter contained nothing important beyond news of plague deaths in London, which was experiencing one of its worst visitations at this time. As Devlin reasonably surmised, this was to try him out. It became apparent to Sir Edward that Hesketh knew nothing of the contents of the letter, but he kept him on at Lathom saying the earl wished to talk to him. The earl used further delaying tactics, time in which he could enquire further and make up his own mind. At last he declared he took so much pleasure in Hesketh's company that he must go with him to court.

Hesketh may have been puzzled by so much attention but suspected nothing untoward. Leaving Lathom, he spent the night of Monday 1 October with his brother at Aughton. The earl had appointed a meeting place for Tuesday 2 October at Brereton, seat of Sir William Brereton, who was another recusant, some forty miles south of Lathom. On the night of 1 October Hesketh wrote two letters, dated 2 October, which he dispatched by Baylie, one to Isabel his wife and the other to his brother Thomas, the lawyer. His excuses to his wife simply made the earl's expressed fondness for his company and his insistence on a visit to court the reason for his not coming to her sooner. Richard's letter to Thomas, known to him as anti-Catholic and careful of his own interests, showed proper caution. Hesketh was a plain man but not naive. 'Having been so long out of the country, I was loth to come to you or any friend I had, before I saw how my lord lieutenant would accept of my coming, and the country think of me.' All had been well: too well, perhaps, for Derby still wished to take him to the court.[29] On 3 October a cavalcade set out from the Derby domain for London. But there is now a gap in the narrative in the course of which Ferdinando got to London and had an audience with the queen. Hesketh meanwhile was put under restraint at Sutton Park, presumably the one in Surrey. Afterwards he was transferred to Ditton Park near Windsor.[30] Just before this he had a passing visit from Sir Robert Cecil.[31] We do not know what Cecil said but apart from making sure that Hesketh still knew very little, he probably encouraged him not to worry for the future but to go on trusting his employers. As for the Hickman letter, it takes no bold stretch of the imagination to suppose that, albeit unknown to the honest or discreet Hesketh, who had not tried to see its contents, it contained some reference to the succession question and Derby's role in it. This explains both Ferdinando's sudden excursion to the royal presence at

---

29 See Devlin, pp 91–2; Hesketh's two letters of 2.10.1593, to his wife, Isabel, and his brother, Thomas, respectively, *Sal. Cal.* iv, p. 381. Sir W. Brereton is referred to as a recusant in CRS, 8, p. 102.   **30** Hesketh was kept after Ferdinando's interview with the queen at Sutton Park and then Ditton Park. Since Ditton Park was near Windsor, it sems likely that the 'Sutton Park' was the estate outside Guildford which was virtually in the vicinity. Cf. Devlin, p. 92, n. 2.   **31** Hesketh's interview with Robert Cecil was indicated in Hesketh's letter of 15.10. in the phrase, 'in respect of that I told your Honour the other day' (*Sal. Cal.*, iv, p. 389). Devlin, p. 94, n. 1). Devlin adds to his note, the evidence 'of a note of Derby's of the 13th implying that Cecil had just returned from the visit' but gives no source.

Windsor and Hesketh's arrest. While Hesketh's relative innocence might have excused, Derby's recusant friends would have been the first to warn him of the danger he was in, the desirability of going straight to her Majesty, and of arresting the letter-carrier in the meantime.

It is significant that Derby went straight to the queen and not to Burghley or anyone by the way. Perhaps he remembered the fate of the duke of Norfolk whose worst mistake had been to trust himself to the courtiers. Derby's interview with the queen was altogether satisfactory. Presumably he showed her the Hesketh letter. She commanded that Hesketh be interrogated. If she made any reference to Hickman, it was carefully omitted from the record. He was never called up for questioning.[32] Many others on the periphery were grilled: Thomas Langton, baron of Newton, recusant, Bartholomew Hesketh, Baylie and others who had nothing to do with it: but not Hickman.

Hesketh's letter 'To Lord Cobham or Sir Robert Cecil' was carefully analysed by Devlin. Of four paragraphs, the first two advised Cecil or Cobham how letters could get through to Stephenson and Falcon without it being suspected that they came from government sources. Hesketh did not want Edward Dyer to know of his arrest or he and his friends would write to Kelley's circle in Prague and rouse the suspicions of the Catholics. Evidently, Hesketh is not now on the side of the papists. The third paragraph claimed that he had made notes of conversations with Sir William Stanley and Dr Worthington in Brussels. These he left with his friends in Prague. He now wished to recover them 'for the satisfaction of your Honour' – presumably Cecil – 'on my behalf'. Evidently, he wished to establish his bona-fide with the principal secretary and to assure him that he was, in spite of any appearances to the contrary, now their honest spy.[33] All the more so since William Waad, a privy council clerk and a man on the way up, had arrived about the time of writing, mid-October, to sift him. Waad began well by claiming that Hesketh was not the alchemist and merchant but Allen's secretary who had come all the way from Rome to stir up Lancashire.

Hesketh's formal confession was delivered on 4 and 5 November. It does little beyond confirming the fact that, far from being Allen's secretary, he 'was never reconciled' to the Church of Rome and had 'no credit with recusants'. He was plausibly throughout the good servant of the English state. He was not allowed to include anything in his confession, at least in what has survived, to make it clear he understood his misfortune arose from the Hickman letter. As Devlin noted, one page of the confession has been badly mutilated. So not for the first time in this tale of treason through a half-century we do not really know what the accused said in his defence.[34]

32 Devlin, p. 93. Cf. Derby to R. Cecil, 13.10. [1593], *Sal. Cal.*, xiii, p. 491.   33 R. Hesketh to Cobham and R. Cecil, see above, n. 27.   34 Same to William Waad 5.11.1593, holograph, mutilated, 2pp, *Sal. Cal.*, xiii, pp 493-4. Devlin, p. 96. It is the confession of a frightened man who hopes by vehemence to be better believed. He repudiates any connection with 'Mr Ormston', a recusant, but refuses to get favour for himself by making false 'supputations' against him or anyone else. 'As concerning that Mr Hesketh which is with the Cardinal ... he is the son of one William Hesketh the elder,

Almost a month later, on 29 November 1593, Hesketh was executed at St Alban's. The same day Waad informed Robert Cecil by letter, 'I was at the arraignment of Hesketh, as I was commanded by my lord keeper, but the man did confess the indictment and acknowledge all his former confessions and declarations to be true' – how many were there? – 'so that there needed no other testimony against him. Nevertheless, Mr Attorney laid open all the plot and course of his treasons for satisfaction of the standers-by, in very discreet sort, and did make collections out of his confessions.'[35]

now so termed of Little Pulton in Lancashire, a continual recusant, which William married the sister of Cardinal Alane and by her had that son and divers others. This William and I came of two brethren between which there was long suit for my grandfather's lands, and there hath not been any great familiarity a[mong] us ...' He admits acquaintance with Doctor Worthington, the eminent exile, and refers in a damaged portion to some matter to be kept 'so secret as might be and as your Honour may think. And I would to God it had been kept from me. I now feel the old grudge to my father in the cardinal is now bestowed upon me; for he might have sent that Hesketh, but being his nephew he spared him and hath made me the enffant perdue as I wrote to the cardinal I thought I should prove.' There follows an obscure sentence. But for 'the affection I bear to my Lord and the hope he would other[wise] have provided for me which way soever he did take the mat[ter] I would otherwise have provided for myself.' He admits, 'I did my message according as I had it in charge with all affection towards my Lord and had obeyed his commandments blinded as many men are with their affections towards noblemen whom they think well of.' This seems to refer, most plausibly in the context, to the letter which he received in Islington for Derby, which he understood from Hickman to be according to either Burghley's or son Robert's will that he deliver it. The fly on the web cannot argue with, still less protest to, the approaching spider. He can only plead. Through obeying what he took to be orders, Hesketh had put himself in a most compromising situation. 'But if it please her Majesty and her Council to pardon my life and conceive well of me and by some mean preserve my credit' which he hoped to have won 'with dealing so sincerely in this matter', he would spend the rest of his lfe in her service. As in the old communist show trials, Hesketh realised his best hope of salvation lay in taking all the blame. 'I confess to have dealt most disloyally towards her Majesty, whose pardon I most humbly pray.' But he made it clear that if he had not supposed the errand came from higher authority than Hickman's own, he would not have undertaken it. 'I would rather have lain in prison during my life or suffered death then I would have done this message for any stranger's behoof.' This declaration for Waad was written at Dytton Park.   **35** Waad to R. Cecil, 28.11.1593, Belsize, holog., *Sal. Cal.* iv, pp 423-4; Devlin, p. 96. Waad was present at Hesketh's arraignment, as lord keeper John Puckering ordered. He 'did confess the indictment and acknowledge all his former confessions and declarations to be true, so that there needed no other testimony against him.' Which? The surviving confessions deny guilt. Did he admit to killing Hoghton? At all events, attorney general Sir Thomas Egerton made a good job of the trial after making 'collections out of his confessions' and 'in very discreet sort'. Much was made of the bad company Hesketh had been keeping abroad. Meanwhile every effort was being made 'to recover the instructions he had of Worthington'. Puckering writing to R. Cecil '[1593, about 24 Nov.], told him that the queen wanted the fact to be mentioned at Hesketh's trial that Derby took the initiative in arresting Hesketh and reporting the matter to her. Egerton 'desireth to be advertised from you of [*vere* 'or'?] some other, that knoweth this to be so, that he may have some warrant of that he shall affirm therein, having otherwise no ground as of himself, either of his own knowledge or by examination, to affirm it.' Puckering reminded Cecil that he told him that the earl himself made him 'acquainted of his dealing therein'. Puckering wanted Cecil to send him 'a few lines either to the justices of the king's bench or to the learned counsel' which he would pass on to them in good time for the trial. It was important that justice should be seen to be done as the Cecils wanted it. What the queen wanted seemed to be much less important; *Sal. Cal.*, iv, pp 421-2.

We do not know what pressure was put on him, or what promises were made, to elicit these admissions at the last moment any more than we know how much Waad told of the whole truth. A later report claimed that at the last Hesketh was extreme in his denunciation of former contacts if not friends. He 'bitterly with tears bewailed their acquaintance, and naming Sir William Stanley and others, cursed the time he had ever known any of them.' Is this all he said? As Devlin summed it up, 'he was trapped in the position familiar to stool-pigeons of the period, of having made declarations in the service of the government and of then seeing the government make use of those very declarations to break his neck.'[36]

The more difficult challenge had now to be faced in the existence of the fifth earl of Derby and his historic claim to the throne. The death of the fourth earl on 25 September had simplified the problem somewhat for the Cecils in so far as there were

---

36 Hesketh's last words; Devlin, p. 96; *Sadler papers*, iii, 20. 'Hesketh's Instructions for treating with the Earl of Derby', for which he was apparently urged by R. Cecil to write to Prague (*Sal. Cal.*, iv, pp 461-3; cf. n. 27 above) raise difficulties as to their authenticity. Hesketh's acceptance of the Hickman letter only on his understanding that delivering it to Derby was a favour to high authority, his almost nonchalant re-entry into England and his general comportment subsquently suggest someone who had nothing much to hide or fear: certainly not his agency for those who wished to take active steps to see that Derby succeeded Elizabeth. At the same time, he had evidently been 'reconciled' during his stay abroad and would have had contact with the exiles and known of their aspirations and increasing interest in the succession in the early 1590s. The 'instructions' were in a sealed packet, apparently endorsed by Hesketh, 'Good Father, if anything happens that I die in this journey, let this packet be burnt without being read of any man, for my oath standeth thereupon.' If Hesketh died, it is difficult to see what point there was in burning the packet, and what oath he made to whom and any reason for it.' Clearly, it smells of forgery. Arthur Gregory and Thomas Phelippes, either singly or as a combined op, would have found no difficulty in handling this further commission. If it was drawn up before Hesketh left Prague, why risk it through the post? The document represented Hesketh as the bearer of an important message to the earl. If he refused to hear it, at least he should, for his honour's sake, see that the bearer was put safely back on the road to his friends. There were 17 gobbets. The 7th contained the nub of improbability. 'To be capable [eligible] it is necessary that he be a Catholic, and that he will bind himself to restore, advance and perpetually maintain the Catholic religion in our country.' That this was 'absolutely necessary' was explained in (8) to (13). The 10th asked him to 'signify what help he requireth' when the time came: 4-5,000 men could be conveniently supplied within 7 or 8 months. Derby was assured (14th) that he had nothing to fear from Europe. Though Philip II 'might invade and conquer the realm, yet he can never possess it in peace, our nation being most impatient of foreign government.' The pope was not eager to have one Catholic monarch too powerful. These items were plausible. The 16th bordered on absurdity. 'It is better now before her death, because he may prevent of competitors, the cardinal and S[ir] W[illiam] Stanley?] are now able to assist, the pope is willing, perhaps another will not be so, the state of France cannot hinder, but rather further, for now he may have some Spaniards, but not too many; it is like some other is provided to challenge it after her death; he hath many enemies that daily seek his overthrow.' That there was 'a draft apparently' of the first ten gobbets attached to the main document makes it clear that this could not have been a document coming from the continent. The draft was probably put together with much editing and probably invention from Hesketh's notes which he indicated in his letter to Cecil and Cobham of 15.10.1593 (v. supra): 'the whole substance abbreviated is in mine your Honour has.' (*Sal. Cal.* iv, p. 389). It does not seem to have used at any point in the susequent pursuit either of Hesketh or Derby. Perhaps it seemed too implausible.

now only two claimants instead of three. The fourth earl had been too old and near the end of his time to have any interest in dynastic prospects. He would probably have been even readier than his successor in the title to repudiate any attempt to push him towards the throne. The new incumbent, young, dynamic, ambitious even if anxious to prove his present loyalty, might well develop a dangerous independence in the years ahead. The ghost of Hesketh, like Caesar in Shakespeare's play, was to continue to play an important role in Ferdinando's drama. What had been achieved through Hesketh was to establish a dangerous and potentially treasonable connection between the continental recusants, especially in Flanders, the dubious circle of magicians and alchemists in Prague, and the house of Stanley, notably the earldom of Derby. Some of the circle, such as Webbe, although an informer, and perhaps Dee, were involved in coining as a more practicable way of transmuting metals into money if not gold. The astrologers were also suspect as being capable of producing horoscopes, including the queen's, to foretell the future succession. This practice was also treasonable. The fourth earl of Derby's wife, Margaret Clifford, had been deeply involved in occultism.[37] It was the more convincing alternative to religion which many found in an age where the Church had lost much of its influence and power to convince: as in the 21st century.

The fifth earl had shown his mettle only the day after his accession. He wrote to Robert Cecil on 26 September 1593 asking him to get his father to use his influence with the queen to see that important offices were returned to the family: 'the office of Chester and lieutenancy of these two shires, of which last her Majesty once thought me worthy, both when my father was in France and Flanders, for then I had the government of these countries under her, and the chamberlainship was never given from this house since her grandfather's time, but by consent, to my lord of Leicester. How near you are to my wife I need not tell you; how near to me, time may with my good fortune make show of.'[38]

It would indeed. This was not the first plea of its kind. The chamberlain of Chester, a county palatine, was 'the mediate officer to all her Highness' superior courts of justice' and the first receiver of all writs and processes. Such claims by Derby served as a warning to the allies of the Cecils in the area, notably Sir Thomas Heneage, chancellor of the duchy of Lancaster. Hoping that his successful interview with the queen after the Hesketh affair would give him the advantage, Derby wrote to Robert Cecil again on 20 October. The answer was a warrant for the arrest of Thomas Langton, baron of Newton, as an accomplice of Richard Hesketh. Ferdinando protested to Cecil but the reponse was left to Waad, in charge of the case, a man well-established by this time for his reliability and lack of scruple. As for Langton, Waad claimed that, 'Hesketh was directed to him. He knowing Hesketh to be come from overseas ... brought him to the speech of the earl'. This Devlin, always careful with his words, dismissed as 'a palpable lie'.[39]

37 Margaret Clifford and the occult: see I. Wilson, op. cit, p. 170.   38 Derby to Robert Cecil, 26. 9.1593, *Sal. Cal.* iv, p. 389.   39 S. to s., [20.10.1593], ibid., p. 392; s. to s., [11.1593], ibid., p. 427;

Derby's last plea for the chamberlainship was put to Robert Cecil on 15 December. As Devlin summed it up, 'it was vital to him both for protection against machinations within his county, and as a sign of the queen's confidence.' The lord treasurer, confident of his sway over the old queen in her dotage, informed Derby by a letter of the 27th that the office was 'of a more large and absolute authority than is meet for a subject'. Shortly afterwards the office was consigned unofficially to Sir Thomas Egerton, formerly a dependent of the Stanleys, who had already provided precedents for giving the office 'to men of much meaner sort'. It was only some months later that the queen formally approved. This year Ferdinando stayed away from the court at Christmas although his company of players had been one of the stays of the season in previous years.[40] Symptomatic of Derby's fall from general grace and favour, and not only that of the monarch, was his desertion by the earl of Essex.

Essex was a politician who had succeeded very well so far in staying afloat on the polluted stream. He had been a prime mover in the overthrow of Sir John Perrot, former president of Munster and lord deputy of Ireland from 1584 to 1588. His trial for treason in 1592 was based on a forged letter from the king of Spain. He was condemned to death on 26 June 1592: and became one more who died disgraced in the Tower, in September. We will consider at some length Essex' role in the Lopez plot. He was also involved in the Yorke-Williams plot of 1594. Yorke had a passport from Essex although Cecil was also involved through his spies Poley and Moody. Some around her Majesty, Rigoletto's vile race of courtiers once again, are busy. Robert Southwell summed it up well in his *An humble supplication*, 'Everyone trampleth upon their ruin whom a prince's disgrace hath once overthrown.'[41]

Devlin, p. 104.   40 S. to s., 15.12.1593, from Lathom, *Sal. Cal.*, iv, p. 437; Alice Derby to s., [11.1593], ibid., p. 427. She foresees her husband would be 'crossed on the court and crossed in his country'; Devlin, p. 104. For Sir Thomas Egerton, attorney general's report to Burghley on the 'office of chamberlain of Co. of Chester', 27.12.1593, from Lincoln's Inn, and its importance, Sal. Cal. IV, p. 446. He justifies refusing it to Derby. 'Albeit of late years the office hath been conferred upon noblemen, as well by Queen Mary as by the Queen's Majesty, yet in ancient times men of much meaner sort for the most part had the place, viz., Sir Richard Mansfield, Sir Randall Brereton, one Delves, one Burnam, and others of like quality.' Egerton got his reward for his cooperation. 'Egerton, a bastard, and formerly a recusant and dependent of the Stanleys, seemed almost to have stepped into Ferdinando's skin. He got his chamberlainship, his private papers, his books, his manor of Brackley, his unfortunate widow (who seems to have had no choice), and the wardship of his daughters the eldest of whom was favourite for the crown in 1600. All this without any personal rancour; he was simply serving Cecil to check every path to the succession.' (Devlin, p. 104, n. 1, quoting from 'Egerton papers 192'). One can only speculate on the kind of pressure put on Alice to accept so unsavoury a second partner after her first.   41 Devlin, p. 106. See Robert Southwell, *An humble supplication to her Maiestie*, ed. R.C. Bald (Cambridge 1953). Based on Inner Temple, Petyt ms 538, no. 36. Written in answer 'to the late proclamation' of 1591, an effort of studied offensiveness in the polemical manner of the times, Southwell pointed out in measured prose the injustices and cruelties suffered by the Catholics, which he was destined himself to receive in fullest degree. We can hardly accept his vindication of Allen and Persons who were described in the proclamation as 'two seditious heads' (p. 4), which from the government's point of view they were. But he is on firm ground in rejecting the

By the spring of 1594, Derby had been effectively isolated from the queen and from any influential friends at court who might have been tempted to intervene at any point and in any way on his behalf. It was time for his exit. The story of his final illness and death was carefully recorded at least in one document endorsed, 'Touching the death of the Earl of Derby'.[42] He fell sick at Knowsley on 5 April. The following Saturday

description of the seminaries as 'a multitude of dissolute young men' (p. 7); on even firmer ground in dismissing the Babington plot as 'rather a snare to entrap them than anything than any devise of their owne, sith it was both plotted, furthered and finished by Sir Francis Walsingham and his other complices who layd and hatched all the particulars thereof as they thought it would best fall out to the discredit of Catholiques, and cutting off the Queene of Scotts' (pp 17-25). He enlarged on the inhuman tortures employed to make papists forswear themselves (pp 33-4). Southwell addressed Elizabeth as 'most gratious Soveraigne' and assumed throughout she was deceived by her ministers into thinking so badly of Catholics, as she undoubtedly was (p. 25). 'Everyone trampleth upon their ruines, whom a prince's disgrace hath once overthrown ... '(p. 1).   42 Derby's death: *Talbot papers*, vol. H, f. 713; Lodge, *Illustrations*, ii, pp 459-61. The account from the *Talbot papers*, is endd. 'Touching the death of the earl of Derby, was published in extenso in *The Month*, vol. 52, p. 166. He fell sick at Knowsley on 5. 4. On Saturday he returned to Lathom and feeling worse sent to Chester for his physician, Dr Case who had treated Alice the week before. On Sunday before the doctor's coming, Derby vomited seven times, the colour 'like soot or rusty iron, the substance gross and fatty, the quantity about seven pints, the smell not without some offence.' His urine resembled the vomit. A glister on Sunday 'wrought five times'. On Monday morning, after a drachm of rhubarb and half an ounce of manna in chicken broth. This 'wrought nine times'. 'On Tuesday, because of his contin-ual bleeding by vomits, he was most earnestly entreated to be let blood [!].' Wisely, he refused; so 'only fomentations, oils, and comfortable plaisters were applied.' On Wednesady, by the advice 'of all his doctors, he took another glister which wrought six times.' On Thursday 'another purge which wrought with great ease nine times.' The same night he took some 'discordium' which eased the vom-iting but it did not cease throughout his illness. On Friday a 'diaphorecion', a sweating medecine, failed to work. That night his urine ceased, and many remedies applied on Saturday produced no effect. Sunday and Monday a catheter 'which the chirurgeon often sucked' produced no result. 'On Tuesday nature declined, and his Honour most devoutly yielded his soul to God.' The physicians declared the cause to be 'long and over-violent exercise which his Honour took four days in the Easter week.' The 'diseases' were 'vomiting of rusty matter and blood, yellow jaundice, swelling of the spleen, melting of his fat, staying of his water, the hiccup.' This report was the politically correct ver-sion. I. Wilson (op. cit., pp 171-4) quotes George Carey, son of the lord chamberlain Henry Carey, Lord Hunsdon, who wrote to his wife, Elizabeth Spenser, sister of Ferdinando's wife, Alice, on 22.4.1594 referring to the late death, 'by villainous poisoning, witchcraft and enchantment, whereof the bottom not yet found, the poisoning made manifest by the judgment of Dr Case and three other physicians all affirming that his disease could be no other but flat poisoning.' Carey related how, when the court was at Greenwich, he had spoken to the queen in intimate conversation. 'With tears ... she professed she thought not that any man in the world loved her better than he [Ferdinando] did, that he was the most honourable, worthiest and absolutely honest man that she had in her life ever known. '(p. 173); Gloucestershire county record office, Berkeley castle Muniments, MF 1161, Letter-book 2. The letter is printed in full on pp 474-5. The queen undertook to see that Alice had the bringing up of her own daughters. She took order with George Carey, with the master of the rolls and the vice chamberlain, Sir Thomas Heneage to appoint commissioners to enquire into the circumstances of Ferdinando's death (p. 475). So that the Cecils could thwart the queen and keep the Stanleys at bay, the wretched Alice had to marry Egerton. The same letterbook includes 'A trewe reporte and obser-vaunce of the sicknes and death of F. late Erle of Derby ... ', by his secretary, John Golborne (p. 434,

he returned to Lathom and sent for Dr Case, his family doctor located in Chester. We need not go into all the finer clinical details, duly supplied, of what happened over the next few days. Until he died on 16 April, there was much vomiting which included blood as well as solid matter. 'In all the time of his sickness he had fifty vomits and twenty-three stools ... vomiting of rusty matter and blood, yellow jaundice, swelling of the spleen, melting of his fat, staying of his water, the hiccup.' The attempted cure included glisters, purges, rhubarb, manna, bezoar stone and unicorn's horn. 'The original cause of all his diseases was thought by the physicians to be his long and overviolent exercize which [he] took four days in the Easter week' – hunting – 'wherein he vehemently distempered the whole state of his body.' According to Devlin, 'modern medical science, going solely on this report would diagnose a burst appendix resulting in acute peritonitis. That, of course, was incurable till the rise of modern surgery; the frequent clysters ordered by the doctors, consisting as they did of mercury in the form of calomel would have increased the inflammation and made death inevitable.'[43] Let doctors comment, but a more obvious cause will occur to the critical reader, and no doubt to doctors of our own time too.

The Great Lord Burghley, who enjoyed so much fortune throughout his life, was undoubtedly lucky in the providential removal of a man so much in his way by means and circumstances with which he apparently had nothing to do. Apart from the working of extraordinary coincidence, there was another and more glaringly obvious cause of Derby's death. Devlin always showed a commendable determination not to be caught in rash judgment. He observed, 'the symptoms of acute peritonitis are difficult to distinguish from those of poisoning by arsenic or some other irritant; and that, after the initial poison had been expelled by purges, mercury in the form of corrosive sublimate might have been introduced through the clyster.'[44] Evidently there was at the time, not surprisingly, suspicion of poisoning since Bezoar stone and unicorn-rhinoceros – horn were used as recognised remedies. Sir George Carey suspected that a member of the Lathom household might have tampered with the clysters – or perhaps anything else.

The countess of Shrewsbury, Bess of Hardwicke's daughter, certainly suspected poisoning and was prepared to name the poisoner although his identity has not penetrated the evidential rampart surrounding the mystery of this case. Her bailiff, Nicholas Williamson, leaving her service in the hope of getting employment with Essex, was arrested a year later and grilled by Burghley. The great man was anxious to gather anything he could hold in hand for eventual use against this other family also potentially dangerous for its relative independence. Williamson admitted, 'My lady also one day told me of the manner and forcible death of my late lord of Derby, say-

n. 11). **43** Ferdinando's death, Devlin, p. 111-112. Stow (1605), Camden (1608). **44** Was Derby poisoned? Devlin, pp 111-113. 'Co lourless, tasteless, odourless, and with no known test to detect its presence, arsenic was a favourite poison for the 16th century, and was certainly suspected at the time. Ferdinando's chief trustee, Gilbert Talbot, who was also under government surveillance, challenged his brother Edward to a duel in the belief he might be plotting this. ': Wilson, op. cit., p. 173, and p. 434, n. 13, *Les Reportes del Cases in Camera Stellata*, ed. Basildon (1894), pp 13-19.

ing that some were of the opinion that my Lord that now is, his brother, had procured him to be poisoned; "but", saith she, "I believe it not".'[45] The poisoner she named was not entered in the record of Williamson's examination although presumably he gave it to Burghley. He would hardly have dared to withold the information. The poisoner was connected with the Stanhopes who had opposed the earl of Shrewsbury in a notorious star chamber case. The Stanhopes were firm allies of the Cecils.

We could not realistically suppose that Burghley would have left any evidence behind of a connection with whoever arranged Derby's demise. It would not have been necessary to produce anything that even remotely looked like evidence. If it were made clear in the right quarter that such a man was in the way, the rest would have been arranged at lower levels down to the actual agent. A postmortem commission into Derby's death was appointed immediately under the direction of Sir Thomas Egerton and Sir George Carey, the brother-in-law of countess Alice, Derby's widow. As one would expect, Egerton, Cecil's man, had the controlling voice. But the beginning of the enquiry was realistic. Carey was able to voice a strong suspicion against Michael Doughty, clerk of the kitchen in Derby's household. Carey wanted Doughty's brother, one of the waiters, to be arrested and questioned. Michael Doughty was MP for Liverpool and a Cecil trusty. He later deposited in Egerton's custody 'a trunkful of Stanley papers sewed up in packcloth and sealed'.[46] More lost evidence? Egerton used

45 Nicholas Williamson's confession to attorney-general Coke, 21.6.1595, from the Tower, *Sal. Cal.* v, pp 251-4. Reference to the countess of Shrewsbury, p. 253, quoted by Devlin, p. 110. The original continues, 'But, saith her Honour, I marvel it is not revenged, for if the like should happen to my Lord as if it doth, it must be by one of these three factions, either Sir Thomas Stanhope with Thomas Markham or his brethren, or the other (whom I understand to be those whom she thought to have poisoned my lord of Derby) by God it shall be revenged upon them all, though it cost full dear; and said further that my Lord at his coming to London, should go forth to dinner but to few places, and should be provided against such practices.' Presumably Williamson in his original examination named the party or parties suspected by the countess to have poisoned Derby but because these were too close to the ruling junta the names were not recorded. Williamson did not expect to be believed against the countess if she chose to deny the truth of what he said. He admitted to answering every interrogatory 'more fully than the words thereof anywise constrained me' (*Sal. Cal.*, v, p. 251). He was sifted on 'What practice I know now of against her Majesty or this realm? and, What plot or practice for the Succession?' He referred to 'the setters forth of the book now in print but not published.' Presumably this was the work usually ascribed, probably inaccurately, to Persons alone: (p. 252) 'And as for ... Huntingdon ... Hertford or my Lord of Derby, I could not learn of any friends or favourers thay had beyond sea; and so as I answered to the first, I say also to this second ... I know not anyone in England, neither vir nobilis, plebeius, vel domina qualiscumque, to plot or practise in any wise for the succession for themselves or any other, or that their practices beyond sea hath any root, support, promise or maintenance anywise by anyone here in England whatsoever' (p. 253). Williamson was one more who wished to come home and enjoy her Majesty's favour having 'left in her Majesty's hands my wife, parents, five brethren and six sisters', and all his patrimony. Could anyone think he would be turned from his allegiance by three weeks' acquaintance with 'one simple and beggarly supposed lord, and of one old, almost doting, Jesuit?' Moody had heard his patriotic speech in public. 'It was the same day he brought the book of Williams' and York's villainous intents to Brussels' (p. 254).   46 The Doughtys and Derby: Devlin, p. 111. The inquest was the subject of Sir Thomas Egerton, master of the rolls, to Sir

his authority to nudge the enquiry away from the obvious to the politically more correct. He was concerned 'not to prejudice the cause'.

So there was no follow-up of suspicion against Doughty. Instead, when the report went to Burghley a week later even Carey had been brought to agree that there was 'greater presumption that the earl of Derby was bewitched than poisoned'. A tall stranger crossed the earl's path twice before he fell ill; an old woman had enquired about his urine which then ceased; a transfixed wax figure was discovered in the earl's chamber; and more nonsense of the kind. George Carey, eldest son of Henry Carey, Baron Hunsdon, was married to Elizabeth Spencer, Alice's sister. This connection with the ruling circle no doubt moved him to accept the witchcraft thesis. Belief in witchcraft as a common cause of ills was widespread even among the sophisticated. However, George wrote to his wife on 22 April to lament the earl of Derby's 'late and hateful death'. His days were shortened not by the ordinary course of nature 'but by the villainous poisoning, witchcraft and enchantment, whereof the bottom not yet found ... The poisoning made manifest by the judgment of Dr Case and three other physicians all affirming that his disease could be no other than flat poisoning.'[47]

Carey included details. Stow accepted the witchcraft theory but he would hardly have dared to do anything else. Not surprisingly, this was the version of events favoured by Burghley. It was not only plausible according to the convictions of the time but forestalled further enquiry, potentially embarrassing, as to whom might have been guilty of his murder. Critical attention turned to the confraternity of witches, wizards and other creatures of the night. These included such people as Dee, Webbe and Kelley as the visible tip of a confraternity concealing a body far from completely under the control of the Cecils. They enjoyed much popular influence but were safe to accuse. That the witchcraft theory was sufficient to satisfy popular curiosity may be proved by the fact that in the period 1587 to 1597 there were more prosecutions for witchcraft on the home circuit than at any time in our history.[48]

Thomas Heneage, vice-chamberlain, 22.4.1594, Lincoln's Inn, *Sal. Cal.*, iv, p. 515. Sir George Carey visited him on 21.4. with Goulbourne and Leigh, 'late servants of the earl of Derby deceased'. Carey had a list of names, not preserved, from which Egerton marked five names 'fittest to be employed in the present service'. Not only 'their love and affection for the earl' but 'their sufficiency every way to perform that which shall be given them in charge': men unlikely to raise, or at least persist in, awkward questions. There would, in any case, be 'no certain and particular articles' but 'the wisdom and discretion' of those presiding would 'from time to time as they shall see cause, devise new questions.' Thus matters would proceed 'without great prejudice to the cause.' Sir George Carey wrote to Heneage and Robert Cecil on 28.4.1594, to pass on Sir Thomas Leigh's report from Lancashire the 'greater presumptions' that Ferdinando had been 'beweeched' rather than poisoned. All the same, 'a vehement suspicion also may be gathered by a letter found by chance, that the younger brother of Dowtie, this lord's secretary, named either Richard or Robert Dowtie, can discover much of this matter.' Carey therefore asked for a warrant for himself or his officers to arrest Dowtie 'now in London,' so that he could be brought before Heneage and Cecil or before Egerton and himself (*Sal. Cal.*, iv, p. 517). Egerton seems to have headed the enquiry away from any pursuit of the Doughtys. **47** Sir George Carey on the manner of Derby's death, see nn. 42-44 above. **48** Witchcraft trials: Devlin,

Burghley toyed with other presentations of the story which alleged Ferdinando's conspiracy with the Catholic exiles. Significantly nothing was published. It was not until 1608 that Camden, working on Burghley's papers, was able to exploit this god-send to the propagandists of the gunpowder plot. By this time an obvious solution was to hand for those who asked, If Derby was poisoned then by whose hand? It was only too evident by now that Derby had been poisoned by the Jesuits. They resented his refusal to go along with their plans for his succession to the throne; still more the fact that he had revealed all to the queen. All this sufficed to justify the revenge they took in poisoning him. Why the Jesuits or other exiles would have wanted to destroy a man who might have been the salvation of the Catholics if he ever came to the throne was nowhere explained. In Cecil's England it would have been dangerous to voice the question whatever the more discerning might think. A more authentic voice from the Catholic exiles was provided by Sir Rowland Yorke in the course of a dinner with Sir William Stanley when the subject of Derby's death came up in the conversation. 'Yorke said, "It is no marvel, when Machiavellian policies govern England. I durst pawn my life that the lord treasurer caused him to be poisoned that he, [Ferdinando] being dead he [Burghley] might marry the young Lady Vere unto the brother of the said earl of Derby".'[49] Small wonder that Sir Rowland was yet another involved in a treason charge along with one Williams who was also present at this dinner. The de Vere marriage took place.

Even with the death of the fifth earl, there were still difficulties remaining for the Cecils with the Derby clan. The manner in which they were overcome illustrates once again the resourcefulness and ruthlessness of the leading family; also the frightening readiness of lesser men, intelligent and ambitious, to do whatever was required of them to serve their own careers and prospects. It boded no good for England that a man cloned after his father in diplomatic and political skills should be able to instal a monarch who was even more dependent on the son than the old queen had been on the father.

The fifth earl did his best before his death to ensure that something at least would be left of the honour and prestige of the Stanleys in their domain. Much depended on the faithful wife, Alice Spencer. She had already done her best for her husband in writing to Robert Cecil at a time when the clouds were gathering over him fast. 'I doubt

---

p. 112, n. 1. 'In the decade 1587-97, prosecutions for witchcraft on the home circuit reached the highest point ever known in our history.' George Carey reported to his wife Elizabeth on 22.4.1594 (see n. 42 above) After offering the proof of poisoning (see above), the other cause was revealed, 'the witchcraft partly by the confession and manifest demonstration in acts of a witch apprehended and in prison for it. The enchantment evident by the finding of his picture framed in wax with one of his own hairs pricked directly in the heart thereof. By practice of some of them your sister [Alice] not aveinte [enceinte?] before with out any cause to be imagined why, brought abed before her time of a boy child' (op. cit., pp 474-5).   49 Yorke accuses Burghley as responsible for Derby's death, intending to marry de Vere's daughter to his brother the 6th earl. Quoted I. Wilson, p. 176, from Leslie Hotson, I, *William Shakespeare* (London, 1937), p. 154; from PRO, SP12/249, no. 92.

not but my Lord shall be crossed in court and crossed in his country, but I imagine his uprightness and honourable carriage will, by means of so good friends as your father and yourself, on whose love and kindness he chiefly and only doth rely, be able to support him against any malice, and to this let me be a mover.'[50] The loving wife, through no fault of her own, had not been able to contribute as much as she could have liked to the welfare of the dynasty. She had produced three daughters, the last seven years before, but no male heir. She now unexpectedly gave birth to a son but it was born dead. In the absence of the male heir, the fifth earl's successor would be his brother, William. Dr Case, educated at St John's College, Oxford, Ferdinando's own college, and a trusted friend, attended the wife during her pregnancy. As a precaution, her husband asked Dr Case to examine his urine. Case pronounced this 'a show of the most sound, perfect, able body that he had seen'.[51] By 11 April this 'most sound, perfect, able body' was close to death. Its possessor, anxious to avoid the succession of his brother, William, of whose ability he had a very poor opinion, arranged with his legal advisers for his estates to become a 2,000-year trust under Gilbert Talbot, earl of Shrewsbury, Lord Buckhurst, Thomas Leigh of Stoneleigh, Ferdinando's brother-in-law, and Edward Savage.[52] A will made the same day stipulated that these estates should not be 'divided and dismembered into many parts and partitions' but Lathom, Knowsley and the rest should pass to his wife Alice 'in augmentation of her dower' for the rest of her life. After that it would go to the eldest daughter, Anne.[53] All this to prevent everything passing to 'the nidicock his brother'.[54]

In fact Burghley made good use of the 'nidicock' brother. Earl William was married to Lady Elizabeth de Vere in the presence of the queen and her court at Greenwich on 26 January 1595. The Cecils lost no time after Ferdinando's demise in making sure as far as they could that the power of the Stanley clan would be nobbled if not broken. On 9 May Ferdinando's widow Alice wrote to Robert Cecil to say she had heard 'of a motion of marriage between the earl my brother [William] and my Lady Vere, your niece ... I wish her a better husband.'[55] The three daughters of the seventeenth earl of Oxford, Edward de Vere, were apparently more attached to their grand-uncle than to their own father. At all events he claimed it to be so. The relationship between this earl and the Cecils is another of the puzzles of the period. Putting it mildly, they did not get on well; and so, as one would expect, the surviving records paint a sombre picture of the earl as contrasted with the baron. De Vere was

---

50 Alice Derby to R. Cecil, [1593 Nov.], *Sal. Cal.*, iv, p. 427; quoted Devlin, p. 104.   **51** Case's diagnosis of Ferdinando's health before the poisoning, 'a show of the most sound, perfect, able body that he had seen'; quoted Wilson, p. 172.   **52** Ferdinando's estate trust; ibid.   **53** His will; ibid., from PRO, Prob. 11/84.   **54** The 'nidicock' brother; I. Wilson, p. 176 and p. 475, from G. Carey's letter to his wife; see n. 42 above. For Ferdinand and William, contrasted, see George Peele, *Polyhymnia*, ed. D. H. Horne, *Life and Minor Works of George Peele* (Newhaven 1952), p. 233 (Wilson p. 109). 'The earl of Derby's valiant son and heir/ Brave Ferdinand Lord Strange ... the golden eagle' ...   **55** Earl William's marriage to Elizabeth de Vere: I. Wilson, p. 177. Alice's assessment of William in s. to R. Cecil, 9.5. [1594], Lathom; *Sal. Cal.*, iv, p. 527.

more or less forcibly obliged to marry William Cecil's daughter Anne under the terms of the harsh wardship laws and conventions of the period.[56] The dowager-countess of Derby struggled on with law suits and legal actions to save the provisions of Ferdinando's will but it would appear to have amounted to little more than a valiant rearguard action. Once again, the Cecils prevailed.

[56] For the Derbys and William Stanley see Charlton Ogburn, The mysterious William Shakespeare, (see above). The book sets out to prove Edward de Vere, 17th earl of Oxford, as the true author of the Shakespeare canon; a theory gaining ground. See also J. T. Looney, Shakespearen identified (London, 1920); B. M. Ward, *The seventeenth earl of Oxford 1550-1604* (see above); *The Bard*, journal of the Shakespearean Authorship Society, especially, Supplement 1, 1976, which analyses critically Samuel Schoenbaum's masterly edition of the documents in facsimile: *William Shakespeare: a documentary life* (Oxford 1975).

8

Polwhele, Annias, Cullen and Cahill

About the same time as the Hesketh plot, another plot, or plots with one inspiration, was bubbling and bursting in the boiling mud of late Elizabethan politics. This plot came between the Hesketh and the Lopez plots. It was concocted by a quartet of panto-mime villains, or characters from the more outlandish reaches of the Commedia dell'Arte. If the reputations of good men were not involved, and the use or threat of tor-ture and the macabre proceedings at Tyburn, it could all be taken as an exercise in black comedy. But it was too black to be truly comic for most tastes. So far the principal, if not the only, inspiration in the earlier plots of the reign was Sir William Cecil, ably assisted by Walsingham; abetted most of the time until their death by Leicester and Sir Christopher Hatton. From this time, however, there was a newcomer on the scene who was anxious to share the kudos for discovering plots. From watching the rival Cecils, no doubt, he concluded this was a sure way to prove his devotion and vigilance in the pro-tection of his queen and also to improve the prospects of an ambitious career.

Robert Devereux, second earl of Essex, had at least one other motive, apart from personal considerations, for his zeal in pursuing plot politics. As Martin Hume put it, a large influence in affairs was 'the war party headed by Essex, who were for ever dis-covering or inventing fresh Spanish plots. The result of all this was a recrudescence of the severity against the recusant English Catholics.'[1] 'It was the fixed policy of the

---

1 Martin Hume, *Treason and plot: struggles for Catholic supremacy in the last years of Elizabeth* (London, 1901), p. 32. It was this power struggle as much as the anti-Catholic policy perhaps, which at this point helped to determine the use of the characters now under review whom A. Jessop described as 'those many restless and discontented spirits who were perpetually passing backwards between England and the Low Countries. A motley throng of hungry adventurers, reckless soldiers of fortune, devout enthusiasts who had ´suffered the loss of all things^a for their religious opinions, seminary priests eager for the crown of martyrdom [?], pensioners of Philip II ready for desperate employment, and pensioners of the English government – the gang of spies in Walsingham's and Burghley's pay.' See *Letters of Fr. Henry Walpole, S. J ... edited with notes by A. Jessop* (Norwich 1873), p. v. Once again, acts of the privy council are missing for this vital period. As Dasent recorded, ''The rest of the letters that were signed by their lordships this 26th of August [1593] are entered in the other register following for this year.ª Sad to say, this other register is missing and with it at least one other volume, as the next manuscript in the council office collection begins ... October 1 1595, a vol-ume of brief extracts from the council register in the British Museum [Library], (Add. 11402) only

Essex party to keep alive distrust and hatred of Spain in order to promote a decisive national war.'[2] Burghley had no more love of Spain than Essex but his motive in fomenting hatred was more realistically directed to curbing the influence of the English recusants in England and making sure of a Protestant succession. He promoted the idea of a Spanish invasion threatening in 1593 in order to keep alive fear of the recusants in queen and nation. In fact he was well aware from the reports of Chateau Martin and others in Spain that any naval preparations being mounted by Philip II were not directed against England. Nevertheless, Chateau Martin, writing to Cecil in April 1593, catching the mood and stoking it, urged that a rumour should be circulated to the effect that Drake was about to attack Portugal so as to keep the Spanish monarch in fear.[3] True, 'Philip was in far more alarm of the possible attacks of English ships upon his treasure fleet, upon his Brittany garrisons, or upon his coasts and colonies, than the English had reason to be of him.'[4] In spite of the odds loaded against him, Philip got considerable reinforcements through to Brittany in the winter of 1593. This had nothing to do with invading England.

Essex was determined not to be outdone in setting up a system of spies and informers abroad. It was part of a significant effort to rival and even outflank the Cecils. This continued until the great showdown of 1601.[4] Dr Morrison, his agent in Scotland wrote to inform him in November 1593 that Philip II was preparing a vast armament for the spring of 1594. Rolston, the earl's spy stationed at Fuentarrabia, informed him on 31 January 1595 that Walter Lindsey, Lord Balgarys, had been well received in Spain as the envoy of the Scottish lords sworn to war against the queen of England. He had been knighted, and had 'obtained all he desired, both for himself and the banished lords, and is coming to Flanders with the cardinal' – Allen? Rolston was wrong. Balgarys remained in Spain, unsatisfied at least in the main object of his mission.[5] But

partially covering the gap': J. R. Dasent, *Acts of the privy council, 1592-1593* (1901), preface p. vii, quoting from p. 489 of the register. More than two years are 'lost'. 2 Essex wants war with Spain: ibid., p. 37. See also E. P. Cheyney, *A history of England from the defeat of the Armada*, 2 vols. (1914, 1926); J. B. Black, *The reign of Elizabeth*, 2nd ed., Oxford 1959; P. M. Handover, *The second Cecil* (London 1959). 3 Chasteaumartin (Salisbury Calendar spelling) to Burghley 30.4. /10.5.1593, *Sal. Cal.* iv, pp 306-7. Stationed in Bordeaux, Bayonne from 7.1593, he sent frequent and detailed accounts of Spanish troop and shipping movements. This volume contains 19 letters. His last was dated from Bayonne 28.3. /7. 4.1594. Thomas Honiman reports to R. Cecil, 4.12.1594 (London, 'Mons. de Chasteau Martin had sometimes a Frenchman sent him to Bayonne when I was there, by ... Walsingham, whom we conveyed into Spain' dressed as a sailor so he was able to move about freely in Spanish ports; *Sal. Cal.*, v, pp 28-9. Samuel Wharton also contacted 'de Chasteau Martin in Bayonne who asked him to go into Spain to spy'; S. Wharton's confession to W. Waad, 26. 4.1595; ibid., pp 184-5. See M. Hume, op. cit., p. 38. 4 *Cal. SP Spain*, iv, p. 596 for Spanish fear of English privateers ravaging the coast of Spain and Portugal. The Venetian ambassador in Madrid reported to the doge on 4.4.1593 (n. s.) 'Although no regular fleet has sailed from England, yet there are about 50 English ships in these waters. They are doing most serious damage every day ... '; quoted in Hume, p. 39, n. 1. This made a further attempt at a Spanish invasion in 1596 almost inevitable. 5 Hume, p. 74, n. 1, Rolston to Essex, 31.1. 1595 (n. s.?) quoting Birch. Hume was mistaken in thinking all British Jesuits favoured a Spanish succession. William Crichton

Essex was clearly in business. All the same, while Essex figured among those accused in the present plot, he took no direct part in organization or discovery.

Even spies with access to what could be taken as reliable sources could be badly mistaken. How much more the amateurs – most of those we are now considering. They were really interested, as always, in what would sell or get them a few crowns from any side. Truth was an irrelevance. Their difficulties were real and circumstances of life hard. At times insupportable. These pressed hardest when the fighting season for all armies and hangers-on came to an end during the closed season of winter. While those who listened to their stories were well aware why they told them, and hardly believed them, they accepted them as an essential weapon in the propaganda war against the popish enemy at home and abroad. The need for continuing the war on the home front was well conveyed by a letter from Tobie Matthew, dean of Durham, to Burghley of 16 October 1593. He advocated no relaxing of persecution in the north-east where recusancy was still strong. 'In case this late commission of enquiry against the wives and servants, when returned to you, be not suppressed, or by respect of persons, unevenly handled, but duly executed, yea, and – as these times and this place require – more severely prosecuted, without such intercessions and mediations from above as have heretofore drawn on [there will be] great inconvenience both to religion and the realm.'[6]

It was not easy to get people to go along with the idea of persecuting for religion especially if such policies were inspired by London, and if one had as friends the people who were being persecuted. One good way of persuading them of the evil of the enemy in the midst was to remind them that their more influential coreligionists aimed at nothing less than the murder of their much beloved queen. That the plots were not genuine need only be known by the government and their spies. But while the spies and informers were essential to government, their trade was fraught with peril. This was well illustrated in the careers of the spies under immediate consideration. We can begin with William Polwhele. The risks for him and many another were only worth running because the alternative might be starvation. There was no shortage of takers. And there were now two employers. 'This keen competition in the discoveries of treason caused the unfortunate priests or suspects who were in or on their way to England

supported James VI. Persons disclaimed any prejudice against James although he wanted a Catholic successor. See Edwards, *Persons*, p. 192. 6 Archbishop T. Matthew reflects a widespread fear that persecution was not as effective against the papists as it should be. See *Cal. SP Dom. Addenda, 1580-1625*, p. 355; from SP12/32, no. 89. This fear bore fruit in the act of 35 Elizabeth (1593) 'for the better discovery of popish recusants.' A 5-mile limit was put on movement from home. The original bill would have confiscated all goods and chattels and two thirds of the income from lands; no public office or entry into the learned professions; wives would have lost their dowers; children would be taken away and brought up in Protestant families. Cf. Conyers Read, *Burghley and Elizabeth* (London 1960), p. 488. See *The penal laws against papists and popish recusants, non-conformists and nonjurors ... from the first year of Queen Elizabeth down to the present year*, printed for R. Gosling in the Savoy, 1723.

to be treated as if each one of them was the emissary of a murder conspiracy or guilty of a design against the State ... [There are] many scores of sheets of depositions of such men, telling under torture or threat, their poor squalid little stories of hardship and suffering, but rarely any more important political secrets than the vague tittletattle of the seminaries or the braggadocio of renegade soldiers and malcontent refugees.'[7]

Polwhele was like most of them, a ham actor who played whatever part the immediate occasion demanded. According to his confession of December 1593, after leaving London with Arthur Canfand, they travelled in Europe: to Flushing, Calais and Rheims 'thence after half a year to Douay to Dr Webb who prevented their returning to England, saying they would be hanged, and sent them to Sir William Stanley with recomendations.' After six months service with Stanley as a page, he served three more in the service of his lieutenant, Jaques Francisco, as a soldier.[8] According to a later confession of 4 February 1594, 'Jaques urged him three or four times to come to England to murder the queen.' He 'refused, alleging the difficulties and his own backwardness therein; Jaques told him the end of a soldier was beggary, to be killed with a bullet, and thrown into a ditch, and that to take such a matter in hand would be glorious before God, she being a wicked creature and likely to overthrow all Christendom.' A previous plotter was parenthetically dragged into it. 'After this Hesketh was sent to England', having first informed a 'Father Sherwood' of his pious intention to remove a tyrant.[9]

Polwhele had to get the approval of Jeffreys, the English agent and merchant in Calais, before crossing over to retail to Burghley a typical story of assassination and plots against her Majesty which he hoped would get credence and reward. Jaques also advised him, while in Calais to 'abide with the spies, then apply to his friends at Court, Mr Fortescue and Mr Sterrell' – alias Robinson. Sterrell knew the court as a spy and right-hand man of Thomas Phelippes. Sterrell's prior knowledge would have assured Polwhele's arrest when he arrived in England. An obviously spurious touch was supplied when Jaques, who had asured Polwhele that killing the queen would be a work of the Holy Spirit, urged him to go to confession – for what? – before giving him sixty crowns and an order to be away next day.[10] He was arrested in England on arrival and at the same time and place John Annias also, an Irishman.[11] Polwhele knew him and

7 Hume, op. cit., p. 90. 'The spies were necessarily persons of questionable life; nearly always sold both to Spain and to England; and it was usually easy to convict them of trechery. It was ... often the policy of their employers to abandon them rather than ... countenance men or methods rendered infamous by accusation; and the agent provocateur, the eager delator, or the vain babbler, was caught in his own lure and sent to ... dungeons or ... a cruel death, while his noble paymaster, who knew ... the true circumstances, affected horror at so much wickedness.' Ibid.   8 Confession of William Polwhele, 12.1593; *Cal. SP Dom, 1591-4*, p. 398; PRO SP12/246, no. 49, 3pp Cf. Hume, pp 97-108. 9 'Notes from the confessions of Polwhele, to be used in charging John Annias and Patrick Collen', 4.2.1594; *Cal. SP Dom*, ibid., p. 424, from SP12/247, no. 39, nearly 4 pp   10 W. Polwhele, confession of 12.1593 (see n. 8). What did Jaques mean by telling him to 'abide with the spies'? Whose spies?   11 John Annias, an Irish adventurer, for his suggestibility, was an ideal subject for interrogation. Which may explain why he was interrogated on at least six occasions. He admitted in a state-

claimed that he met him and an associate, one Tompson, at Lille, on the way to England. They had it in mind to set the queen's navy on fire. This and taking the Tower were fairly common projects for such enthusiasts.[12] Polwhele also spoke of another Irishman known to them all, Patrick Collen, already in England, who had already been sent over to kill the queen.[13] He had a jewel to present to the earl of Essex

ment 'set down by himself and delivered to Mr lieutenant of the Tower' on 8.2.1594 that 'when before the council he had no memory and was afraid.' All the same, he 'did not mean to conceal anything'; *Cal. SP Dom.*, ibid., p. 429; SP12/247, no. 54. He had in any case been severely softened up at or before a previous examination, undated, being put in the manacles by justice Young 'until he was almost dead'; *Cal. SP Dom.*, ibid., p. 421; SP12, ibid., no. 33. The principle charge against him seems to have been his association with Tompson, an expert in 'fireworks'. Annias left England for France in 1586. He had taken a commission in the light horse under Parma but was never in Rome or Spain and never served under Stanley or Jaques Francisco. He was acquainted with Patrick Collen but not Polwhele. Nevertheless, he had seen a passport that Polwhele had from Jaques and told Tompson 'that they were of one company and probably of one business' (ibid.) Annias' information on Polwhele was no doubt brought to his notice so that the latter was willing enough to suggest a list of embarrassing questions involving Annias' employment of Tompson at Dieppe. Polwhele met Annias and Tompson at Lille (*Cal. SP Dom.*, ibid., p. 423, [4.2.]1594; SP12, ibid., no. 38). **12** It seems sufficiently evident from John Daniell/Danyel's declaration of 21.2.1594 that he was an agent-provocateur in the employ of Burghley. His main object was to embroil James Archer, S.J., William Stanley and Hugh Owen with some 'mischievous practices' against Elizabeth which they communicated to him. Archer and Holt asked Daniell 'to make choice of one of his countrymen' an Irishman 'for that purpose' (*Cal. SP Dom.*, ibid., p. 438; SP12/247, no. 79). He had to be a 'tall soldier, an Irishman but not of the Irish regiment' (Daniel, declaration of 25.3.1594, 6pp, *Cal. SP Dom.*, ibid., p. 442; SP 12, ibid., no. 91). Archer's known career rules him out as a cheap assassin. He was rector of Salamanca from 1592 to 1605, and in 1606 first prefect of the Irish mission in the Irish college, Rome. (H. Foley, *Records* ... , vii, pt. 1, p. 15) Daniel's report of 21.2. says he persuaded Hugh Cahill 'to take it in hand but not to put it into execution', 'it' being understood as the murder of Elizabeth. Archer gave Cahill 100 crowns with a promise of 2,000 more when the work was done, and 30 crowns pension for life on return. Daniell got the Jesuits to procure Cahill a passport through the earl of Ormond for 6 months on the pretext of going to England to bring back 'his wife and children'. Daniell meanwhile came to England 'and detailed the circumstances at large to the lord treasurer at Gunnersbury.' All this took place, in the early days of May 1593. This is clear from Daniell's Declaration of 25.2. which brought William Holt into the plot and added the crafty detail that the Jesuits reminded Cahill of the story of Judith and Holofernes to confirm him in his purpose. It also added dates which, even if not true, gave an air of accuracy and authenticity, as in other plot stories. So the passports were ready on 5.6. when Archer gave Cahill the 100 crowns received from Owen. Daniell and Cahill took leave of the Jesuits on 7.6. who exhorted them to hurry 'as there were an Englishman and a Scotchman appointed for a similar purpose.' They set out for St Omer and Calais on 17 June, and sent letters to Burghley and Ormond by Thomas Jeffrey, the 'English merchant'. Six weeks later, Ormond sent Daniell Burghley's passport. They arrived in England on 24.8. It is difficult and unnecessary to believe that any of them kept so accurate a diary of events. Avoiding excessive accuracy was the time of their reporting to Cecil: some time 'in September'. They did not go eventually unrewarded, it seems. Thomas Windebank reported to Robert Cecil on 27.2.1594 that he asked Elizabeth to sign a warrant 'for money to be distributed to certain Irishmen.' She hesitated, telling Windebank to tell Cecil, 'no part of the money should be given to Daniell and another whose name she had forgotten' Cahill? So the warrant was deferred for the Cecils to make the final determination. (*Cal. SP Dom*, ibid., pp 443-4; SP12/247, no. 96). **13** Patrick Collen/Cullen was examined before Sir Thomas Wilkes, attorney general Egerton, solicitor general Edward Coke and Richard Young on 6.2.1594. He served three years in Stanley's regiment and knew Jaques well, but not for two years past because he

whose henchman he would become. Essex's alleged pretensions to the crown were sometimes included or implied in the confessions of other prisoners. These were extracted under suggestion or oral pressure, not necessarily torture, by those whose sympathy lay evidently with the Cecils rather than Devereux.[14]

Annias, Polwhele and Collen were not only aware of one another's business but were quite prepared to sell one another down the pass to escape any hook that dangled over them. Their stories told for this purpose were only for the credulous. Another man, Tompson,[15] a dealer in 'fireworks', who stayed on the continent, was also in their

had Edmund Keasley, Collen's kinsman, executed on suspicion 'he purposed to serve the queen'; *Cal. SP Dom.*, ibid., p. 427; SP12/247, no. 45. An examination of 21.2. gave him 4 years service mainly under Jaques Francisco, Stanley's lieutenant, as one of his company. Their influence procured him 15 crowns a month pension from Philip II which replaced a gentleman's pay of 50 shillings a month (ibid., p. 436; ibid., no. 76). He saw Jaques at Brussels in October 1593 before coming to Calais. Jaques asked him to do the king a good service to be indicated 'the next morning'. Meanwhile Oliver Eustace warned Collen to beware of Jaques as 'a cunning fellow' who 'sought to set himself up with the fall of others', and not to get involved with any enterprise against England or Ireland. Jaques' commission revealed next day was to murder Antonio Perez with a pistol, and gave him £30 'for his voyage' (Examination of 6. 2.). On the whole, it is possible, even likely, that Collen had some kind of commission to kill Perez, Philip's traitor. This was later turned into a plot to kill the queen and bolster the evidence against Lopez and his company (see n. 16 below). Since Collen possibly told the truth about a plot to kill Perez, and could not be trusted to depart from the truth at official dictation, like Hesketh, he was eliminated. As Coke reported to Puckering, about mid-year 1594 giving details of recent plots on one Lingen, pensioner of Philip II, who 'accompanied with Patrick Cullen, already executed for treason.' *Cal. SP Dom.*, ibid., p. 516; SP12/249, No. 9.   14 An undercurrent in the examinations flows against the reputation of Essex. As Hume noted, 'bringing in the name of the earl of Essex was made the most of by his enemies'; Hume, op. cit., p. 104, n. 1. Hugh Owen reputedly reported that he was 'told that Heskett [*sic*] executed some months past, upon pretence of being sent to the Earl of Derby, &c. [*sic*], upon being examined as to whether the earl of Essex would take part with the earl of Derby or not, said that the writer told him that one Robinson had said that the earl of Essex meant to have the crown himself if he could' (Hugh Owen to Phelippes, 3(?). 1594, from Brussels; *Cal. SP Dom.*, ibid., p. 475; SP12/248, no. 53). 'Notes from the confessions of Polwhele' (see above) claimed 'Annias had a jewel which he was to have presented to the earl of Essex at his coming into ngland, meaning to have become his lordship's man.' Annias claimed (exam. of [4.11.1594], see above) that Tompson had the jewel to give Essex, although he admitted, 'he Annias would be half with him. '   15 Tompson figured largely in the confessions of Annias. His first (? *Cal. SP Dom.*, p. 421, see above) claimed that this expert in 'fireworks' offered to Stanley to fire the queen's ships by night. Annias knew Tompson but never told him of 'Collen's business for England ... Tompson would have promised to do anything if he should have got money, and tried to cozen the writer in hopes.' 'Questions suggested by Polwhele to be put to Annias' (ibid., p. 423, see above) claimed that Annias met Polwhele at Lille where he saw his passport and told Tompson Polwhele was on the same 'service' as Collen 'but that Tompson should deceive them both and relieve Polwhele of some of his money. Tompson told Polwhele Annias meant to deceive him, keeping him there till he sent in Tompson first to kill the Spaniard' Antonio Perez. Or did Annias and Tompson intend to get Polwhele drunk and cut his purse at Gravelines so he could not go over; or did they just want to rob him? Or did Polwhele simply hand his purse over to Tompson since 'he was in fear they would have his purse and his life?' The answers, whatever they were, are less important than the questions, maybe, which indicate the kind of company who dealt in this plot whatever it really was. Their plight

company. Polwhele accused him of stealing his purse and escaping into France. So it was that Polwhele, as he claimed, had to depend on Jeffreys to give him money sufficient to go to England to tell-sell his story. Polwhelc, Annias and Collen all told their tales in gaol – independently of one another being held incommunicado – each putting all the blame for a real intention to complete various crimes on the others while maintaining his own posture as an honest spy or agent-provocateur. The crimes mutually ascribed were normal: burning the queen's ships, murdering Antonio Perez, Lord Burghley and, inevitably, the queen herself.[16] Collen may have been if not commis-

and motivation for the risks they took in entering Cecil's web were indicated in the examination of James Garrett, Irishman, before Richard Young on 16. 4.1595. During some six years soldiering in the Low Countries, he was for four months one of the 150 English and 71 Irish serving in Stanley's regiment. He left three months before, 'coming to England to do his country service'. La Mothe, Stanley and 'Count Charles' were in trouble with Duke Ernestus 'for keeping money and munition from the soldiers in France whereby they died for hunger.' The commanders held back 'contribution money' from their soldiers so they were obliged to 'rob and spoil' the country in order to survive. A Walloon colonel had recently been beheaded for this. After Count Mansfeldt's departure, 'the governor' gave order that all the soldiers should be paid monthly; *Cal. SP Dom.*, ibid., pp 486-7; SP12/248, no. 73. If the order had been obeyed presumably Garrett would still have been with the forces overseas. 16 This Polwhele plot has a connection with the Lopez plot, which also appears to have been a plot to murder Antonio Perez, and becomes metamorphosed for propaganda purposes into a plot for killing the queen. Collen's confession of 6. 2.1594 (see n. 13 above) was quite clear that any intended victim was Antonio Perez. It was the accommodating Annias who connected his group with the Lopez plot through Tinoco. Annias knew Manuel Luis Tinoco and promised him 'good news' that he intended to steal some letters coming from Philip II from a Spanish captain at St Omer 'and thus do her Majesty service'. Tinoco was a servant of Don Antonio, the Portuguese pretender, so he wanted to know what was in them. Annias wrote from St Omer to Tinoco in Calais asking him to delay his voyage to England for six days while Annias completed his job. Annias admitted he had served Philip II but now intended to become 'a true subject of the Queen'. He had sent John Daniell to England for his pardon. When he got it, he would accompany Tinoco to England and 'discover' what was intended against queen and state. At the end of 1593, Richard Stanihurst in Spain, asked Captain Oliver Eustace to see Stephen Ibarra, secretary of the council of war in the Low Countries, about procuring Antonio Perez' assassination in England. Annias, no doubt under suggestive pressure from his examiners, Sir Thomas Wilkes, Egerton, Coke, Waad and Richard Young, gave it as his opinion that it was not about killing Perez but the queen; examination of 5. 2.1594, *Cal. SP Dom.*, ibid., p. 425; SP12/247, no. 44. According to official notes, undated, taken from matter allegedly supplied by Annias, Tinoco amd Hugh Owen, Tinoco 'set down the practice for Antonio Perez' while Collen was employed by Jaques to kill Elizabeth, although he left his passport at St Omer(!): 'he was to use the show of killing the Spaniard'(ibid., p. 430 and no. 58). Annias' 5th examination on 11.2. was before the same examiners as before although Young, the rackmaster was absent. Annias no longer needed intimidation, if he ever did. Collen now told Annias that Holt and Jaques had sent him to kill the queen and made him swear not to reveal it. Polwhele also told Annias Collen had come over to kill the queen. Collen told Annias 'he knew of his employment' three months before he was sent. 'Jaques has many friends in the court of England, and one ... to whom he directs the persons whom he employs for any service in England.' Plots laid overseas were mainly against the navy and the queen. 'Polwhele and Collen can tell who are Jaques' friends'. The net could be cast as wide as the government chose. 'They have great hopes of Sir Thomas Tresham, and some lawyers in the inns of court' (ibid., p. 431 and no. 60). Annias' sixth confession of 12.2. included a damning piece of gos-

sioned then not discouraged to put an end to Perez, Philip II's declared traitor. None of them had any intention of murdering Burghley, the queen or any other English figure. The main business was to confess these intentions as coming from the expatriates working and fighting with or alongside Spain. The Catholic soldiers, the Jesuits, especially Father William Holt, and Hugh Owen, the intelligencer, were dragged in and made responsible for suggesting and financing these ambitious murder attempts. Collen claimed to have received £30 in gold apparently for the murder of Antonio Perez. If he did, it was not from the Jesuits who rejected the idea of assassination. Certainly, they had no access to large sums of money to waste on undisguised swashbucklers. Annias claimed that the order for Perez' assassination had come from Esteban de Ibarra, Spanish secretary of state for war, then in Flanders. But there was no agreeement among these pantomime knaves as to the victim really intended, whether Perez or the queen.[17] Plausibly neither.

The absurdity of all these claims are sufficiently evident from the confessions of the first two, but Polwhele's contribution set the mark of absurdity on the rest. The unhappy Polwhele received the full attention of rackmaster Richard Topcliffe, who loved his work only too well, although the examinee on this occasion presumably needed little persuasion. He claimed to have approached the Jesuit, Sherwood, although there was none of this name. Perhaps it was an alias Polwhele picked up somewhere. There were several priests of this name operating at this time.[17] 'Sherwood' not only assured Polwhele of the meritoriouness of killing Elizabeth but even reproached him for sloth: 'that he was a fool for not having undertaken it sooner, when he was first moved to it, as he then might have had the honour of it; but now Collen had gone on the same service, and more were going every day'.[18] Sir William Stanley was supposed to have spoken in the same crude terms of killing Elizabeth. Polwhele claimed he 'had often heard Jacques say they did not esteem killing Antonio Perez, who had done all the hurt he ever could do ... nor the killing of anyone else save the queen.'[19] Father Holt thought likewise. Jacques' intention was the talk of Brussels.

In February 1594 an Irishman by name of Hugh Cahill[20] came over to regale Topcliffe at Burghley House in the Strand with a parroted repetition, as it seems, of

sip, naming Bennet 'as one about the queen of whom he has often heard it said that Jaques spoke well' (ibid., p. 431 and no. 62). See also n. 13.   **17** For Sherwood see G. Anstruther, *The Seminary Priests*, i, 1968: five priests of this name about this time. This one was seemingly Richard, brother of Henry and John, also priests: (p. 314). See William Holmes examination of 21.4.1594, *Cal. SP Dom.*, ibid., p. 485; SP12/248, no. 75. Holmes was 'late servant' to Lady Stourton and served Sir John and Lady Arundel, his widow 13 or 14 years. He knew 'John Sherwood, priest, now deceased, lived with them 8 years.' John does not seem to have gone abroad after his studies.   **18** Polwhele's examination, 21.2.1594; *Cal. SP Dom.*, ibid., pp 435-6; SP12/247, no. 73.   **19** Ibid.   **20** The 'Voluntary confession of Hugh Cahill' before Richard Topcliffe at Burghley House in the Strand on 21.2.1594 recounts briefly the career of Daniell's assistant: born in Tipperary, he served under Leicester in the Low Countries in Captain Hidgecock's company and then in Captain Thomas Shirley's 'band of horse'. He was taken prisoner by Taxis' 'freebooters of Zutphen'. Taxis offered him the choice of serving him or being hanged. So like many Irishmen Cahill took an oath of service to the king of Spain and

the same plot. All these plotters seem to have been acquainted with one another and would have known, even if they had not discussed with one another, the stories that sold best in England. It is noteworthy that Burghley usually left this sort of visitor to a subordinate. It was clearly beneath his dignity to deal directly with them himself. Cahill named the Irishman, John Daniell, in fact his director, who had come over with permission in August 1592 to tell his own repetitive story. In February 1593, even while Cahill was being interviewed, Daniell, a professional agent provocateur and accepted as such by Burghley, told his story about blowing up the Tower of London.[21] Cahill claimed that after a search by Sir William Stanley, Holt and Hugh Owen for someone suitable to kill the queen, Daniell had offered him the commission and the prize-money.[22] It was agreed that they should both go to England and reveal the miscreants to Burghley. Cahill related that Daniell took him to the priests Holt and Archer in Brussels who agreed to give them 100 crowns down, 2,000 more and a pension when the job was done.

Daniell took Cahill with him to Calais in August 1593 and, with official permission, went to England leaving Cahill in Calais. Fathers Archer and Walpole found Cahill there and fumed at his delay in carrying out the commission. At their urging, Cahill crossed the Channel without permission, and was introduced to Burghley by Daniell.[23]

served until Easter 1592. So far, factual enough we may suppose; *Cal. SP Dom.*, ibid., pp 436-7; SP12/247, no. 78.   **21** John Daniell to Richard Young, 6. 2.1593/4. A plot to blow up the Tower involved a vault containing brimstone and gunpowder over it. Two men would gain access through 'a trap door which doth stand much open'. They would use time fuses. 'Moody is the man that descried the place in the Tower' with the brimstone and powder. There was also supposed to be a device on foot 'to set the ships at Billingsgate on fire and the houses also, and to set the inns and woodstacks in London, on fire'; *Cal. Sal.* iv, p. 474; cf. Hume, op. cit., p. 106, n. 1.   **22** In May 1592 'John Daniell, an Irish gentleman', told Cahill on pledge of secrecy that Sir William Stanley, Holt and Hugh Owen wanted 'a tall, resolute and desperate Irishman to go to England to kill the queen'. If Cahill agreed, they would give him money, and he Daniell, would go with him to England to reveal it to the queen or the lord treasurer. So Cahill with Daniell visited Holt, Archer and Owen, all together, in Brussels. They commissioned Cahill to kill Elizabeth 'a most blessed deed' 'with a sword or a dagger, at a gate or narrow passage, or as she walked in some of her galleries.' Proper recompense was arranged. Cahill promised to do it 'although he never had any such intention.' It was Daniell who brought him two or three days later 100 gold crowns saying 'Archer the Jesuit had sent it from Hugh Owen' with a passport from Count Mansfeldt to go to France and then Calais; voluntary confession of Hugh Cahill, 21. i. 1594; see n. 20.   **23** After receiving his money in May 1592, Cahill, as he claimed, moved to Calais where Daniell obtained a six-month passport for him through the Jesuits to go to England 'for his wife and children', as Daniell put it (declaration of 21.2.1594, see n. 12) or 'on pretence of fetching his wife and children into the Low Countries' as Cahill put it (voluntary confession of 21.2.1594, see n. 20). Cahill stayed 'there and about St Omer' till November 1592 waiting for a passport from the English side. In the interval of waiting, and while Daniell was priming Burghley in England, Archer and Henry Walpole, 'a short, well-set black man, with black hair very like a Spaniard, about 33 or 34 years old', found Cahill at Calais. According to Daniell, the Jesuits were looking for a ship to Spain. They persuaded Cahill 'to come over to England secretly with Sir John Skidamore's son, a priest' alias Walkin according to Cahill, who 'lent him 16 or 17 crowns', as the Jesuits asked, and paid his charges (voluntary confession). This was plausible: a genuine commission from the Jesuits to Cahill,

In collusion, they both told the same story. It is hardly necessary to point out that there was no sort of evidence for these claims. Neither the ministers of Spain nor the responsible representatives of the Catholic expatriates, laymen or priests, would conceivably have employed the characters we are meeting here to buy a sack of anachronistic potatoes let alone carry out assassinations of the kind suggested. Neither the ministers of Spain nor the Jesuits, who agreed with them in much if not in everything, would have stooped to this solution of their difficulties. We have seen this already and will see it again.[24]

and the only one. Cahill and Skidamore landed at Margate. 'On his arrival at Westminster, [Daniel] informed Burghley and brought Cahill as he ordered to him.' Cecil was 'very sick', and since he could not examine Cahill – there was no question of examining Daniell – he thought of putting him in the Marshalsea, but such was Daniel's influence that 'upon the writer's word, that he should be forthcoming delivered him to the writer's charge, in which he has since remained' (Daniell, declaration of 21.2). **24** The main object of the present plot(s), as presented through the examinations and confessions of the plotters, as we have seen, was assassination, whether plausibly of Antonio Perez or, most unlikely, of Elizabeth. The men behind the projects were supposed to be the organisers and commanders of English subjects serving in the Spanish forces (including Irish and Welsh), Sir William Stanley, Hugh Owen, and Jaques Francisco, and also the Jesuits who stood by to encourage as chaplains. They were mainly responsible for making the murder attempts seem moral. As Perez was a traitor, his killing might have seemed morally justified as proper retribution. Collen may therefore have reported correctly when he claimed that when Jaques dealt with him for killing Perez he objected to it as murder. Jaques denied it, or to kill 'the greatest whatsoever that was an enemy ot the king of Spain.' Jaques took Collen to Holt. 'Holt said that he was a churchman, and wished that Jaques had not acquainted him with the enterprise, but that he saw no reason why he might not lawfully do what Jaques wished'; confession of Patrick Collen before Wilkes, Egerton and R. Young, 16. 2.1594, *Cal. SP Dom*, ibid., p. 436; SP12/247, no. 64. Cahill, Daniell's tool, as one would expect, was most forward in making the Jesuits countenance not merely Perez' but Elizabeth's assassination 'a most blessed deed'. See voluntary confession, 21.2., n. 20 above). A liar is never trusted even by his own. Daniell reassured Burgley (declaration of 25. 2, see n. 12 above), 'notwithstanding the great confidence he had and has in Cahill, never suffers him to come within the court gates, nor in any place where he might come near her Majesty.' Doubtless he realised that Burghley, who trusted none of these people, himself included, would think less of Daniell for trusting even his own lackey. A more reliable account of Jesuit attitudes was supplied by Henry Walpole, the Jesuit, in his confession of 13.6.1594 before Edward Drewe. Jaques Francisco aka Jacomo Francischi asked if it were desirable to kill the queen. Walpole 'dissuaded it', although Cahill, whom Archer had given him as a companion to England, 'accused him of seeking her Majesty's death'. Walpole 'was told by Fr Persons at Valladolid that some in England confessed their purpose to have killed her.' Persons believed 'Catholics, especially religious men, ought to suffer violence but offer none, especially to princes; that their means were persuasion and prayer, and that the seminaries would in time reduce England to their faith. He believed if any member of his society had been known to deal in such a horrible enterprise, the general would cast him out'. He protests 'that he abhors to think of it, and never did nor would move any man thereto.' He bore 'a most reverent, dutiful and loving mind towards her Majesty'; *Cal. SP Dom.*, ibid., pp 517-20; SP12/249, no. 12. Persons' views rejecting assassination were made clear in his *A temperate wardword ...* See Edwards, *R. Persons*, pp 85-6 and passim. Not that Persons or his friends rejected recourse to arms. Walpole confessed that he 'heard Englefield say that the Catholics in England were much to be blamed' for although they wanted their religion restored, '*yet they would not allow of the only probable means of admitting the Spaniards*' (confession of 13.6).

Hugh Owen got to hear of it all and may have been the one who inspired a disclaimer to Phelippes, as it was conjectured, regarding the accusations made against him and his colleagues by what seemed to be dubious contacts of the earl of Essex. The writer insisted that the earl had no part in their negotiations at any time. The interest of Cecil supporters in besmirching the earl is only too evident even if the Cecils themselves could have truthfully repudiated any responsibility. Party and partisan interest was evident in the claims put forward that Owen and Stanley intended to kill the queen.[25] In refuting the notion, Owen's apologist claimed credibly never to have seen Collen in his life and had only a passing encounter with Cahill or Polwhele. He was justifiably indignant that his reputation should depend in the slightest degree on 'perjured jacks who could not in any Christian commonwealth bear any credit for witnesses'.[26] Owen countered with the information that the duke of Parma was for ever receiving information about plots against him being contrived in England, and offered by much the same sort of people with the same motives as those who flocked to London. Far from using them, Parma's policy was to ignore them. 'If the queen and her council would do the same, they need never unquiet themselves as they do, nor so

---

25 [Hugh Owen to Phelippes], 3(?). 1594, Brussels? ; *Cal. SP Dom.*, ibid., pp 475-6; SP12/248, no. 53. The writer was someone 'wholly depending upon the earl' which clearly excludes Owen. So he repudiated accusations against Essex as well as against Owen. They were made 'by some lately executed, and by others yet living.' He had no connection with Hesketh or his alleged plot to embroil Essex as well as Derby in the succession issue. He swore to the falsity of Daniell's and Cahill's assassination charges against Stanley, 'the writer' and others to kill the queen, giving them money for the purpose. The writer was 'out of the country' while this was supposed to be going on, and 'did not know of it until his return from Rome the Christmas following.' He 'dares swear the same for Sir William Stanley.' He hardly knew Cahill but 'did Daniell divers particular pleasures, worth a better recompense than ... his false accusations. Daniell in the Low Countries gave it out that the writer 'had correspondence with the council' so how could he want to kill the queen? This is not in itself a watertight argument, Daniells and company being the men they were. Daniell and Polwhele gave evidence against Collen at his trial involving Stanley, 'the writer and others'. The writer 'protests that he never saw Collen, and the poor man said as much, both at his arraignment and execution, but all would not help; such force had iniquity and injustice against simplicity and innocence.' Daniell, 'thinking to curry great favour' gave Burghley an imaginary list of Burgundians, English and Irish' anxious to kill the queen. Among the names was that of John Annias, 'a great friend of Daniell's', but 'a sorry fellow' who could 'make white powder', but 'would not kill a cat if she looked him in the face.' Daniell in naming him had not foreseen his coming into England and Annias had no idea he was on his friend's list. He had 'of late fled into England after murdering and robbing a Spaniard who of trust had put himself into his hands; and notice having been given by the lord treasurer in all the ports and landing places of [Daniell's] list, he was on his arrival forthwith carried to the Tower.' The writer naively supposed that now his 'former offences' would receive their just reward 'as it will not now lie in Daniell's power to clear him of aught that he has falsely accused him of.' It is clear why Collen was, apparently, the only victim of the gallows at this time. And if he or others insisted on their innocence, this too could be ascribed to deceit. As the obliging Polwhele confessed on 21.2.1594 (see n. 18) when Jaques commissioned him to kill Elizabeth, he persuded him, 'if he were taken and even brought to the gallows, not to confess that he meant any hurt to the queen but to protest that he meant her no more hurt than he did to his own soul, which he might truly say, as he wished her in heaven.' 26 Ibid.

easily permit false juries to cast away so many innocent men.'[27] Parma may have had no use for such people but some in England did. Essex was now one of them. The Cecils certainly were too intelligent to believe their own propaganda or to have any regard for the tools they used while they used them. Apart from the use of plot stories against papists and undesirable characters picking up dangerous military experience on the continent, the atmosphere of peril and distrust created made it possible to isolate the queen from her subjects and critics of the regime ever more effectively. Whatever else seemed to be threatened with instability in uncertain times, the Cecilian hegemony was not.[28]

27 Ibid.   28 The follow-up to the 'plots' meant more limited access to court and queen was indicated in 'directions for apprehending suspicious persons from overseas at the cinque ports etc. [*sic*]. No Irish suitor could be preferred without a certificate from the Lord deputy 'or some of the Council'. There was a clampdown on Irishmen in London, 'or about the court'. A proclamation would forbid all who had served under Stanley or Philip II to come into England. Anyone coming without leave would be imprisoned and punished as an enemy. Anyone who detected such 'shall have good reward and not be made known to the offender.' An usher and assistants would 'attend daily all coming to court for her Majesty's service or to see any principal person.' Masters of the requests were 'to have a room without the court gates' to receive callers and suitors. All back doors were to be kept shut. Anyone lodging within two miles of the court had to be 'in the porter's books' or 'allowed by a master of requests, or by special warrant of any lord.' For defaulters, it was examination, prison 'and not delivered until licensed'; *Cal. SP Dom.*, ibid., pp 432–3; SP12/247, no. 66. It was all very reasonable – precautions always are. But the Cecils and their allies would have known that this was an excellent way of making sure that the queen for all practical purposes would come under no influence but their own.

9

The Lopez plot

About the same time as the preceding, an equally unsavoury and improbable sequence of events took place which passed into history as the Lopez plot. On 7 June 1594 three Portuguese were executed at Tyburn for treason: Rodrigo, or Ruy, Lopez, Esteban Ferreira da Gama and Manuel Luis Tinoco. They were accused of trying to poison Elizabeth. An interesting and unusual feature of this plot is that even historians of established repute agreed until recently that it had no real foundation in fact. Professor David Katz in his impressive study, the best to date, reverses this general verdict. Much depends on the extent to which we are prepared to accept the official version of the story, carefully prepared by William Cecil, and the reliability of accounts extracted from witnesses under torture or the threat of it. To question the truth of the plot as given in official sources cannot be done without casting a shadow on the reputations of both Cecils and of the earl of Essex for truthfulness. But what we have seen so far surely gives us the right to be doubtful once again of the transparent integrity of the main accusers. The earlier consensus, and the fact that it has been explored by four historians of note at different times, could provide a distant justification for judging critically those other plots which have until now been largely taken for granted as true.[1]

Dr Lopez was one of a numerous community of Portuguese physicians living in England who were taken to be Jews at least by inner conviction.[2] Lopez had lived in England for some forty years; in London from about 1558, achieving a certain fame and modest fortune as a medical practitioner of ability. He treated Walsingham and

---

1 Sources: *Cal. SP Dom. 1591-4*; *Cal. SP Spain, 1567-1603* and documentary sources indicated therein. W. Murdin, *State papers*, 1759, pp 669-75. A standard account for the government: based on W. Cecil's careful editing and organisation of the material; Waad submitted a draft to Cecil on 4.2.1593/4 (see also *Cal. SP Dom.*, 1591-4, pp 452-3, and *Sal. Cal.* iv, p. 485); another draft by Cecil is in *Cal. SP Dom.*, p. 558; further correspondence of Waad, Cecil et al. in C. Read, *Burghley and Elizabeth*, p. 498; Sal. ms 139, nos. 41-8); Katz, (see below), pp 96-8. Godfrey Goodman, *The court of King James I*, Brewer ed. (London 1839), i, pp 147, 150-6. Martin Hume, *Treason and plot* (London 1901), pp 115-53; he gives a useful list of sources on p. 116, n. 1. P. M. Handover, *The second Cecil* (London 1959), pp 117-19, 121, 123, 152. Alan Haynes, *Invisible power* (Stroud 1992), p. 111-20. David S. Katz, *The Jews in the history of England 1485-1850* (Oxford 1996), chapter 2, 'The Jewish conspirators of Elizabethan England', pp 49-106: this is the most complete study so far. He concludes that Lopez was quilty of conspiracy against the queen.   2 Goodman, p. 150.

became the household doctor of the earl of Leicester. Some critical spirits would say the fact that he was also by repute a poisoner went not ill with this appointment. In 1567 he was house physician at St Bartholomew's, presiding over a matron and twelve nursing sisters. Although he was criticised at one point for neglecting the poor of the hospital, by 1575 he was among the chief doctors of London along with his conational and colleague, Dr Hector Nuñez. By 1586 he was principal physician to the queen. The queen gave him the revenues of a parsonage procured by her from the bishop of Worcester. A wealthy patient gave him a house so that his son, a student at Winchester and Oxford, bade fair to continue and even improve the family fortune. It is not on the face of it likely that an intelligent foreigner so relatively well established would stoop to anything so foolish as to destroy his most influential employer and protectress.[3] True, the unlikely can happen.

For the purposes of our story, the international aspect of Lopez's career could be taken as beginning in 1581, the year following the Spanish occupation of Portugal. The death of Sebastian I at Alcazarquivir in North Africa on 4 August 1578 left the throne without an obvious successor. The problem came to a head with the death of Cardinal King Henry. Philip II was probably the best claimant in law. Four rival contenders were descended from Emmanuel who died in 1521. Philip II's mother was a daughter of Emmanuel. The father of another prominent contestant, Don Antonio, was a son of Emmanuel but illegitimate. Advised by Granvelle, and sustained by the military prowess of the duke of Alva, Philip, who had the wherewithal to make the nine parts of the law effective, drove Don Antonio into an exile hovering between France and England. From the first, Don Antonio was seen in England as a possible stick with which to beat the Spaniards. And by no one more than Robert Devereux, earl of Essex. Lopez became perilously involved in the politics surrounding Don Antonio when he allowed himself to be drafted into the earl of Essex's spy service from about 1590. Essex had married the daughter of Sir Francis Walsingham after the death of Sir Philip Sidney, her first husband. The earl certainly did not marry her for money since Walsingham was relatively poor. Nor seemingly for love since he reportedly assured his father-in-law when he sought her hand, 'only that he might be so enabled by his good counsel ... to do his prince and his country some service. Whereupon his father-in-law did assure him that what directions he could give him should not be wanting.'[4] The queen, was so put out by the earl's marriage, as she was by almost any marriage of her trusties, that he found it expedient to leave the court for a time. Walsingham died suddenly in 1590. Essex hoped to take over his papers and records but the sure-footed Burghley got in first, persuading the queen to let him take them over for the good of the state. Essex

---

3 Hume, pp 117-118; Katz, pp 49-53 for the early career of R. Lopez and family. In the 1580s, he lived in Wood Street, leaving his house near Barts Hospital. Of his 9 children, 8 are recorded in the parish of St Bartholomew the Less. He later took a house in Mountjoy's Inn, Holborn, and also had property rented from Winchester College; Katz, p. 55. Nuñez and Lopez, leading physicians in London, in the 80s, had business contacts with W. Cecil, Shrewsbury and Leicester. 4 Goodman, p. 147.

never saw them. Not to be outdone, he still resolved to carry on Walsingham's work in espionage himself.[5]

Essex made contact with a number of Walsingham's associates and undercover agents. These included Lopez. The earl put it to him that he was ideally suited to act as a spy for Elizabeth while seeming to work for Spain. Lopez saw the dangers attached to becoming, according to the appearances, a double-agent. Goodman reconstructed very plausibly his objection put to Essex, although one wonders if he would have been quite so candid. 'My Lord, this is a very great business and a dangerous; you are now in favour, but how long you may continue we know not. You may die and then the whole treason will be laid upon me.' [6] Lopez got time to consider. He wisely consulted Elizabeth before giving his consent. The queen was shrewdly non-committal in her reply. It was hardly a doctor's business to become a spy, but the decision was his. If he did her good service it would not go unrewarded. Essex had already acquainted the queen with the project but wisely at this stage Lopez took no chances.

An important factor in the Lopez story was the arrival of Don Antonio in England in 1586. After unsuccessful efforts to unseat Philip, including the failed expedition to

5 Ibid., pp 148–50. Paul E.J. Hammer, *The polarisation of Elizabethan politics* ... (see Bibliography, above). From the viewpoint of the presetnt work, the most interesting chapter of this well-documented study is chapter 5, 'Matters of Intelligence' (pp. 152–98). From 1593 and his appointment to the privy council, Essex began to build up his own system of contacts abroad which included Florence, Venice and Germany as well as France. This was encouraged by Elizabeth. Essex' system only began to falter when Robert Cecil received his formal appointment as secretary of state in 1596 and seriously set about reinstating a system which had been allowed to atrophy, it seems, after the demise of Walsingham in 1590. Essex no less than Walsingham and the Cecils was prepared to make use of dubious characters in the service of the state. Essex made use of Roger Walton, 'a rogue of the first order who had dealings with several councillors duting his chequered career' (p. 156). Walton's speciality was egging on others 'to vow dangerous deeds and then reporting on them'. Richard Verstegen, the Catholic intelligencer and no mere propagandist, recorded that he had brought some half a dozen to the gallows in this way. Essex and Thomas Phelippes were well aware of what Walton had been up to. Hammer admits that this 'provides circumstantial evidence to support allegations by modern historians that Essex and other privy councillors used agents actually to foment conspiracies against the queen.' Also, 'The Babington Plot, for example, which ultimately brought death for Mary, Queen of Scots, was largely driven by *agents provocateurs* employed by Walsingham' (pp. 156–7, and nn. 21–23). Nevertheless, Hammer concludes that Essex had the right of it in his dealings with Lopez and his company in the eponymous plot. 'By driving Lopez to the gallows, Essex not only demonstrated his mastery of intelligence, but exposed and triumphed over any remainingdoubts about his capacity as a councillor; (p. 138). There is no attempt to investigate the plot in depth. No discernible motive emerges for Lopez' alleged betrayal of Elizabeth, but it is evident that his efforts to forestall the earl in laying his intelligence before the queen made him look foolish when he turned up with the same thing a little later. Hammer reinforces the traditional picture of Essex as a proud and sensitive man who was capable of deep and bitter feuding with anyone who crossed or made a fool of him. But there was a deeper motive for sinking Lopez arising from Devereux' deep hatred of Spain and anxiety to keep hostilities alive. 'The charges against Lopez scuttled plans for renewed contact with Spain about peace talks which Essex bitterly opposed. Moreover, by destroying Lopez, who had important contacts in Constantinople, Essex delivered a devastating blow to any future diplomatic overtures which might involve Elizabeth's mediation between the emperor and his Turkish enemies' (ibid.).
6 Ibid., pp 150–1.

the Azores of 1583, he was allowed to settle in England. The pretender was set up in a kind of minicourt at Eton College. Inevitably, he became a focal point of anti-Spanish intrigue with his life in jeopardy. But Essex who hated all things Spanish was fully behind him. Lopez had to accept Don Antonio since he had now thrown in his lot with the earl. Not that Lopez' ultimate ambition lay in politics. This was rather to make enough out of his medical practice and a monopoly in aniseed and sumac to take him to Antwerp; thence to Constantinople and a more tranquil climate in all senses. The Turkish connection was one already well-established for Lopez and also Nuñez a friend and ally. Hector Nuñez was from 1554 Fellow of the College of Physicians and also of the College of Surgeons. He was naturalised as an Englishman in 1579. He and Lopez were the leading physicians in London in the '80s. Alvaro Mendez, another associate, later known as Solomon Abenaes, was known to Philip II; and to Walsingham who valued him for his influence in France. In 1585 Solomon Abenaes went to Turkey to succeed Joseph Nasi as the principal Jewish agent in that court. He acquired wealth and influence as a customs farmer and was very active in Anglo-Turkish politics. English merchants had been active in the Levant since Anthony Jenkinson came to an understanding in 1553 with Suleiman the Magnificent. Dr Lopez was Abanaes' agent in England. The Turkish connection became more significant after 1580 when Sultan Murad III granted a charter to English merchants. Before this they had only traded under French protection. From 1583 to 1588, William Harborne became Elizabeth's agent and ambassador to the Sublime Porte. Lopez from this time was a man to be noticed and handled with care and even respect.[7]

Lopez took up the cause of Don Antonio with apparent enthusiasm. From about 1586 the trio of Lopez, Nuñez in London and Abenaes in Constantinople pushed for an Anglo-Turkish alliance against Spain. Cecil and Walsingham were in favour. At least once, Walsingham forwarded a packet from Don Antonio to Abenaes. Lopez, much trusted by her, used his influence with the queen for the pretender. But Lopez' allegiance to his cause was questioned in Spanish circles. On 26 March 1587 Bernardino de Mendoza, Spanish ambassador in Paris, instructed Alonso de Idiaquez to say that, according to one Montesinos, 'Antonio de Vega wished to gain over Dr Lopez to purge our friend [Don Antonio], as he is in the habit of doing every fortnight ... but he had not ventured to speak plainly about it but only by hints.'[8] If Lopez was required to purge him in an even fuller sense with an effective poison, it was only hinted at. Lopez had not taken the hint. Would Antonio become another Ferdinando Stanley?

Since de Vega was Portuguese, it is not surprising if Lopez had dealings with him. Lopez, like Parry and others in their dangerous side-profession, was bound to have contacts with opposing factions. Mendoza informed King Philip on 28 March 1587 that Lopez was now a friend of Antonio de Vega, key Spanish agent in London.[9] Vega informed Mendoza on 30 April that he had won over Lopez 'to his Majesty's service

7 For the Turkish connection, see Katz, pp 52, 55, 59-61.   8 Mendez to Alonso Idiaquez, 26. 3.1587; *Cal. SP Spain 1567-1603*, , pp 49-50; Katz, p. 59.   9 S. to Philip II, 28.3.1587; *Cal. SP Spain*, ibid., p. 48; Katz, p. 60.

with good promises, and he has already done wonders in trying to get him [Don Antonio] turned out of here ... ' Mendoza, an old hand at diplomacy, had his doubts. He wrote a note on the back of Vega's letter asking why, if Vega was so certain of Lopez' new allegiance, he had not already done the necessary as far as killing the pretender was concerned.[10] At all events, Lopez was now inserted into the Spanish espionage system. This does not mean, of course, that he had switched his true allegiance from the English side.

Don Antonio's fortunes were now at low ebb. In the spring of 1587 he was described, no doubt with hyperbole, as almost starving. By the summer of 1587, his fortunes promised to turn. Elizabeth seemed favourable to plans for a naval expedition to Portugal. But it was at this juncture that Don Antonio fell out with Lopez because it had come back to him that the doctor had reported to Leicester the pretender's unfavourable view of him. Had Lopez overdone at this point his policy of keeping in with everyone; not excluding the Spaniards? They now put pressure on Vega to get Lopez to end the quarrel since an estrangement would mean the end of an influence which could solve the pretender problem once and for all. This was achieved.[11] Vega was the one who collected most of the information sent on to Philip but some of it may have come from Lopez' careless or calculated talk about what he picked up in court. The Jewish network of Lopez, Nuñez and Abaenes may have received and passed on through their other contacts the first news of the preparation of the Armada.[12] The impression of Spanish agents working in England was that the Portuguese Jews were all working for England against Spain; likely enough, since however unfriendly the English attitude to Judaism it was mild compared with the usual attitudes in Iberia.

Lopez and Nuñez certainly supported the attempt on Lisbon in 1589 by Drake and Sir John Norris following the failed challenge of the Armada. By this time Abenaes in Constantinople had been replaced by David Passi at Don Antonio's behest. He was angry at what he took to be Abenaes' lack of energy in working for a Portuguese follow-up after the Armada. The English agent in Constantinople, Edward Barton, thought Passi was pro-Spanish. One object of the Lisbon expedition was to rouse the Portuguese to rebellion against the Spanish. It was treated more or less as a commercial venture, a joint-stock company, with the queen among the leading shareholders. The enterprise was bigger than the Armada in the planning stage. But planning flaws forced the queen to increase her investment considerably. The worst flaw was basic disagreement in the top direction as to the main purpose. Elizabeth was chiefly concerned to destroy the fifty or so ships which had limped back to Santander and San Sebastian after

---

10 De Vega to Mendoza, 30.4.1587; *Cal. SP Spain*, pp 76-8. Mendoza declared, 'What he [Vega] says about my having sounded Dr Lopez through Suygo is a great lie. If Vega is so certain about Rodrigo Lopez, why has [he] not already disposed of 'his uncle' [Don Antonio]? Lopez offered to 'purge' another Portuguese, Bartolome Bayon, for Guerau de Spes, but dropped the recipe on the way to the apothecary, which was found and Lopez was in the Tower for 6 months. Bayon was murdered but there is no proof that Lopez was in the Tower for that; *Cal. SP Spain*, ibid., pp 76-8; Katz, p. 61.   11 Katz, p. 62.
12 First news of the Armada preparations; Katz, p. 63.

the Armada. Drake and Norris aimed at nothing less than the conquest of Portugal. So they set sail on 18 April 1589 with considerably more soldiers than would have been necessary for Elizabeth's more limited objective. Essex joined them unofficially on the *Swiftsure* in an enterprise that proved neither swift nor sure. Once at sea, the expedition ignored Elizabeth's orders. They bypassed the Spanish fleet and made for Lisbon. The intention was to plunder Portugal and put a friendly king back on the throne. Sinking ships, as Elizabeth wanted, would have brought nothing to the shareholders. But poor organisation, sickness, and Elizabeth's not surprising refusal to allow a relief expedition to throw good money after bad made sure the enterprise was a complete fiasco.[13]

The failure of the Lisbon enterprise meant that from this time much of the activity was at cross purposes in anti-Spanish circles. All were anxious to recoup as far as possible considerable financial losses. Essex, as anti-Spanish as ever, now looked for a better alternative to Don Antonio as the restored king of a freed Portugal. He favoured the duke of Braganza. Don Antonio's reputation was at low ebb; and along with it that of many of the exiles who had shown ardour in his support, including Rodrigo Lopez. Certainly, Don Antonio showed little political ability and no sense of security. In July 1589, after the return of the failed expedition, Don Antonio told Esteban Ferrera de Gama to send letters to him through Lopez. He knew that Lopez was serving Elizabeth but was she the only one he was serving? Taking a Spanish pension presumably, was Lopez also in reality serving Philip II? At all events, Don Antonio entrusted a packet of letters for Escobar, his agent in France, to Lopez, and he in turn entrusted them to Manuel Andrada. Andrada claimed later that these fateful letters were taken from him after he was captured.[14]

The precarious state of the pretender's status and prospects after the failure of the Lisbon project meant that the Portuguese exiles felt obliged to keep their options open; serving all parties while trying to offend none, but keeping their personal interests in main view. Spain, incredibly lavish and optimistic in distributing its pensions, at least on paper, even to very dubious friends, did sometimes get information in return. Among the circle of Portuguese expatriates trying to stay afloat in this welter of loyalties, and well-known to Lopez, was a group destined to have a determining effect on his life and career. These too might have qualified as the cast for an early Italian opera. Manuel de Andrada served Don Antonio, Philip of Spain and Elizabeth. His ultimate allegiance was doubtless to himself. Why not? None of the people he served had any regard for his Jewish religion, which he had to dissemble most of the time, while he could only be looked on as a tool to be used while he was useful, and discarded when he ceased to be. It hardly needed the intelligence of a Levantine Jew to convince him or his conationals how little they counted in the higher echelons of politics. So he worked for Don Antonio and spied for Spain, supplying Mendoza with reliable and up-to-date information on English naval affairs and on Antonio himself. Lopez was as close a friend as such a man could have.

13 Haynes, op. cit., pp 113-14; Katz, pp 70-1.   14 Katz, p. 72.

Proficient in French and Flemish, Andrada carried out missions for Don Antonio abroad. In 1590, having despaired of further help from Elizabeth, the pretender gave secret instructions to Andrada to freight a ship to take him to Gravelines, Dunkirk, or even Brazil or Constantinople. Andrada contracted with the Flemish captain for 10,000 crowns to alter course at sea and run to Dieppe where Antonio could be picked up by the Spaniards. Andrada's letter to Mendoza in the spring of 1590 revealing the scheme was intercepted and deciphered by Phelippes. Andrada was imprisoned and would have suffered the extreme penalty at the hands of Don Antonio but for the strenuous intervention of Lopez with the queen and privy council.[15]

It is likely that the real cause of Andrada's good fortune was that Walsingham realised he might be used as a spy on Spanish doings under cover of negotiating peace even if in fact Essex and Walsingham had no real interest in the cessation of hostilities. Andrada, whose bona fide seemed well established with the Spanish by his recent exploit, was sent to Spain about the end of 1590. He went with a companion, Pedro Marques, who drops immediately out of the story. Andrada was well received by Don Cristobal de Moura/de Moro, member of the consejo de estado and adviser on Portuguese affairs, and may have had a brief audience with the king. De Moro gave it out that Andrada's purpose was the opening of peace negotiations with England through Lopez. His propositions included an assurance that Don Antonio would never leave England. Lopez would somehow see to that. But if Don Antonio did manage to stay alive, he would then be obliged to leave England. Andrada also conveyed the offer of a brother-in-law of Lopez to do a secret service recommended to him by Andrada but so far unrevealed to Lopez. This could be taken to mean, and could only mean, the dispatching of Don Antonio. Aware that such an offer might put him in a suspect category, Andrada explained, 'he never on his conscience urged the persons to do this; yet seeing that although the heretic queen had been merciful to him, Don Antonio had tried by all means to have him killed, he, Andrada, in revenge for such cruelty, is now disposed to do everything against Don Antonio, even to have him killed. Nothing will be done, however, without his Majesty's orders'. There is no mention anywhere, be it noted, of any lethal intent regarding Elizabeth. Nor for that matter in the official minutes is there any specific mention of killing Don Antonio, only of keeping him in England. The state of the Spanish treasury hardly allowed for extravagance. By way of reward Andrada got no more than 300 reals with a vague promise of a pension of 30 reals. A jewelled ring, 'one of the old jewels from his Majesty's caskets', solicited for Lopez' daughter was worth another £100. All this was to be inflated into evidence against Lopez for a design on the queen.[16]

15 Ferreira's offer to Philip II; Haynes, p. 115; Hume, p. 119; this refers to *Cal. SP Spain*, iii & iv in general and iv, p. 12, for the specific reference to an assassination to be paid for with 25-30, 000 ducats. Lopez extricates Andrada; Hume, pp 119-21; Haynes, pp 113-14.   16 Andrada's mission to Madrid, the 'false peace negotiations', and Lopez' brother-in-law to kill Don Antonio; see Hume, pp 124-5, and the 'old jewel' story, pp 162-4; Katz, p. 75. Hume emphasizes that this negotiation was the basis for the

Andrada was shipwrecked on the way back from Spain but got to le Havre with his papers intact. On 2/12 August 1591 he wrote to Burghley for leave to come to England. He had asked for a passport at Dieppe to come to England but the Huguenot governor, by a sound instinct, arrested him as a suspicious character. He was taken to England as a prisoner. Burghley, who knew of his journey to Spain and remembered his former betrayal of Don Antonio, treated him with reserve but did not dismiss him. On Burghley's instructions, he was grilled by Mills, Don Antonio's minister Botello, and Lopez at Rye on 2 August 1591 about his intentions and doings on interrogatories supplied by the older Cecil. Andrada unburdened, completely or not, to Mills on 13 August. He had given out abroad that he was a Spanish agent of Philip II on his way to redeem Spanish prisoners in England. He had also written to Don Antonio begging forgiveness for past misdeeds. Andrada told his interrogators that his Spanish commission was to lead the English on with false hopes of peace while they prepared another Armada; and also to organise the death of Don Antonio. He revealed the offer of Lopez' brother-in-law, though without naming him, to kill Don Antonio for a price. And somewhat more. William Cecil was reliably reported as largely incredulous. All the same, Andrada gave a correct list of Spanish spies still in England, cited Mendoza's letter recommending him to Philip II, and plausibly insisted on his own motive as being the freeing of Portugal from Spanish tyranny and vengeance for relatives who had succumbed to Spanish persecution. In the end Burghley decided that, at least for the time being, Andrada would be more useful alive than dead. He consigned him to the custody of Dr Lopez.[17]

At this time, Andrada and Lopez were agents working for both sides and up to a point trusted by both sides. All the same, the Spaniards wanted a letter of credence from Elizabeth before proceeding further in the peace negotiations real or false. They also required Lopez to supply intelligence through Andrada who, presumably, they trusted rather than Lopez, a man they had never seen. Lopez had so far exercised no little skill in keeping in with all sides. But by this time, apart from the queen and apart from Essex to whom he had promised his service, he was effectively on his own. Leicester died in 1588 and Walsingham in 1590. Burghley was too shrewd to trust Lopez; or Andrada either. If ever they lost their usefulness, no question of regard for past services would affect any future relationship with them. The queen was bound to

accusation later that the real victim intended was Elizabeth. For this there was never any foundation or the remotest likelihood that Philip or his ministers would countenance it. Hume quotes the documents relevant to the accusation in full from Paris, Archives Nationales, K. 1578, nos. 7 & 11, maintaining they 'prove conclusively the falsity of much of the evidence upon which Lopez was convicted. They are in the form of minutes from the secretary of state, Moura, to Philip, for his consideration and approval, and although they bear no date, they are correctly included in the papers for 1591'; Hume, appendix to chapter v, pp 162-4, especially p. 163. In these minutes the killing of Don Antonio is only interpretatively referred to as 'the secret service'. The only clearly expressed intention regarding Don Antonio is to keep him in England (p. 162). For Andrada's tortuous relations with Philip, Don Antonio and Lopez, see Katz pp 72-6.   17 Lopez' examinations; Hume, pp 124-5; Katz, p. 76.

stand fairly aloof. Essex was Lopez' main suporter but might not have stood by him in need. In any case, Lopez was reported to have made a fatal error in his handling of the earl. It would not have taken the shrewd doctor long to sum up the earl's defects of character and despise him for them. He began to treat him with a certain humorous disdain. Any enthusiasm for the man whom the earl had, as he supposed, taken into his service, rapidly cooled for at least one good reason. Essex had hoped to make himself the sole channel to the queen of any information from Lopez. But Lopez far from content to let Essex have all the credit for his fact-finding wanted most of it for himself. So 'as soon as ever Lopez had received any intelligence, he went instantly to the queen and acquainted her Majesty therewith; and afterwards he went to the earl of Essex and acquainted him; then did the earl of Essex come to the court and acquainted her with the same; and the queen knowing it before, did but laugh at the earl of Essex; and so it fell out several times.' Essex never enjoyed being laughed at. The doctor's casualness burgeoned into indiscretion. During the holidays he would go to Eton 'where Don Antonio ... together with the king of Spain's secretary [Antonio Perez] who had fled out of Spain did then reside; and making merry with them, Lopez began bitterly to inveigh against the earl ... telling some secrecies, how he had cured him, and of what diseases, with some other things which did disparage his honour. But as soon as Lopez was gone, they went instantly to the earl of Essex, and, to ingratiate themselves in his favour did acquaint him with all the several passages.'[18]

After this, even if Essex did not consider Lopez sufficiently important to call for special revenge, any use to which he might be put to further personal advantage would not be ruled out from any consideration for Lopez. An element of revenge doubtless entered into the further relations of the earl and the physician and its conclusion. At the least it would have been evident to the earl by now that Lopez was expendable. Another of Lopez' circle who attached himself to Essex was Manuel Luis Tinoco. Of no notable calibre, he became his agent abroad.

In April 1593 the lord treasurer decided to use Andrada again. He was sent on a mission to the Netherlands on 24 April with ten pounds in his pocket – all he ever received from Burghley, it seems – to act the spy. He sent several letters to Burghley but of no great consequence. Already in August 1593 he wrote letters expressing discontentment with his lot and even threatening to go where he might get better recognition. It was just as well for him that he never came back to England.[19] Lopez spent 1592 and the first six months of 1593 in his spying business, working apparently for all sides.[20] Esteban Ferreira da Gama, another of his circle, offered his submission to Philip II in 1593 so that he could return to his estates. He told Lopez this. Da Gama was an assiduous disseminator of malicious rumour, or retailer of unwelcome truths as some might believe. With good reason Lopez did not trust him. Da Gama claimed

18 Goodman, pp 152-3. Tinoco becomes the servant of Essex; Haynes, p. 115.   19 Andrada's exit 1593: see Hume, pp 129-130.   20 Katz thinks the time was spent 'by all accounts' in 'negotiations with Spanish agents for payment towards a plot against the queen' but presents no solid evidence.

that Don Antonio would be poisoned as soon as he fell ill; and quoted Andrada as alleging that Lopez was willing to poison not only Don Antonio but Queen Elizabeth for good measue. It had been reliably reported as early as 1586 that Philip II was willing to have Don Antonio poisoned. This was not a contradiction of Philip's ethical stand on the subject because as Idiaquez, the king's secretary informed Mendoza, the Spanish ambassador in Paris, 'the deed might be done without scruple as Don Antonio is a rebel and has been condemned to death by law'.[21]

Antonio de Vega, held to be the chief Spanish agent in London, claimed that he had won over Lopez to handle the Don Antonio commission. Certainly, as his professed friend and doctor, Lopez was in an ideal situation for exercising his alleged talent for poisoning. But allegation is one thing and proof another. Andrada's unsatisfactory examinations and papers left behind after his escape to Europe were to be used as the foundation of a plot by which Lopez and the two mentioned at the head of this narrative were supposed to kill not Don Antonio but Queen Elizabeth. Lopez was now in perilous isolation. His situation was not dissimilar from that of Ferdinando, Lord Strange, although the characters of the two men were utterly unlike. By 1593 Lopez was in the position of the perfect fall-guy, a man of secondary importance with important connections, but none that would stand by him in a crisis. He could therefore be represented as attempting almost anything the government or any other enemies had a mind to. The blow was to fall suddenly. Meanwhile he continued to enjoy the favour of the court. In his circle of Portuguese expatriates there were two who were destined to be associated with him in ruin.

Esteban Ferreira da Gama, the Portuguese nobleman living with Lopez in Holborn, who had endangered the reputations, such as they were, of many, now had a taste of his own poison. In mid-October 1593, Elizabeth was told that, being disillusioned in his service with Don Antonio, da Gama had offered his services to Philip II together with Don Manoel, Don Antonio's eldest son. His services included a readiness to organise Don Antonio's death. Elizabeth gave orders for Essex to arrest him. On 18 October 1593 he was handed over to Don Antonio at Eton.[22] Orders were sent to the cinque ports for the interception of all correspondence from abroad for Portuguese addressees. Soon after da Gama's arrest, Gomez d'Avila, a 'mean, base fellow' who lived near Lopez, also in Holborn, was arrested with a letter on him as he came from Flanders. Addressed from Francisco de Torres to one Ferrandis, it could fairly be taken to refer to commercial transactions. Only interpretation could make it even remotely incriminating. As much was to be made of it, it calls for quotation in its essential parts. 'The bearer will inform your worship in what price your pearls are held.' The receiver of the letter would get further advice as to 'the uttermost penny that will be given for them' and wanted to know what arrangements had been made 'for the conveyance of the money, and wherein you would have it employed'. The bearer would also relate where the negotiation stood regarding 'a little musk and

21 Esteban Ferreira de Gama; see Hume, pp 132–3.   22 Hume, pp 132–3; Katz, p. 84.

amber, the which I determined to buy. But before I resolve myself I will be advised of the price thereof.' For the rest the writer thought that between them they would make a 'good profit'. That was all. Not surprisingly, Gomez d'Avila as the mere letter-carrier could give no further explanation of what he carried.[23] Evidently officialdom had something brewing since d'Avila was imprisoned and the fact kept secret.

About this time a large packet of letters was seized on a Portuguese at Dover addressed to Manoel Luis Tinoco in Brussels. These included a letter from Ferreira da Gama to Secretary Moura enclosing another from Lopez to Ferreira written before the latter's arrest. Lopez' letter simply passed on to Ferreira harmless court gossip.[24] Lopez meanwhile was using his influence with the queen to secure the release of da Gama, Don Antonio's prisoner at Eton. There was no better person than Ferreira da Gama, he assured her, to negotiate peace between England and Spain, if this is what she wanted. If not, Ferreira would be still be a good person to use 'to cosin the King of Spain'.[25] Elizabeth no more than Philip of Spain approved of attempts by commoners to make fools of crowned heads even if they were enemies. Lopez was sharply rebuked.

It fell to Essex to sift Gomez d'Avila. Emulating his late father-in-law, we may believe, he left no stone unturned whether it was to find the truth or to pin on the victim such evidence as was needed to make a plot. Typically Essex soon became impatient. Gomez d'Avila was grilled daily by Essex on the real meaning to be attached to the pearls, musk and amber in the letter he carried. D'Avila could reveal nothing but he was understandably becoming very anxious. The day came when, waiting for his daily interview, he managed to convey a message to Dr Lopez by way of someone who spoke Spanish to tell him of his imprisonment. It was not surprising that he approached Lopez. Lopez was well-known. Much might be won from his influence with queen and court. Essex seized on this communication as an excuse to show d'Avila the rack. With or without further prompting, d'Avila admitted or declared that he had been sent by da Gama two months previously to Brussels to Manuel Luis, now identified as Tinoco, and to secretary Ibarra some two months before that. The answer referring to amber and musk had been intended for da Gama.[26]

23 Hume quotes (p. 135) from Yetswirt's *True report of sundry horrible conspiracies* (London 1594). 'The bearer will inform your worship in what price your pearls are held. I will advise your Worship presently of the uttermost penny that will be given for them, and crave what order you will have set down for the conveyance of the money, and wherein you would have it employed. Also this bearer shall tell you in what resolution we rested about a little musk and amber, the which I determined to buy. But before I resolve myself I will be advised of the price thereof. And if it shall please your Worship to be my partner, I am persuaded we shall make good profit.' On the strength of this Gomez d'Avila was imprisoned, this fact being kept secret.   24 Hume, p. 134.   25 Ibid. Hume uses and quotes from W. Waad's account of the written correspondence between Lopez, d'Avila, Ferreira, Caldeira, Tinoco, and the Spanish authorities, from Calthorpe ms 33, f. 148f. The facts are probably substantially as he gave them but Waad knew how to embellish and slant his story to put their doings in the worst possible light. This was his business.   26 Hume, p. 135.

Da Gama, meanwhile, still Don Antonio's prisoner at Eton, established some kind of contact through his young Spanish warder with another Portuguese, Caldeira, who belonged to the French ambassador's household. Caldeira avoided personal contact with da Gama; but the latter according to William Waad, admittedly an unlikely source from which to recover simple truth, sent a note, 'a little ticket', to Caldeira through young Pedro his guard. The note urged Caldeira to see Dr Lopez and warn him to prevent Gomez d'Avila against leaving Brussels for England. We only have Waad's account as to what was in the note. Only copies of the notes seem to have been available so what was in the originals if there were any could only be guessed. We have been here before! Waad did his duty in writing up an account of proceedings according to what he was given. According to this note, da Gama claimed that if d'Avila 'should be taken, the doctor would be undone without remedy'. It also declared, 'All the diligence that hath been used doth not condemn Dr Lopez as yet any whit, for I have bravely diverted anybody from that.' We may certainly agree with Waad that it was all 'very suspicious'.[27] Our suspicions need not be confined to Lopez and Ferreira da Gama. Essex, as we have seen, had a double motive for eliminating Lopez: first the personal one, and second Lopez' influence with Elizabeth which he used to encourage her to make peace with Spain. Undoubtedly, her physician stood at the centre of such influence in government as was enjoyed by the Portuguese exiles. They must have seemed far too friendly to Spain.

It is not easy to believe that da Gama would have been so naive as to write even a little note containing such sinister import and without necessity. Would he have entrusted such a note to a Spaniard, even a young one, normally hostile to all things Portuguese, and even if he were Don Antonio's servant? Perhaps young Pedro had been chosen with this in mind. In the event, he informed his master Don Antonio about Ferreira's attempts to get in touch with Lopez. In consequence Caldeira was arrested and imprisoned at Ditton Park. Apparently knowing this, Lopez still felt it necessary to send a note to Ferreira to reassure him. It was written on another scrap of paper sent in a handkerchief from the laundry – vaguely reminiscent of the arrangement with the brewer of Chartley! According to this, Lopez assured Ferreira that 'he had sent twice or thrice to Flanders with that object and would spare no expense, if it cost him £300'.[28] Could Lopez have been so naive? As Katz pointedly reminds us,

27 Hume, p. 136; Haynes, p. 118. Only copies, or alleged copies, of Ferreira's notes exist. Katz claims, 'the involvement of so many untrustworthy characters in a plot to kill Don Antonio and to kill Elizabeth was Lopez' first mistake' (op. cit., p. 83). But Katz seems to rely too heavily on what was put down later in the examinations and confessions extracted under torture or the threat of it, and no doubt put to them in fair detail as to what was required. The whole tale depends on Tinoco's and de Gama's admissions under torture.   28 Ferreira's 'little note' to Caldeira said that he should warn Lopez to prevent Gomez d'Avila coming over from Brussels 'for if he should be taken, the Doctor would be undone without remedy', and further, 'all the diligence that hath been used doth not condemn Dr Lopez as yet any whit, for I have bravely diverted anybody from that', moved Waad very reasonably to regard this as 'very suspicious'. One cannot easily believe that Ferreira, not being a com-

'This was the first time that Lopez had actually committed himself to paper.'[29] The note was of course intercepted. Da Gama was confronted with it. He was induced to admit that Lopez was a principal negotiator for the submission of Don Antonio's son and heir to the king of Spain. Lopez had procured Andrada's release from prison three years before so that he might go over and arrange with Mendoza the poisoning of Don Antonio. None of this was new to the examiners.

Essex' next move was to put pressure on the 'base fellow' Gomez d'Avila. He was brought to confess, presumably with no difficulty, that a large sum of money – up to 50,000 crowns – was to be sent to da Gama in England to purchase the adherence of Don Antonio's eldest son Don Manoel for Spain. Confronted with this, da Gama admitted the musk and amber reference was in a letter intended for him and that it referred to the question of Don Antonio's successor. Da Gama was also prevailed upon at some point, it was claimed, to say that Lopez sent letters to Moro assuring him of unreserved service to Philip II even if it meant Elizabeth's death, and for this commission Lopez wanted 50,000 crowns: 'the exact sum Don Antonio had given Lopez to be paid in Portugal.' If caught out, Lopez would be able to explain away the two payments as one and the same. It was only da Gama's word that Andrada once told him Lopez would be willing to poison Elizabeth as well as Don Antonio.[30] Andrada, a key witness, was safely abroad. Essex was making progress.

Whatever Manoel Luis Tinoco had been party to, it did not occur to him that any of his activities so far could reasonably be taken to stir the suspicions of the English state. In December 1593, he arrived at Calais from Brussels with the Spanish answer to the proposals for peace negotiations proposed before by Lopez and Ferreira da Gama. Tinoco asked the English consul in Calais to get him a passport to come to England. Significantly, he wanted Burghley to be approached and not Essex although it was the earl's commission he had received originally to sound out Braganza's attitude to the succession. Tinoco must have known of Essex' opposition to peace with Spain: and of the tension between Essex and the Cecils. He represented himself at Calais as a friend of Don Antonio. His only wish was to serve Elizabeth. He had important secrets picked up in Brussels to reveal to Burghley. Tinoco was aware before he left France that da Gama and d'Avila were under arrest but evidently it caused him little concern.[31] Tinoco got his safe-conduct to enter England sent to him by the artful Waad. It allowed entry but made departure a matter for the discretion of the

plete fool, would have put provocative hints of this kind into the message. Waad would not have been tempted to challenge what was presented to him as 'evidence', and he would have had nothing presumably to do with the manufacture of forged evidence; see Hume, p. 136 and n. 2.; Katz, p. 83.   29 If de Gama's 'little ticket' to Lopez telling him not to send 'further incriminating letters to Antwerp' was an error, Lopez 'compounded the error' by replying, telling de Gama all would be arranged for his release. Katz discerningly points out that 'this was the first time' Lopez 'committed himself to paper'. But if he had been so careful so far, was he really careless on this occasion? It is surely suspicious that, as Katz admits, both letters were 'immediately intercepted'. Essex now put him under formal surveillance. Katz, p. 85.   30 Katz, p. 83.   31 Haynes, p. 117.

English government. Taking no note of this small print, Manoel Luis crossed the Channel. On arrival in England, he was immediately arrested, taken to London and imprisoned on 14 January 1594.

It was claimed that Tinoco had with him bills of exchange for large sums of money as well as two letters which could be taken as compromising. A letter signed by count de Fuentes, governor of Flanders, dated 2/12 December 1593, was addressed to Ferreira. It was a testimonial for the bearer, Tinoco, and further invited da Gama to go to Spain via Portugal for private conference with Don Cristobal de Moura. Its terms were general and contained nothing compromising. The same could be said of the other letter from Ibarra. It referred da Gama to Tinoco who knew their decison in the unnamed affair, whatever it was. Ibarra ended with a fine flourish. 'He is persuaded that da Gama will do his endeavours, and he may be assured himself to obtain all that is to be expected of one [Philip II] who can do so much, and is so willing to recompense what is done in his service, which is so much for the benefit of the world.'[32]

Much in the letters was made to depend on Tinoco's knowledge. Inevitably he was subjected to very pressing enquiry. Significantly, Burghley was happy to leave the pressing to Essex.[33] Burghley would not have been averse to clearing the board of interfering foreign amateurs in the nation's affairs. It could be left to Essex to do it. The baron preferred to deal with bona fide merchants rather than foreign renegades for his information. The queen herself was more than somewhat favourable to the Portuguese presence. So let the earl risk the odium of pruning their numbers. Grilled at interviews with Essex, Waad and others, no doubt with the threat of torture in the background if he failed to come up with the right answers, Tinoco told a tale that hovered between plausibility and absurdity. Plausibly he admitted that he was the source of the de Torres letters to Ferreira.[34] Absurdity soon followed. Archduke Ernest, the new viceroy of Flanders, intended to invade England by way of the Isle of Wight. A priest and a Jesuit were coming from Dieppe to kill the queen with a 'device of fire'. Plausibly again, he was brought by leading questions to aver that he had been sent to England to join with Lopez to execute 'a service' for Philip II. He was pressed on the letters from Fuentes and Ibarra to Ferreira da Gama. Although he admitted relinquishing the cause of Don Antonio, he denied that the letters had anything to do with him. The most significant admission to which he was drawn was that Lopez was to be the principal agent of Philip's service. This and the 'evidence' of da Gama's notes, real or alleged, was sufficient to put Lopez where Essex wanted him. The earl had him arrested on 21 January 1594.[35]

Lopez had his house searched but nothing incriminating was found. The Cecils now appeared actively on the scene. He was examined by Essex and both of them at Burghley House. The Cecils cleared Lopez of sinister designs although Burghley knew of his connections with Spanish agents. Andrada had revealed his legitimate interest in the peace negotiation two years previously. This was the opportunity which

32 Hume, pp 138-9.   33 Haynes, p. 118.   34 Ibid.   35 Hume, pp 140-2.

they had probably been waiting for to reduce an aspiring rival to size. Robert Cecil lost no time in sending a messenger to Hampton Court to tell Elizabeth not only that Essex had arrested her personal physician but that subsequent examination showed him to be innocent. This was nicely calculated to exacerbate relations further between the queen and Essex with whom she had been quarrelling since Christmas. The queen was provoked by the arrest. At a subsequent meeting with Essex, when Robert Cecil was present, she flared up, not for the first time. Essex was dismissed as 'a rash temerarious youth'. It was all music, no doubt, in the ears of the man described by Hume not very kindly but not inaptly as 'Cecil, the prim, sly little hunchback'.[36] This other Robert also took the trouble to inform her that 'in the poor man's house were found no kind of writings of intelligences of which he was accused. Or otherwise, that hold might be taken of him'.[37] To make matters satisfactorily worse, it seems that Elizabeth had already received notice of her favourite's dealings in the matter of Braganza's projected succession in Portugal. This had been kept secret from her as well as from the privy council. She reasonably regarded it all as an invasion of her own prerogative.[38] Essex left the queen's presence to sulk for two days and no doubt devise a way in which he might recover so much lost ground. Perhaps it did not take him too long to realise that Lopez had to be guilty.

On 24 January Anthony Standen, one of the more competent and significant members of the earl's entourage, arrived at Hampton Court where Achilles was still sulking. Evidently on the earl's inspiration, for he could hardly have gained the information elsewhere, Standen wrote an account for Anthony Bacon on the 30th of Lopez' examination on the 21st. He claimed that 'Lopez had been detected of a design to poison the queen'.[39] Next day Nicholas Faunt, another of Essex's retainers, wrote to Bacon from London to say, 'It was most true that Dr Lopez was most deeply touched in the particular working of the queen's destruction, and was discovered to have been the King of Spain's pensioner for seven years past.'[40] On 23 January, after due or undue pressure, Essex got from Tinoco an admission that da Gama had promised the Spanish ministers that Lopez was ready to serve the king of Spain. The story of the jewel for Lopez was thrown in for good measure.

Burghley remained unmoved. 'In folly I see no point of treason intended to the queen but a readiness to make some gain.'[41] On Tuesday 29 January Lopez was transferred to the Tower. On the 28th, Essex had written to Anthony Bacon a dramatic letter announcing his great discovery.[42] 'I have discovered a most dangerous and most desperate treason. The point of conspiracy was her Majesty's death. The executioner

---

36 Hume, pp 142-6.   37 Katz, p. 86.   38 Haynes, p. 119.   39 Hume, p. 143.   40 Ibid.   41 Tinoco exam on 23.1.1593/4 was crucial. Katz, p. 87, quoting from *Cal. SP Dom.*, *1591-4*, pp 416-17; W. Cecil to Robert Cecil, 23.1.1593/4, Cambridge University Library, ms Ee. 3-56, No. 15, quoted in C. Read, *Burghley and Elizabeth*, p. 498.   42 The date of Lopez' transfer to the Tower is variously given. Hume and Katz (p. 87) put it on 29.1.1594. Haynes says, 'by 5 February', using as his authority A. Standen to Anthony Bacon, p. 119. The date is given in Handover, op. cit., as 29.1. who also gives the date of the Standen/Bacon letter as 30.1.1594, quoting from Birch, op. cit., i, p. 150.

should have been Dr Lopez; the manner poison. This I have so followed as I will make it appear as clear as the noonday.'[43] It was suspiciously premature.

All this time the examination of the other prisoners proceeded. Since the basic loyalty of each was only to himself, with the threat of the rack hanging over them all, they squealed like pigs in the slaughter-house. The standard trick of telling each prisoner what the other had confessed against him was completely effective. Tinoco was told that da Gama, threatened with torture, had saddled him with high treason. Tinoco did not allow himself to be outdone in his anxiety to tell his captors what they wanted to hear.[44] Waad was the Cecils' man but he was allowed to tell Faunt, who wrote to Bacon on 11 February, to pass on some 'secret' news which could only have been for Essex' encouragement. The enquiry itself was credibly 'very strict' but the items released all seemed to help the earl's case. Faunt, quoting Waad, says Lopez admitted receiving letters from Spain soliciting his services. But he never, as he said, committed himself. 'Yet one letter was found in which he offered all his service to the king, saying that he only stayed in England to do him acceptable service, which, being done, he would think himself happy to retire and die in his Majesty's dominions.'[45]

We will not be surprised to learn from Hume that this letter cannot be traced. As Hume commented in dry understatement, 'Mr Faunt's hearsay assertion of its existence is not conclusive.' Nor is much credence to be given to Ferreira da Gama's confession of 18 February. According to this, he received from Lopez two letters at his dictation for de Moura which offered to do all that the king of Spain desired. The wording was purposely obscure so that nothing certainly treasonable could be proved. Heavily leaned upon, Da Gama gave it as his opinion that 'the doctor would have poisoned the queen if required'. Hume again: 'this is an instance of the way in which the evidence was built up. From these extorted admissions to the confident statements that Lopez had written to the Spaniards offering to kill the queen was but a step.' Da Gama in the same confession also claimed that shortly before Andrada left England in 1593, he told him that if King Philip wished, Lopez would poison either the queen or Don Antonio. Da Gama afterwards repeated this to Lopez himself who replied, 'As for the king [Don Antonio], he shall die with the first sickness that shall happen to him, but for the queen we have no answer yet from the other side.'[46]

It will be evident by now from the nature of the case against Lopez, and the other two under suspicion with him for that matter, that two men of the acumen of William

---

43 Hume, p. 144; Handover, p. 114 and n. 7. 'As Essex refers in the letter to A. Bacon, Monday, 1594, (Birch, p. 152) to his retirement for two days, the Monday would be 28 January.'   44 Hume, ibid.   45 Ibid. Faunt to A. Bacon, 11.2.1594, 'wrote ... some news he had heard secretly from ... Waad about the Lopez case, which he now mixed up vaguely with the Collen, Annias, and Polwhele conspiracies ...'
46 Confession of Stephen Ferreira da Gama before Essex, Sir John Wilkes and Waad, 18.2.1594; *Cal. SP Dom.*, ibid., p. 434; SP12/247, no. 70; Hume, pp 145-6 and 146 n. 2. Katz admits (pp 87-8) that the first three weeks of examinations produced no hard evidence. But he thinks that this confession of 18.2. constituted a major breakthrough. Hume seems to dispose effectively of this. It all depends on the word of da Gama, a man under threat of torture.

Cecil and his no less astute son could not have been taken in by the flimsy evidence on offer. It is evident from their recorded reactions that so far they believed none of the charges. The attitude of the queen was also important. Throughout she remained as incredulous as the Cecils regarding the charge against Lopez. She remained so to the end. At first she held back, but when Tinoco was arrested in January 1594 after his arrival in England, she chose this moment to counterbalance the Essex influence. She appointed Burghley to examine him.[47] It was after this examination, which uncovered nothing much, that Tinoco was brought to the lodge in Hampton Court park to be grilled by Robert Cecil and Essex together. Essex conducted the examination, in French as it happened, since, unlike Cecil, he knew neither Italian nor Spanish; something else to the examinee's great disadvantage and perhaps to the earl's. It was only on the strength of an admission by Tinoco that da Gama had been sent to England to win Lopez over to Philip II's service that Essex had Lopez arrested in the first place. Lopez was examined at Burghley House in the Strand by the two Cecils and Essex. Lopez denied all.[48] As we have seen, Robert Cecil declared that nothing was found in his house to compromise or contradict him.

At some point early in February the Cecils were involved in a complete volte face. If it was not the force of the evidence, what was it that brought them, together with Essex, to work up the flimsiest of cases into a show trial in Guildhall? How could Robert Cecil come to declare at one point with so much passion and venom, referring to Lopez, 'The vile Jew said that he did confess ... it, that he had talk of it, but now he might tell further he did belie himself; and did it only to save himself from racking, which the Lord knoweth on my soul's witness to be most untrue ... and judgment passed against him with the applause of all the world.'[49]

P.M. Handover was explicit in connecting the destruction of the Lopez group with the tense relations between the Essex and Cecilian factions in court and government. This makes complete sense of the U-turn of events which led to the death of the Portuguese for high treason. We have seen the struggle in the background between the Cecilians, who were not averse to peace with Spain, and the Essex faction which was. In order to discredit Spain in the eyes of Elizabeth, reverse his temporary eclipse in her favour, and queer the pitch of the Cecilians, Essex claimed the credit for uncovering this plot to murder her. So the Cecils were excluded from the first 'revelation' of the plot when Essex arrested Ferreira da Gama in Lopez' house in mid-October 1593 and turned him over to Don Antonio at Eton. Arrests and interception of letters and their misinterpretation in the interests of Essex' plot followed inexorably. So far the Cecils held aloof. They had a Portuguese interpreter who dealt in 'the business of Antonio

47 'Advertisements delivered by Emanuel Louis Tinoco, 15.1.1594; *Cal. SP Dom.*, ibid., p. 411; SP12/247, no. 12; Handover, p. 113. 'Amid much wild talk he revealed that Ferrera had been sent to England 'to try and win Dr Lopez' to do 'service for the king of Spain'. On the strength of this statement which again could have meant little or nothing Essex had Lopez arrested. 48 Handover, p. 113 and n. 3, quoting Ferreira to Fuentes, 1.2.1594, *Cal. SP Dom.*, p. 422. 49 Hume, p. 150; quoted from SP12/247, no. 97; *Cal. SP Dom.*, p. 444. See below, n. 72.

Perez and others' staying in one of their Strand houses so they would have known what was going on.[50] One could not imagine William Cecil or his all-seeing son being kept in the dark about anything of importance. Meanwhile, Essex saw the way out of a predicament. But the Cecils stood in his way. They enjoyed influence as much as anything because they were the queen's stalwart defenders against frequent attempts, as it was alleged, on her crown and life. If Lopez and his accomplices really were potential assassins, and the case could be proved against them and aginst the defending Cecils into the bargain, Essex would have an opportunity to repair his reputation with the queen and snatch a triumph from his rivals. Nothing would impel her to listen to him as much as a discovery by him of a plot to kill her. Essex soon convinced himself that there was indeed a plot and he had uncovered it. All the same the obstinacy of the Cecils in failing to see it was an obstacle. Could it be overcome?

There was a matter at this time which affected all parties closely, especially the Cecils. The appointment of an attorney-general was in the air. This appointment was also important to Essex since the influence of this official in the management of justice and especially state trials was paramount. It will be evident that by this time the apparatus for treason trials had become a killing machine to remove enemies of the state and of those who governed it. They were a vital factor in the power game. The attorney-general and the clerks of the council, notably Waad at this time, edited and provided the evidence on which judges or triers were obliged to conduct their case. The evidence had to be selected, edited and presented in such a way that only one reasonable verdict was possible – death. Essex as an aspirant to more power, and the Cecils who already had most of it, were all vitally interested in having a friend or subordinate who could be relied on in this important office.

After Essex put Lopez in the Tower on 29 January 1594, Essex and Robert Cecil went to examine him next day. Robert Cecil let the other Robert do the pressurising. Lopez reacted as a man who was frightened, as well he might be, and cursed and swore his innocence. Nothing was proved against him, and Robert Cecil knew how little had been revealed. So, presumably, did Essex. On the way back to the Strand on this 30th of January Essex and Robert Cecil shared a coach. Cecil brought up the subject of the new attorney-general. Elizabeth was going to make the appointment in five days' time. Cecil wanted to know, as if he did not know already, Essex' favourite for the post. The earl said that everyone was aware that he wanted the appointment of Francis Bacon. Cecil claimed that he was too young and inexperienced. 'Give me one only precedent for the appointment of so raw a youth to that place of such moment.' Essex replied at once. 'I could name a younger than Francis Bacon, of less learning and of no greater experience, who is sueing and shoving with all force for an office of far greater importance, greater charge and greater weight than the attorneyship.' Robert knew that the reference was to him and his hope of becoming principal secretary, and said so. He modestly referred to the merits of his father, who had taught him, rather than his own.

50 Handover, p. 113.

As for Bacon, 'If at least your lordship had spoken of the solicitorship, that might be of easier digestion to her Majesty.' Essex, as always when baulked, stormed in his fury: 'The attorneyship for Francis is that I must have; and in that I will spend all my power, might, authority and amity, and with tooth and nail defend and procure the same for him against whomsoever; and whosoever getteth this office out of my hands for any other, before he have it, it shall cost him the coming by. And this be you assured of, Sir Robert, for now do I fully declare myself.'[51]

Cecil typically remained unruffled and reported all to his father. They sought out and informed Elizabeth. She seems to have decided after their exposition of the situation that this was another occasion when a refractory horse should be starved of his oats. The Cecils exploited their opportunity not only to make sure that Edward Coke should be the next attorney-general, but also to put in office Sir Edward Stafford and Robert Cecil as secretaries, appointments to be announced within a few days. But the Cecils were too worldly-wise to want a powerful enemy waiting at their elbow on the lookout for revenge. It was not their way to make enemies openly and Essex could still be dangerous. In view of a volte face by the Cecils *vis-à-vis* Lopez and company, one has to conclude that some arrangement was made behind the scenes to allay the furious resentment of the wounded boar. True, this involves an example of extrapolation which is only to be allowed when an evidential link is lacking but one knows it must have been there. But because it is lacking, as so often in these darker corridors of history, one has to allow the right of those who refuse to judge except on certainty. The reader has as much right as the writer to reconstruct the scene or scenes at the making of a pact – or to reject it. The fact is that from this time forth there was no disharmony among the principal engineers of the almost inexorable progress of the wretched Portuguese towards the scaffold. We hear of no more protest on the part of Essex against the appointments. Robert Cecil concurs fully in the sentence delivered against the 'traitors' although there was no new and startling adjunct to the evidence previously available and hitherto rejected: only admissions after threat of torture. Nothing has so far come to light in writing even in private letters. Perhaps we should not expect it. But to suppose that no agreement was reached must, in the light of all the rest, seem to most of us unrealistic.[52]

Certainly, from the time of Ferreira da Gama's examination of 18 February 1594 no further obstacle was placed in the way of a verdict that was now desired by all parties to the prosecution. Da Gama admitted on the 18th that he had received a hint from Andrada that Lopez would poison Elizabeth. So it was agreed there was sufficient evidence to proceed. The interrogation procedures from this time were much rougher, after the presumed agreement between the earl and the Cecils. In spite of the threat hanging over them, the Portuguese seem to have been guarded enough in their replies

---

51 Ibid., pp 115-16 and n. 9, quoting A. Standen to A. Bacon, 3.2.1594; Birch, i, pp 152-3. 52 Katz has nothing to say on this aspect of the rivalry between Essex and the Cecils and the probable way in which it was resolved.

for the first three weeks to come up with nothing that put any of them in danger. That Andrada could not now be examined was never deemed an obstacle. 'Tinoco's admissions were used as levers for parting still further the lips of Ferreira; and the two prisoners were so cleverly handled with fear of torture, and by a desire to ingratiate themselves with their examiners, that the story soon looked circumstantial enough to ensure the hanging of Lopez.' By 22 February, da Gama's last denials in the Tower were broken down and on the 26th Tinoco was brought to the manacles. Nothing they said in the circumstances now could be taken as anything more than an effort to get themselves too literally off the hook; even if it meant incriminating one another. 'When the evidence, such as it was, was pieced together, it appeared from the declarations that the reference to "peace" and "service" really meant the murder of the queen by Lopez.'[53]

Tinoco was reported to have admitted on the 26th, 'The letters I wrote to Ferreira by Gomez d'Avila concerning the point which speaketh of pearls, and the price of them, was to give him to understand that the news which he had sent that Dr Lopez would kill the queen were very greatly accepted, and much esteemed of count de Fuentes and secretary Ibarra.'[54] On the 22nd, even without the manacles, Tinoco had already confessed that Andrada told Fuentes 'that Dr Lopez bound himself to dispatch the queen by poison; whereof it behoved him [Fuentes] to advertise the king of Spain thereof with all speed.' Philip declined to proceed further in such a matter through a personage as discredited on all sides as Andrada. Thus Tinoco.[55] The 50,000 conjectural crowns from Spain, which had been mentioned earlier in connection with the peace negotiations, and which were presumably the sum proposed to bring over interested and influential parties to the idea, now became the sum which Lopez demanded for his dispatch of Elizabeth. It was earlier suggested that this was the sum demanded by Lopez for killing Don Antonio but it is sufficiently unlikely that so vast a sum would have been paid out to so problematic a character as Lopez even if Philip had approved.

As Hume reminds us, 'It was not in accordance with the Spanish principle to pay beforehand – if at all – and according to the confessions the matter hung fire until Ferreira was sent by Lopez to Flanders with the two letters already referred to again

---

53 Hume, p. 146; Handover, p. 117. Katz, like John Bossy and other writers of this school, seems to think that, if the use of torture could not be approved of, at least it revealed the truth. This is surely naive. From this point in his well-ordered and well-documented narrative Katz seems to be too ready to take the assurances of government sources for truth.   54 Hume, p. 146, n. 1 quotes Tinoco's confession as of 26. 2.594. (*Cal. SP Dom.*, date is [23 Feb.], p. 439) from Yetswirt: 'The letters I wrote to Ferreira by Gomez d'Avila concerning the point which speaketh of pearls, and the price of them, was to give him to understand that the news which he had sent that Dr Lopez would kill the queen were very greatly accepted, and much esteemed of count de Fuentes and secretary Ibarra. And touching the point concerning musk and amber, the count de Fuentes did tell me that he did look for a resolution of the king of great importance; and when it came there should be as great matter.'   55 Hume, p. 147 and n. 1; Katz, p. 88.

offering his service in obscure terms.'[56] Obviously, Tinoco's confessions 'were all directed to prove his own innocence at the expense of Lopez and Ferreira, whilst the latter sought to shift the principal burden upon Lopez. Both the prisoners, however, admitted the main point, namely, that the conspiracy really aimed at the queen's death.'[57] Had the victim intended been Don Antonio, it might have been plausible; that it was the queen may be regarded as absurd.

Elizabeth could not do less than appoint the lord admiral, Essex and Robert Cecil to reexamine Lopez. This took place on 26 February when Tinoco by his first full confession corroborated da Gama's charges. At first Lopez refused to admit the charges. He 'kneeled down, very solemnly lifting his hands, his eyes and countenance towards

---

56 Tinoco's depositions were crucial to the government case. On 16.1.1594 he claimed in a letter to W. Cecil, his letters written from Calais, the secrecy of his journey, and being accompanied by two servants of the 'captains of Dover castle', and his desire for a speedy return, all proved his loyal intentions towards Elizabeth. His recent examination needed explanation: he 'was confused and encumbered by the cunning demands of the earl [Essex] and faltered in three respects.': first, language, since the examination was in French; second, the sight of so many Portuguese committed to prison; thirdly, he 'was confused with the manner of that secret examination, though his heart was devoted to the service of the crown.' He is glad that 'his honour' accepted his offer of service. He 'gives his word as a gentleman to serve the queen ... by giving secret advetisements of all things.' He 'will declare anything that Cecil desires to know and not conceal anything.' He served Don Antonio for thirteen years and thereby lost all he had in Portugal. He will now serve Elizabeth. He desires to be known as Cecil's servant. In a word, Tinoco is now another Annias who will say whatever he is told. Cf. Haynes, p. 116; Hume, p. 148.   57 Tinoco and Ferreira put the whole burden on Lopez. Cf. 'Advertisements delivered by Emanuel Louis Tinoco' of 15.1.1594, 4½ pages endorsed by Cecil as Tinoco's 'memorials' translated out of Portuguese, *Cal. SP Dom.*, pp 411-414; SP12/24/, no. 12: also 23.1., Tinoco's statement, *Cal. SP Dom.*, p. 416; SP12, ibid., no. 19: 8.2, Tinoco's declaration before Waad, ibid., p. 428 and no. 51: 18.2, and 19.2, confessions of Ferreira da Gama were put before Essex, Wilkes and Waad, ibid., p. 434 and no. 70 (the 2 confessions). On 8.3. da Gama made a confession, ibid., p. 455 and SP12/248, no. 12. On 9. iii. a 'brief declaration' of Lopez's treasons was drawn up, taken from 'those already calendared': a 6½ page document, damaged, written by W. Cecil's clerk, and corrected by himself with additions by solicitor general Coke. Basil Fitzgibbon considered it a 'forgery'. See ibid., p. 455 and no. 15. Tinoco made a further declaration from the Fleet to W. Cecil on 1.3. (o. s.). He claimed that he denied all until he was certain that da Gama, fearful of torture, confessed all he knew. R. Cecil showed to Tinoco da Gama's confession. It said nothing about Lopez but 'that he should confess 'the business that is to result in the good of all Christendom.' Tinoco 'did all this' so that da Gama should confess all he knew. Tinoco thought that he 'has thus lost his excellency's [Burghley] and Sir Robert's favour.' Evidently, this gave the Cecils the pretext for joining with Essex in regarding Lopez as guilty for forensic purposes from now on. Tinoco further claimed that in 'order to cause Ferreira to confess' he wished to be tortured himself so that 'Ferreira would then have been assured that he would have discovered all'. Evidently, it would not have occurred to da Gama that Tinoco would refuse to come out with whatever was wanted, and to save himself unnecessary pain, da Gama would have corroborated all. Tinoco had to admit that concealing these things 'has been much to his cost'. Finally he 'confesses that he has wilfully erred and asks mercy. ': *Cal. SP Dom.*, pp 456-7; SP12/248, no. 20. Katz observed that it is only after da Gama's confession of 18.2. that the poisoning charge against Lopez appeared for the first time in an official document: *Cal. SP Dom.*, p. 434 and Katz, p. 88.

heaven, [and] besought God ... to heap vengeance upon him and his here and in the world to come if there were any such thing.' He also suggested, rather charitably, that Tinoco and Ferreira were drunk when they made their confessions. The threat of torture, which he mentioned at his trial, now made him change his mind completely. 'Calling himself better to remembrance', he confirmed all the accusations laid against him by the other two.[58] According to Philip Gawdy, writing to his brother, Lopez had to endure more than threats. 'Dr Lopez hathe bene often examyned, and divers tymes uppon the racke.'[59] The Cecils did nothing now to thwart the course of injustice since the destruction of the Portuguese was, in effect, the presumed price to be paid for the appointment of Coke as attorney-general. In political terms the price was not excessive. They may well have been the principal cause of the literal turning of the screw on the wretched prisoners. The task now was to have all the alleged facts at hand for the preparation of a consistent story for public consumption. The work was well done, probably by Waad. As Katz justly observed, 'the details of their stories preserved in the state papers are extraordinarily consistent.'[60] Knowing by now the competence of both Cecils and their chosen servants, one would not expect them to be otherwise.

The elimination of the Portuguese influence as a political excrescence was fully in accord with Cecilian policy. The whole affair was very much in the public eye but there was no danger of awkward questions being asked by the generality. Judaism was hated and despised, if also feared, as much as popery and Jesuitism. This comes through clearly in Shakespeare's play. But Marlowe's *The Jew of Malta*, probably first performed about 1592, and much less subtle, was now revived, it seems, by the admiral's men, Shakespeare's rivals.[61] As the admiral had himself been involved in the pursuit of Lopez it would have been helpful and appropriate. Certainly, it was nicely timed to stir poular fury against the Lopez group and divert the attention of critical spirits, if

58 Handover, p. 118 and nn. 11-15. Her account here is based on BL Harleian ms 871. 'This ms is a contemporary record of the examination', referring immediately to Lopez's examination of 30.1.1594. **59** Katz, p. 89, quoting from HMC report 7, App (1879), 522b. **60** Katz, p. 88. Undoubtedly much trouble went into the preparation of the trial material to make it sound convincing. On 4.3. Waad wrote to R. Cecil from Wood Street to tell him that, as Burghley had commanded, he had 'drawn a narration of Dr Lopez's treasons'; *Cal. SP Dom.*, p. 452 and SP12/248, no. 7. This was accompanied by the report itself, 22½ pages long, based on the evidence produced at his arraignment and trial. It showed 'the discovery was made by an intercepted ticket which Ferreira wrote after his apprehension, from his care to conceal the doctor, whereupon Manuel Luis was stayed on his return to England. On this the doctor's altered countenance betrayed his guilty conscience; he was taken, examined, and after vehement denials, at length confessed all.' ;ibid. and -/7.1. A memo on Lopez of 9.3. included, 'he confesses he is a Jew though now a false Christian.' He was taken before he could get to speak with Ferreira, yet they agreed upon their examinations, and confessed all that was alleged against them. 'Lopez wrote and signed his own confession.' Also, 'about the time of this conspiracy, several English and Irish were found ... corrupted with money, and animated by certain English Jesuits with promise of salvation' to kill the queen. Of these 'divers taken ... some condemned and some spared, because they have with great sorrow confessed their offence, and utterly detested their setters on, and their devilish ghostly Fathers'; ibid. and -/ no. 16. This explains how the spies got off and the relatively innocent were made to suffer. **61** Katz, p. 102.

any, from the more bizarre aspects of the case. It was never difficult to stir popular dislike of the foreigner especially those originating in the Mediterranean. That they were Jews made it even easier. Most would have concluded that the whirligig of time was only bringing in his just revenges where the Portuguese miscreants were cocerned.

A show trial was put on at Guildhall on 28 February 1594 by a special commission of fifteen judges of which the lord mayor, Lord Charles Howard, the lord admiral, Lord Buckhurst, Sir Robert Cecil, Sir Thomas Heneage, Sir John Popham, chief justice of the queen's bench, Essex and his brother-in-law, Lord Rich, were prominent members. William Cecil was noticeably absent.[62] It was time for Coke to perform his first significant forensic service for the Cecils, and incidentally for Essex. 'That unpleasant, urgent bully', as Haynes calls him, although still only solicitor-general, was put on as prosecutor. It could be taken as his apprentice piece for the more important office. No official account is extant of the trial so it may be that he allowed his enthusiasm, never in short supply on these occasions, to carry him to excess. He obliged on this as he would on future occasions when a politically correct verdict was needed by the regime in such trials. Many times over he was to prove himself a man who knew his place and knew how to be grateful. Essex himself was soon to realise how grateful.

It is reported that Coke began by showing that all the plots against the queen were the response to 'her constant defence of Christ's cause and His Holy Word against the pope, and for protecting her dominions against the ambitions of the king of Spain'. The root cause of all the trouble was 'the cursed bull of Pius V'. When Philip 'and his priests' despaired of 'prevailing by valour', they turned to 'cowardly treachery'. What cannon could not do gold pieces would. So the navy was to be burned 'with poisoned fireworks', some of the nobles were to be seduced to rebellion, and finally 'the blood of a virgin queen' was to be poured out. So 'many needy and desperate young men are seduced by Jesuits and seminary priests with great rewards and promises to kill the queen' with heaven and canonisation as their reward in prospect.[63]

Eventually Coke came to the point. 'This Lopez, a perjured murdering traitor and Jewish doctor, worse than Judas himself, undertook the poisoning.' What made it unforgivable was that he was the queen's 'sworn servant, graced and advanced with many princely favours, used in special places of credit, permitted often access to her person,

---

62 Katz points out 'no official account of the trial has yet been found. '(p. 90) It is not included in the State trials volumes. Francis Bacon was present as Essex's man but took no active part in it. See G. B. Harrison, *The Elizabethan journals 1591-1603*, part 1, pp 288-291 from SP12/247, nos. 97, 102, 103. Katz noticed Burghley's absence (p. 89). Doubtless he was anxious to keep communications open with Elizabeth who was unhappy with the whole proceedings against Lopez. Cf. Handover, p. 118; Haynes, p. 119.   **63** G. B. Harrison, p. 289. The 'heads of the indictment against Dr Lopez', [28. ii.], nearly 2 pages, consists of a list of letters dated with the excessive accuracy frequent in such trials to convey the illusion of precision. So, for example, on '31. Jan. 1590, he conspired the death of the queen, and to stir up a rebellion and war within the realm ...' On '20 Jan. 1593, Em. Andrada conferred with him for poisoning the queen, which he undertook to do, 20 Feb. 1593 through Andrada.' Eleven dates are given in all. See *Cal. SP Dom.*, p. 445, from SP12/247, no. 100.

and so not suspected' least of all by the queen herself. He only delayed action until 'payment of the money was assured. The letters of credit for his assurance were sent'. Once
again, marvellous chance came into it. 'Before they came to his hands, God most won-
derfully and miraculously revealed and prevented it.' The way the miracle worked was
described in some detail. Some followers of Don Antonio, disillusioned with their master, offered their services to the king of Spain for any treason required whether against
Antonio or against the queen. While outwardly pretending loyalty to, and working for,
Don Antonio, Lopez too was 'a secret instrument for the king of Spain'. So he continued 'for many years by means of' Andrada, Mendoza 'and others'.[64]

Lopez was trapped by the interception of a letter from Andrada to Mendoza telling
him he had won over Lopez. But it was Andrada who was arrested. Lopez tried to tell
Andrada what he should say at his examination. In fact he said it so well that he was
released. Philip was so pleased with the outcome thus far that he sent Lopez a jewel.
After this, Andrada dealt with Lopez for poisoning the queen. His willingness was communicated to Fuentes and 'Ibarra, the king's secretary'. Andrada then went to Calais to
provide liaison between Lopez and the Spanish side. Ferreira da Gama became
Andrada's agent to maintain direct contact in England with Lopez. Gama was told 'that
he might commit all things to Lopez, who hoped to do one great service to the king and
a remedy for Christendom, which was to poison the queen the king paying for it.' Why
Coke's hated 'Jewish doctor' should put himself in jeopardy to provide a remedy for
Christendom was not explained. But undoubtedly the money was good, or rather the
promise. Lopez undertook to provide the service for 50,000 crowns. Da Gama signified
this 'by letters' to Fuentes and Ibarra. He even wrote to de Moura to assure him of the
doctor's 'affection to the King of Spain'. Lopez 'also sent two packets of letters to
Count Fuentes, de Moro [Moura] and de Ibarra, wherein he promised to do all the King
of Spain should command'. But to disguise the fact that there was no real evidence for
all this, it was brazenly claimed that, 'since the king knew the business, as [Lopez] told
Ferrara, he made him write in obscure and covert words'. Lopez enquired often about
the acceptance of his service, and the money which would be paid in Antwerp where
Lopez was preparing a house for himself before he moved on to Constantinople.[65]

In addition to Ferreira da Gama, it was claimed that Tinoco was now used as a go-
between. He was arrested most conveniently 'with the letters from the Count Fuentes
and Ibarra, letters of credit for the money being found upon him'. Not without
naïveté, as it must seem in the light of pressures known to be used, an attempt was
made to use the separate times and separation of those arrested as proof that their
agreeing and consistent statements upheld the truth of the declared tale. Tinoco and
de Gama 'agreed in all things concerning the plotting of the treason'. All the same, the
difficulty in making the evidence stick could not be effectively concealed. 'In handling
of these treasons Lopez was so careful that he never wrote anything himself nor treat-

64 Ibid., p. 290.   65 Ibid., p. 291. Cf. Francis Bacon, *A true report* ... , p. 287; Birch, *Memoirs* ... , 1,
pp 59-60; Katz, pp 90-1.

ed directly with Tinoco, but used Ferreira de Gama as a means between them. Nor did he ever discover any part of their proceedings or pretences to her Majesty or any of the Council.'[66]

With Walsingham and Leicester dead, Essex desiring only Lopez' destruction, and the queen sufficiently remote from it all, the allegation could be made in court with all safety. According to Goodman, after Lopez' arrest and imprisonment in the Tower, 'he sent divers messages to the queen, and did appeal to her Majesty's knowledge: to whom the queen graciously returned this answer, that for such things as he had revealed to the queen, he should suffer no loss; but if any other things should be objected against him, it was fit for the honour and justice of the state that he should make his defence.'[67]

In the course of his examinations Lopez had denied 'with blasphemous oaths and horrible execrations' that he had ever been involved in any such matter. But he was brought eventually to confess 'that he had indeed spoken of it and promised it but all to cozen the King of Spain'. Even this was later contradicted when he said, altogether credibly, that he had 'belied himself only to save himself from racking'.[68] The speciousness of the accusations in the trial will be evident from what has gone before but Hume's final summing up deserves quotation. 'It must be recollected that the letters purporting to be written by Andrada in Calais to Count Fuentes connecting Lopez directly with the plot to kill the queen were recited on the recollection of Tinoco, who asserted that they had been shown to him in Brussels by the secretary of Count Fuentes.'[69]

According to quasi-official accounts the accused offered little in the way of telling criticism of all this. 'At the bar Lopez said little in his own defence, but cried out that Ferrara and Emanuel [Tinoco] were made up of nothing but fraud and lying', drawn out of them, he might have added, as in his own case, by fear and/or application of the rack. 'He had intended no hurt against the queen, but abhorred the gifts of a tyrant; he had presented the jewel to the queen that was sent by the Spaniard; and he had no other design in what he did but to deceive the Spaniard and wipe him of his money.'[70] Francis Bacon claimed that when Lopez was confronted with da Gama he 'confessed the matter, as by his confession in writing, signed with his own hand, apeareth. But then he fell to that slender evasion, as his last refuge, that he meant only to cozen the king of Spain of the money; and in that he continued at his arraignment; when notwithstanding at the first he did retract his own confession; and yet being asked whether he was drawn either by fear of torture or promise of life to make the same confession, he did openly testify that no such means was used towards him.'[71]

It is unlikely that Lopez was given the opportunity to say much in his defence; certainly not without interruption. 'In accordance with the usual procedure in such cases, the accused was browbeaten and abused unmercifully by his judges and prosecutors ...

66 Harrison , p. 291.   67 Goodman, 1, p. 154.   68 Harrison, p. 291.   69 Hume, p. 149, n. 1.   70 Harrison, p. 291.   71 Katz, p. 91, quoting F. Bacon's 'Abstract of the evidence ... ', *Cal. SP Dom.*, ibid., pp 445-8.

Lopez, guilty or innocent, was doomed long before, and on his own statement he was condemned to death as a traitor. Cecil was as eager as Essex now to wash his hands of sympathy for the fallen wretch, and directly he left Guildhall he wrote to a friend that "the vile Jew sayd that he did confess indead to it, that he had talk of it".' Of course it was untrue, said little Robert, that the fear of the rack entered into any of his utterances. 'And the most substantial jury I have seene have found him guilty in the highest degree of all treasons; and judgment passed against him with the applause of all the world.'[72] 'All the world', in the Globe or wherever, had been stirred up by a relentless propaganda orchestrated by Essex. Christopher Marlowe's *The Jew of Malta* had done its work with the populace to make it receive the correct verdict with open arms.[73] The audiences may have been limited but a stone thrown into a pond sends ripples in all directions.

Ferreira and Tinoco were put on trial at Guildhall on 14 March before the commissioners. 'Tinoco was arraigned upon an indictment from his own confession: that he had secret messages and intelligences to the king of Spain and his ministers' in order to organise their forces against the queen. De Moura, 'one of the king's most secret counsellors, wrote letters to de Gama touching his services to the king.' Tinoco brought the letters to London, and came from Brussels to London 'to deliver a message and an embrace from the Count Fuentes' and also a credence from Andrada to Lopez for himself'. Further, 'that he' – Tinoco or Andrada? – 'wrote word to Lopez that Count Fuentes ... was glad that he was such a good servant to the king of Spain'. He would be liberally rewarded. The letter also required 'Lopez to procure the treaty of peace between the queen and the king to be renewed as the king desired it; meaning by "peace" her destruction by poison; which letters he delivered to Lopez.' He wrote under a false name to de Gama referring to the price of pearls 'by which was meant the poisoning of the queen'. The other reference to musk and amber meant 'the burning of the queen's ships'. Fuentes told Tinoco 'on oath of secrecy that he had received order from the king of Spain to give Lopez whatever he required for poisoning the queen, and that he delivered to de Gama in London several letters written by him in obscure words in the Spanish tongue concerning it ... which letters were found upon him when apprehended. These matters being declared to him through a Portuguese interpreter, he affirmed them from point to point, acknowledged his faults and called for mercy.' Needless to say, he got none. 'Stephen Ferrara de Gama being also indicted pleaded not guilty; but his former confessions and other proofs being produced against him, confessed all to be true; whereupon he also was convicted by judgment of the court for imagining and compassing the death of the queen.'[74]

Hume's conclusion on all the above – a scholar well-versed in the Spanish sources – still seems to be valid. The proofs against Lopez 'are absolutely confined to the declarations of his two accomplices, and especially Tinoco, who confessed himself a per-

---

72 Hume, p. 149-150; Handover, p. 118 and n. 16 quoting R. Cecil to Windebank, 28.2.1594, SP12/247, no. 97.   73 Handover, p. 117; Katz, p. 102.   74 Harrison, pp 293-4.

jurer ... The evidence of Philip's complicity is for the most part demonstrably false' – only for the most part? – 'whilst that against Fuentes and Ibarra' – that is, for the alleged murder plot against Elizabeth – 'rests likewise on extremely unsubstantial foundations.' The surviving 'original documents ... were compatible with the objects of the conspiracy being: the simulation of peace negotiations to obtain information; the winning over of Don Antonio's eldest son and his adherents; the "cosening" of King Philip for the benefit of the conspirators; and the murder of Don Antonio or of Antonio Perez.'[75]

Even after the sentence pronounced at Guildhall, the case of Cecil's 'vile Jew' was by no means closed or hopeless for him. As we have seen, he appealed in a kind of desperation to the queen after his arrest. Her response was sympathetic if reserved. Clearly, she could not prevent the trial taking place. 'Being found guilty, he was carried back to the Tower; then did he more petition than ever, and appeal to the queen's own knowledge and goodness; and did ever receive these gracious answers from the queen: that not a hair of his head should perish; wished him to be content and to have patience, that all things might be done with the honour of the state; it should be but a short imprisonment and a little loss of practice in his profession, which cannot countervail the credit of the state, which her Majesty did so much respect.'[76] Appearances had to be preserved; but Elizabeth, as a disinterested party, could not have been deceived by the forensic farce which had just ended. At the same time, she had no desire for even the appearance of a collision between the throne and the system or her chief ministers over such trivial persons as those condemned: wise woman, no doubt. But we need not doubt that she intended to rescue Lopez at least if she could. Acting too independently would cost Charles I and James II the throne, and the first, his head as well.

Lopez, as the queen's prisoner while he was in the Tower, was safe since her permission was needed for either release or execution. Doubtless, she had it in mind to play a waiting game until the whole affair had blown over. Lopez could then be released into the exile he coveted. It now became a battle of wits and wills between the sovereign and an unholy alliance of her overmighty subjects, the Cecils and Essex, to make sure that Lopez did not escape – no doubt to tell a very uncomplimentary tale abroad. It is likely that William Cecil, who had been careful not to take an active part in the trial, stood by Elizabeth's ear to comfort, distract, and justify what followed. He drafted a speech for her thanking God for her escape; but, not surprisingly, she never seems to have delivered it.[77] Abenaes in Constantinople did not desert Lopez in his hour of need. He sent Judah Serfatim to plead Lopez' cause in London. Abenaes and Lopez shared a common ground for dislike since Don Antonio had been spreading tales in Turkey that Abenaes had obtained his wealth by fraud. Don Antonio wanted the Turks to confiscate Abenaes' property, giving him half. Lopez had been in contact with Philip II to discredit Antonio and defend Abenaes. Serfatim requested at least the stay of the doctor's execution. He did not leave London before 10 April.[78]

75 Hume, pp 151-2.   76 Goodman, p. 154.   77 Katz, p. 93; C. Read, Burghley, p. 584. From *Cal. SP Dom.*, p. 462.   78 Katz p. 93. It is remarkable that Katz, against all previous scholars, finds the evi-

It seemed that the queen's will would prevail. The elimination of Lopez and his companions in misfortune was not to be a simple matter. On 18 April 1594 Sir Michael Blount, lieutenant of the Tower, informed Sir Robert Cecil that he had the attorney-general's warrant to deliver Lopez, da Gama and Tinoco to the sheriffs of London to be executed on 19 April at 9 a.m. 'But since your Honour doth signify that her Majesty will have the executions stayed till I hear further of her Highness' pleasure therein, I will stay the prisoners accordingly.'[79] On the 18th, Buckhurst and Sir John Fortescue informed Robert Cecil they 'had taken advice' with the lord chief justice and the attorney general, 'and the unanimous legal opinion' was that Lopez and the rest must be executed within the short time left before their commission expired.[80] The queen having her own ideas on Lopez' destiny refused to be persuaded. It was no doubt at this point that Sir Robert, or less probably Sir William, Cecil, having put himself in the clear *vis-à-vis* the queen, persuaded the willing Essex to be the catspaw. 'At this time, Popham was preferred to be lord chief justice of the king's bench, and by the means of the earl of Essex who was then the great favourite; and Popham by the persuasion of the earl of Essex, made means that Lopez might be removed unto the king's bench prison in Southwark.'[81] And removed he and his companions were.

Lopez and the others were now outside the queen's protection. According to Stow and Camden, 'Roderick Lopez, with the two other Portuguese ... were conveyed from the Tower of London by the lieutenant to the Old Swan, and thence by water to Westminster, where being brought before the king's bench bar, the lieutenant was called to bring in his prisoners, which he then delivered and was discharged of them.'[82] Seemingly the same day, 7 June, Lopez 'was brought to the king's bench bar, and they demanded what he could say for himself why the sentence of death pronounced against him should not be put in execution. Dr Lopez replied, that he did appeal to

dence against the Portuguese so convincing. Unless other plots are studied in a general context perhaps it is easy to believe that justice could not have gone so far astray in the days of Good Queen Bess and the Great Lord Burghley.   79 Katz, p. 95, from *Sal. Cal.* iv, p. 513.   80 Ibid. The law officers are very much under the direction of the Cecils. On [14.3.]. Lord keeper Puckering wrote to R. Cecil: should he proceed against Ferreira and Tinoco in the absence of the lord chief justice? He encloses the attorney general's letter which requires expedition. He thinks Daniell, serjeant elect, 'may suffice instead of a judge.' Fenner was on circuit. Daniell sat as 'a commissioner on the former proceedings against Lopez.' The attorney wanted directions 'in regard to the inconvenience if he should die before execution.' If they proceeded with the commission the next day, Puckering, R. Cecil and Essex should 'come thither'; *Cal. SP Dom*, pp 459-60; -/248, no. 26. Attorney-general Egerton writing to Puckering enclosed a letter of 14.3.1594, from Lincoln's Inn, ibid., and -/248, No. 26.1. The lord chief justice is too ill to attend. The commission is adjourned to 7 a. m. on [15. 3.]. There is great expectation of speedy proceedings. 'Dr Lopez has kept his bed for the most part since his trial, and whether he practises anything by slow poison may be doubted [believed]. If this instant trial should be deferred and Lopez should die before execution great dishonour and scandal might ensue ... Deferring the proceedings may be more dangerous to her Majesty, and more dishonourable in the opinion of the world than is meet to adventure.' Puckering knows Daniell is 'learned and wise' and sufficient 'to direct in form of law and manage the pro ceedings. A judge's name gives countenance but adds nothing to learning'.   81 Goodman, pp 154-5.   82 Harrison, p. 303.

the queen's own knowledge and goodness for the acquitting of him.'[83] It was probably Ferreira, the more sophisticated party, who followed Lopez and 'began a long narration to open things from the beginning, and how he was ensnared. The court willed him to be short; but he said he could not be, but would open the business from the beginning. Then they willed him to hold his peace.' [84] He tried to make his point 'by a writing in his own language, which being read by an interpreter, the attorney general bade stay for it was not true.'[85] Appointed to his new post on 10 April, this contribution came from Sir Edward Coke, a man who could be relied on by his patrons to say what was to be taken as true and what was not.

'Then the marshal of the king's bench was called and charged with the prisoners to convey them to the prison of the king's bench and there to deliver them to the sheriffs of London with a writ to see them executed. So they were conveyed by water to Westminster from the bishop of Winchester's stairs in Southwark, from thence to the king's bench, there laid upon hurdles and conveyed to the sheriff of London over the bridge, up to Leadenhall and so to Tyburn.'[86] Goodman had the tale of what followed 'from a very credible man that was then present'. Just as 'the former narration [he] heard from a very honest man, who had it from him that did solicit Dr Lopez' business, and was the messenger between the queen and him'. Not quite direct; but as good as much that passes for historical evidence. 'Being brought to the place of execution, Lopez began to speak and to acquaint the people with the whole business. But there were some that stood afar off, some in one place and some in another, and they cried to him, "Speak out, speak out." Others that were in some nearness unto him, cried aloud, "Hold your peace! Hold your peace!" And thus was the whole time spent, and the poor man could not be heard a word, and so was turned off the ladder.'[87] An early example of 'rentacrowd'. Hume retails a story for what it is worth from Lee's *The Church under Queen Elizabeth* regarding the end of another of the three. 'Probably Tinoco, as he was the youngest, recovered his feet after the hanging, and, mad with pain and desperation, attacked the executioner. The crowd applauding his pluck, broke through the guard and made a ring to witness the fight. Two burly ruffians came to the executioner's help, but one was immediately felled by a blow from the prisoner, who kept the other two at bay for some time. The half-strangled creature was at length stunned with a blow on the head, and the disembowelling then proceeded.'[88] According to Haynes, 'the fluent Ferreira da Gama' may have been spared the rope and knife to go on a mission to Morocco to save the son of Don Antonio who was being held in Fez seemingly as a hostage. Don Antonio died in 1595. [89]

83 Goodman, p. 155.   84 Ibid. Goodman agrees with Stow's Annals ... and Camden's Elizabeth which he may have been following. Cf. Harrison, ibid., pp 303-4.   85 Ibid., p. 304. Handover mentions Coke's appointment as attorney general on 10.4.1594.   86 Harrison, p. 304. From Stow, *Annals* ... and Camden, *Elizabeth*.   87 Goodman, p. 155. Goodman's witness was Sir Henry Savile, provost of Eton and friend of Essex. Cf. Katz, p. 98.   88 Hume, p. 151 and n. 1, quoting from Dr Lee's *The Church under Queen Elizabeth*.   89 Haynes, p. 120.

The queen's part in the whole affair, as in all these plots, was evidently the least blameworthy. Indeed, she showed herself not for the first time to be the prisoner of court and courtiers. One is reminded of her situation *vis-à-vis* William Parry. This time she resented more strongly the original arrest of her personal physician, and was instrumental in seeing that the two factions, Cecil's and Essex's, shared the trial procedure. It may be she was hoping that the well-known antagonism of the two would prevent any condemnation of Lopez. Had the question of a new attorney-general not intervened, it might have done. In the end she was out-manoeuvred by the impregnable alliance of the Cecils and Devereux. She could not save Lopez from death but she was able to save his wife from the depredations normally following a successful outcome for treason. His lady, Sarah Lopez, 'petitioned the queen for his goods; to whom the queen gave them all, and would not suffer her to lose one farthing'.[90] The restoration was made in March 1595 and included a lease in Mountjoy's Inn from Winchester College. All the same, Elizabeth kept the Lopez ring and wore it publicly.

Elizabeth 'did not readily forgive [Essex] for the part he had played' throughout the whole affair, although she must have been aware of the influence of the Cecils in the background. They played their part discreetly and respectfully towards her, leaving the rougher work to Essex who lacked their finer sensitivity and reticence in dealing with the queen. She would have perceived this. The Cecils played their game cleverly: but one man was not deceived. Antonio Perez, a man well-versed himself in the theory and practice of skulduggery, pinned to Robert Cecil the soubriquet 'Robertus Diabolus' – Robert the Devil, a title which clung to him for the rest of his life. As Handover summed up in a good example of understatement, 'So concluded an episode from which no one, in retrospect, emerges with credit.'[91] Lopez, da Gama and Tinoco were none of them men to be admired, but if they received justice in all this it was only of the poetic kind. Not so disgraceful as the destruction of the Christian peers Norfolk and Derby, the elimination of the Jewish group, though not so innocent, was sordid enough.

At all events, the Cecils could not only feel contentment in Coke's appointment on 4 April as attorney general but also feel exonerated from any further obligation to Essex if such there had been. However upset Elizabeth may have been for a time by Essex's high-handedness, she was not prepared to see the balance of court power destroyed by Devereux' complete eclipse. It was reported that when an expedition to Brest had been finally resolved on 25 July, Essex was among those eager to take part. 'The queen using very gentle words to him says that his desire to be in action and give further proof of his valour and prowess is to be liked and highly commended; but she loveth him and her realm too much to hazard his person in any lesser action than that which shall import her crown and state, and therefore willeth him to be content.' To help his contentment, in spite of her reputation for parsimony, she gave him a warrant for £4,000. There was a hint in her last reported judgement on this occasion that,

90 Goodman, pp 155-6; Katz, p. 100.   91 Handover, p. 119, quoting Birch, i, p. 352 and ii, p. 227.

while not using the words of Perez, she herself was aware of the serpentine qualities of her other preferred favourites. 'Look to thyself, good Essex, and be wise to help thyself, without giving thy enemies advantage; and my hand shall be readier to help thee than any other.'[92] However much she knew she had to rely on them, she could not have enjoyed being outwitted by the Cecils even if Essex was for the moment an accomplice. Perhaps she was as troubled at the end of it all, as we might be, that there was no discernible motive for the treason of Lopez and his associates.

92 Harrison, pp 308-9, from Birch, *Memoirs* ... , i, p. 181. Katz concludes, 'What has been consistently misunderstood by modern writers is that it is not necessary to establish that Ruy Lopez actually plotted to poison the queen, that he procured the materials and set about working according to a secret plan. By the terms of the treason laws then current, Lopez' *secret contacts with the Spanish crown and his numerous discussions about the possibility of poisoning the queen* [my italics], were more than enough to hang him many times over.' But after he undertook to do spy work for Essex and Walsingham, his contacts with Spain were not secret from the council. His discussions about the possibility of poisoning Elizabeth, and we do not know if they took place, were part of his espionage task. Katz sees the force of an objection. 'It may be that in some ways he acted as a double agent, and that one of the many Elizabethan court factions' – were there that many? – 'was kept aware of his Spanish contacts. If this was so, it was effectively hidden from the judges.' The judges may well have acted correctly on the tainted evidence supplied. But this does not exonerate those who supplied it. Katz concludes, 'those who would defend Lopez's innocence have yet to make their case.' After all the above, the reader must judge if the case against Lopez and his fellow-accused really established their guilt. Essex and the Cecils could still be taken as the ones who need to make their case.

10

Edmund Yorke and Richard Williams

In the same month that the Portuguese trio were tried and condemned, yet another 'plot' came to light which may well have influenced the queen in her early reinstatement of Essex as her favourite.[1] On 23 June 1594 Edmund Yorke wrote to Essex from Calais.[2] He was the son of Sir Edmund and nephew of Sir Rowland Yorke who had enjoyed a significant if not distinguished career before going over, like Sir William Stanley, with his English regiment to the Spanish side at Zutphen.[3] Whatever other reasons may have influenced their change of allegiance, both must have been exasperated by the experience of service against the Spaniard in France and Flanders at this time. Some account of which provides important background for what followed. On 30 January 1591 it was decided that Sir Edmund should be sent to the French king to stir him to some activity and determine the conditions on which English forces should be sent to his aid. Elizabeth thought it 'strange' that in the four months since the Spaniards had invaded Brittany the king had told her nothing of his intentions and had given no assistance to the prince de Dombes who now only had 1800 men. The Spanish were mounting an offensive to conquer Brittany. Dombes had asked her for 2000 men to be paid for by the king but she wanted a request from the king himself before proceeding further. Doubtless she wanted some kind of guarantee that her bill would be paid. The Spaniards now possessed all the ports save Brest. Elizabeth had already tried an approach through her ambassador but he had met with no response. Sir Edmund was to go over and get decisions and especially the free use of Brest for English ships and soldiers.[4]

In one of her typical mind-changes, fourteen days after Burghley drew up letters and warrants for 2000 pikemen to be dispatched, on 12 February 1592 the queen refused any further aid for France. She was piqued that he had not taken Rouen.[5] On the 14th, however, Parma captured Neuchâtel[6]. By the 24th, this galvanised Elizabeth into placing £1000 worth of supplies and 1600 men with Sir Edmund to be conveyed

---

1 Main sources: *Cal. SP Dom.*, 1591-4; 1595-7; PRO Kew, SP 12/248, 249. Martin Hume, *Treason and plot* (London 1901), pp 153-161; G. B. Harrison, *The Elizabethan journals ...* , 1591-1603, part. 1, 1955 ed. n.; William Camden, *The history of ... Princess Elizabeth*, 4th ed. n (London 1688), p. 495. 2 E. Yorke to Essex, 23.6.1594, *Cal. SP Dom.*, 1591-4, p. 522; SP12/249, No. 18. 3 Hume, p. 153, n. 1. 4 G. B. Harrison, i, pp 7-8; Rymer, Foedera, xvi, p. 89. 5 GBH, p. 102; *Unton correspondence*, p. 319. 6 GBH, p. 103; *Unton corr.*, p. 330.

into Normandy. However, he was to stay at Dieppe and relieve the forces of the allies only when and if it seemed strictly necessary.[7] According to a report of 25 March 1592 'Sir Edmund Yorke with twelve companies arrived at Dieppe on the 18th.'[8] This attempt at remote control from London before the days of radio communication was to be attempted later with Essex with even more disastrous consequences.

The report which mentioned Sir Edmund's arrival also indicated the prevailing cynicism and disillusion in the ranks of the allies. Rouen at last was now under pressure from the French king. So '2000 French that had disbanded have rejoined the army and more return daily in the hope of spoil at Rouen.' In the event, by mid-April Parma had raised the siege of Rouen although his own camp was successfully pillaged on 7 May. However, the blow was not decisive, and not enough to raise notably the poor morale of the English. 'The English soldiers in these days are much harried and many disband daily for want of money and victuals.'[9] Desertion was common. Sir Edmund's original instructions of 1 March 1592 had decreed that after he arrived in Dieppe 'no vessel should take on any English soldier who cannot show his licence to depart'.[10] It was not applied very effectively. An order in the privy council of 13 May 1592 tried to solve the problem at the English end. Notwithstanding the council's previous orders to prevent the unlicensed return of the soldiery from service in Normandy, over 200 men 'of strong and able bodies are landed at Dover and places near without passport, in the company of some few sick men, and without stay'. They 'beg in the county, with the pass port of the mayor, using most slanderous speeches of the queen's service and entertainment, tending to the great discouragement of such as be willing to serve'. The mayor was to give 'good bonds' and 'all soldiers that of late are landed without passport to be stayed and punished'.[11] On 21 May 1592 the council recorded Sir Edmund Yorke's report before his death that the Normandy companies were 'decayed' down to about 1500. Since then they had become even weaker through 'sickness, famine, escaping and other indirect means'. There were nineteen captains but not enough men for more than eight companies. So the queen was 'much abused' in her belief in the strength of her forces. All the same, she was charged 'as if the companies were full and complete'. Sir Roger Williams was to make a muster and reduce all to eight companies or more at the rate of a hundred men to a company under the best captains left.[12] This then was the working background of this latest group of 'plotters' which explains much in their subsequent conduct.

Probably rejected as one of the 'best captains', with father and uncle dead, and with no easy prospect of obtaining his inheritance from Sir Rowland of what was described

---

7 GBH, p. 105; *Acts of the privy council*, xxii, pp 273, 279.   8 GBH, p. 116; Unton corr., p. 391.   9 GBH, p. 129; *Unton corr.*, p. 130.   10 GBH, p. 110.   11 Ibid., p. 131; *Acts of the privy council*, xxii, p. 448.   12 GBH, p. 132; *Acts of the the privy council*, xxii, p. 478; see also, estimates signed by the council for imprest of 10 captains and 150 men to be sent to Normandy with a reinforcement under Sir Edmund Yorke, 24.12.1592; SP12/241, no. 61; council to treasurer and chamberlains of the exchequer authorizing payments at her Majesty's command for 1600 men and officers to join the force in Normandy to aid the king of France; ibid., s. d., -/241, no. 62.

as a considerable property in Flanders, Captain Edmund was one more who was tired of exile and anxious to return. His letter of 23 June shows an awareness that he might be exchanging the frying pan for the fire. He admitted departing without licence and so was 'an offender'. But in spite of his nominal captaincy he claimed he had 'never borne arms or conspired against her Majesty'. Edmund begged Essex for forgiveness, basing his optimism, it seems, on previous acquaintance with the earl. He wanted it taken into consideration that, although a Brussels court had recognised his claim to his uncle's inheritance, 'his right would not be granted without a trial of his allegiance in service'. This Edmund refused. Perhaps his real reason was less loyalty – evidently he had been well-regarded by Sir Rowland – than to escape direct involvement in the nightmarish situation on all the fronts outlined above. His best hope now was to exploit whatever remained of any relationship with Essex. Remembering the nature of court rivalries and the sensitivity of the earl, he assured him he had 'reconciled himself to none others of the Council, hoping through him only to attain pardon'.

Edmund referred to two more gentlemen with him who were hoping to shelter under his umbrella in a return to England. 'One went with him out of England and the other has been with Stanley's regiment three years.' The former was presumably Richard Williams and the other, Henry Young. Williams had served under Essex in France. Evidently Young was in an extremely precarious position and would have to work hard and cooperate very fully to get off a potentially lethal hook. 'They also crave pardon, and rely on the writer for it, being unknown to his lordship; they promise service to him and her Majesty.' There was a fourth whom we will meet later; and possibly a fifth.

It was known that Edmund Yorke had been received into the Catholic Church by the Jesuit, William Holt. Williams like Yorke may well have been relatively bona fide. Whatever he knew or suspected, Essex gave them all permission to come to England. Perhaps he was already hoping to discover another plot to enhance his prestige; something easier to handle than the Lopez affair and one which would be more acceptable to her Majesty. The quartet was kept under close observation from their first landing in England. 'Young was a rogue pure and simple, and hastened in the usual way, when he found that suspicion was entertained, to be the first to betray his companions.'[13] He had his reasons however ignoble. Untramelled by loyalties, the lesson he had learned on the fighting front was to look after himself. No one else would. He did not necessarily relish selling Yorke and Williams down the pass, but if this was the condition of survival, and to avoid the attention of the rack-master, what else was there to do? His first examination took place on 30 July 1594.[14] His confession for his examiners, whoever they were, gave out a story of the usual kind. He may have been an informer already.

It is impossible to believe that Yorke, coming to England cap in hand to get what favour he could, was really on the way to raise rebellion. Young must have been large-

13 Hume, pp 154-5.   14 H. Young's confession, 30.7.1594; *Cal. SP Dom.*, 1591-4, pp 531-2, pp 531-2; SP12/249, no. 41, 2½ pp

ly prompted by his interrogators to tell a story he was happy enough to repeat if that was what they wanted. And they did. The more lurid the story the more useful and even convincing as propaganda; and the greater the likelihood of the teller escaping the rack and the hangman's rope, not to speak of other reward. Henry Young was of a coterie familiar by now in this narrative. According to Young, Sir William Stanley and Holt the Jesuit persuaded Captain Yorke to take Richard Williams with him to England, a Welshman with many Catholic friends in those parts, as a prelimnary to raising rebellion in North Wales. The rebellion would begin after Christmas by taking Conway castle in one night by Williams' means. 'He heard this from Yorke and Williams' speeches.' Young may have gleaned the names of local magnates from conversation with Williams but their connection with an attempted rebellion could only have been suggested by his interrogators. So the money for the enterprise was to come from Williams' uncle, Ralph Sheldon, and a Mr Pew, a rich Anglesea squire and merchant. With at least recusant sympathies, their elimination could only be a good thing. Young offered the means. Suspected absurdity is fully confirmed when we learn that Young 'heard this at a conference with [Dr William] Gifford and Holt at Dr Worthington's chamber'. The idea of Holt and Gifford, who were always on opposite sides, and the very correct Worthington, being involved in such an affair was ludicrous.[15] Someone else the government was willing to be rid of was one Middleton, a captain of one of the queen's ships. He would come with his craft which would assist in blocking possible interception by other ships of the queen's. Middleton had a brother in Antwerp. Young heard all this in a conversation between Yorke and Williams in the latter's house in Brussels. A crafty touch which doubtless required more than Young's ingenuity to devise claimed that Yorke's story about not getting his uncle's property was substantially false. Yorke was advised, seemingly by Holt, 'to make it appear that he left the court at Brussels because he could not obtain his uncle's substance, though order has been taken, as the examinate knows, by Fr Holt for all that is due to him'. In fact – Young's 'fact' – Yorke had already 'received £250 in money which Young is privy unto', and 'by Holt's device', Yorke brought over his uncle's will with a copy of a decree in Italian to the duke – Parma? – also a letter of Fr Fenn, 'his uncle's executor'. This gave a list of Rowland Yorke's goods which graf Harmord should detain. These were safe in Fenn's hands for his use except some money and jewels which Yorke had brought over with him to England. To reinforce the illusion of being discontented with Sir William Stanley and the English, 'they sold their cloaks and were denied a passport by Stanley'; and to make the deception even more convincing, they were to

15 For William Holt, William Gifford, Thomas Worthington and their mutual relations, see Dnb, vol. 21, 1890, for Gifford; vol. 27, 1891 for Holt; vol. 63 1900, for Worthington: Peter Guilday, *The English Catholic refugees on the continent 1558-1795* (London 1914), passim. T. F. Knox, *Letters and memorials of William Cardinal Allen 1532-1594* (London 1882), passim, especially for W. Gifford: H. Foley, *Records of the English province S.J.*, vii, part 2, 1883, pp 230-46 for W. Holt: L. Hicks, 'The exile of William Gifford from Lille in 1606', *Recusant History*, 7 (1964), pp 214-38. F. Edwards, *Robert Persons*, passim.

be 'stayed at Artois' and imprisoned, care being taken 'that news thereof might reach Calais'. A detail to make good Protestants shiver, Yorke made Young 'receive the sacrament that he would be true to him', while Williams and Yorke both were set by the incompatibles Gifford and Holt to 'sift' Young's zeal for their religion; for in England he was known to have contact with Cholmely 'who had dealings against them'. Young was cleared on Yorke's word. Presumably unknown either to Holt or Gifford, Yorke, Williams and Young had not otherwise disguised their intention in Brussels to return to their allegiance in England.[16]

Young's allegations were all that was required to bring Yorke and Williams to the Tower. Essex, determined to vindicate himself as a sleuth, and eager, no doubt, to obliterate the dubious memory of Lopez, took the initiative in the examinations. Yorke's first, a week after Young's, took place before Essex and Lord Cobham, warden of the cinque ports. He would already have been known to both by disrepute. On 2 March, Burghley had received a letter from Dieppe accusing Yorke of 'suspicious' speeches. 'He has left the town and is thought to have gone over to the enemy.'[17] An informer to the bailiff of Dover a few days later claimed he was going with Yorke to Antwerp where Yorke would have his uncle's regiment, presumably Sir Rowland's.[18] An intercepted(?) letter from Yorke to a contact in Dieppe of 21 March expressed sorrow that fortune had crossed them, urged patience but gave no further clues. Perhaps the command of the regiment had been refused.[19] More damning was the report of another informer recently from Europe and ready to serve up anything to get a meal in return. Richard Blundeville in mid-April reported Yorke's 'speeches' systematically by date. It was done before examiners in London who no doubt helped him to 'remember' dates exactly to make it all more convincing for future forensic purposes.

On 27 February 1594 Blundeville went to Yorke's chambers where he found Richard Bonker and his man Harry Young, son and heir of Young of Kent worth £60 per annum: so Henry was a gentleman at least in the technical sense: one of the many decayed. Yorke invited him to enter the emperor's service. Fifty gentlemen were coming over for this and some 'would be made dukes'. At a visit on 2 March Blundeville got Yorke to divulge the names of some of these aspirants to imperial service. One was Franklin from Yorkshire who was worth £500 per annum, 'and some gentlemen who were like himself very good in making poison': Harry Young 'was very good too'. On 3 March he learned that 'Yorke's sworn brother had come over to serve the emperor.

16 H. Young's confession, 30.7.1594, see n. 14 above. Another copy, 3½pp , *Cal. SP Dom.*, p. 532; SP12/249, no. 42. Cf. Hume, pp 154-5.   17 Otwell Smith to W. Cecil, Dieppe, 2.3.1594; *Cal. SP Dom.*, p. 451, extract from the French Corresp. of 2.3.   18 Edward Browne to William Atkins, bailiff of Dover, 8.2.1594; *Cal. SP Dom.*, p. 455; SP12/248, no. 13.   19 E. Yorke, Abbeville, to William Munning, at Mons. Ercknells, Dieppe, 21.3.1594; *Cal. SP Dom.*, p. 469; -/-/42. Endd. by Burghley, 'Young Edmund Yorke's letter to Monyns'. According to Richard Blundeville (15.4.1594, ; *Cal. SP Dom.*, p. 485). Munning was a Catholic friend of Yorke's. Blundeville went with him on 6. 3. to dine at Huepe's, a Protestant. Munning told Yorke that when his man came with his money, Blundeville would have 500 crowns.

Better still, on 28 March Bonker dropped the information that Captain Mostyn and Yorke's brother had come over to join Edmund, and 'they mean to come to the burning of London, and to pluck Justice Young and the other officers'. Yorke said "my Lord" was a blood-sucker and that he would lay a coal of fire upon the stairs in a privy place and put poison upon it so that as many as came up the stairs would fall down dead.' Bonker also reported that certain young courtiers referred to 'my lord as a caterpillar and a chamberling'.[20] On 17 April Blundeville and Richard Barker confessed to Waad that Thomas Langdon and Munning were good friends of Yorke. Munning promised to pay Yorke's debts when his money came, and to take him to Italy.[21]

By the time Edmund Yorke came to the question at least two of his own letters were in the hands of his interlocutors. On 6 June he wrote to another uncle, Sir Edward by name, expressing surprise that he had not answered his letters and asking him to send money as requested. 'If his pardon is granted, begs £15 and when settled will repay him.'[22] On the same day that he wrote to Essex for leave to return, 23 June, he wrote again to uncle Edward telling of his plea to Essex, 'his lord and master', for his pardon. When Sir Edward saw the pardon, he wanted his uncle to give him £10 'to defray charges and bring him up to council and not to think hard of him that he departed until he knows the cause'.[23] Evidently, Sir Edward, being well aware of the dangers of becoming too involved with his wayward nephew, was hardly forthcoming. Edmund Yorke's first examination took place in the Tower on 12 August 1594 before Essex and Lord Cobham.[24] Doubtless, what the council had already been told about him or learned from Young was brought to his notice early in the interview so that the grant of a pardon swiftly ceased to be a foregone conclusion. Yorke emphasised his submissiveness from the first: the service he offered in his letter to Essex 'was anything the queen should command'; which was to say anything her councillors commanded or even hinted. The first part of the confession could be taken as true. Holt wanted to send him to Scotland 'but [Yorke] knows not on what business'. He met three priests in Abbeville. One, Fr Ingrams, went with him to the Low Countries where he was 'reconciled' by Holt. So was Young. Yorke 'told Williams of his mission to Scotland, and Williams told Willis, Sir William Stanley's secretary, that one day he would be known as an honest man.' Holt gave him twelve crowns when he left and told him to 'stay Catholic'.

So far so good. But then alleged statements by Young enter the narrative which suggest that, if they were true, Young was already playing the part of agent provoca-

20 'Speeches of Captain Yorke, son of Sir Edmund Yorke. Report by [Richard] Blundeville', 15. 4.1594, no indication of where it was written, 3pp; *Cal. SP Dom.*, p. 485; SP12/248, no. 69. It reports Yorke on 2. iii. as showing an interest in the Lopez case.   21 Joint confession of Richard Blundeville and Richard Barker before Waad, 17. 4.1594; *Cal. SP Dom.*, p. 488; -/-/ no. 74 Notes by W. Cecil on Blundeville's notes show he was taking a backseat interest in the case; *Cal. SP Dom.*, p. 536; -/-/ no. 46. Blundeville seems to have been a professional informer and soon dropped out of the proceedings. 22 Edmund Yorke to Sir Edward Yorke, 9.6.1594; *Cal. SP Dom.*, p. 516; -/249/ no. 8.   23 Same to same, Holborn, 23.6.1594, from Calais; *Cal. SP Dom.*, p. 522; -/249, no. 18.   24 Ed. Yorke's 1st examination, 12.8.1594, 3pp; *Cal. SP Dom.*, p. 539; -/249, no. 63.

teur. 'Young said he had offered to Fr Holt in writing to kill her Majesty on condition of a sum in hand and more afterwards.' Williams said – Young's report still – that he would do it for much money 'and advancement of his house as he should be sure to die'. Yorke's mission to Scotland was now clarified. He would go in a man-of-war, while Stanley said, if the queen were dead, he would take his regiment to Scotland, 'make it strong, and go to the earl of Derby, as would all the English'. What we have seen above regarding the real state of the English regiment at this time makes Stanley's boast sufficiently unlikely. In any case, Stanley would not have suggested killing the queen. Mention of Derby is, of course, significant since the government, through the Hesketh plot, had been doing its best to bring the family into disrepute. Williams was reported to have said, presumably by Young, that if he came to England, 'he would make a rebellion' after robbing some great house to cover its expenses. Along with Derby, the government was anxious to bring leading recusant families closer to ruin. So Williams was supposed to have said that after forces were mustered he would make Pew of Anglesey, 'a man of good living', join him, 'sell his land worth £500 a year and help him with the money'. As a tailpiece a little possible truth was mixed in with the rest. 'Until lately', Williams always received his brother's pension in England. Perhaps it was also true that 'Williams sent to Owen before leaving Brussels, offering service, and Young wrote the letter.' Young again. So it was just as possibly false.[25]

Yorke was examined again on 12 August. This time he was brought to admit that Young swore to kill Elizabeth and William Cecil, while he and Williams 'wished they had enough money to try if they would do it'. Jaques Francisco valued Williams highly 'and had him for his bed-fellow'. Williams was ready for anything. Hearing of trouble in Ireland, he wished he was there with 2,000 men. But this time Yorke had no idea what Williams was supposed to be doing in England. 'He should have come into England about some service but did not say what.'[26] Young himself made a 'declaration' on 12 August, which suggests something volunteered rather thah extracted under threat or promise. Williams was represented as a rakehell who, with Captain Dyer, lieutenant to Sir William Stanley, Captain Duffield and other stole £1,800 worth

---

25 Hume takes the view that the initiative in 'shopping' the other two was taken by Yorke. But the order of the confessions, Young's first on 30.7. and Yorke's first on 12.8., makes Young the initiator. It is not clear where Young was interrogated or who interrogated him so that whoever made leading suggestions, probably Waad, would not be known to have done so. It is significant that Young escaped the gallows. He admitted writing the letter for Williams in his 2nd 'declaration' – note the word – of 12.8. (*Cal. SP Dom.*, p. 540; -/249, no. 66). Williams wrote to Dr Gifford for 'emplyment and 200 crowns' plausible – 'and advancement for his house if he perished in the action'; not plausible. Young said Williams suggested killing the queen. Yorke replied, 'that they were fools to think of killing the queen; she was always mewed up in a chamber. It would be better service to kill the lord treasurer's horse, for he would take it so grievously if the old jade were dead that he would die too.' Here we have a hint of how agent provocateurs' accusations could be built up plausibly on the silly talk which the soldiery and others doubtless produced in their cups and even when sober. Cf. Hume, pp 155-6. 26 Yorke's 2nd examination, 12.8.1594; *Cal. SP Dom.*, p. 540; SP12/249, no. 63 (NB. Same number as for the first examination).

of plate from 'Winchester church' to turn into coin. This was done in Sir Griffin Markham's chamber in Grey's Inn and a number of gentlemen shared the proceeds. Further information was offered to discredit Ralph Sheldon, member of another well-known Catholic family. The craftiest touch was that, in admitting he wrote letters for Williams to Stanley, Charles Paget, Sir Thomas Throckmorton and Owen about his lack of resources and inability to remain longer abroad, Young claimed that this was a device of Stanley's to hide the real reason for Williams and Yorke going to England. This was to kill the queen. The intention was that her 'many spies in Brussels would think they were going back to England for poverty and discontent and not to perform what they had taken in hand'. This was contrived by Stanley, Holt, Gifford and Wright, an Irishman. To maintain the illusion of poverty – which was probably the truth – Yorke forced Williams to walk cloakless about Brussels, having sold his cloak through Wright, a 'man of many words'. Among Young's many words, he averred that Yorke as well as Williams intended to raise rebellion in North Wales. To cover expenses, they intended to use 'the same engine they used at Winchester', to rob Elizabeth of her plate at Whitehall. Indeed, they had already tried it, but one of them lost his nerve and cried out so they called it off. They wounded him and threatened him with death if he did not keep his mouth shut. So no one ever heard of it. As a parting shot, once again the Derby clan was smeared. Williams' company included Edward Bushell, servant to Lady Strange.[27]

Williams was also examined on 12 August; twice, the first time before Essex, Cobham and attorney-general Coke. It is likely he fell for the usual trick of volunteering or confirming information when he was told that his colleagues had already informed on him. Again, it is likely that his examiners helped him along, with threats veiled or otherwise. Certainly, if his story had not helped the propaganda machine, his shrift would have been short. In the first examination, he admitted offering Owen and Gifford 'service in England but they made slender answer': plausible. He had heard Young and Yorke discussing the queen's assassination and admitted making Pew of North Wales sell his land to which Williams would add the proceeds of robbery to raise rebellion: not plausible. It was possible that a certain Jones came to Anglesey 'to fetch over the nephew of Dr Lewis, bishop of Cassano', while one Bishop from Warwick worth £400 a year, often came over.[28] Williams' second examination before Essex and Cobham gave further details of the Winchester robbers. He conceded that he had committed a robbery in England and afterwards went to France with Essex to serve under Sir Thomas Baskerville to avoid possible consequences. He had deserted to the enemy. One Harrison had shown him tools to open locks and break holes in brick walls. Harrison and Dyer were often together, and they and Henry Duffield did the Winchester robbery. Williams 'heard that Harrison intended robbery at Whitehall', and that he had offered Gifford to do anything for money 'but Gifford did not like such

27 Henry Young, 'declaration', 12.3.1594; *Cal. SP Dom.*, p. 540; -/249, no. 64, 2pp Cf. Hume, ibid.
28 R. Williams, 1st exam., 12.8.1594; *Cal. SP Dom.*, p. 541; -/249, no. 68.

offers from strangers'. Williams claimed that he was persuaded by Holt to join Dyer 'in some service for the king of Spain'.[29]

Some of it was plausible, but not the idea that he, a nobody, had come to England to raise rebellion. He had offered his prospective services in England to Holt and Gifford but, credibly enough, they were not encouraging. Certainly, they would not have been encouraging or discouraging in unison since there was between Gifford and all the Jesuits deep antagonism. Williams admitted much chatter going round in Brussels about killing the queen. One wonders who really started this kind of rumour. Also that Young had agreed to do it for money. Williams was examined again before Essex and Cobham on 13 August. 'Torture soon wrung from the poor wretch further avowals. He gave particulars of all the Catholics and priests he knew, and was ready to confess everything.'[30] This admixture of falsehood and exaggeration was not enough for Williams' captors. Torture, or the threat of it, made him give particulars of all the priests and Catholics he knew, which may have been true. But he also confessed much which in the circumstances could only be taken as evidence of his extreme fear, as in the case of the Portuguese in the Lopez plot.

Young's place in all this as the principal songbird was indicated in a letter of 13 August to Cobham at the court in Greenwich. He will say whatever he is told to say. He 'cannot repeat his former articles from memory, but will abide by them and maintain them, if confronted with Yorke and Williams, should they make exceptions.' He 'wishes what he has written to be read in their hearing' and 'will manifest his allegiance to his prince'.[31] On 15 August Yorke and Williams were examined again, separately of course, before Essex and Cobham. By this time, both had capitulated completely to pressure from their captors, admitting everything that was demanded of them however absurd, and corroborating one another. So Holt promised Yorke or any confederate

---

29 R. Williams, 2nd exam., 12.8.1594; *Cal. SP Dom.*, p. 541; -/-/70. Hume commented that the violent talk 'was the usual swashbuckling gossip of the Brussels refugees, directed especially to the inculpation of Young and Williams, whom Yorke suspected of betraying him'; op. cit., p. 155.   30 R. Williams, Confession, 13.8.1594; *Cal. SP Dom.*, p. 541; -/-/72. Cf. Hume, p. 157. Hume states that torture was used but does not give any reference. It is likely that the threat or the sight of the instruments was enough to extract or gain assent to all that was required. Only some priests and Jesuits under torture had sufficient stamina or motivation to resist: notably Robert Southwell, John Gerard, and probably Edmund Campion and Henry Walpole. The last named was under question at this time. On 14.8. interrogatories were prepared for Yorke, Williams and Young; *Cal. SP Dom.*, p. 542; -/-/78. Williams seemingly made the main contribution to 'names of sundry persons that are diversely charged', with later notes as to their fate: Williams' brother, Pew of Anglesey 'a kinsman of Williams', Bishop of Wolvered in Warwicks, Ralph Sheldon, who kept Williams' wife and children in his absence; another Williams and his sister in Louvain were to be arrested if they came to England. Captain Middleton with 'a brother with the enemy', Henry Duffield, Harrison and Bushell 'who were at the Winchester robbery and at the attempt on Whitehall', with a few more names, were to be rounded up. The list was drawn up on 16. 8. Most were to be arrested and sent up for examination by Waad at Wood Street; *Cal. SP Dom.*, p. 544; -/249, no. 87. Also of 16. 8., three conjecturally, are four more documents, three drafts of the above, and the 4th a 'list of persons named in the above paper'; ibid.; -/249, nos. 88, 89, 90, 91.   31 H. Young to Cobham, 13.8.1594; *Cal. SP Dom.*, p. 542; -/249, no. 74.

100,000 or 200,000 crowns to raise rebellion 'or do some notable act'. Williams and Young were to raise rebellion in North Wales, or at least take and fortify Conway. Williams and Dyer were to have taken Portsmouth by way of preparation for an invasion by Stanley from the Continent. Williams looked for help from Pew and Ralph Sheldon, Catholics, Captain Duffield 'and other gentlemen'. In a word, whoever the government wished could be drawn into the net of persecution. Another Williams was Sheldon's sevant. He was formerly at Rome, but 'is now with Mrs Allen and does all the cardinal's business'. Young gave Yorke a book written by his own hand about poisoning. Admitting he had a pension of twenty crowns a month from the king of Spain, Williams agreed, 'the rest of Yorke's articles are true'.[32] Whatever the English Jesuits wanted, it is certain that they never at this time had 100,000 crowns to lavish on tragicomedians of this kind.

Henry Young made another of his 'declarations' on 16 August. It was mainly embellishment of what had preceded. Yorke was to raise rebellion in the north where there were many Catholics. Williams preferred North Wales. Winchelsea was mentioned as a place where Stanley might land with one or two thousand men to start a rising. Evidently there were recusants here to be terrorised. Ralph Sheldon had escaped the consequences of his recusancy through his friendship with chancellor Hatton. Involvement with Yorke and Williams could be taken to blow this precious cover. They had needed it for their real intentions. 'They were to pretend discontent and a wish to return through lack of maintenance. By order of Holt and Gifford, they were examined at Brussels, imprisoned a day or two and then let go ... Holt promised Captain Yorke he should want for nothing, and that there should be safe conveyance of his packets.' Yorke received a jewel worth £30 and £250 in cash for his use. 'Yorke was at first to follow Lord Essex, and show himself dutiful at court. The rising was to be when Dr Gifford came after the Christmas holidays.' One curious touch has the ring of truth. It is difficult to see why or how Young would have invented it. 'Yorke said he believed the lord treasurer had poisoned the young earl of Derby to marry the young Lady Vere to the earl's brother, England being governed by the Machiavellian policy of those who would be kings, and whom it is time to cut off.'[33] This in itself would have been a pass to Tyburn. It would have supplied the sufficient reason for his destruction with nothing further added.

The results of one examination in the whole series may probably be taken as the simple truth. This was the examination of Antony Johnson, aged fifteen, on 17 August. He was the fourth who came to England with the other three. From Gelderland, he 'served an Englishman in ... Stanley's regiment; also Richard Williams in Captain Bostock's company, who promised to bring him to England. Williams kept company chiefly with Fr Sherwood, and their interviews were private; Yorke with Fr Holt. Yorke

32 Edmund Yorke, examination, The Tower, 15. 8.1594, 2pp, *Cal. SP Dom.*, p. 543; -/249, no. 79; copy of the above, 2pp, -/249, no. 80. Exam. of R. Williams, -/-/81; copy, -/-/82.   33 H. Young, declaration, 16. 8.1594, 6pp ; *Cal. SP Dom.*, p. 545; SP12/249, no. 92.

and Williams lived together in the market-place, Brussels.' [Johnson] 'had no money of Williams who was very poor, but some mean apparel. Williams had a fray with his host to whom he owed money. Yorke promised to procure Williams' pardon if he would go to England with him.'[34]

By this time it would have been evident that Yorke, with his Jesuit connection, some financial resources, leader of the group, and having bad thoughts on Derby's death, was the man who needed most to be leaned on. Williams was a secondary figure but he had been most useful in helping to set the mastiffs on to an important group of recusants. His part in any 'plot' might therefore have been played down. This is hinted by his examination on 20 August before Sir Michael Blount, Francis Bacon and William Waad. It was now evident to those at the top that men of the second echelon could take up the pursuit. Essex and Cobham could safely leave further examinations to those named, although these were by no means insubstantial or unreliable. By this time they would have to sift men who knew already what they were supposed to say – and the terrible consequences of not saying it. So Williams merely informed on a namesake, Edward, who had contacted Allen in Rome and said 'his old master, Mr Sheldon, was as good a Catholic as any in England'. Richard was allowed to claim that he had 'been privy to no practices'. He 'refused Holt and Owen's request to undertake something because they would not give him the money they demanded.'[35]

Tried the same day before the esame examiners, Yorke was obliged to make much more damning admissions in a more coherent account of the plot: more coherent but by no means free of absurdities which hardly need further pointing up.[36] Holt persuaded him 'to come over on the queen's pardon, and to live in the court as one fled away, having the money due to his uncle sent for his maintenance, and an assurance on oath of 40,000 crowns with prompt payment guaranteed by the secretary Stephen de Ibarra, if he performed the required service of killing the queen, by his own agents, or by Tipping, or Garret, ensign to Jaques, who were to be sent over.' Previous absurdities were maintained. 'At the conference thereon, Sir William Stanley, Throgmorton, Charles Paget, Drs Worthington and Gifford and Williams were present. Some spoke of a poisoned arrow or rapier, or a dagger as she walked in the garden' – here is a curious echo from the Parry plot. Yorke, it seems, 'had 40 crowns from Gifford, but they kept him in want to make him take the matter in hand'. By way of preliminary, Yorke 'was to have served the earl of Essex, Williams the lord admiral, and Young the lord

---

34 Antony Johnson's exam., 17. 8.1594; *Cal. SP Dom.*, p. 546; -/249, no. 95. It seems Robert Williams was a fifth who came over in Yorke's party. A Dubliner, he had fought with Essex in France; subsequently served months with Stanley but 'departed secretly': deserted? 'Wishing to come over with some English gentleman, he was engaged by Mr Yorke; did not know him but had seen Mr Williams in Stanley's regiment'. R. Williams, exam. before Thomas Fane [at Dover?], 6. 8.1594; *Cal. SP Dom.*, p . 537; -/-/56.   35 R. Williams' exam. before Sir Michael Blount [lieutenant of the Tower], Francis Bacon and William Waad, 20.8.1594, 1½ pp ; *Cal. SP Dom.*, p. 546; -/-/96; -/-/97 is a copy. Bacon and Blount were Essex trusties. Waad too knew what was expected of him.   36 E. Yorke, exam. before Blount, Bacon and Waad, 20.8.1594, 3pp ; *Cal. SP Dom.*, pp 546-7; -/-/98.

chamberlain. They swore on the sacrament to do it and were absolved by Father Holt.' It is glaringly absurd that, if Holt thought murdering the queen was a crime or a sin, he could absolve it before it was committed. This likewise came out of the wellworn ragbag of ideas on the peculiar ways of papists.

Opportunity was taken to connect this plot with Hesketh's and the entanglement of the earl of Derby. Yorke was forced to declare in this confession, 'Moody is come, or will soon come over, [to kill the queen, and will have money from Throgmorton and Paget]. They will offer the crown to the earl of Derby with the king of Spain's assistance. They assemble two or three times a week to devise means of destroying her Majesty.' Sheldon was the man they would have gone to for help if they had succeeded, and 'if they failed, they were to move some rebellion in the earl of Derby's name though he were not privy to it.'[37] One thinks of Mary, queen of Scots and the bond of association.

The next day, 21 August, Yorke under pressure in another examination before Essex and Cobham, added impressive details no doubt intended to improve the air of authenticity. He 'was first moved to destroy the queen by Father Holt in the Jesuits' college, Brussels, last May, in ... Stanley's presence; they spoke of the difficulty of receiving his uncle's money unless he performed some service and told him that the duke of Parma had praised his uncle, Rowland Yorke, as the truest English subject the King of Spain had.' Was this to promote jealousy among the rest when they heard it? The next time, Drs Gifford and Worthington, Throckmorton and Charles Paget were present, 'and they promised him 40,000 crowns and told him many at court would be glad and were looking for it. Throckmorton said if his brother had been a man of any resolution, it would have been done.' Yorke wanted 'a resolute man to execute the part, to further and rescue him if he could'. They promised him 'Richard Williams, Throckmorton's cousin' – Francis was executed in 1585. One notes a certain system in this attack on a connected, if loosely connected, group of recusants It would happen again at the time of the gunpowder plot. Yorke had money from Holt to settle his debts at Brussels, 'being threatened for non-payment of rent for his lodgings'. This could have been true. But not that 'they solemnly swore him to perform the service, and Holt confessed him, and gave him the sacrament'. Yorke now completely implicated Williams who 'swore to kill the queen, Yorke to aid him, and to do it if he failed, by poisoned arrow, pistol or rapier. They hoped for help from Captain Duffield and Bushell, who served Lord Strange' – another thrust at the Derby Stanleys. Moody got a further dishonourable mention. He 'Tipping and Garret are coming over to kill her; and if the English fail, a Walloon and a Burgundian from Stanley's regiment are to be employed.'[38]

---

37 E. Yorke, exam., 20.8.1594. See n. 36. The passage in the above quotation in square brackets 'is from the marginal abstract in the subsequent paper.' This is a copy of the above with marginal abstracts. Appended is a note that Yorke 'acknowledged this confession on 21 August before ... Essex and ... Cobham'; *Cal. SP Dom.*, p. 547; -/249, no. 99.   38 E. Yorke, confession, 21.8.1594, before Essex and Cobham, 9pp; *Cal. SP Dom.*, p. 548; -/-/103. Five more documents of 21.8. touch the

By this time, the three main accused had been reduced to the point where they were ready to admit or say anything. Young never had any difficulty, it seems. Nevertheless, Williams may now have shown some recalcitrance. In some notes taken, conjecturally by Waad on 21 August, the item was included, 'To forbear to deal with Williams for a few days, and then Bacon and the writer' – Waad – 'to deal with him.'[39] It would be possible to read too much into it, but it sounds as if Richard needed to be brought 'to know himself', to use a graphic phrase of Burghley's. A few days solitary confinement to brood on the realities of his situation may have been necessary at this point to curb some spirit of protest in an evidently explosive character.

Yorke was examined on 24 August before Blount, Bacon and Waad. He did not now 'remember who told him that Tipping and Ensign Garret were to be employed to kill the queen, but Fr Holt told him of the Burgoman and Walloon, many English having failed to execute it'. Williams told Yorke that 'Moody, a resolute man, was come, and had money from Paget and Throckmorton'. Moody we have met already as a spy for the English state. Yorke and Williams, according to this confession, were both very eager for the murder. Imaginative details were added that 'Stanley should deny them a passport; that the governor of "Burborow" should stay them; that Williams should seem to be in want', while Yorke would approach Essex by letter for Williams' pardon. Yorke came over 'poor but was to have 100 crowns in London' – from whom? He already had 'twenty crowns from Fr Holt, but to colour the matter, gave him a bill for it'. In short what was claimed originally from Holt as a gift was only a loan: which is plausible. 'Williams prevented his coming over without a passport lest he might damn himself, having taken the sacrament to kill the queen, by being taken and forced to confess it.'[40]

It would have occurred to critical spirits then and later that the generous admissions of their own guilt by Yorke and Williams owed no little to the threat or application of torture. Some attempt to forestall this suspicion was provided in a 'declaration' by the accommodating Young on 24 August. 'Yorke said at Calais that he wondered at any man's wronging his friends for a little torture, and that he was armed for any torture, and boasted of the duke of Parma's praising his uncle for his constancy under torture

case, all on *Cal. SP Dom.*, p. 548; copy of first, -/-/104, 5½ pp Another copy, 6pp , -/-/105. Yorke acknowledges to E. Coke that Young wrote to Holt offering to kill Burghley: addressed to Waad, clerk of the Council; -/-/106. Interrogatories for R. Williams; ibid., -/-/107. R. Williams, exam. before Essex and Cobham, mainly the replies to the preceding; SP12/249, no. 106. Williams thinks Moody has already come to England. Particulars of Williams' dealings with Yorke, 1½pp; -/-/108. A copy of -/-/108 is -/-/109. Notes by [Waad, 21.8.] for Essex to write to Flushing for the arrest of Moody and his extradition to England. More information required from Yorke and Williams on Ensign Garret, the Walloon and the Burgundian. 'To forbear to deal with Williams for a few days, and then Bacon and the writer to deal with him.' Bushell must be properly identified; -/-/110. [Edmund Yorke], depositions, 21[?]. 8. Williams when in Burgundy wished his sword in the queen's belly, the deed done and themselves back again; -/-/111.   **39** *Cal. SP Dom.*, p. 548; -/249, no. 110. See also n. 38.   **40** E. Yorke, exam, 24.8.1594, 4pp; *Cal. SP Dom.*, pp 549-50; -/-/112. A copy of the same, 3pp; -/-/113.

... Williams said he would die rather than betray his friends, and if he said anything when on the rack, would deny all again when free from it.'[41] Young said, presumably at the time, that 'if they were so foolish as to go, they might be hanged, racked or tormented'. The absurdity of a 'council for the state of England' consisting of incompatibles who met every morning in the Jesuits' college was again put forward.

Richard Williams, was examined twice on 27 August: the first time before Blount, Coke, Bacon and Waad with the addition of Edward Drew; the second time before Drew, Bacon and Waad. Neither added anything notably significant to what had been said before except that on the second occasion Williams claimed he 'heard Young affirm with great oaths that he would kill her Majesty'.[42] On 28 August Yorke and Williams confronted one another before the commissioners Blount, Drew, Bacon and Waad. 'Yorke swore that they took the sacrament to kill the queen, and that Williams had wished his sword in her belly. Williams denying this, Yorke told him he denied it on account of his oath, but it was unlawfully taken and may therefore be broken.'[43] The meaning is obscure.

Little now remained, it seemed, save to draw up an indictment from the examinations of Yorke and Williams. Notes and memoranda of attorney-general Coke, stressing the 'aggravated nature of their treason' pointedly omitted any reference to Henry Young.[44] Young in two letters written at the end of August makes his role of informer, at least by now professional, very evident. Writing to Waad on 30 August, he enclosed 'speeches' he had heard from two unfortunates who conversed while he was listening. It could have been nothing compromising except by way of interpretation since they both wished 'to be examined thereon'. Young also wanted 'Williams' boy to be sent to him, to utter what he might fear to tell any other'. Far from fearing trial, Young was expecting speedy enlargement. He asked Waad to use his influence with Essex and Cobham to get him released.[45] The letter to Cobham of 31 August suggests that Young had been doing spy work before this latest contribution to the government cause. He had been 'importuned by Bagnall, keeper of the prison, to write certain conversations which Bagnall had with Pettit in his sickness' and from which Bagnall had learned much. It was for Cobham to sift this Bagnall.[46]

41 H. Young, declaration, 24.8.1594; *Cal. SP Dom.*, p. 550; -/-/114. 'The Council of State for England consisting of Stanley, Paget, Thomas Throgmorton, Owen, Captain [William] Tresham, Drs Gifford and Worthington and Holt confers every morning after Mass in the Jesuits' college.' As an additional absurdity L. Hicks noted that Throckmorton was not then in Flanders. 42 R. Williams, 2 exams., 27. 8.1594, the Tower; *Cal. SP Dom.*, pp 550-1; -/249, no. 117, 1st exam., notes by Essex say the confession was acknowledged before him, and Williams 'will avow it to his death and before Yorke's face': 2 copies of the preceding; -/-/118, 119: another copy without the notes; -/-/120: 2nd exam., Thomas Greenfield, keeper of the earl of Arundel, escapes to Scotland; -/-/121: 2 copies of the preceding; -/-/122, 123: extracts from the confessions of Yorke of 21.8., and of Williams of 27. 8., 3pp 43 'Certificate by Blount, Drew, Bacon and Waad', 28.8.1594, the Tower; *Cal. SP Dom.*, p. 551; -/-/125: 2 copies of the preceding; -/-/126, 127. 44 E. Cokes' notes and memoranda on the exams of Y. and W.; *Cal. SP Dom.*, p. 553; -/249, no. 134, 3pp [August, 1594]. 45 H. Young to Waad, 30.8.1594; *Cal. SP Dom.*, p. 552; -/-/130. 46 Same to Cobham, at the Court,

Among Coke's notes indicated above, presumably for the preparation of the indictment of Yorke and Williams, was a reference to the 'numerous and treacherous designs of the king of Spain against her Majesty'. Essex's inspiration as the head of the war party is transparently obvious. But as Hume observed, 'the evidence of the complicity of secretary Ibarra depends only upon Yorke's statement that Holt had said that he guaranteed the payment; and in Lord Burghley's breviate a note points out that "this is all against Ibarra or any other Spaniard"'. [47] Burghley also noted for his private purposes the absurdity of the idea of Charles Paget, Worthington, Gifford and others being associated with the Jesuits in such an enterprise – or in any enterprise at all, one might add. This absurdity was emphasisied by Young, as we have seen, in his 'council of state for England, which met in the Jesuit College at Brussels every morning'. Hume was too well acquainted with Spanish sources to be led astray by Young's nonsense. Unacquainted with Jesuit sources, however, he was not sufficiently critical of statements implicating Jesuits. All the same, he noted at least one suspected falsification in a contemporary account. 'In Yetswirt's *Sondry horrible treasons*, written almost immediately after the event, it is stated that Yorke confessed that "Hugh Owen showed him at Brussels an assignation in writing, signed by Ibarra, for assurance of payment of 40,000 crowns, to be given to him from the king of Spain if he should kill the queen, or should assist Williams or any other to perform the same. The assignation was afterwards deposited with Holt the Jesuit, who also showed it to Yorke, and swore on the sacrament to pay the amount as soon as the fact should be committed." I can find no such statements in Yorke's confessions in the state papers. The main point, apparently, was to connect Spaniards with the plot.'[48]

Williams had to undergo three more recorded examinations: two on 12 September 1594, and one, seemingly the last, on 1 February 1595. Essex and Cobham left the task to subordinates.[49] They added nothing of significance to what had been said before. The most important points, perhaps, in the first two confessions touched the recusants, particularly Sheldon, which had been Williams' special contribution. As Hume concluded, 'the plot of Holt, Yorke and Williams, like that of Lopez, served as fresh

Greenwich, 31.8.; *Cal. SP Dom.*, p. 552; -/-/131. I have found no other references to Bagnall. **47** *Sal. Cal.*, iv, p. 607; quoted Hume, pp 159-60. **48** Hume, p. 160, n. 2. **49** R. Williams, 1st exam. of 12.9.1594, before Blount, Edward Drew, Waad. Dyer told Williams that Constantine Throgmorton, Henry Duffield, Harrison and his brother, and a brother of Lord Grey, took part in the Winchester robbery. Dyer did not take part in the Whitehall attempt: 'they were hindered by one of their number being drunk'; *Cal. SP Dom.*, p. 555; -/250/6. The 2nd exam. before 12.9. before Blount, Drew and Bacon gave details of Edward Williams, Ralph Sheldon, and Clitheroe living 'chiefly at Antwerp'; -/250, no. 7. The exam. of 1.2.1595 'before Coke and three others' added nothing much to details of Williams' service and contacts in the Low Countries; *Cal. SP Dom.*, 1595-7, p. 7; SP/12/251, no. 11. Some time in September evidence was collected from the examinations of Yorke, Williams and Young 'concerning persons connected with the conspiracy against her Majesty: viz. Stephen Ibarra, Sir William Stanley, Fr Holt, Thomas Throgmorton, Hugh Owen, Dr Gifford, Charles Paget, Dr Worthington, Tipping, ensign Edward Garret, Moody, a Walloon and a Burgundian'; 5 pp ; *Cal. SP Dom.*, 1591-4, p. 559; -/250, no. 12.

fuel for the fire of hatred which it was the object of the Essex party to keep raging between England and Spain, it being represented that Philip and his ministers, both in the Lopez case and this, were the first instigators of the murder of the queen.'[50] It was all drawn up, probably in September, in a treatise over fifteen pages long: 'A discourse showing the secret practices of the king of Spain against the person of Queen Elizabeth and her estate'. It was recognised that 'a great number, not carried away with inordinate affection to either, suspend their judgment' – evidently the document was intended for consumption in France and Flanders. 'The secret and dishonourable attempt made on the queen's life by Dr Lopez' and companions, and 'the other by Yorke and his company, provoked thereto by great reward proposed by secretary Ibarra, make the matter manifest to the world how barbarously and inhumanly these foul actions proceed from Spain, from whence also are maintained by sundry pensions, a multitude of persons adjudged traitors to their native country and fugitives from the same , who yield no other service to the king but to be instruments of such kind of barbarous actions, or to be spies for the king of the actions of their country, etc. [*sic*].' Elizabeth on the other hand 'has never been privy to any practice against the king of Spain's life, nor have her ministers. Neither has she received into her kingdom any rebel or person condemned by the king of Spain.'[51] The piece was overseen and 'corrected by Lord Burghley'. Presumably it was shown to Elizabeth.

'News from London' of 19 November reported 'no mention of peace' while the queen wanted any peace to include France and the States. Evidently in a state of high sensitivity, she was 'much displeased' with a letter from the archduke, never using 'your Majesty' and ending with 'your cousin'. This was taken to prevent the going over to negotiate peace of Thomas Wilkes. But 'the Spaniard neither can nor will have a general peace unless reduced to the last'.[52] So Essex had won a signal victory over the peace party and all the good Protestants had made another advance against the papists.

Yorke and Williams passed out of general history by the end of 1595. That there was an arraignment and a trial in which there could only have been one verdict, is sufficiently attested by a letter of John Daniell to Robert Cecil of 5 August 1595. Daniell who had a wife, nine children and no money, reminded Cecil of the services which he hoped would get him a job. 'At the arraignment of Yorke, Williams and Southwell the Jesuit, I was nominated the first discoverer of the late practices intended against her Majesty and her dominions. Lord Burghley, the lieutenant of the Tower, and Justice

---

50 Hume, p. 160, n. 2.   **51** 'A discourse' on Philip II's 'secret practices' against Elizabeth, September(?) 1594, 15¼ pages, 'corrected by Lord Burghley', *Cal. SP Dom.*, p. 558; -/250, no. 10. This is followed by a 'catalogue of the rebels and fugitives in the Low Countries', 30 under Stanley, 30 under Jaques, 16 under Bostock, and 38 more under others named. The names of 35 English 'fugitives' serving in the Low Countries, and receiving pensions from 20 to 200 crowns a month, is headed by Westmoreland, Lord Dacres, Sir William Stanley, Hugh Owen, Charles Paget and Michael Moody. There were also 25 Jesuits and priests, 9 laywomen or nuns, and 16 in the court at Brussels; *Cal. SP Dom.*, p. 559; -/250, no. 11, 7¼ pages.   **52** News from London, 19.11.1594; *Cal. SP Dom.*, p. 564.

Young, if he were alive, could report my readiness to give all the information I could.'[53] No official or even unofficial record seems to survive of the arraignment and trial of Yorke and Williams.[54] Camden has the clearest references to the execution. 'In the second month of this year [1595] Edmund York, nephew to that York who betrayed the fort at Zutphen to the Spaniards, and Richard Williams, both apprehended the last year ... suffered death at Tyburn for high treason.' Yorke was the main culprit who confessed that Holt, Hugh Owen, Jacomo de Francisco 'and others' offered him 40,000 ducats 'subscribed with the hand of Ibarra the Spaniard' to kill the queen or assist Williams in the deed. 'This assignment lay in Holt's hands for his use; that Holt, kissing the consecrated host' – a recurrent absurdity – 'sware that the money should be paid as soon as the murder was committed; and that he bound York and Williams by oath and the sacrament of the Eucharist to dispatch it.' Camden had further interesting comments. 'The villainy of the fugitives in relation to such wicked attempts was notorious about this time; while some encouraged murtherers to commit parricide upon the queen; others greedy to get their money offered themselves to commit the fact, and being once hired to do it presently revealed the same; and others, false and treacherous among themselves, put one another forward to their destruction before they were aware of it, intrapped one another with cunning devices and many times charged one another with notorious falsities.'[55]

The unhappy pair were obscure enough to deserve oblivion, no doubt, but it is possible that, like Edward Squier in what follows, they said the wrong things in their scaffold speeches which called for the severest censorship. It is to be noted, as we might expect, that there was no mention of Henry Young in Daniell's letter or in the last scene at Tyburn. He probably survived to go on doing the job which Daniell so coveted; one of those indicated by Camden as ready trap his comrades with 'cunning devices' and charge them with 'notorious falsities' for his own profit. Camden, of course, gives no hint as to who might have been the real employers and encouragers of such people.

---

53 John Daniell to R. Cecil, 5. 8.1595; *Cal. SP Dom.* 1595-7, p. 85; SP12/253, no. 62.   54 The London, 1816 enlarged edition of T. B. Howell, *A complete collection of state trials ... earliest to 1783*, has nothing between Sir John Perrot 1592 and Robert Devereux 1600. The 12-part edition of E. Coke's *Reports* ... , published in the Savoy in 1738 likewise has nothing. J. Willis Bund, *A Selection of cases from the state trials*, i, *Trials for treason 1327 to 1660* (Cambridge 1879), p. 303, has a brief reference to 'Cullen, Yorke and Williams who were also sent over to kill the queen, were each tried and convicted; the last two were also charged with a design of firing the fleet with balls of wildfire.' Holt and the Jesuits were behind it. No source is given. Alfred Marks, Tyburn Tree, its History and Annals (London, 1908), p. 168 gives a few details ultimately deriving from Camden. See n. 55.   55 William Camden, *The history of ... Princess Elizabeth*, 4th edition (London 1688), p. 495.

Edward Squier's plot

Arguably the most bizarre of all the plots at this time attached itself to the name of Edward Squier. This brewed up between 1597 and 1598 from ingredients collectted over a few years previously. So bizarre was it that even methodical historians of the period such as J.B. Black, D.H. Willson and P.M. Handover did not think it worth even a mention in their standard works. It may well be that this grotesque episode was not of primary significance in the general history of the times. True, it brought no credit to those responsible. Nevertheless, in the overall context of the runup to the gunpowder plot it is decidedly important in giving a further insight into the devious ways of government. It also illustrates the mind of Sir Robert Cecil and a rare determination inherited from his father to stop at nothing to achieve the end of destroying enemies and rivals. Aiming at the elimination of Catholicism, it targeted particularly the Jesuit presence in the country as a principal obstacle to true religion. This time the Jesuits got to know more about it and were able to put a finger on some of the absurdities.

Lord Burghley died on 5 August 1598. The Squier plot may therefore be taken as Robert Cecil's first truly independent excursion into the dark realm of plot management.[1] It revealed a hand not yet practised enough to make a convincing success of it, although it owed something to experience gained from the Lopez plot. The Squier plot involved a double brace of villains; John Stanley and William Monday, with Edward Squier and Richard Rolls playing opposite them. Stanley and Monday were more characters out of Robert Greene's underworld. Rolls was a shadowy figure. The fallguy, as he proved to be, Edward Squier, was less a villain than an unlucky adventurer who happened to fit the needs of Cecilian statecraft at the time. He corresponds to Babington, Ballard, Parry, Ferreira, Tinoco, Lopez and Yorke in previous plots. The most authentic villain, John Stanley, was used as the means of trapping Squier. He, William Monday and Richard Rolls, described optimistically perhaps at one point as a gentleman, escaped with their lives after playing their part: but not before they had passed at least a year in prison to give public attention time to forget them and the whole sordid story. They were then thrown back in the sea no doubt to scavenge in the polluted shallows as hitherto.

1 F. Edwards, S.J., 'The strange case of the poisoned pommel. Richard Walpole, S.J., and the Squire Plot 1597-1598', *Archivum historicum S.J.*, vol. LVI, 1987, pp 3-80; 'Sir Robert Cecil, Edward Squier, and the

The technique in setting up the plot, as in the case of Lopez and others, was to take circumstances in themselves innocent, or relatively so, and interpret them in the most sinister light possible. As we have seen, Lopez and the Portuguese had Spanish contacts which, while proving nothing formally reprehensible from the English viewpoint, were made to bear the interpretation of an attempt to kill the queen. In the Squier plot, it was the contacts between Squier, and for that matter, Rolls, with the English Jesuits in Spain which was made the basis of a plot to poison her Majesty, and for good measure, the earl of Essex. Richard Walpole, S.J., based on Seville, where the English Jesuits had founded a college in exile, and to a lesser extent Robert Persons, and Martin Array, a scholarly secular priest and close cooperator of the Jesuits, were Cecil's main target.

The vital factor in a plot of this kind was at least one man who was malleable, suggestible and sufficiently lacking in scruple to regurgitate as his own whatever judicial examiners wished him to declare. John Stanley, another Henry Young, was the man who sang in perfect tune what was piped to him in the Tower by the examiners. One could say tormentors since another essential ingredient in the total contrivance was, yet again, the threat of torture hanging over all the prisoners to make them tell something more useful than the truth. Edward Squier, with considerable reluctance, agreed eventually to give back to the examiners all they wanted to hear. But it was only after five hours of torture, as it was reported, that he could be brought to perjure himself satisfactorily. The good effect was ruined when eventually he contradicted on the scaffold all that he had admitted in his prison.

In trying to judge the truth or otherwise of the story, it helps to examine what is known from other sources of the main characters involved. As David said, all men are liars, but some more than others. In trying to discern the truth, one looks for any sudden or unlikely development in the story at every point in their examination. Important is the principle of probability. The Squier story, once again, teems with absurdities.

What witnesses were more likely to be telling the truth? The most reliable may be taken to be Thomas Fitzherbert. The Fitzherberts, like the Walpoles who produced Cecil's prime villain of this piece, Richard the Jesuit, were a recusant family of much honour and distinction in their locality, Swinnerton in Staffordshire. Born in 1552 and educated at Oxford, Thomas married in 1580 Dorothy East of Bledlowe, Buckinghamshire. When persecution of Catholics became intense in England, he went to France in 1582, and after his wife's death in 1588, moved to Spain. The Spanish king was happy to accept the services of a man excluded from probable distinction in his own country only by the accident of religion. After a time in Rouen as an intelligencer, in 1596 Fitzherbert became Philip II's English secretary. He gave what help he could to the recusant exiles and published some seven books. In 1601 he retired to Rome where, after ordination to the priesthood in 1602, he filled a number of important offices before joining the Jesuits in 1613.[2]

poisoned pommel', *Recusant History*, vol. 25, no. 3 (May 2001), pp 377-414. The 'Squier' spelling of his name seems to be the one the 'plotter' preferred and is so rendered here. No account of this strange plot is to be found in Protestant sources, it seems.   **2** For the Fitzherberts of Swynnerton, especially,

Fitzherbert's most important work in the present context was *A defence of the Catholyke cause ...* published in 1602. It was prompted primarily by this Squier plot. That Fitzherbert served the king of Spain did not mean that he wanted to see his own country under Spanish rule. 'Amongst many malicious slanders wherewith ... heretics seek to make us and our cause odious to all men, of the principalest is that we desire the conquest of our country by the King of Spain.'[3] Not that this could have comforted the present regime in England since Fitzherbert's aim was 'to restore and assure Catholic religion there by establishing a Catholic king with whom they might renew ... the ancient league so long continued in times past betwixt the two kingdoms of England and Castile ... '[4] So Sir Robert Cecil had a genuine problem. Should concocting or even encouraging such a plot as Squier's have been part of his solution? If it achieved the end, the means, he clearly believed, were altogether justified: a principle he ascribed to, but which was not accepted by, the Jesuits whom he hated so much.

Fitzherbert seems to have summed up well the character of John Stanley, a vital witness, in pithy Elizabethan prose. 'No man here hath other opinion of him than that he is a notable drunkard, a common liar, a pilfering, cosening and cogging companion, yea and (as he himself hath made no bones to boast) a pursecatcher upon the highway, and as I have credibly heard, a common horsestealer, for the which and such other virtues of his I understand he hath scoured sundry gaols in England, and should have flowered the gallows long ere this if he had had his rights.'[5] Fitzherbert was not talking from hearsay. He had experience of the man himself in Spain after he had obtained his release from gaol through Jesuit instrumentality. 'And as for his behaviour here ... within a few days after he was set at libertie ... we were both weary and ashamed of him, for besides his vile and scandalous life, too bad to be told, he would sometimes ... blaspheme God ... and sometimes threaten to make himself away because he was not regarded and rewarded according to his expectation.' He betrayed his fellow-prisoners in Seville, revealing plans they had in hand for their escape. 'He discovered an English ship that arrived there, not for any zeal to this king's service, but in hope to get a third part of the goods.'[6] There was more.

Thomas, see Dnb, 19 (1889); L. Hicks, *Letters of Thomas Fitzherbert 1608-10*, CRS 41 (1948); Dom Bede Camm, *Forgotten shrines* (London, St Louis 1910), 'The tragedy of the Fitzherberts', pp 1-74, pedigree p. 398; H. Foley, *Records ...* , ii, 1875, pp 198-230; Wood's *Athenae ...* , 1815, ii, pp 661-4; Joseph Gillow, *Bibliographical dictionary of the English Catholics*, ii, 1885, pp 284-8, mentions several Fitzherberts.	**3** T. Fitzherbert, *An apology of T. F. in defence of himself and other catholyks, falsly charged with a fayned conspiracy against her Majestie's person, for the which one Edward Squire was wrongfully condemned and executed in ... 1598. Wherein are discovered the wicked and malicious practices of some inferior persons to whose examinations the causes of Catholykes are commonly committed and their impious manner of proceeding; not only against the sayd Squire but also against many Catholykes that have been unjustly condemned for like fayned conspiracies against her Majesty and the state* [Antwerp 1602] 8v. This treatise of 104 pp was appended to *A Defence of the Catholyke cause ...* 144 pp	**4** Edwards, p. 33, n. 86. The references under my name in this article refer to the earlier article in *Archivum Historicum*. See n. 1.	**5** Ibid., p. 28, n. 74. **6** Ibid., p. 29, n. 76.

Some part of Stanley's own account of himself may be cautiously accepted as true. A soldier of not much fortune, he was a prisoner of the Spanish from 1589 until 1592. 'Converted' in gaol near Cadiz by Father Robert Persons, as he claimed, he was allowed to go free. Back in England he was imprisoned once again for three more years. Francis Drake used his influence to get him out of prison so that he could join what proved to be his last expedition. At the end of another chapter, Stanley found himself once again in a Spanish prison at Vatallo, this time with William Monday, a fellow adventurer and rakehell in the Squier story. They signed a joint statement of their experience on 1 November 1597.[6] Their depositions varied with the country where they were made. In Spain, Stanley described himself as a devout Catholic devoted to Philip.[7] In England he was a good Protestant whose only desire was to serve the queen. Once again Stanley and Monday secured their release in Spain. Stanley, bringing letters from Spain when he got back to England, was sent to the Tower, a fact reported by John Chamberlain to Dudley Carleton on 3 October 1598.[8]

According to admissions made later in the Tower, Edward Squier was a scrivener at Greenwich who had worked for a time in the queen's stables. He was unsettled in his profession and accompanied Drake, like Stanley, on his last voyage of 1595 to 1596. He was on a ship called the Francis, or Frances, which was captured by the Spaniards, so that Squier, along with Richard Rolls, found himself in the prison of the inquisition at Seville. Richard Walpole and Joseph Creswell, Jesuits stationed in the city, came to visit them as they usually did English prisoners. They encouraged Rolls and Squire to become Catholics; but they were careful to drop no word, it was plausibly claimed, against the English queen. Before arrangements were completed for their release, however, Squire and Rolls managed to escape on their own initiative. Back in England, Squire contacted a member of the privy council, possibly Sir William Knollys, controller of the household, to get himself decontaminated of any suspicion after contact with the Jesuits. The information got back to Sir Robert Cecil but nothing was done to prevent Squier and Rolls from joining Essex's ill-fated expedition to Terceiras in 1583. Later Squire served in Essex' flagship which got back to Plymouth on 26 October 1597.

Squier continued his maritime career until about the beginning of September 1598. He was then 'called home from the seas' to be lodged in the Counter in Wood Street. Some time before 18 October he was 'sent for hence into the Tower', presumably by the same men who recounted the salient facts of his arrest and imprisonment in a document signed on 28 January 1599. These were the lord keeper, the earl marshal, the lord admiral, Lord North, Lord Buckhurst, Mr Comptroller, and inevitably, Mr Secretary Cecil.[9] As in the case of Lopez, Squier's fate could be taken as sealed long before any formal trial for treason. His death was doubtless foreseen by his captors, and especially by one, as something more useful than his life, or anything he had done in it hitherto.

7 Archivo Nacional, Simancas, E. 182, unfol., (no. 77).   8 *Cal. SP Dom.*, 1598-1601, p. 102.   9 J. R. Dasent, *Acts of the privy council*, new series, 29 (London 1905), p. 506.

Meanwhile John Stanley had been busy in the Tower helping some privy councillors with their enquiries. He had been there with William Monday since about mid-year 1597. To wile away the tedium of his imprisonment, and to ingratiate himself with his captors, Stanley composed a 62-page autobiography offered to the lords of the privy council. It has marginal comments by Cecil who observed at one point, 'when the fox preaches beware goslings'. It seems unnecessary to summarize even briefly for present purposes this roving and rambling life beyond remarking that the writer fully admitted contact with Richard Walpole, Joseph Creswell and Thomas Fitzherbert. Two thirds of the way through his disjointed but not dull narrative Stanley switched to a completely new subject with its own heading, 'Of Richard Rolls and Edward Squier'.[10] This implies, does it not, that the subject had been suggested to him. Stanley claimed not only to have met them in prison but also to have been present at the conference with his captors concerning a ransom. There is strong suspicion of fabrication. He claimed that Squier and Rolls were to receive 1500 ducats for some service they had promised the king of Spain. The last part of his narrative contained disjointed notes on Englishmen in Spain and Spanish officials. This would have told the councillors nothing they did not know already from better sources. It is noteworthy that there is nothing in the narration that hints even remotely at the bizarre plot with which Rolls and Squier were to be charged later.

Nor was there anything notably compromising in the first confession of John Stanley made at the Tower on 23 September 1598. Stanley claimed that 'Walpole, one Davys and Owen' came to see them in their Seville prison to convert them to Catholicism. But Walpole 'did noways deal with him or with Monday to his knowledge any way to persuade them to do any service against the queen's Majesty or the estate of the realm, but of themselves they did devise to offer service to the king to procure their liberty.'[11] Stanley's examiners pressed him on whether he had heard before leaving Spain that Squier and Rolls 'had done service to her Majesty sithence their coming over'. Stanley at first denied any knowledge of what Rolls and Squier were doing. But 'in the afternoon' on a threat of confrontation with Monday, he agreed that Creswell had said how 'they had played the villains and broken their vow' to serve the king. The examination was signed at the foot of each page by Stanley. The effect desired by this confession, no doubt, was to convince any later reader that if Rolls and Squier were brought to Stanley's memory by his examiners it was not with any intention of accusing them prematurely or unfairly.

William Waad, a Cecil trusty, reported to Essex on 17 October, 'We were all at the Tower this afternoon urging Stanley upon the two letters which he brought.'[12] One was allegedly from Walpole and the other from a Fitzherbert, presumably Thomas. The examiners brought him to admit that he had devised them himself and got a

---

10 Salisbury mss, 233/5, f. 1v. BL Microfilm M 485/59. The pages in the original were numbered subsequently with 4 pages left unnumbered. Hence the '60' pages given in the calendar.   11 Edwards, pp 44-5, and n. 124, p. 47 for Stanley's afternoon confession of 23.9.1598.   12 Ibid.

Spaniard to write them. Clearly he was in the position of a man who from now on either did and wrote what he was told or else faced serious consequences. We cannot suppose that Stanley experienced any crisis of conscience in agreeing to go along completely with all that was now required of him. He made a second declaration in his own hand in the presence of Essex and Robert Cecil on 18 October 1598. The fact of cooperation and appearance of harmony between these two key figures was still holding. William Waad was also present with them at this examination.

The declaration of 18 October blossomed into a fully fledged assassination plot in which not only priests and Jesuits but even the king of Spain and his ministers were involved. On 5 August 1597 – again a nice detail of dating enhanced the appearance of verisimilitude – Stanley was brought to the king's presence by Creswell after being sworn to secrecy. He was sent to William Monday to collect 'a perfume which should be cast in the way of her Majesty to cut off her life'. For good measure, 'Also I was employed to help Monday to burn her Majesty's navy.' [13] The name of Thomas, Baron Arundell of Wardour, was also dragged in although not with any suggestion that he was part of the murder plot. Stanley and Monday's perfume plot was now tied in with Rolls and Squier who were predestined to be the principal accused. 'Walpole told me at my departure from Seville to Madrid' – where Stanley met Fitzherbert – 'that Rolls and Squier were employed about her Majesty's person, and how they had received money for the same' – presumably the killing. The same day at seven o'clock, 'John Stanley having deliberately read over again this declaration ... did affirm and justify the same to be true in all things in the presence of Essex, Robert Cecil, Edward Coke'.[14] The names were signatures. Stanley's was among them.[15]

No time was lost. Edward Squier came to examination in the Tower on 19 October. Squier, a man of very different clay from Stanley, suffered the ordeal of one who was forced unwillingly for purposes of state to say things that were simply false. Confronted with Walpole's plot in its developed form as it was supposed to be presented to him in Seville, 'he denied that anything of the kind had ever passed in his conversations with Walpole. He was put to torture.' Overcome by its ferocity, 'he confessed whatever the wiles of those who concocted these stories thrust upon him'. No details of the torture are available but according to Array it lasted for no less than five hours. 'Standing thus between fears of condemnation if he drew back, and hopes of pardons if he accused others' he began 'to frame the tale that in his confession is set down'.[16] Squier confessed that Walpole gave him instructions in compounding poisons. The one preferred for the task in hand was a mixture of opium and 'white mercury water'.

13 Regarding Stanley's transfer to the Tower about 18.10.1598 and his second declaration before William Waad, Essex and R. Cecil, the important detail of the signatures of the last two at the end of the confession on f. 168r., as well as Stanley's, was omitted by H. Foley (Records ... , ii, pp 241-3) which for the rest is substantially accurate. Original in SP12/268, no. 82. Cf. *Sal. Cal.*, 396.   14 Foley, ii, p. 241.   15 Ibid., p. 243. Foley omits the reference to the 7 p. m. session and the signatures of the leading councillors. Cf. Edwards, p. 50, n. 139.   16 Edwards, *The Elizabethan Jesuits*, p. 279.

The substance was to be kept in a double bladder pierced with holes which Squier would press down on the queen's saddle. She would get it on her hands and take it with her food. The detail was supplied at this stage that Squier should get five different people to buy the ingredients from different apothecaries to avoid suspicion.

An important object of the government at this time, which scarcely needed to be openly avowed, was to set Jesuits and secular priests at loggerheads so that the trouble of destroying them all them would be much reduced if they fell to maiming one another. Here was another thread which was to be woven into the Squier plot. One of the most articulate and vociferous of the Catholic critics of the Jesuits was Dr Christopher Bagshaw, a secular priest who had been captured on landing in England in 1585 and sent to Wisbech castle: a kind of oflag for priests set up for this purpose since the 1580s. A plot at no time plausible was now rendered even less so by the fact that Squier was supposed, according to this confession, to have been recommended to Bagshaw by Walpole. This was because he knew 'all these courses the Jesuits do hold'.[17] Walpole was further supposed to have given Squier a letter for Bagshaw but 'he threw it into the sea after he came past Plymouth'. If Squier had any difficulty about preparing the poison, 'he should receive further directions therein, either from Bagshaw, or that Bagshaw knew' someone who could instruct him further. 'This latter conference together with the letter and directions in writing were had and delivered in May [1597] in the English College at Seville, in Walpole's presence no other person being present.'[18]

In short, all depended on Squier's word, or rather the word imposed upon him by his examiners either by the threat or use of torture. The examination was carried out by John Peyton, E. Fleming, Francis Bacon, William Waad, Edward Coke and signed by them all. They all knew their duty to their careers and their masters, more especially Coke. This was one of his early commissions as attorney-general. He would know how to be grateful for his prestigious appointment. A postscript added to Squier's examination made him purchase the ingredients at different apothecaries' shops in London. They probably belonged to papists or suspected papists whom it was intended to compromise. The postscript too was signed by the same examiners. It was presumably set down after Squier had been tortured since it was in a clerk's hand and signed in one place only by Squier. It was substantially a flowing narrative and had doubtless been prepared before the show.[19] According to this, by way of afterthought, Walpole exhorted Squier, 'It were a very meritorious act to stab or kill the earl of Essex, if you can come at him, but this against the queen is all in all.' Essex was in the background for the rest of it; but such references helped to hold his interest, and make him even less critical of motivation for another chance to strike at Spain.

---

17 Aray, *The discoverie and confutation of a tragical fiction devysed and played by Edward Squyer yeoman soldier, hanged at Tyburne the 23 of November 1598 ... by M. A., preest, that knew and dealt with Squyer in Spayne*, no place of publication given, 1599, 3v. Scolar reprint 71 (1971).   18 Foley, II, 244.
19 Edwards, 'The strange case ...', *Archivum Historicum* ... , see above n. 1, p. 52-3.

It was all very maladroit. Further attempts at embellishment made it all the less convincing for anyone who knew anything at all about Jesuits and their ways. Fortunately for the government, the populace, for whom this kind of propaganda was mainly intended, did not. There is, or was, in the Society of Jesus what was known as the rule of touch, which means that no one was allowed to embrace or handle anyone else. Nevertheless, according to this examination of Squier, Walpole at one point, 'put his left arm about my neck in a kind of hugging manner, and held me fast, making the cross, but I understood not what he said, save in the beginning of his speech I understood Dominus, and when he had done he said, "God bless thee, and give thee strength, my son".'[20] All this too was included in the Authentic Memoirs of that 'exquisitely villainous Jesuit Father Richard Walpole' by an author unknown but who had evidently been allowed to inspect Squier's deposition. The book was published some five or six weeks after Squire's execution. If the author had been present, or at the trial, the memory could be presumed to be still fresh.

In fact there is reason to suppose that the author of *A letter out of England ...* was none other than Francis Bacon who had been given the task of writing up this official and contrived account of events from Squier's 'confessions' taken in the Tower. By this time the tide of prejudice was running a course full enough to lead most to believe anything about papists, especially Jesuits. Provided it was bad enough, no matter how absurd, it must be true. In the event the government at the time did its best to obliterate vital parts of the record of a plot that failed in its purpose for important respects. These would be corrected in subsequent attempts of the kind, especially the last and greatest, the gunpowder plot. A curious feature of Squier's first examination is that it virtually ignored any part played by Rolls. It also introduced a third character, Jackson, who soon dropped out of the story. It was also claimed that Squier was allowed to depart from Spain and did not in fact make his escape. There was some by-play in a complicated story which could well have allowed for the main characters' return to England in secret to negotiate the ransom of some Spaniards taken prisoner in the Cadiz raid. This was not allowed to spoil the even flow of the main narrative for public consumption.

Squier's second examination, that is, the next of which there is surviving record, took place on 23 October. Impressive detail was added to the account of his attempt in the Islands expedition to poison Essex. He smeared his poison on the earl's chair: but with no result. Undiscouraged, on returning from the sea, he treated likewise the pommel of Elizabeth's saddle: with no more success. Compromising details were added to embroil the Woodhouse family, well known recusants who lived at Breccles in Norfolk.[21] Squier's third examination took place on 24 October. It was brief but important since it now claimed that he 'received the confection of poison at the hands of Walpole, the Jesuit. Which composition was to the quantity of a garden bean'. Squier did not know what it was made of since Walpole did not tell him.[22]

---

20 SP/12/268, no. 86, ff. 175r-176r. Squier's signature is at the foot of f. 175r. Edwards, 'The strange case ...', p. 54.   21 SP12/268, no. 89, ff. 180r-181v; Foley, ii, pp 248-50.   22 SP12/268, f. 185r/v;

William Monday and Richard Rolls were brought to examination on 3 November.[23] Monday was careful to repudiate any connection with the others in the murder attempts. 'And utterly denieth that he had ever any speech with Squier or Rolls about any atttempt or matter against the queen's person ... ' Rolls' examination on the same day rejected the idea of promising any service to King Philip let alone poisoning the queen. It is possible that Rolls was handled so delicately because it is likely he received a genuine commission in Spain to treat for the ransom or exchange of prisoners. True, Rolls was a 'gentleman' to Squier's 'yeoman'. But this would not have saved him from torture. Stanley and Monday, professional villains, might be useful to government on a future occasion, and so they survived. Clearly they did not need torture to help them remember. Monday made an important statement that Walpole and Fitzherbert thought they had been let down by Rolls and Squier and so they betrayed them to the English privy council. This was the story retailed by Camden.[24]

It was concluded that all the data necessary for a successful treason trial was now in place. It fell to Sir Edward Coke as attorney-general to prepare the case for the prosecution. Making no mention of Rolls, Monday or Stanley, Coke wrote to inform Cecil, the man behind it all, that he had drawn up the indictment against Squier in due form of law. This was the second test of Coke's skill and devotion to his master since his appointment. He was very anxious to please. He asked Cecil for further corrections and instructions. 'But yet what is convenient to be inserted and what omitted, it is my part to be directed by those that are able to give directions in so great a cause'.[25] It might seem good to those who knew better to involve other Jesuits as well as Walpole. 'Albeit the whole composition of it do, as seemeth to me, tacite set forth the whole manner of the contriving of it to be not by P. Walpole alone.'

Squier's trial took place in Westminster Hall, the usual venu for such occasions, on 9 November 1598. Squier, brought to the bar by the lieutenant of the Tower in time-honoured practice pleaded not guilty. John Popham, another trusty servant of the crown, was the presiding judge with Edward Anderson, Francis Gawdy and Edward Fenner. The names of the jury are also known.[26] The indictment described Squier as 'lately of London, yeoman', accused of intending to kill the queen on 20 April, in Seville. And on other days before and after both in Seville and other places overseas, he not only sought to deprive the queen of her throne but also of life, and to raise sedi-

Foley omitted this confession altogether. On f. 185r appears 'Exam by Edw. Coke' in Coke's hand, and a signature, 'Edw. Squier'. His signatures in all these confessions shows no deterioration in spite of torture. Are they his? **23** PRO, ibid., no. 103, f. 203r/v. **24** W. Camden, *Annals ...* , English ed. (London 1635), p. 498. **25** Edward Coke to R. Cecil, 3.11.1598, holog., from the Temple, endd. 'Mr Attorney'; *Sal. Cal.*, 8, 421; ms 65/40. **26** PRO, KB/8 Pouch 55, Baga de Secretis; cf. deputy keeper's report, appendix II to 4th report, pp 291-2, Latin. Pouch 55 contains 12 membranes, the legal instruments neccessary for Squier's trial; no. 7 is justice Roger North's precept for the return of the petty jury for the trial; no. 8 is a list of 26 names from which 12 were chosen; no. 9 is the justice's precept to John Peyton, lieutenant of the Tower, to have Squier at Westminster great hall on Thursday 9.11.; no. 12 is Elizabeth's writ of Mandamus of 6.11. to form a commission of oyer and terminer.

tion and slaughter among her subjects. On 22 May 'at Seville he conspired with the late King Philip II and public enemy of the queen and false traitor who had prepared a great fleet and army to invade England and bring it into a wretched and everlasting captivity.'[27] The rest of the indictment recounted the story of the plot with its latest revisions which made Walpole hand the poison to Squier. The king of Spain was fully implicated. The plot intended the death of Essex as well as of Elizabeth. Squier made his attempt on the queen on 11 June 1597, and on Essex about 27 or 28 September.

No adequate account of Squier's arraignment and trial has so far come to light. What could be taken as deliberate suppression could only mean that the whole proceeding went wrong from the government viewpoint. It is likely that a fairly full account was forwarded to Rome by Henry Garnet, the superior of the Jesuits in England. If so it was among the many items in the English College, Rome, lost or destroyed at the time of the suppression of the Society, or subsequently. Fitzherbert commented, 'If it be true that is here reported' – in Spain – 'as it is like to be, for that we hear it uniformly from divers parts, that Squier was condemned without witnesses presented at his arraignment upon some light presumptions and his own confession extorted by torment, as he said himself at the bar, and also at his death, it is clear that he was wrongfully condemned, for that no law can allow that such a confession should suffice for the condemnation of any man without some other evident proofs.'[28] As Fitzherbert further observed, 'This Stanley testified nothing upon his own knowledge against Squier but only upon hearsay from us here which cannot suffice in law to condemn any man, especially in this case, seeing it was acknowledged by M. attorney that we of whom he was supposed to have heard it, had suborned him to overthrow Squier, and besides to do some great mischief in England under colour to accuse Squier of that matter, so that both he and we are supposed to have conspired to betray Squier ... Stanley being Squier's accuser, he could be no witness against him, for that in law they are to be distinct persons.'[29]

Although Fitzherbert's criticisms are just enough in themselves, the convention by this time was well established, as we have seen, that no witnesses needed to be called in a trial for treason. The accused could even be denied counsel.[30] Fitzherbert took the further trouble to deny that, as far as he knew, he had ever had any contact with Squier, whether by mouth or letter, and was never 'any way privy to any other man's conspiracy of the death of her Majesty or of my lord of Essex'.[31] According to Martin Array, Squier, while denying any attempt at murder in England himself, was ready to accuse Walpole of such intentions. 'And in this he stood stiffly all the time of his arraignment until he understood first by the chief judge that he laboured in vain, for that the very concealing of the matter treated in Spain for so many months was treason of itself, though it had never been attempted to be put in execution within England itself. And secondly ... he perceived divers speeches and large discourses made unto him by

27 Edwards, 'The strange case ...', p. 60.   28. Fitzherbert, 2v.   29 Ibid., 9r/v.   30 Edwards, *The marvellous chance*, pp 213-14.   31 Fitzherbert, 1r.

sundry councillors, but especially by secretary Cecil, exhorting him to confess the whole, that except he yielded to all as it lay in the first tale, there was no hope of favour and mercy. And then he falling down upon his knees confessed all again. But yet afterwards, when he found also by experience that this would would not save his life nor keep him from execution – whereof it is likely that he had hope if not full promise – he denied the matter again at his death as they can witness who were present at the same and heard him, whereof also some have written the same hither.'[32] Fitzherbert commented on his and Walpole's alleged part, 'As I understand that Mr Coke ... was a principal actor in the tragedy of Squier ... and ... a notable calumniator in belying and slandering me with F. Walpole and others, charging me not only with discovering the matter to Stanley ... but also with imparting it to the king my master ... making his Majesty thereby an abettor of the imaginary conspiracy, I cannot forbear to answer him briefly ... I have not got so little experience and skill of kings' humours in these fifteen or sixteen years ... that if I should have employed Squier or any man else to kill her Majesty I would have acquainted any king or foreign prince therewith, whereby they might take me for a queen- or kingkiller. For howsoever the act might turn to their benefits ... I am sure they would say with Augustus Caesar, I love the treason but I hate the traitor; besides ... they hold it for a necessary point of state to maintain the sovereign majesty of princes as sacred and inviolable, yea though it be of their very enemies ... [Philip's] royal heart was no more compatible with murders and mischiefs than [Coke's] base mind is capable of kingly conceits ... I must hold you either for the simplest or else the most malicious man that ever occupied your place.'[33]

Like the trial, there is no satisfactory record of Squier's execution. But it is evident that the stage management failed to make it work out convincingly for Cecil. As Henry More observed, 'the entire tragedy was indeed a hollow sham apart from the death of Squier which was real enough.'[34] At all events, he had not long to wait for the end. He was executed at Tyburn on 13 November according to the ghastly ritual customary for traitors. Some who saw it wrote to Fitzherbert who commented, 'This I affirm as well upon divers relations that I have seen thereof in writing, as also upon the credible report of a credible person who was present at his execution with whom I have spoken here in Madrid ... ' Squier at the end repudiated all part in it so that the sheriff 'was kindled with great choler against the poor man for denying it, but also ... all the assistants and beholders who were much amazed to hear matter so far from their expectations there uttered by him that died.'[35]

'When all this got back to Walpole himself, his first reaction was to laugh at it as the idle imagining of a lunatic.'[36] Nevertheless when he heard how the bizarre story was being exploited in England to discredit him and his Society the smile soon faded. So

32 Aray, p. 12. 33 Ibid., p. 15r. 34 Edwards, *The Elizabethan Jesuits*, p. 281. 35 Fitzherbert, p. 38v. In the latter part of this treatise (37v-43r) he takes the author of the *Authentic Memoirs* to task, for his untruths against Squier as well as his attacks on the Society of Jesus. The same pamphlet was discussed and answered also in an appendix to *The discoverie and confutation*, pp 12v-14v. 36 *The Elizabethan Jesuits*, p. 279.

slight was Squier's acquaintance with Walpole that he did not even remember his name aright. In Squier's trial and examinations, the Jesuit is referred to as 'William' throughout. We need hardly recount Walpole's obvious points offered to refute the absurdities of the story. He concluded, 'No doubt Divine Providence saw to it deliberately that matter patently absurd should be mixed in with the rest' so that no one unblinded by prejudice or party spirit could fail to read the true meaning.[37] 'Who doth not see it were too childish to imagine I would build so important an enterprise upon so slight a foundation as was the weak conceit which I had of Squier's integrity? ... Lastly what likelihood, I pray you, that if I had used Squier so confidently in a matter of such moment, he would have stolen away with such fear and secrecy not daring to make me privy thereunto?'[38]

Walpole was under no illusions as to the mind which lay behind the plot, but Robert Cecil's manoeuvres were still clumsy compared with Burghley's. 'Herein the young cub seems nothing so cunning as the old fox his father.'[39] But the young cub was learning all the time. He would improve dramatically until in the gunpowder plot he produced a masterpiece; or at least a contrivance flawless enough to deceive for centuries many well-intentioned people as well as those willing to be deceived. There are still those, understandably, who have no motive for delving too deeply beneath the surface of a story which has fitted the national mythology so well and for so long.

Although the kind of analysis from sources which we can make in our own day, and the knowledge of each other and of their Society possessed by the Jesuits in that day, are sufficient to demonstrate the absurdity of the plot, it was by no means unsuccessful as propaganda. Someone like Francis Duckett, who had presumably not been present at the execution, could write, 'My wife hath kept such company since my going to London, and is so obstinate in a dangerous course touching religion as I fear the troubles such undutiful courses do deserve. And though my opinions have sometimes been addicted that way, yet I protest, since I saw the treacheries revealed of the Jesuits by Squier the traitor in Michaelmas term last, I have abjured their irreligious and damnable courses against the state.'[40] Such a plot, flimsy by the evidence offered, doubtless provided many waverers with a good excuse and honourable pretext for abandoning a faith which was costing its adherents increasingly dear. All the same, it represented a great flaw in this kind of propaganda that the victim might ruin the effect by going back on earlier statements and confessions once he arrived at the scaffold. A final maintenance of innocence destroyed most of the value of what went before.

It was a cynical world but less unbelieving than our own. Most men in Squier's position believed sufficiently in the afterlife and retribution, and the ultimate demands of truth, to prevent them from wanting to go before the God in whom they still firmly believed with a grave lie or calumny on their consciences. Even the villains believed

---

37 Ibid., p. 208.   38 Ibid.   39 R. Walpole to Henry Garnet, from Seville, 12.5.1599, signed original?; English College archives, Valladolid, ms Ser. II, L. 1, unfoliated.   40 F. Duckett to R. Brother, 31.5.1599; *Sal. Cal.*, 9, pp 186-7. Ibid; ms 70/67.

in their own fashion. So a means had to be found to convince those involved in any future rigged plots that they could go safely to the scaffold with their lies; nay, witness the shadow of the axe over their necks, and still be convinced that if they played their part and upheld the charade they could put off telling the truth until a later date. The means would be found.

It seems only fair before leaving the subject of Squier and his infamous treatment by Cecil and his trusties in government to admit that similar injustices were not unknown abroad. Thomas Fitzherbert, a witness whose integrity we can hardly doubt, underwent a similar experience in Brussels in 1595 when he was working for the duke of Feria. 'I was through the rigorous if not malicious proceedings of a certain judge brought to be accused by two several persons, not only to have intelligence with Sir Robert Cecil, whose honour knoweth how ignorant I am thereof – but also to have conspired together with them the burning of the king's munition at Mechlin.'[41] Fortunately for Fitzherbert, Archduke Albert and his council knew him well enough to arrange for an interview at which he was easily able to clear himself. The fact emerged that the original judges in the case 'had not only given two torments to [two] prisoners without just cause, and so forced them to accuse both me and themselves wrongfully, but also confronted them together in such sort, that one instructed the other what he should say. Yea, and that he razed their depositions that were different and made them agree by his own art. Whereto the prisoners consented also for fear of new torments, choosing rather to die than to endure the same, and determining to discharge their consciences at their deaths, as well for their own purgation as mine.'[42] So it would be unjust to suppose that Cecil and his friends were doing something unprecedented in manoeuvring the machinery of state for the darker purposes of revenge or statecraft. It would be naive to suppose that while it happened abroad, it could not happen in England. As for Fitzherbert, was it Cecil who began the false rumours against him?

---

41 Fitzherbert, p. 3v.   42 Ibid.

Robert Devereux, earl of Essex

We come to the elimination of Robert Devereux, second earl of Essex. We cannot talk of a plot in the sense in which the term has been applied to events so far described. Nevertheless, the manner in which Robert Cecil stalked his prey from perhaps as early as 1593, and more discernibly from 1599, shows the second Cecil possessed of the same kind of resourcefulness, single-mindedness and patience of the hunter displayed if less maturely in plots more deserving of the name. He also showed a singular ability for interpreting the ambiguities of a rival's situation so as to make it look the worst for him and the best for himself. The exploitation of weakness was an art brought to perfection by the Cecils. Because of these men of genius, the earl of Essex, like the fourth duke of Norfolk, though his flaws were quite dissimilar, made himself in the long run the inevitable loser in any trial of strength with Sir Robert. The Lopez and Yorke-Williams plots revealed an ugly side to Essex, but it was one he shared with many of his generation. Cecil was no better but much more competent. As a man who made bad mistakes, and above all as a loser, historians have not been kind to Essex. Perhaps E.P. Cheyney took the kindest view possible. 'If the earl of Essex had been born a king, he would have been a gracious, popular and reasonably happy monarch. Adventurous, alertminded, quick to reward merit, appreciative of devotion, affable, liberal, he would have rejoiced in the popularity it was so easy for him to win. Born a subject as he was, under the repressive authority of the queen, and restricted by the rival influences of other statesmen and courtiers, his limitless ambition, his desire for glory and applause, gave him no rest or satisfaction in life.'[1] And in the end destroyed him.

Robert Cecil's ambition, like his father's, was limitless, but he never forgot his place as a subject. While he did his best, and successfully, to make himself, like Burghley, indispensable to the queen, he never presumed on any occasion to treat her Majesty even approximately as an equal. Essex did. So while he strutted arrogantly to his ruin the Cecils slipped discreetly into the position of prince consorts if not uncrowned kings. There can be no doubt about the superior intelligence of the Cecils, William and Robert, over the rest of their generation. Monarchs might not love them for it, but

---

1 E. P. Cheyney, *A history of England from the defeat of the Armada to the death of Elizabeth* (London, 1926), ii, p. 421.

they found they could not dispense with their loyal and discreet services. The riches they acquired for their house and line could thus be easily excused.

Sir Robert Cecil received his formal appointment as principal secretary on 5 July 1596. He lost no time in consolidating his position with the queen. Essex was still in near eclipse, largely self-imposed since he had not reacted magnanimously or diplomatically to recent setbacks. The queen had not been happy with the Lopez affair. And Essex continued to sulk over appointments to office which were not to his liking. While he sulked in the shadows, the secretary made the most of his time in the sun. He spent most of the day with Elizabeth, influencing her 'rather by his tongue than his pen'.[2] He procured the appointment of Lord Burgh as the new lord deputy for Ireland and Richard Bancroft as the bishop of London. This 'gave Cecil virtual control of all printing and publishing' since practically all the printers were in London.[3] While Cecil consolidated his position by staying as close to the skirts of royalty as possible, Essex accepted on 12 March 1597 a post which could take him even further from the royal presence. This was against the advice of his astute protégé Francis Bacon. Master of the ordnance, Essex was now set on the military career which would keep him away from court, and enable rivals, including Cecil, to manoeuvre against him to their heart's content. Cecil slipped easily into the place of his father as the principal confidant of the aging and doting queen.

In October 1597, Cecil became chancellor of the duchy of Lancaster. This gave him the determining influence in the north-west. A new circumstance this year promised improved relations among the great courtiers. All seemed to herald peace and light as preparations were made for war in the Islands expedition of May 1597. This was planned by Essex, Ralegh and Cecil together. Experienced courtiers remained unconvinced of Cecil's sincerity. Sir William Knollys, Essex's uncle, warned him in a letter of June 1597, 'If we lived not in a cunning world, I should assure myself that Mr Secretary were wholly yours ... I will hope the best, yet will I observe him as narrowly as I can.' He wrote again, 'Mr Secretary remaineth in all show firm to your lordship, and no doubt will, so long as the queen is so well pleased with you.'[4] The difficulty was, her Majesty's favour tended to go in and out like the sun behind passing clouds.

Cecil was absent in France in 1598 in connection with the peace of Vervins between France and Spain. In that time, 'Essex made no attempt to injure Cecil'.[5] But as Cecil understood only too well, gratitude, even if it is sometimes a political virtue, cannot be allowed to stand in the way of true progress. Nor could it be interpreted as ingratitude to manoeuvre a rival into a position where, by his own choice, he became less of a rival. While Cecil was on his embassy, Essex seemed to do his best to injure his own cause. He succeeded in bringing about a cool reconciliation between his mother, Lettice

2 P. M. Handover, *The Second Cecil: 1563-1604* (London 1959), p. 152. Her insight into the politics of the court and period makes her book essential reading still.   3 Ibid., p. 153.   4 W. Knollys to Essex, June 1597; T. Birch, *Memoirs of the reign of Queen Elizabeth*, 2 vols. (London 1754), ii, p. 351 and pp 351-2; quoted Handover, p. 156 and n. 14.   5 Ibid., p. 174.

Knollys, and the queen. But although his wife was pregnant, he had an affair with Elizabeth Brydges, a royal maid of honour. Elizabeth, if she found out, would not have been amused. He produced an apology defending his anti-Spanish policy but it 'was not a constructive document but rather a glorification of the pomp and circumstance of war'.[6] It appeared in print in June 1598. The earl affected astonishment, but as it had been in the form of a letter to Antony Bacon, his reaction at its appearance could hardly have been sincere. For the rest he showed little interest in the daily drudgery of office correspondence or in the reports which came to him from the agents set up for him by Antony Bacon in an 'extensive and efficient service'. He was adequate on theory: 'intelligence is the light of a state'.[7] But clearly, he lacked the intelligence and staying power needed to exploit a situation where he might have repeated former success and increased his influence. The Cecils were professionals. Essex was an amateur and perilously close to being a playboy for too much of the time. Elizabeth, like an understanding aunt, indulged him like a spoiled and adolescent nephew. But this could not go on for ever. If he had not the capacity to be a serious rival to the Cecils, he still had too much influence to be left on a destructive course as a loose canon. The shape of things to come was already present before the Irish campaign.

An ambivalent opportunity for both Roberts came with the need to pacify Ireland and to find someone who would undertake what most took to be an extremely thankless task. More than one English reputation had in the past been engulfed in the bogs of Ireland. Before real trouble began, harmony was early threatened. Essex wanted Sir George Carew, a friend of Cecil, to be given the command. Elizabeth overrode Essex and designated Sir William Knollys. Essex, typically, could only take this as a personal slight. In a colourful incident at court, he gave way to temper to the extent of swinging round and turning his back on the queen. Roused to fury, she boxed his ears. Essex then spontaneously laid hand to his sword. It needed the lord admiral standing by to restrain him. Still out of control of himself, the earl strode angrily from the chamber declaring that he would not suffer such insult even from an Henry VIII. One courtier commented, 'I know but one friend and one enemy my lord hath; and that one friend is the queen and that one enemy is himself.'[8] The queen could be surprisingly long-

---

6 Ibid.   7 Essex to Dr Hawkins, 27. 2.1596; Birch, i, p. 429; quoted, Handover, p. 174.   8 F. Bacon, *Apothegms*, quoted in Spedding, ii, and in Handover, p. 178. For the earlier career of Essex, see P. E. J. Hammer, *The polarisation of Elizabethan politics: the political career of Robert Devereux, 1585-1597* (Cambridge 1999). This study on the demise of Essex was completed before the appearance of Hammer's work, a work of monumental scholarship. The sources indicated in notes and bibliography are rich in information. The author, as has been noted elsewhere, shows the common reluctance of scholars to admit that the frequent plots apparently occurring throughout the reign were, more probably than not, contrivances of government to bring enemies and rivals to ruin. Nevertheless, *The polarisation of Elizabethan politics* ... is by no means an essay in whitewashing, and the credibility of the thesis of the present book emerges from his well-documented survey of the court of Elizabeth and her courtiers at the time under review. Essex emerges as a character to be taken seriously many ways, as a soldier, organiser, and servant of the state. Undoubtedly, the loss of opportunities in so many directions, which were acquired by Robert Cecil when he became secretary of state, a place

suffering. Perhaps she feared to destroy the equilibrium set up by the rival factions in the court which centred on Essex and the Cecils. So Essex did not fall completely from grace. But how long could he survive? Handover justly commented on this piece of folly, 'When by such actions he failed to destroy her tolerance of him, Cecil could only wait.'[9] He did not have to wait long. Nor could he do less than work quietly for the earl's downfall since Essex made no secret that he still regarded Cecil as his principal enemy. In this at least the earl's judgement seems to have been sound.

Essex returned to court and favour in October 1598. After much manoeuvring by his critics and enemies, and against the better advice of truer friends, especially Francis Bacon, he assumed the command of the expedition to pacify Ireland. The earl himself was well aware of the dangers of the task. He had some inkling of the damage enemies and rivals at court, especially Cecil, and to a lesser extent Cobham and Ralegh, could inflict on him in his absence. By this time, for most commentators, Essex can do nothing right and responds only foolishly or wrongly to circumstances. We have seen that there is justification for a harsh judgement if we only consider his performance as a courtier. All the same, his acceptance of the command, knowing the risks it entailed, surely argued public spirit even if mingled with love of glory and a desire to strut in the public eye. Hammer's careful study of the earl's earlier career fully bears this out.

Essex set out for Ireland on 27 March 1599. On the controversial Irish camapaign to bring the earl of Tyrone and others into subjection, J.B. Black's comments still seem valid. The main task was to overcome Tyrone who prevailed in the north. But Essex decided first to reduce Leinster and Munster. As Black observed, 'Some critics assert that the earl ought now to have hurled all his available forces against Ulster in a single concentrated blow, regardless of risk, with a view to capturing the rebel and destroying his hideout; but this is mere armchair tactics, betraying a complete misunderstanding of the military situation. If Essex had attempted, in response to the angry promptings and bitter criticisms of the queen, to launch an all-out offensive against Tyrone with the troops at his disposal, in the existing state of their morale, he would have courted irretrievable disaster.'[10] If one ask why the queen, an amateur in the role of Boudicca, was so critical of Essex, the obvious answer could be taken without prejudice to lie primarily in the presence of Cecil who was almost constantly at her elbow and the ablest of the voices advising her.

coveted by the earl, relegated Essex almost automatically to second place whatever else he achieved. Add to this the rivalry and the determination to oust all rivals on the part of the new secretary, even if it meant their destruction, which gave the earl scant prospect of survival let alone success. This rivalry is clearly shown in Hammer's book and the inevitability of the outcome which still lay in the future in 1597. Meanwhile, if the portrait of Essex is given the third dimension it deserves, warts and all, the traditional view of Essex and his ascent and decline are not radically changed from the traditional view of Essex given by earlier writers. His prowess as a soldier was clearly vicdicated by J.B. Black in the 2nd edition of his *The reign of Elizabeth* (Oxford 1959). 9 Handover, Ibid. 10 J. B. Black, *The reign of Elizabeth: 1558-1603*, 2nd ed. (Oxford 1959), p. 434. See also L. W. Henry, 'The earl of Essex and Ireland, 1599', Bulletin of the Institute of Historical Research, vol. xxxii, no. 85, May 1959, pp 1-23.

Essex was not supported in his reasonable demands for reinforcements, especially for pack horses, which were not available in Ireland. But even Sir William Knollys supported Cecil in encouraging him not to send the horses as demanded.[11] Could it be that Knollys, a shrewd statesman and careful of his own interests, had decided by now that his nephew's cause was already as good as finished? If so, his conclusion should have been immature. Black commented, 'we might almost conclude that the Cecilian party in the council were none too anxious for the expedition to succeed'.[12] It is significant that when later on Mountjoy was sent to replace Essex in the command no difficulty was made in meeting his need for horses. Mountjoy was predestined for success, Essex was not. It was not simply due to fate. 'It has been customary with historians', declared Black, 'to condemn Essex for "wasting his time" fruitlessly in the south. But it should be borne in mind that the decision to move into Leinster was taken on purely military grounds, was unanimous, and represented the considered opinion' – of men on the spot – 'who knew what they were talking about.'[13] Furthermore, Essex had prior warning, it seems, of Tyrone's intention of making a raid into Munster. It is noteworthy that 'Mountjoy followed the same tactics a year later without any disapproval from London'.[14]

On 25 June 1599 the earl sent a report to the queen which summed up the difficulties of the situation in which any English commander would find himself. Unfortunately, if Essex showed himself a good judge in matters military, he showed no skill in concealing unpleasant truths from those who could and would present them in the worst possible light. Thus he admitted that the war would be 'great, costly and long'.[15] What was worse, he allowed his suspicion of Cobham and Ralegh's dealings behind his back to slop over into open criticism of the queen's favour towards them. Soon after, Blount, Southampton and Rutland were recalled. In three more letters the queen further clarified her displeasure at Essex's proceedings. A letter of 30 July even cancelled his leave to return for England for consultation when and if he should see fit. Essex did not conceal the low state of morale. 'Your army which never yet abandoned the body of any principal commander being dead, doth now run away from their chief commander being alone and in fight; and ... your people had rather be hanged for cowardice, than killed or hurt in service.'[16] She remained unimpressed and presumed to dismiss his council of war as 'men of slender judgment'.[17] In all of this we could reasonably discern the influence of his most effective and most relentless rival who at least would have done nothing to support him in the queen's presence.

A curious rumour reached the court in August 1599 to the effect that a Spanish fleet had landed in the Isle of Wight. It was a false rumour, but Cecil made it the excuse for calling out a general muster and letting it be believed that another Armada was on the way. This could be seen as an excuse for continuing to refuse necessary reinforcements and supplies which Essex continued to demand quite reasonably for Ireland. Cecil must have known full well the unreality of the latest threat. Ominously, early in the

---

11 Black, p. 430.   12 Ibid., p. 432.   13 Ibid.   14 Ibid.   15 Ibid., p. 435.   16 Ibid.   17 Ibid.

alarm, Elizabeth told Essex to stay in Ireland. He was now in a situation, ideal from his enemies' viewpoint, where even friendly observers, given his well-known propensities, could only expect him to go from bad to irretrievable blunder. Which he obligingly did. The truce with Tyrone arranged on 8 September 1599 was in the circumstances unavoidable; but it was unwise to let it take place without witnesses. Black concluded reasonably that, although it was agreed either side could end the truce on fourteen days' notice, in effect it left the initiative to the Irish earl.[18]

It seems unnecessary to recount for present purposes in much detail a story often told. The basic facts seem incontrovertible. Worth noting is the part played by Robert Cecil in the unfolding of the last act of the Essex tragedy. Cecil had no serious rival to the queen's attention while Essex was plodding literally and metaphorically through the Irish bog. Little Robin was thus able to consolidate his hold on sovereign and state by doing his own kind of plodding. According to one observer, the queen 'is wholly directed by Mr Secretary, who now rules all as his father did'.[19] Unquestionably, he was efficient, reliable, hardworking and patient so she had no reason to withhold favour. On 21 May 1599, he became master of the court of wards, a most important step for several reasons. First, it was highly lucrative. Lord Burghley had drawn £1,000 per annum from the sale of wardships apart from the profits of the eight he kept for himself. Furthermore, 'with perquisites on such a scale, it was possible to limit financial manipulation to this one source, where the small staff made secrecy possible, and so to preserve reputation as well as financial stability.'[20]

The wards office was an important factor in the Cecilian war on popery. 'The court of wards was a chief weapon in controlling the Catholic families, for Catholic wards were given to guardians who would bring them up in the Protestant faith.'[21] Essex, who also aspired to the post, which was finally conferred during his absence in Ireland, would probably have dealt more chivalrously with the children of Catholic parents although no Catholic himself. But as Handover put it, with her kind of realism, 'a long memory and a ruthless vigilance were essential qualifications; and Essex had neither'.[22]

As we have seen, in the first week of September 1599, Essex met Tyrone in a fateful interview at the river Lagan, on the edge of County Monaghan. He had reduced Tyrone to the point where he was forced to seek a truce – as he had done before. It was not defeat for Essex but neither was it victory. Essex granted the truce on 8 September and wrote to the queen recommending that it be granted. In the days before the telegraph it was the kind of decision which a commander in the field had to make on his own initiative. In England his predicamnent was not appreciated. Seeing the truce as anti-climax if not equivalently defeat, Elizabeth under the influence of her advisers in London, sent a peremptory refusal. On the receipt of her letter on 24 September,

18 Ibid., p. 436. See also Cyril Falls, *Elizabeth's Irish wars* [1560-1602] (London, 1996), 2nd edition. 19 F. Cordale to H. Galdelli, 21.7.1599; *Cal. SP Dom.*, 1598-1601, pp 251-2. Quoted Handover, p. 191. 20 Handover, p. 190. See also Joel Hurstfield, *The Queen's wards* (London 1958). 21 Handover, p. 181. 22 Ibid., p. 196.

Essex put the army under the command of the earl of Ormonde and left Dublin forthwith for London. He did not return alone. With him came 'Southampton, Rutland, Sir John Harington, his personal household, most of the knights he had created, and the better part of the captains and gentlemen of the army'.[23] At the end of his tether – his tethers were never long – Essex had ignored the queen's order not to return. On 28 September 1599 he was at Nonesuch presenting himself to the queen in her bedchamber at 10 a.m. before she was even properly wigged and gowned. Overcome by surprise, her first reaction was still not unfavourable; but she soon recovered herself and her sense of what was fitting. Essex, magnanimous in success and victory, and impatient – almost petulant and childish in adversity – had reacted with his usual precipitancy and lack of foresight. In the next few months before his execution on 25 February 1601, his enemies might have dictated almost everything he did to make sure of his final defeat.

Essex' sudden and unexpected return to Nonesuch on 28 September presented a problem for court and government alike. Cecil's behaviour as already an astute and practised politician was exemplary at the meetings of queen and council convened to deal with the problem earl. From the first, on 28 September and subsequently Sir Robert never erred. Essex, when he became aware of his real predicament, proceeded with uncharacteristic caution for a time: so circumspectly in fact that it seemed he might even now secure reinstatement. The queen would have been willing to see him restored in honour and influence since she understood the principle of divide et impera in managing court and government. The Lopez affair had most recently revealed the danger to her authority when her leading courtiers were at one. At a third meeting of the council on the same day, 28 September in the afternoon, convened once again to examine the charges against the earl, only Cecil, Hunsdon, North and Knollys could be found for a sparse gathering. A turn in the earl's fortunes seemed so likely that some who had been ready to censure now felt it discreet to melt into the background. The handsome and dashing favourite might still prevail over the deformed, diminutive first secretary. And the earl might wish to visit retribution on any who had seemed to oppose him. Few were ready to face the possibility of his political vengeance. While the careful ones stayed away, Sir Robert kept cool and unafraid. He made the most of a memory for recent events far superior to the earl's and put him in the shade several times in argument. Nevertheless, Essex at this meeting acquitted himself well.

But the end was still a long way off even if the queen's indignation still burned brightly. Essex 'was not permitted to see his wife: he was suffering from stone in the kidney; and his beseeching letters to the queen were unanswered ... At Michaelmas he was deprived of his monopoly of sweet wines, the proceeds of which formed the main part of his income. ' "An unruly beast", remarked Elizabeth, "must be stopped of his provender".'[24] He was told at the end of the meeting on 28 September to keep to his rooms.

23 Black, pp 436–7.   24 Handover, p. 197.

On 29 September he was brought before a full council 'where he had to stand bare-headed before the table while he endured a heavy grilling lasting five hours'. 'He bore this treatment with good humour, for he was still convinced that he could explain everything so satisfactorily that he would be restored to favour, and that Cecil then would pay the price.'[25] But the end result was far from what he had wished. The council's report – it took them only a quarter of an hour to compile – to which Knollys acquiesced with the rest, found his truce with Tyrone indefensible and his unauthorised departure from Ireland tantamount to desertion of duty. He was given into the custody of Lord Keeper Egerton at York House. If Essex still had a long way to go, for Cecil the worst was already over.

On 6 October Egerton, Buckhurst and Cecil visited Essex at York House. After a three-hour discussion the earl announced that he would accept the advice offered him to retire into private life. All parted amicably, with Cecil assuring Essex that he would do everything possible for his contentment for which Essex expressed thanks.[26] But his supporters did their best to maintain his dislike of Cecil, and Cecil was aware of the fact. 'Of course, the entire populace was with Essex: the Church preached clemency, and prayers were offered up for the sufferer; while pamphlets and papers were scattered broadcast in the streets praising his virtues and libelling his supposed enemies.'[27] Cecil therefore did his best to give the impression that the last person in the world to wish harm to Elizabeth's falling favourite was her principal secretary. Too conveniently, perhaps, he heard from Ireland a few days later – who was his informant? – that Essex 'had no resolution to do other than betray the kingdom as soon as he could get advantage, towards which he did prepare all things'.[28] This information was conveyed to Sir Henry Neville on 24 October. Neville was among those who joined the Essex faction later. It is likely that this honest man already had misgivings about any charge of treason levelled at Essex.

It seems certain that Essex, during his confinement at York House, was in touch with James VI with a view to enlisting his diplomatic support. To compound the complications of the situation, the negotiation was carried out secretly by Mountjoy, an Essex supporter. But Cecil also was to make contact with the king before Elizabeth's death in connection with the forbidden, and what she took to be the treasonable, subject of the succession.[29] Meanwhile Essex' cause had to face the fatal setback presented by Tyrone's threatened resumption of the offensive in Ireland at the end of the six-week period agreed in the truce.[30] In October, Mountjoy was appointed to replace Essex as lord deputy in Ireland. Cecil did not attempt to block it since he knew

25 R. Whyte to R. Sidney, 13.10.1599; Arthur Collins, editor, *Letters and memorials of state*, (the Sidney papers), 2 vols. 1746, ii, 133; quoted Handover, p. 199.   **26** Black, p. 437.   **27** R. Cecil to Sir Henry Neville, 24.10.1599, *Winwood's memorials*, i, p. 118; quoted Handover, p. 199.   **28** Handover, p. 200. See *The secret correspondence of Sir Robert Cecil with James VI of Scotland*, E. Goldsmid's edition (Edinburgh 1887). See n. 92.   **29** Tyrone to Sir William Warren, 29.10.1599, PRO SP Ireland 1599-1600, p. 205. Quoted Handover, pp 199-200.   **30** R. Whyte to R. Sidney, 13.12.1599; *Sidney papers*, ii, p. 150. Quoted Handover, p. 201.

Mountjoy was a man to be trusted by all sides, and also that this would be a way to wean him from his loyalty to Essex.

Meanwhile, Essex, always vulnerable to even the bluntest arrows of outrageous fortune, gave way to despair and fell seriously ill. Cecil, who always had a sensitive finger on the public pulse, and a perfect understanding of the need to maintain correct appearances, obtained permission for Lady Essex to visit her husband. He also had him moved to the lord keeper's own apartments at York House.[31] On 28 November 1599, at the end of the law term, and according to precedent, Cecil gave a lengthy speech in the star chamber at a meeting between council and judges justifying government policy. It included a description of the earl's 'disobedience and desertion' to justify his continued detention and disfavour. It was intended to percolate into the country and win the nation from the earl to the administration. Its success was partial. 'Since he was unpopular, it was counted against him, and the legend of Robertus diabolus received new accretions.'[32] Not until 5 June 1600 after eight months of confinement was Essex brought before eighteen commissioners for formal trial, presided over by lord keeper Egerton. Others present included Thomas Fleming, Francis Bacon and inevitably Robert Cecil. Some two hundred 'men of quality' and from the professions witnessed the scene. Coke managed the prosecution. On his knees, the earl had to listen to the charges of making too many knights, campaigning through Munster, conferring with Tyrone and deserting his post. Rather surprisingly, when the time came for the verdict the commissioners could not agree. Handover admitted, 'the case against Essex had misfired. There was too much insistence upon the knighthoods conferred, and the appointment of Southampton to be master of the horse against the queen's wish.'[33] Although these were matters the queen found of great importance, 'Cecil had tried to divert her from her concentration upon points which weakened the case against Essex'.[34] All the same, Cecil adroitly succeeded in conveying the impression to many that he had actually used his influence on behalf of the earl. 'By employing his credit with her Majesty on behalf of the earl, he has gained great credit to himself, both at home and abroad.'[35] Essex, found guilty on several charges, was punished by deprivation of his public offices and returned to virtual confinement.

Not until 26 August 1600 was he finally set free although still forbidden to come to court. Already the unaccustomed show of humility and acceptance throughout was turning to exasperation. 'The queen had thrust him down into a private life; and he could not serve with base obsequiousness.'[36] Never a model of patience, by November 1600 the earl broke under the strain. In Sir John Harington's words, 'he shifteth from sorrow and repentance to rage and rebellion'; so much rebellion, at least in word, that he did more than mutter scorning phrases regarding the queen. Far from beautiful,

31 R. Whyte to R. Sidney, 13.12.1599; *Sidney papers*, ii, p. 150. Quoted Handover, p. 201. But Lady Essex was only allowed visits to her husband during the day. See Black, p. 437. 32 Handover, ibid. 33 Handover, p. 206. Cf. Black, p. 438. 34 Handover, p. 207. 35 J. Petit to Peter Halins, 14.6.1600; *Cal. SP Dom.*, 1598–1601, p. 442. Quoted Handover, p. 207. 36 Black, p. 438.

she was 'cankered' with a mind 'as crooked as her carcase'.[37] He was convinced, and at least in this he was surely right, that he was surrounded by enemies at court who desired his overthrow; not least Sir Robert Cecil. Cecil's attitude could not be attributed simply to rivalry or malice but to what he took to be the demands of Realpolitik.

The rest of the earl's story, centred on the 'rising', until he came to be tried before his peers on 19 February 1601, needs no retelling in the present context. Suffice it to say that the published lists of those who took part in this ill-considered and badly managed affray make it clear that this was no Mayday riot. The names reflected the popular hatred of the Cecilian regime and the desire of many in high and responsible places to establish an alternative to the reign of a second King Cecil. Besides Essex and Southampton and their immediate supporters were the earls of Rutland and Bedford, noble lords such as Monteagle, Sanders, Arundell, and representatives of leading families – Sir Charles and Sir Jocelyn Percy, Sir Henry Carew, Sir Ferdinando Gorges, Sir Robert Vernon, Sir Henry Lumley, Sir Carey Reynell, Sir John Scot. There were among them responsible statesmen like Sir Henry Neville and Sir Henry Bromley. Already the gunpowder plot looms on the horizon. Noteworthy is the number of names involved later as important figures in the plot story. Lord Monteagle, Francis Tresham, his close friend Robert Catesby, John Grant and John and Christopher Wright.[38]

Robert Cecil, as might be expected, after Essex' failed attempt to rid Elizabeth's court by force of his party once and for all, knew exactly what to do. And did it. Without delay, examinations were made and evidence taken even while the world was recovering from the general confusion. On 9 February it was Cecil who began arrangements for the trial and did most of the day's work on several days. Cautious souls on the council still showed 'a tendency to vanish'.[39] Buckhurst felt the onset of an ague, Fortescue went lame, and most of their colleagues, no doubt, were anxious not to take the initiative in what might even now be a perilous undertaking. The situation was certainly resolved by 13 February when key members of the privy council, sitting as the arbitrary court of star chamber, made a public statement. This followed the Cecil line in most of the charges. The earl was attacked for his 'ingratitude' to Elizabeth, favour shown to both puritans and papists, 'intrigues' with Tyrone and lesser matters. Cecil even claimed that 'he had been devising five or six years to be King of England; had wit, and much power put into his hand, and meant thus to slip into her Majesty's place'.[40] This last absurdity was too much even for a court so committed to political correctness, and at the trial this charge was not pressed.

The formal arraignment took place in Westminster Hall, the customary scene of such show trials, on 19 February. As was usual, the triers were appointed by the coun-

37 Ibid. 38 F. Edwards, *Guy Fawkes: the real story of the gunpowder plot* (London 1969), pp 44–5. See Sal. Cal., 11, p. 214. As Handover writes, 'To [Essex's] misfortune he was surrounded by men whose advancement depended upon him alone; young, hot-blooded and hot-headed, restless and reckless as the long reign of Elizabeth spun with intolerable slowness to a close.' (p. 220). But this was only one element in his misfortune. 39 Handover, p. 224. 40 Ibid.

cil, meaning primarily Cecil. Lord treasurer Buckhurst was the lord high steward. The triers included Cobham and Grey, but Essex was not allowed to challenge their presence since they were his peers. Ralegh was present as captain of the guard with forty of the queen's guard 'to attend the service'.[41] Cecil could not be one of the twenty-five noble peers who were triers but he witnessed the proceedings in a place of concealment, a deus ex machina to make sure that all went well. The lieutenant of the Tower was called upon to 'return his precept, and bring forth his prisoners, Robert, earl of Essex, and Henry, earl of Southampton'. The earls kissed one another's hands and embraced each other. They pleaded not guilty to the indictment.

The main charge was that on 8 February Essex 'went about with armed men very rebelliously to disinherit the queen of her crown and dignity'.[42] Like Catiline in his Roman venture, 'Essex entertained the most seditious persons ... to join with him in his conspiracy ... none but papists, recusants and atheists.' The day's events on 8 February were recounted in some detail. Coke showed that to raise 'power and strength in a settled government ... is construed as in case of high treason'. It was also treasonable to assemble power, as Essex had done, and refuse 'to dissolve his company when called on by the sovereign to do so'. He also 'levied power to take the Tower of London, and to surprise the queen's own court'. [43] He ordered 'that if he and his complices should miscarry in London then the counsellors which he caused to be imprisoned in his house, should be slain'. Essex asked for leave to speak against these 'slanders' but he was interrupted so that Henry Witherington's examination could be read. An eye-witness of events, he claimed he heard cries of, 'Let us make and end of them,' referring to the imprisoned councillors, and 'that order was left' to kill the lord keeper and lord chief justice if things went wrong in London.[44] Essex denied the cries for murder. 'Mr Witherington came voluntarily to my house unsent for, and in the forenoon did come into our company, and took to heart as much as we did whatever we went about: and these are but reports, for he that is the witness, is now sent into the country about some employments.' The councillors were locked up 'intending only to save them lest they should take hurt' from the mob. Egerton, Worcester and Popham then declared they heard the words, 'Kill them. Kill them' but 'would not charge ... Essex that they were spoken either by his privity or command'.[45] The 'declaration' of these three recounting the events of 8 February was then presented to the court by Popham and how they were detained by Essex. He shouted out 'that he should have been murdered in his bed; that he had been perfidiously dealt with; that his hand had been counterfeited, and letters written in his name'. Popham assured him that if it were so justice would be done 'whomsoever it concerned'. Southampton complained of an attack on him by the Lord Grey but Popham told him Grey had already been 'imprisoned for it'. Essex' defence for refusing to stand down on being ordered by Egerton to lay down

41 State trials, 1730, I, p. 190, col. 1.   42 Ibid., p. 191, col. 1.   43 Ibid., col. 2. The point was made that in this 'rebellion ... no man racked, tortured or pressed to speak anything further than of their own accord'; p. 192, col. 1.   44 Ibid., col. 2.   45 Ibid., p. 193, col. 1.

their arms was that they were in danger of attack from outside. This 'put them into such a fear and ecstasy that it was not in my power suddenly to dissolve them'. The prosecution insisted on the heinousness of refusing to stand down when called by authority to do so on their allegiance.

As for dealing with papists, Essex averred, 'papists have been hired and suborned to witness against me; as by the means of one Sudall ... a seminary priest sent into Ireland to deal with Sir Christopher Blount, whom he thought to be inward with me, to touch my honour and reputation. Then Bales, the scrivener in the Old Bailey hath confessed under his hand to ... counterfeit my hand in at least two letters.'[46] Coke claimed that this was by the contrivance of one of his own men but Essex countered that this was done by John Daniell, 'an arrant thief, one that broke a standard of mine, and stole a casket of my wife's and many other things ... It is well-known who set him at work to attempt against me so much as ... to procure my hand to be counterfeited'.[47] The point was not taken up by the prosecution, but after charges that Sir John Davis and Blount were papists, the confession of Sir Ferdinando Gorges was read. Gorges, summoned to London by Essex to assist him in a crisis, took part in two meetings at Drury House which discussed the alternatives; 'first to surprise the court, or to take the Tower of London, or to stir in the city'. They decided to surprise the court. Davies drew up the details of the plan of action. But Gorges, aware of their small numbers, advised Essex 'to submit himself to the queen's mercy [rather] than proceed any further'. Southampton at Essex House called for action. Sir Charles Davers' examination was presented next. He claimed that before Christmas 1599 Essex wondered 'how he might secure himself to have access to the queen's presence without resistance'. Essex then wrote certain articles to Southampton how to surprise the court. After 'divers consultations', it was agreed to take the Tower, as commanding London, and then surprise the court. Or perhaps to surprise the court first. Essex would then immediately 'have called a parliament to reform disorders and private grievances'. Davers 'utterly disliked of these courses' and when the alarm was raised in the court, he advised the earl to flee into Wales or overseas' rather 'than to trust to the city'. Davers claimed he had only been drawn in 'for the love he bore to ... Southampton'.[48]

The examinations of Davis and Blount which followed added little to the preceding but Blount made one interesting admission. 'Being asked ... whether ... Essex did not give him comfort that if he came to authority there should be a toleration for religion, he confesseth he should have been to blame to have denied it.'[49] Blount's second

46 Ibid., p. 194, col. 1.   47 Ibid.   48 Gorges' and Davers' confessions, ibid., p. 194, col. 2 to 195, col. 2. 'Papers relating to Essex's conspiracy' from the Salisbury mss, complete transcripts, include Sir John Peyton to Nottingham, Hunsdon and Sir Robert Cecil of 18, 2, 1600, one letter of Henry Cuffe to R. Cecil and two to the the council, undated, and his examination on 8.3.1600, his will, a letter of Southampton to the council and another to Cecil, and his confession, all undated, Sir Charles Danvers' declaration. ascribed by L. Hicks to November 1599, and Sir Christopher Blount's examination of 13.2.1600 are in *Correspondence of King James VI ... with Sir Robert Cecil and others in England ...* , Camden Society, vol. 78 for 1861, editor John Bruce, pp 80-110.   49 Davis' and Blount's

confession not only admitted that he had been 'reconciled to the pope' but Essex said, 'he looked not any should be troubled for religion, and liberty of conscience'.[50] As Rutland's examination made clear, this did not mean that Essex had acquired any sympathy for Spain. Whatever the rights and wrongs of the Essex case, it meant that there could be no question of a more enlightened policy on religion if Cecil prevailed. England could only look forward to becoming for ever another Protestant Northern Ireland. Confessions of the Lords Sandes, Cromwell and Monteagle as reported added nothing to the status quaestionis. Coke reemphasised the fact that the truth had come to light through these confessions 'without rack or torture to any of them'.

Essex in reply pointed out that, 'the selfsame fear and the selfsame examiner may make these several examinations agree all in one were they never so far distant'. The examinees were all 'men within the danger of the law, and such as speak with a desire to live'.[51] With his own intimate experience of the trials of Lopez, Yorke and Williams, he clearly knew what he was talking about. Far from intending to take the Tower, he claimed his only purpose was 'to have come with eight or nine honourable persons, who had just cause of discontentment ... unto her Majesty, and so by petition, prostrating ourselves at her Majesty's feet, to have put ourselves unto her mercy'.[52] She would have been asked to 'have severed some from her ... who by reason of their potency with her, abused her ... with false informations': to wit, 'Cobham, Cecil and Ralegh'. He took Cobham to be the more malign influence.

Gorges was present in the court, and in a dramatic appeal, Essex asked that he be called upon to give his witness viva voce. Coke must have been tempted to point out that such an appeal was not a part of the treason trial procedure. The lord admiral, however, got in first and asked that Gorges 'might unfold openly what other secrets have passed between him and ... Essex touching the state'. Gorges said, 'All that I can remember I have delivered in my examination; and further I cannot say'. But after further pressure from Essex and Southampton he was brought to admit, 'by the oath I have taken I did never know or hear any thought or purpose of hurt or disloyalty intended to her Majesty's person by my Lord of Essex.'[53]

The lord admiral insisted on knowing if Essex ever issued 'any articles in writing under his hand ... laying open the projects for ... surprising the court and Tower'. This seems to have been satisfactorily dealt with. The next intervention was by Southampton who admitted the folly of the action of 'going through the town' but insisted that Essex' intention in having men 'planted at the court was [because] he feared hindrance by private enemies that would have stopped his passage to the queen'. After that he intended no more than a direct appeal to the queen. Francis Bacon made his unkind cut at this point comparing Essex's action to Pisistratus in antiquity who had likewise made an armed appeal to the populace. Essex' appeal had failed but what if it had not? The best thing the earl could do now would be 'to confess and not to justify'. Essex

confessions, State trials, p. 195, col. 2.   **50** Blount's 2nd confession, ibid., p. 196, col. 1.   **51** Essex' defence, ibid., p. 196, col. 2.   **52** Ibid.   **53** Gorges' testimony, ibid., p. 197, col. 1.

countered that 'when the course of private persecution was in hand' Bacon had offered to be a 'means to the queen', composing a letter in Essex' name 'and in his brother [*sic*] Sir Nicholas Bacon's name', which he intended to show the queen. The letter 'appointed them out that were my enemies as directly as might be'. Essex knew that Cecil had seen the letter 'and by him it will appear what conceit he' – Bacon – 'held of me', although he had now passed to the other side.[54] Bacon rejoined, 'I spent more hours to make you a good subject than upon any man in the world besides'. His letter would not 'blush' since it showed only Bacon's good intentions towards the earl. At this point the trial took an unexpectedly dramatic turn when Essex claimed, 'I can prove thus much from Sir Robert Cecil's own mouth that he, speaking to some of his fellow counsellors should say that none in the world but the Infanta of Spain had right to the crown of England'. The charge forced Cecil to break cover. In a coup de theatre turn, Cecil stepped out from behind a tapestry concealing a door to a room where he had been listening at the keyhole, so to speak. Already he anticipated the verdict of the court. 'The difference between you and me is great; for I speak in the person of an honest man, and you, my lord, in the person of a traitor.' He continued in a speech typical of his oratory at its best. The bland face of his portraits claimed, presumably without a blush, 'I have innocence, truth of conscience, and honesty to defend me against the scandal of slanderous tongues and aspiring hearts.' He loved Essex before he saw 'his ambitious affections inclined to usurpation'. In appearance the earl was 'humble and religious. But God be thanked, we know you: for indeed your religion appears by Blount, Davies and Tresham, your chiefest counsellors for the present, and by promising liberty of conscience hereafter'. Cecil stood for loyalty, Essex for treachery. Cecil admitted he had said the king of Scots was a 'competitor', and the king of Spain likewise. But so was Essex who wished to depose the queen, make himself king of England and call a parliament. Cecil was sorry for all those 'noble persons and gentlemen of birth' who had been drawn in. 'For my part, I vow to God, I wish my soul was in heaven and my body at rest so this had never been.'[55]

At this point, Cecil challenged Essex to name the councillor who had reported his support for the Infanta as the rightful heir to the throne. It was Southampton who named 'Mr Comptroller', Sir William Knollys as their informant. Cecil, fully exploiting the drama of the occasion, then fell on his knees and thanking God for that day asked that with the queen's permission Knollys be sent for. Knevet, the messenger, was warned not to tell Knollys why he was sent for. Knollys came. He was fully obliging to Cecil. 'I remember once in Mr Secretary's company there was a book read that treated of such matters; but I never did hear Mr Secretary use any such words or to that effect.'[56] Cecil could only thank God that 'the earl stood there as a traitor yet he was

---

54 F. Bacon's attack on Essex, ibid., col. 2. Nicholas Bacon was the father of Francis, not his brother who was Anthony. 55 R. Cecil's speech. Ibid., p. 197, col. 2, to p. 198, col. 1. 56 Knollys' witness, ibid., p. 198, col. 2. The book in question was presumably Doleman's conference on the next succession known under the title *The book of succession* published in 1594; Handover, pp 226-7. For the suc-

found an honest man'. He forgave Essex from the bottom of his heart for the wrong done him and besought God to do no less.

Southampton moved on to profess ignorance of the law which might have construed some outwartd act of his as treason but he never intended harm to her Majesty in thought or intention and could only throw himself on her mercy. For the rest he was so joined to Essex in friendship, kinship and marriage that it was inevitable he should join him in any enterprise not intending harm to the queen. His intention was only to assist Essex 'in his private quarrel'.[57] He rejected Rutland's claim that he had incited Essex to the action; and as for being a papist, 'I protest most unfeignedly, I was never conversant with any of that sort. I only knew one White a priest that went up and down the town yet did I never converse with him in all my life.' Essex made a similar protest after insisting on his desire simply to have had access to the queen for justice against his enemies and not with any intention of shedding 'one drop of their blood' himself. 'I was never papist, neither did I ever favour any sectary ... For my religion it is found, and as I live, I mean to die in it.'

Bacon resumed the attack. 'How weakly he hath shadowed his purpose, and how slenderly he hath answered the objections.'[58] A former duke of Guise had acted similarly in Paris with eight men, and at the unsuccessful end, had also claimed it was all a private quarrel. Essex could only admit, 'it was my fault to stand out', and commended those who had only followed him in loyalty to himself, but not against the queen, to her Majesty's mercy. The triers then went apart to consider their verdict after the chief judges had told them that for a subject to bring a sovereign to change his mind by a superior display of force was rebellion, and rebellion always intended 'the death and deprivation of the king'. After a deliberation lasting half an hour the peers triers unanimously found Essex and Southampton guilty. Essex accepted the verdict without further demur. 'I owe God a death, which shall be welcome, how soon soever it pleaseth her Majesty.' He emphasised that his conscience was 'free from atheism and popery'. Southampton reiterated that it was ignorance of the law that had made him go so far, and he could only submit to her Majesty's mercy. Sentence was pronounced by the lord high steward: the usual death for treason by hanging, drawing and quartering at Tyburn. Both earls received it resignedly; indeed, cheerfully. They knew the system. They could expect nothing else in this kind of trial. Essex only asked that he be allowed his usual chaplain, and that Lord Thomas Howard and the lieutenant of the Tower should take the Anglican communion with him at the end to bear witness to his true religion.

It could be seen as tragic for the country that Essex lacked those qualities of statesmanship which could have made him an adequate opponent to Cecil's policies. He led

cession question, see L. Hicks, 'Sir Robert Cecil, Fr Persons and the Succession 1600 1601', *Archivum Historicum*, An. xxiv, fasc. 47 (1955); art. in *Recusant History*, 4, pp 104-137; T. Clancy, *Papist pamphleteers* (Chicago 1964), passim especially p. 241; A. J. Loomie, 'Philip III and the Stuart succession in England, 1600-1603', *Revue belge de philologie et d'histoire*, 43, no. 2 (1965), pp 492-514).   **57** *State trials*, p. 199, col. 1.   **58** Ibid., p. 199, col. 2.   **59** J. Chamberlain to D. Carleton, 24.2.1601, *Cal. SP*

those who saw a problem for the future but his clumsy approach to its solution laid him open to the most serious charge which the lawyers, conscious of their duty to state and career, and polished in their skill, knew how to build upon even if a foundation of real evidence for treason was flimsy or non-existent. But Essex' subsequent behaviour makes commiseration difficult. It was a return to the Essex of the Lopez plot. In an interview with Cecil, Egerton and others who had taken a principal part in the trial, Essex not only admitted his 'guilt but proceeded to lay open the plot, and impeach some persons not yet called in question'.[59] He was prepared to climb out of the pit into which he had fallen by his own maladroitness on the backs of others whom he had pulled in with him.

The verdict of the trial was all that Cecil could have wished. Essex, Southampton, and four others were all sentenced to death. Southampton was pardoned, apparently through Cecil's intervention with the queen, but the others paid the supreme penalty. As in the case of the fourth duke of Norfolk in 1572, the queen was not eager to proceed to the extreme measure at least where Essex was concerned. She recalled one warrant. When Cecil had the second he saw to it that there would be no mischance by having two headsmen on the scene so that if one fainted or defaulted the other would be ready to step in.[60] The earl's death had its sympathisers. Sir Henry Wotton, some years later, observed that the queen could not be entirely exonerated from the sadness of the time. Essex 'had to wrestle with a queen's declining, or rather with her setting age, which ... is of itself the more umbratious and apprehensive, as for the most part all horizons are charged with certain vapours towards their evening.'[61]

The 'offenders' in the Essex treason were divided for official purposes into four categories. Those who were executed – six: those tried and forgiven, among whom were John and Christopher Wright, Sir Charles Percy and Sir Jocelyn Percy. 'Persons living that are condemned' included the earl of Southampton, Sir Edmund Baynham and John Littleton. A fourth category contained 'the names of those that are fined and reserved to her Majesty's use'. Among these were Sir William Parker – fined £4,000 – Robert Catesby, who was fined 4,000 marks, and Francis Tresham 3,000 marks. Sir Henry Neville, Sir Henry Bromley and Sheriff Smith were also in this group.[62] The phrase 'fined and reserved to her Majesty's use' has a subtle ambiguity about it. It could simply mean, to be dealt with at her Majesty's pleasure, meaning as things now were, as Cecil thought fit. Or it could take the meaning, and almost certainly did, that these people were to be employed for various purposes of statecraft, much as Ridolfi

Dom., 1598-1601, p. 590. Quoted, Handover, p. 227. See abstract of Essex's confession, 21.2.1601, *Cal. SP Dom.*, ibid., p. 588 for more evidence of Essex' attempt to throw the blame on his subordinates, including Cuffe, his secretary. For a detailed description of Essex' end and Ralegh's presence, see State trialS, ibid., p. 201, col. 2. **60** Council to constable of the Tower, 24.2.1601; *Cal. SP Dom.*, ibid., p. 591. Quoted Handover, pp 227-8. **61** Black, p. 441. **62** *Sal. Cal.*, part xi, p. 214. Although only six conspirators are here recorded as executed, others, like John Littleton senior may have died without record so far noticed; Edwards, *Guy Fawkes ...* , p. 46.

had been used after being shown where his best interest lay as a prisoner in Walsingham's house at the time of the eponymous plot.

It is certainly extraordinary that Francis Tresham, Robert Catesby and Parker – Baron Monteagle – to name no others, should have been ready to put their heads so near the hangman's rope and chopping block only a very few years later by their alleged voluntary participation in the gunpowder plot. It must be remembered that their fines did not buy them a pardon, only exemption for an unspecified time from arraignment and trial. According to John Throckmorton, a friend of the Treshams and Catesbys, 'the queen and council were more incensed against' young Francis Tresham 'than any whatsoever'.[63] Lady Katheryne Haward tried three times to get Tresham's 'arraignment and attainder' held up; for the verdict in any such trial was for all intents and purposes a foregone conclusion. Tresham had dared to mount guard at Essex House over the lord chief justice, and lord keeper, Essex' prisoners at the time of the affray. Lady Haward finally had recourse to John Throckmorton who obligingly 'engaged [himself] to three most honourable persons, and one especial instrument' from whom he had received his 'former good'; whatever this was.[64]

The bribe, as it was in effect, which bought Tresham temporarily off the hook, was the very considerable sum of £2,100 which was to be paid within three months 'to save his life attainder in blood, and such lands as either in possession or reversion might thereby accrue to her Majesty'. Throckmorton had to admit that it had been a hard bargain: 'the which, I protest, was the most – and is reputed here by the wiser to be the hardest cause ever carried over – of this whole tragedy.' The councillors in fact held out to the last possible moment. 'It was eleven o'clock on Tuesday night before there was resolution of any warrant for the recall of what was passed against him.' Tresham 'should have this day have been arraigned with Sir Christopher Blount, Sir John Davies, Sir Charles Danvers, Sir Gelly Mericke, Cuffe and others that must die as the principal actors'.[65] Sir Thomas Tresham, father of Francis, had to indemnify John Throckmorton for this outpouring of bloodmoney. Throckmorton had already done as much for Tresham's nephew, Robert Catesby. The fact that they came from recusant families could not have helped their case. If John Throckmorton had not professed the correct religion, his pleas would surely have gone unheard.

With the death of Essex, the supremacy of Robert Cecil was there for all to see. It is not out of place, perhaps, to consider the character of the man as he now was as seen through the eyes of a friendly biographer. 'There was a ruthlessness in his character that prevented him from being soft-hearted, a clarity of judgment and an acceptance

---

63 John Throckmorton to Sir Thomas Tresham, 5. 3.1601 BL, Add. ms 39830, ff. 51r-2v; HMC, Series 55, *varia III*, pp 109-10; Edwards, op. cit., p. 45. Much will be found on the Treshams at this time in the Clarke-Thornhill mss, BL Add. mss 39828-39836 (see Varia 55 above).   64 Egerton claimed at Essex' trial, 'We did often re quire Sir John Davis and Francis Tresham to suffer us to depart, or at the least, to suffer some one of us to go to the queen's Majesty to inform her where and in what sort we were kept. But they answered that as Essex commanded that we should not depart before his return, which, they said, would be very shortly'; *State trials*, i , p. 193, col. 2.

of harsh facts that he inherited, perhaps, from his mother [Mildred Cooke]. By comparison, his half-brother was squeamish. Of three prisoners, men likely to escape, Thomas asked if they were to be "kept in irons in the low dungeon?". If so, he wrote, "I desire it may be set down in plain words in the letter, or else they may impute this severity to me, wherein I desire to be cleared." Cecil would never have allowed the opinion of his fellows to deflect him from a course he believed politically correct and just.'[66] Doubtless Robert laid the emphasis on what was politically correct. He gave the impression of crisp, direct dealing with the problems of his office although he could sometimes show signs of wavering especially when the queen herself could not make up her mind and gave him no cue. This was because he needed to wait upon her every mood, making sure that he made no mistake that might affect his influence.

The death of his father seems to have affected him deeply. He owed much if not everything to him. 'The loss sapped his natural warmth of heart. Their relationship ... combined with his deformity ... had the result that his father boxed in his emotional life. Burghley was irreplaceable to his son. And so Cecil became more withdrawn and inscrutable, and his closest associations were not to be deep friendships, for there was a final sincerity and a last spasm of affection that he could no longer give.'[67] From now on one could say that he lived only for his work: this was to consolidate his hold on power and remove all possible rivals. He believed that all this was for the good of the country as much as for himself and his house. To attain his ends, as for his father, every means was justified especially in an emergency. And most of the time was emergency. No rivals or potential rivals could be allowed to interfere with his grasp of power and control of policy. Anyone near the seat of power who attempted to exercise judgment independent of his, or even act in matters of state without first consulting him, was his enemy and destined for removal. Like his father, he stalked his victims carefully, keeping well downwind until the moment came to strike.

65 Edwards, *Guy Fawkes* ... , p. 45.   66 Burghley to R. Cecil, 6. 9.1601; *Sal. Cal.*, xi, p. 382. Quoted in Handover, p. 209.   67 Grey to Cobham, 21.7.1598; Sal. Cal., viii, p. 269. Quoted in Handover, pp 179–80. R. Cecil had a reputation as a libertine as well as a man of extraordinary resource not to say cunning. It seems he took Sir Anthony Shirley's wife; see D. W. Davies, *Elizabethans errant*, p. 73. Bodleian Library, ms Tanner 299, has no less than 13 uncomplimentary funerary verses written soon after his death. Typical is the following (ff. 11r-13r): At Hatfield near Hartford there is a coffin A hart griping harpy of shape like a Dolphin; Whose plots and whose projects did all of them tend, To cousin the king and the state to offend ... But yet though he had all the sleights of a fox He could not prevent her that gave him the pox. No other contemporary statesman attracted such hostility. Sir Walter Cope who worked well with him, recorded another view: 'The late lord treasurer for wisdom and integrity exceeded the most, or all, that went before him, whom living the world observed with all admiration and applause; no sooner dead, but it seeketh presently to suppress his excellent parts, and load his memory with all imputations of corruption'; Bodleian Library, Tanner ms. 278, pp 503f., printed in Gutch, *Collectanea curiosa* ... (Oxford 1781), pp 119-133.

Index

PLOTS AND PLOTTERS IN THE REIGN OF ELIZABETH I

By the same author:

The dangerous queen (London 1964)
The marvellous chance (London 1968)
Guy Fawkes: the real story of the gunpowder plot? (London 1969)
The gunpowder plot: the narrative of Oswald Tesimond alias Greenway (Folio
   Society, London 1973)
The Elizabethan Jesuits (London and Chichester 1981; a translation from the
   Latin of the first six books of Henry More, S.J.'s *Historia missionis Anglicanae
   Societatis Jesu*, Saint Omer 1660)
The Jesuits in England from 1580 to the present day [1983] (Tunbridge Wells 1985)
Robert Persons: the biography of an Elizabethan Jesuit, 1546–1610 (St Louis, Mo
   1995)

FRANCIS EDWARDS, S.J.

Plots and Plotters in the Reign of Elizabeth I

FOUR COURTS PRESS

Set in 10.5 on 12.5 point Ehrhardt for
FOUR COURTS PRESS LTD
Fumbally Lane, Dublin 8, Ireland
e-mail: info@four-courts-press.ie
and in North America
FOUR COURTS PRESS
c/o ISBS, 5824 N.E. Hassalo Street, Portland, OR 97213.

A catalogue record for this title
is available from the British Library.

ISBN 1–85182–614–9

Printed in Great Britain
by MPG Books, Bodmin, Cornwall

Contents